DICTIONARY OF HEALTH INSURANCE AND MANAGED CARE

David Edward Marcinko

MBA, CFP©, CMP©

Editor-in-Chief

Hope Rachel Hetico

RN, MSHA, CPHQ, CMP©

Managing Editor

SPRINGER PUBLISHING COMPANY

NEW YORK

Springer Publishing Company, Inc.
11 West 42nd Street
New York, NY 10036

Acquisitions Editor: Sheri W. Sussman
Production Editor: Sara Yoo
Cover design by Mimi Flow
Typeset by Compset, Inc.

06 07 08 09 10/ 5 4 3 2 1

Library of Congress Cataloging-in-Publication Data

Dictionary of health insurance and managed care/David Edward Marcinko,
    editor-in-chief.
        p. ; cm.
    Includes bibliographical references.
    ISBN 0-8261-4994-4
    1. Insurance, Health—Dictionaries.   2. Managed care plans (Medical care)
—Dictionaries.   I. Marcinko, David E. (David Edward)
    [DNLM: 1. Insurance, Health—Terminology—English.   2. Managed Care
Programs—Terminology—English.   W 15 D554 2006]
RA413.D53 2006
368.38′2003—dc22

2005029976

Printed in the United States of America by Banta Book Group.

Contents

Dr. David Edward Marcinko, MBA, CFP©, CMP©, is a health care economist and former board-certified surgical fellow from Temple University in Philadelphia. In the past, he edited four practice-management books, three medical texts in two languages, six financial planning books, and two CD-ROMs for physicians, financial advisors, accountants, attorneys, and business consultants. Internationally recognized for his work, he provides litigation support and expert witness testimony in state and federal court, with clinical publications archived in the Library of Congress and the Library of Medicine at the National Institute of Health. His thought leadership essays have been cited in many scholarly journals (e.g., *Physicians Practice, Managed Care Executives, Medical Interface, Plastic Surgery Products, Teaching and Learning in Medicine, Orthodontics Today, Podiatry Management,* the *Journal of the American Medical Association* [JAMA.ama-assn.org], and *Physician's Money Digest*); by professional organizations (e.g., the Medical Group Management Association [MGMA], American College of Emergency Physicians [ACEP], American College of Medical Practice Executives [ACMPE], and American College of Physician Executives [ACPE]; and by academic institutions (e.g., the Northern University College of Business, UCLA School of Medicine, Medical College of Wisconsin, Southern Illinois College of Medicine, Washington University School of Medicine, University of Pennsylvania Medical and Dental Libraries, University of North Texas Health Science Center, Emory University School of Medicine, and the Goizueta School of Business at Emory University). Dr. Marcinko also has numerous editorial and reviewing roles to his credit. His most recent textbook from Springer Publishing Company is *The Advanced Business of Medical Practice.* A favorite on the lecture circuit and a linguistic docent often quoted in the media, he speaks frequently to medical and financial services societies throughout the country in an entertaining and witty fashion.

Dr. Marcinko received his undergraduate degree from Loyola College (Baltimore), completed his internship and residency training at Atlanta Hospital and Medical Center, earned his business degree from the Keller Graduate School of Management (Chicago), and his financial planning diploma from Oglethorpe University (Atlanta). He is a licensee of the Certified Financial Planner© Board of Standards (Denver) and holds the Certified Medical Planner© designation (CMP©). He obtained Series #7 (general securities), Series #63 (uniform securities state law), and Series #65 (investment advisory) licenses from the National Association of Securities Dealers (NASD) and a life, health, disability, variable annuity, and property-casualty license from the State of Georgia. Dr. Marcinko was also a cofounder of an ambulatory surgery center that was sold to a publicly traded company, a Certified Professional in Health Care Quality (CPHQ), a medical-staff vice president of a general hospital, an assistant residency director, a founder of a computer-based testing firm for doctors, and a president of a regional physician practice-management corporation in the Midwest.

Currently, Dr. Marcinko is chief executive officer and provost for the Institute of Medical Business Advisors©, Inc. The firm is headquartered in Atlanta, has offices in five states and Europe, and works with a diverse list of individual and corporate clients. It sponsors the professional Certified Medical Planner© charter designation program. As a national educational resource center and referral alliance, the Institute of Medical Business Advisors©, Inc., and its network of independent professionals provide financial solutions and managerial peace of mind to physicians, emerging health care organizations, and their consulting advisors.

Hope Rachel Hetico RN, MSHA, CPHQ, CMP©, received her nursing degree from Valpariso University, and master's degree in Health Care Administration from the University of St. Francis, in Joliette, Illinois. She is operations editor of a dozen textbooks and a nationally known expert in managed medical care, medical reimbursement, case management, infection control, health insurance and risk management, utilization review, National Committee on Quality Assurance (NCQA), Health Plan and Employer Data and Information Set (HEDIS), and Joint Commission on the Accreditation of Healthcare Organizations (JCAHO) rules and regulations. With a well-documented history of identifying innovations in education and accelerating their adoption by the medical, insurance, and financial services industries, she is frequently quoted in the health care business media and brings a decade of entrepreneurship and creative leadership skills to the Medical Business Advisors National Network© of independent advisors. Prior to joining the Institute of Medical Business Advisors©, Inc., as president and chief operating officer, she was a senior hospital executive, financial advisor, licensed insurance agent, Medicare, Medigap and long-term-care specialist, certified professional in health care quality (CPHQ), and distinguished visiting instructor in health care administration for the University of Phoenix, Graduate School of Business and Management, in Atlanta. Ms. Hetico was also regional corporate director for medical quality improvement at Abbey Healthcare, a public company in Costa Mesa, California. Now, she is responsible for leading www.MedicalBusinessAdvisors.com to the top of the exploding business-to-business educational marketplace, while continuing to nurture the company's rapidly expanding list of medical and financial services clients and colleagues.

Preface

"When I use a word," Humpty Dumpty said, in a rather scornful tone, "It means just what I choose it to mean—neither more nor less."

"The question is," Alice said, "whether you can make words mean so many different things."

"The question is," said Humpty Dumpty, "which is to be master, that's all."

Lewis Carroll,
Through the Looking Glass

Medical insurance and managed care is a component of the protean health care industrial complex. However, it is not contained in a separate space, and its language needs to be codified and documented to avoid confusion over terms of art. Health, Medicare, Medicaid, dental and vision insurance and worker's compensation, disability, and long-term-care insurance represent financial products that play a critical role in Americans' personal and professional lives. However, the field is rapidly changing in their cost-constrained economic environment. More products, technology, and terms have reached the marketplace in the past few years than in all previous decades, and the introduction of new words is indeed rapid. Moreover, with its quixotic efforts, the U.S. Department of Health and Human Services, along with the private sector, has created a labyrinth of new programs with confusing terminology, eponyms and jargon, as well as related accounting, Health Insurance Portability and Accountability Act, finance, and economics abbreviations.

And so, the *Dictionary of Health Insurance and Managed Care* was conceived as an essential tool for doctors, nurses, clinics, and hospitals; health care administrators, financial advisors, and business consultants; accountants, actuaries, and benefits managers; health maintenance organizations, preferred provider organizations, and insurance companies; as well as medical, dental, business, and health care administration graduate and doctoral students.

The *Dictionary of Health Insurance and Managed Care* can also be used as a handy quick reference source and supplement to sales literature for insurance agents, brokers, actuaries, underwriters, and managed care product professionals, and to answer prospect questions and inquiries about servicing. Fast, succinct, and technically accurate responses to such questions can sometimes mean the difference between closing and not closing a sale or reducing costs when purchasing a health insurance or managed care product.

And, let us not forget about savvy consumers who will find the *Dictionary of Health Insurance and Managed Care* a wealth of information in readily understood language. It is astonishing that the health insurance purchase decision is often made directly by the layman without sufficient basic knowledge of the various acronyms, definition, and policy provisions!

With 5,015 definitions, 3,010 whimsical abbreviations and acronyms, and a collection of 2,015 resources, readings, and nomenclature derivatives, the *Dictionary* is actually a three-in-one reference tool. It contains more than 10,000 entries that cover the language of every health care industry sector: (a) layman, purchaser, and benefits manager; (b) physician, provider, and health care facility; and (c) payer, intermediary, and insurance professional. We highlight new terminology and current definitions and include a list of confusing acronyms and alphabetical abbreviations. The *Dictionary* also contains definitions and offerings of the recent past that are still in colloquial use. These definitions are expanded where appropriate with simple examples and cross-references to research various other definitions or to pursue relevant or related terms.

Of course, by its very nature the *Dictionary of Health Insurance and Managed Care* is ripe for periodic updates by engaged readers working in the fluctuating health insurance and managed health care milieu. It will be periodically updated and edited to reflect the changing lexicon of terms, as older words are retired, and newer ones are continually created. Accordingly, if the reader has any comments or suggestions or would like to contribute substantive unlisted abbreviations, acronyms, eponyms, or definitions to a future edition, please contact us.

David Edward Marcinko
Hope Rachel Hetico
www.MedicalBusinessAdvisors.com
Norcross, Georgia
MarcinkoAdvisors@msn.com

Foreword

Why do we need the *Dictionary of Health Insurance and Managed Care?* And, why do payers, providers, benefits managers, consultants, and consumers need a credible and unbiased source of explanations for their health insurance needs and managed care products?

The answer is clear!

Health care is the most rapidly changing domestic industry. The revolution occurring in health insurance and managed care delivery is particularly fast. Some might even suggest these machinations were malignant, as many industry segments, professionals, and patients suffer because of them. And so, because knowledge is power in times of great flux, codified information protects all people from physical, as well as economic, harm.

For example, federal government forecasts reveal that total expenditures on health services will surpass $2 trillion in 2007, and account for 17% of the gross domestic product. As a country, Americans spend dramatically more total dollars on health care, and more as a percentage of the economy, than they did two decades ago. Along with these growing expenditures, the government is assuming greater control. Currently, almost 50% of health care costs are under federal or state mandates through Medicare and Medicaid entitlement programs. The recent prescription drug program and implementation of the Health Insurance Portability and Accountability Act add more confusion for medical providers and facilities, insurance agents, health plans, and patients. This tumult occurred so rapidly that Americans can no longer assume operative definitional stability. The resulting chaos is as expected.

Fortunately, the *Dictionary of Health Insurance and Managed Care* provides desperately needed nomenclature stability to health insurance policy issues and managed care procedural concerns. With almost 10,000 definitions, abbreviations, acronyms, and references, the *Dictionary* is the most comprehensive and authoritarian compendium of its kind, to date.

Health care economist Dr. David Edward Marcinko, and his colleagues at the Institute of Medical Business Advisors®, Inc., should be complimented for conceiving and completing this laudable project. The *Dictionary of Health Insurance and Managed Care* lifts the fog of confusion surrounding the most contentious topic in the health care industrial complex today. My suggestion, therefore, is to "read it, refer to it, recommend it, and reap."

Michael J. Stahl, PhD
Director, Physician Executive MBA Program
William B. Stokely Distinguished Professor of Business
College of Business Administration
The University of Tennessee
Knoxville, TN

Acknowledgments

Creating the *Dictionary of Health Insurance and Managed Care* was a significant effort that involved all members of our firm. Major source materials include those publications, journals, and books listed as references, as well as personal communication with experts in the health insurance and managed care industry.

Over the past year, we also interfaced with public resources, such as various state governments, the federal government, the Federal Register (FR), the Centers for Disease Control and Prevention (CDCP), the Centers for Medicare and Medicaid Services (CMS), the Institute of Medicine (IOM), the National Research Council (NRC), the U.S. Department of Health and Human Services (HHS), and the Office of Civil Rights (OCR), as well as numerous private institutions, physicians, nurses, and managed health care experts to discuss its contents. Although impossible to acknowledge every person that played a role in its production, there are several people we wish to thank for their moral support and extraordinary input.

These include: Timothy Alexander, MS, vice president of Library Research, and Robert James Cimasi, ASA, CBA, AVA, FCBI, CMP©, president and founder, Health Capital Consultants, LLC, St. Louis, Missouri; Jerry Belle, president, Aventis Pharmaceuticals North America; Gary A. Cook, MSFS, CFP©, CLU, RHU, CMP©, Content Developer for COOS Development Corporation, Huntersville, North Carolina; Dr. Charles F. Fenton, III, Esquire, health-law attorney, Atlanta, Georgia; Professor Gregory O. Ginn, PhD, CPA, MBA, MEd, Department of Healthcare Administration, University of Las Vegas, Nevada; Timothy R. Hetico, CEO, Hetico Insurance Agency, Springfield, Ohio; Dr. Jay S. Grife, Esquire, founder and CEO, Medical Malpractice Consultants, Inc., Jacksonville, Florida; Dean L. Mondell, MD, president, Rehabilitation Specialists, PC, Las Vegas, Nevada; Paul A. Valle, Jr., MD, Family Care Associates at the Greater Baltimore Medical Center in Maryland; and Sheri W. Sussman, Senior Vice President, Editorial, Springer Publishing, New York, who directed the publishing cycle from conception to release.

Dedication

The *Dictionary of Health Insurance and Managed Care* is dedicated to Mackenzie Hope Marcinko of Atlanta; Rachel Pentin-Maki, board of directors, Finlandia University, Hancock, Michigan; and Ray Hirvonen, Raymond M. Hirvonen Foundation, Marquette, Michigan. They constantly reminded us to present concepts as simply as possible, as we endeavored to create a comprehensive *Dictionary* relevant to the entire health care industrial complex.

INSTRUCTIONS FOR USE

Alphabetization
Entries in the *Dictionary* are alphabetized by letter rather than by word, so that multiple-word terms are treated as a single word.

Cross-References
Contrasting or related terms may be cross-referenced in the *Dictionary* to enhance reader understanding. Once an entry has been fully defined by another term, a reference rather than a definition may be provided (e.g.,: health maintenance organization. *See* MCO. *See* IPA).

Definitions
Because many academic words have distinctly different definitions depending on their context, it is left up to the reader to determine their relevant purpose. However, the various meanings of a term have been listed in the *Dictionary* by bullets or functional subheading for convenience. Older terms still in colloquial use are also noted. *See* Unusual Definitions.

Disclaimer
All definitions, abbreviations, eponyms, acronyms, and information listed in the *Dictionary* are intended for general understanding and do not represent the thoughts, ideas, or opinions of the Institute of Medical Business Advisors©, Inc. Care has been taken to confirm information accuracy, but we offer no warranties, expressed or implied, regarding currency and are not responsible for errors, omissions, or any consequences from the application of this information. Furthermore, terms are not complete because many are written in simplest form. The health insurance and managed care industry is evolving rapidly, and all information should be considered time-sensitive.

Italics
Italic type may be used to highlight the fact that a word has a special meaning to the health care industry. It is also used for the titles of publications, books, journals, articles, and white papers referenced in the *Dictionary*.

Unusual Definitions
Unique trade or industry terms that play an active role in the field of health insurance and managed care are included in the *Dictionary* along with a brief explanation, as needed.

Abbreviations and Acronyms
Abbreviations with multiple meanings are included in the *Dictionary* because the industry does not possess a body of standardized acronyms and abbreviations.

Bibliography
Collated readings from a variety of sources for further research into specific subjects of interest.

TERMINOLOGY: A–Z

A

'A' TIER: The top and usually most expensive level of drugs available from a health insurance policy or managed care plan formulary.

ABSENTEEISM POLICY: Guidance within an organization or business about how to manage the state of chronic absence from work. Absenteeism is usually addressed through progressively stricter disciplinary measures that can result in the termination of the individual's employment. This is generally governed by the organization's absenteeism policy. See Presenteeism.

ABSOLUTE: A complete or final ruling or order on health insurance, without conditions.

ABSTRACT: A collection of information from the medical record by hard copy, charts, or electronic instrument.

ABUSE: Actions that do not involve intentional misrepresentations in health care billing but which may result in improper conduct. Consequences can result in civil liability and administrative sanctions. An example of abuse is the excessive use of medical supplies. See Compliance, FBI, Fraud, and OIG.

ACADEMIC MEDICAL CENTER: A group of related institutions including a teaching hospital or hospitals, a medical school and its affiliated faculty practice plan, and other health professional schools.

ACADEMY OF MANAGED CARE PHARMACY: A trade organization of pharmacists who work for the managed care insurance industry.

ACCELERATED DEPRECIATION: A method in which larger portions of depreciation are taken in the beginning periods of asset life, and smaller portions are taken in later years. See Depreciation.

ACCELERATED PAYMENT: The partial advancement of funds to temporarily pay for delayed healthcare claims.

ACCEPTANCE: The agreement to an offer of a health or managed care insurance contract.

ACCEPT ASSIGNMENT: Physician agreement to accept the fees allowed by an insurance plan, HMO, prospective payment system, or by Medicare.

ACCESS: A patient's ability to obtain medical care. The ease of access is determined by components as the availability of medical services and their acceptability to the patient, the location of health care facilities, transportation, hours of operation, and cost of care. See Applicant and Policyholder.

ACCESS FEE: The managed care or health care insurance plan fee to access its panel of member medical providers.

ACCESSIBILITY OF SERVICES: Ability to get medical care and services when needed.

ACCIDENT: In the context of health insurance, it is an unintended, unforeseen, and unexpected event that generally results in injury or loss. See Illness, Injury, Hazard, Peril, and Loss.

ACCIDENTAL BODILY INJURY: Unforeseen and unintended bodily injury resulting from an accident. Generally considered a more liberal term or definition in accident insurance policies, as distinguished from a technical interpretation of the term "accidental means." See Accident.

ACCIDENTAL DEATH: Death as the result of accidental bodily injury (i.e., injury that is unintended, unexpected, and unusual). Contrasted with death by accidental means, which means that the cause of the accident itself must be accidental (slipping off a ladder, etc.). Thus, a broken neck as a result of an intended safe dive into a swimming pool is accidental death, but not death by accidental means. See Accident.

ACCIDENTAL DEATH BENEFIT: An extra benefit that generally equals the face value of a health insurance or managed care contract or a principal sum payable in addition to other benefits in the event of death as the result of an accident. See Accident Insurance.

ACCIDENTAL DEATH AND DISMEMBERMENT: A policy or a provision in a disability income, life, or health insurance policy that pays either a specified amount or a multiple of the weekly disability benefit if the insured dies, loses his or her sight, or loses two limbs as the result of an accident. A lesser amount is payable for the loss of one eye, arm, leg, hand, or foot.

ACCIDENTAL DEATH AND DISMEMBERMENT BENEFIT: A policy provision that pays a stated benefit in case of death or the loss of limbs or sight as a result of an accident.

ACCIDENTAL DEATH AND DISMEMBERMENT RIDER: A supplementary benefit rider or endorsement that provides for an amount of money in addition to the basic death benefit of a life or health insurance policy. This additional amount is payable only if the insured dies or loses any two limbs or the sight of both eyes as the result of an accident. Some riders pay one half of the benefit amount if the insured loses one limb or the sight in one eye. See Accident Insurance.

ACCIDENTAL DEATH INSURANCE: A form of life or health insurance that provides payment if the death of the insured results from an accident. It is often combined with Dismemberment Insurance in a form called Accidental Death and Dismemberment. See Accidental Death and Dismemberment.

ACCIDENTAL DISMEMBERMENT: The severance of limbs at or above the wrists or ankle joints or the entire irrevocable loss of sight. Loss of use, in itself, is not usually considered to be dismemberment. See Accidental Means and Accidental Means Death Benefit.

ACCIDENTAL MEANS: An unforeseen, unexpected, unintended cause of an accident. The means that causes the mishap must be accidental for any claim to be payable.

ACCIDENTAL MEANS DEATH BENEFIT: An optionally available health or life benefit providing for the payment of a multiple (usually double) of the face amount of the policy in case of death by accidental means. The benefit usually covers death resulting from bodily injury affected solely through external, violent, and accidental means, independently and exclusively of all other causes, and within 90 days after such injury.

ACCIDENTAL MEANS, DEATH BY: Death resulting from a cause that is accidental, so that both the cause and the result are accidental. See Accidental Means.

ACCIDENT FREQUENCY: The rate of occurrence of accidents. See Accident.

ACCIDENT FREQUENCY RATE: The total number of disabling injuries suffered by employees per 1,000,000 employee-hours of work on an annual basis. See Accident Frequency.

ACCIDENT HEALTH INSURANCE: Insurance under which benefits are payable in case of disease, accidental injury, or accidental death. Also called health insurance, personal health insurance, and sickness and accident insurance.

ACCIDENT INDUSTRIAL: An unforeseen, unintended accident that has occurred as a result of one's employment or occupation.

ACCIDENT INSURANCE: A form of insurance against loss by accidental bodily injury.

ACCIDENT POLICY: Health or life insurance that provides indemnities for loss resulting from accidental bodily injuries. See Accident Health Insurance.

ACCIDENT SEVERITY RATE: The number of days lost from disability injuries or death per 1,000 employee-hours of work, with 6,000 days charged for death.

ACCIDENT SICKNESS INSURANCE: See Accident and Health Insurance.

ACCOUNTABLE: Subject to penalties relative to accepted responsibilities.

ACCOUNTABLE-HEALTH PARTNERSHIP: An organization of doctors and hospitals that provides care for people organized into large groups of purchasers. See Accountable.

ACCOUNTABLE HEALTH PLAN (AHP): A joint venture between medical practitioners and institutions (insurance companies, HMOs, or hospitals) that would assume responsibility for delivering medical care. Physicians and providers work for or contract with these health plans. As independent delivery systems (IDS) form and demonstrate their ability to manage capitated care, they begin to struggle with issues of ownership or alliance partnerships with HMOs, insurance companies, or other financing entities. An accountable health care system describes an IDS plan with a financing component. When an IDS plan operates one or more health insurance benefit products, or a managed care organization acquires a large-scale medical delivery component, it qualifies as an accountable health system or accountable health plan.

ACCOUNTING PERSPECTIVES: Perspectives underlying decisions on which categories of goods and services to include as costs or benefits in an analysis.

ACCOUNTS PAYABLE: The amount of money a health care organization or insurance company is obligated to pay vendors. Also known as APs. See Accounts Receivable.

ACCOUNTS RECEIVABLE: The amount of money a health care organization or insurance company is due from insured patients or vendors. Also known as ARs. See Aging Schedule and Accounts Payable.

ACCOUNTS RECEIVABLE INSURANCE: Insurance coverage for uncollected accounts (ARs) and health insurance or managed care premiums, plus the expenses of record reconstruction and various other collection fees, but without the physical, paper, or electronic devices, computer disks, tapes, or memory sticks. See ARs.

ACCREDITATION: The process used to certify and recognize that a predetermined set of standards has been met.

ACCREDITATION CYCLE FOR MEDICARE + CHOICE DEEMING: The duration of CMS's recognition of the validity of an accrediting organization's determination that a Medicare + choice organization (MEDICARE + CHOICE) is fully accredited. See CMS (Centers for Medicare and Medicaid Services).

ACCREDITATION FOR PARTICIPATION: State requirement that plans must be accredited to participate in the Medicaid managed care program.

ACCREDITED HOSPITAL: A hospital or similar entity whose medical quality standards are accepted by the Joint Commission on Accreditation of Healthcare Organizations.

ACCREDITED INVESTOR: Rule 501 of Regulation D of the Securities Act of 1933, requires a natural person whose individual net worth, or joint net worth together with a spouse, exceeds $1,000,000. Alternatively, under the same rule, an accredited investor is a natural person with an individual income in excess of $200,000 in each of the two most recent years or joint income with a spouse in excess of $300,000 in each of those years and has a reasonable expectation of reaching the same income level in the current year. Often used in private placements for health care facility bonds and securities.

ACCRETE: Medicare term for adding new enrollees in a health plan.

ACCRUAL: The amount of money that is set aside to cover health insurance expenses. The accrual is the plan's best estimate of what those expenses are and (for medical expenses) is based on a combination of data from the authorization system, the claims system, lag studies, and the plan's prior history. See Accrual Basis of Accounting.

ACCRUAL BASIS OF ACCOUNTING: A method of accounting that attempts to match health insurance revenues with medical expenses and claims by recognizing revenue when a service is rendered and expense when the liability is incurred irrespective of the receipt or disbursement of cash. See Accrual.

ACCRUE: To accumulate, as in debt or revenue. See Accrual and Accrual Basis Accounting.

ACCRUED EXPENSES: Incurred, but not yet paid, expenses. See Expenses.

ACCRUED INTEREST: Interest dollars added to the contract price of a hospital bond from the last interest payment date. It is always computed up to, but not including the settlement date.

ACCUMULATED DEPRECIATION: The total accumulated amount of depreciation recognized as an asset by a health care organization or managed care or insurance company, since purchase. See Depreciation.

ACCUMULATION: Total utilized medical services per dollar limited of covered benefits.

ACCUMULATION PERIOD: Specific time period for incurred health care expenses that are at least equal to the deductible or similar amount, to begin insurance or managed care benefit period.

ACID TEST: A managed care liquidity financial test that measures how much cash and marketable securities are available to pay all current liabilities of the organization. See Acid Test Ratio and Quick Ratio.

ACID TEST RATIO: A managed care liquidity ratio that measures how much cash and marketable securities are available to pay all current liabilities of the organization. (Cash and marketable securities or current liabilities.) See Acid Test and Quick Ratio.

ACQUISITION COST: The cost of soliciting and acquiring health or managed care insurance business premiums and insured members.

ACTIVE: A currently in-effect insurance status.

ACTIVE, FULL-TIME EMPLOYEE: Working for an employer on a regular basis in the usual course of business to be considered eligible for health insurance or disability insurance coverage. Usually, a minimum number of regular work hours are needed. See Full Time Equivalent.

ACTIVELY-AT-WORK: Describes a health insurer's policy requirement indicating that a member is actively and gainfully employed.

ACTIVE RETENTION: Self-pay. Accepting the costs and risks of not possessing health insurance coverage.

ACTIVITIES OF DAILY LIVING (ADL): An index or scale that measures an individual's degree of independence in bathing, dressing, using the toilet, eating, and moving across a small room. See Long-Term Care Insurance.

ACTIVITY-BASED COSTING (ABC): Defines costs in terms of a health or managed care organization's processes or activities and determines costs associated with significant activities or events. ABC relies on the following three-step process: (a) activity mapping, which involves mapping activities in an illustrated sequence; (b) activity analysis, which involves defining and assigning a time value to activities; and (c) bill of activities, which involves generating a cost for each main activity. See Activity-Based Management.

ACTIVITY-BASED MANAGEMENT (ABM): Supports health insurance operations by focusing on the causes of costs and how costs can be reduced. It assesses cost drivers that directly affect the cost of a product or service and uses performance measures to evaluate the financial or nonfinancial benefit an activity provides. By identifying each cost driver and assessing the value the element adds to the health care enterprise, ABM provides a basis for selecting areas that can be changed to reduce costs. See Activity-Based Costing.

ACTIVITY RATIOS: Financial ratios that measures how effectively a health care organization is using its assets to produce revenues. See Liquidity Ratios.

ACT OF GOD: Accident without human intervention, unforeseeable, and a result of natural causes.

ACTUAL ACQUISITION COST: Net payment, after expenses, for provided medical care or services.

ACTUAL CHARGE: The amount of money a medical provider or health care facility submits for payment from a health insurance carrier. It is usually more than received.

ACTUARIAL: Refers to the statistical calculations used to determine the managed care company's rates and premiums charged their customers based on projections of utilization and cost for a defined population. See Actuary.

ACTUARIAL ASSUMPTIONS: In establishing premium rates, scheduling policy provisions, and projecting future cost increases, a MCO, HMO, or insurance company must make certain estimates. The most important assumptions are based on probabilities of illness, accident, or death using large numbers of insureds (so called mortality and illness assumptions) and assumptions about interest and capital gains, as well as sales commissions and other health insurance expenses.

ACTUARIAL BALANCE: The difference between the summarized small market insurance (SMI) income rate and cost rates over a given valuation period.

ACTUARIAL COST: A cost derived through the use of actuarial present values.

ACTUARIAL DEFICIT: A negative actuarial SMI balance. See Small Market Insurance.

ACTUARIALLY SOUND: A health plan is considered to be actuarially sound when the amount of money in the fund and the current level of premiums are sufficient (on the basis of assumptions on interest, mortality, medical, claims, and employee turnover) to meet the liabilities that have accrued and that are accruing on a current basis. See Actuary.

ACTUARIAL PRESENT VALUE: The current worth of a health care amount payable or receivable in the future, in which each such amount is discounted at an assumed rate of interest and adjusted for the probability of its payment or receipt.

ACTUARIAL RATES: One half of the expected monthly cost of the Small Market Insurance program for each aged enrollee (for the aged actuarial rate) and one half of the expected monthly cost for each disabled enrollee (for the disabled actuarial rate) for the duration the rate is in effect. See Actuary.

ACTUARIAL SOUNDNESS: The requirement that the development of capitation and insurance rates meet common actuarial principles and rules. See Actuary.

ACTUARY: A person who determines insurance policy rates, reserves, and dividends, as well as conducts various other statistical studies.

ACUITY: A benchmark of illness severity used to establish medical or allied medical staffing needs.

ACUPOINT (acupuncture point): Any of an indefinite number of points on or near the surface of the body that are allegedly susceptible to healthful activation.

ACUTE CARE: A pattern of health care in which a patient is treated for an acute (immediate and severe) episode of illness, for the subsequent treatment of injuries related to an accident or other trauma, or during recovery from surgery. Personnel with complex and sophisticated technical equipment and materials render acute care in a hospital. Unlike chronic care, acute care is often necessary for only a short time. See Acute Care Certificate.

ACUTE CARE CERTIFICATE: Physician attestation indicating why a patient should remain in a hospital. An advisory committee can review the certificate and decide that the doctor's certificate should be revoked. Health funds are only required to pay the equivalent of the benefit that would be payable to nursing home patients, which is less than the acute care rate. See Certificate of Need.

ACUTE DISEASE: Illness characterized by a single episode of disease and constrained to a fairly brief period of time.

ADDITIONAL BENEFITS: Health care services not covered by Medicare and reductions in premiums or cost sharing for Medicare-covered services. Additional benefits are specified and are offered to Medicare beneficiaries at no additional premium. Those benefits must be at least equal in value to the adjusted excess amount calculated in the ACR. An excess amount is created when the average payment rate exceeds the adjusted community rate (as reduced by the actuarial value of coinsurance, copayments, and deductibles under Parts A and B of Medicare). The excess amount is then adjusted for any contributions to a stabilization fund. The remainder is the adjusted excess, which will be used to pay for services not covered by Medicare or will be used to reduce charges otherwise allowed for Medicare-covered services. See Average Cost Rate, Medicare Parts C and D, and Medicare Advantage.

ADDITIONAL DIAGNOSIS: Any diagnosis other than the primary or admitting diagnosis. See Comorbid Condition.

ADDITIONAL DRUG BENEFIT LIST: Prescription drugs listed as commonly prescribed by physicians for long-term use. Subject to review and change by the health plan involved. Also called a drug maintenance list. See Medicare Part D.

ADDITIONAL MONTHLY BENEFIT: Riders added to disability income insurance policies to provide additional benefits during the 1st year of a claim while the insured is waiting for Social Security benefits to begin.

ADHESION INSURANCE: Life, health, or managed care insurance contracts issued on a take-it-or-leave-it basis. See Contract and Aleatory Contract.

ADJUDICATION: Processing health insurance claims according to contract. See Mediation.

ADJUSTABLE PREMIUM: A premium change, by classes of insured, in a health insurance policy.

ADJUSTED ADMISSIONS: A measure of all patient care activity undertaken in a hospital, both inpatient and outpatient. Adjusted admissions are equivalent to the sum of inpatient admissions and an estimate of the volume of outpatient services. This estimate is calculated by multiplying outpatient visits by the ratio of outpatient charges per visit to inpatient charges per admission.

ADJUSTED AVERAGE PER CAPITA COST (AAPCC): (1) Actuarial projections of per capita Medicare spending for enrollees in fee-for-service Medicare. Separate AAPCCs are calculated, usually at the county level, for Part A services and Part B services for the aged, disabled, and people with end-stage renal disease (ESRD). Medicare pays risk plans by applying adjustment factors to 95% of the Part A and Part B AAPCCs. The adjustment factors reflect differences in Medicare per capita fee-for-service spending related to age, sex, institutional status, Medicaid status, and employment status. (2) A county-level estimate of the average cost incurred by Medicare for each beneficiary in fee for service. Adjustments are made so that the AAPCC represents the level of spending that would occur if each county contained the same mix of beneficiaries. Medicare pays health plans 95% of the AAPCC, adjusted for the characteristics of the enrollees in each plan. See Medicare Risk Contract and U.S. Per Capita Cost.

ADJUSTED AVERAGE CHARGE PER DAY: The average charge billed by hospitals for one day of care, which is adjusted total charges divided by total days of care. See Adjusted Total Charges.

ADJUSTED AVERAGE CHARGE PER DISCHARGE: The average charge billed by hospitals for an inpatient stay (from the day of admission to the day of discharge), which is adjusted total charges divided by number of discharges.

ADJUSTED COMMUNITY RATING: The process of determining a group's premium rate in which an HMO adjusts the standard or pure community rate premium by adding or subtracting an amount that reflects the group's past claims experience. See Rating, Risk, Hazard, and Peril.

ADJUSTED COVERAGE PER CAPITA COST: Estimate of average monthly benefits cost, after certain adjustments. See AAPCC.

ADJUSTED DRUG BENEFIT LIST: A small number of medications often prescribed to long-term patient or required for long-term chronic care. Also called a drug maintenance list, which can be modified from time to time by a health plan, CMS, or third party administrator. See Drug Formulary or Formulary.

ADJUSTED EARNINGS: Net earnings from a health or other insurer's operations, plus the estimated value of additional insurance in force or of the growth in premiums written. See Net Earnings.

ADJUSTED NET GAIN FROM OPERATIONS: Referring to a health or managed care insurer, the net gain from operations, plus the estimated value of increases in the amount of insurance in force or the growth in premiums during the year.

ADJUSTED NET WORTH: The worth of a managed care, health insurance, or other company, consisting of capital and surplus, plus an estimated value for the business on the company's books. See Net Worth.

ADJUSTED PAYMENT RATE (APR): The Medicare capitated payment to risk-contract HMOs. For a given plan, the APR is determined by adjusting county-level AAPCCs to reflect the relative risks of the plan's enrollees. See Adjusted Average Per Capita Cost.

ADJUSTED TOTAL CHARGES: Because OSHPD regulations require that hospitals report charges for the last 365 days of a stay; only total charges for a patient who stays more than 1 year must be adjusted upward (increased) to reflect the entire stay. Thus, for patients staying longer than 1 year, the average daily charge for the last year of the stay is calculated and applied to the entire stay. The formula is: (Total Charges ÷ 365 = Charge per Day) × Length of Stay = Adjusted Total Charges. *See* OSHPD.

ADJUSTMENT: A change made to an insurance claim or medical bill.

ADJUSTMENT REASONS: A schedule of insurance code information to explain medical bill or fee schedule changes.

ADMINISTRATION: The cost center that includes the overall management and administration of the health care institution, general patient accounting, communication systems, data processing, patient admissions, public relations, professional liability and non-property-related insurance, licenses and taxes, medical record activities, and procurement of supplies and equipment.

ADMINISTRATIVE COST CENTERS: Health care organizational support units responsible for their own costs. *See* Administrative Cost Centers.

ADMINISTRATIVE COSTS: Medical costs related to utilization review, insurance marketing, medical underwriting, agents' commissions, premium collection, claims processing, insurer profit, quality assurance programs, and risk management. Includes the costs assumed by a managed care plan for administrative services such as billing and overhead costs. See Administration and Expenses.

ADMINISTRATIVE LAW JUDGE: Hearing officer settling a dispute by a health care insurance, managed care, or other administrative agency.

ADMINISTRATIVE PROCEEDING: Adjudication by a health care insurance, managed care, or other administrative agency.

ADMINISTRATIVE PROFIT CENTERS: Health care organizational support units responsible for their own profits.

ADMINISTRATIVE SERVICES ONLY (ASO): A contract between a health insurance company and a self-funded plan in which the insurance company performs administrative services only and the self-funded entity assumes all risk.

ADMINISTRATIVE SIMPLIFICATION COMPLIANCE ACT: Signed into law on December 27, 2001, as Public Law 107-105, this Act provided a 1-year extension to HIPAA "covered entities" (except small health plans, which already had been extended until October 16, 2003) to meet HIPAA electronic and code set transaction requirements. Also, allows the Secretary of HHS to exclude providers from Medicare if they are not compliant with the HIPAA electronic and code set transaction requirements and to prohibit Medicare payment of paper claims received after October 16, 2003, except under certain situations.

ADMISSION: The process of administrative registration for a patient in need of in-patient or outpatient medical care services.

ADMISSION CERTIFICATION: A method of assuring that only those patients who need hospital care are admitted. Certification can be granted before admission (preadmission) or shortly after (concurrent). Length-of-stay for the patient's diagnosed problem is usually assigned upon admission under a certification program. See Acute Hospital.

ADMISSION, HOSPITAL: The number of patients formally admitted for a certain type of care in a hospital facility. Includes the discharge from acute and formal admission to nonacute, and vice versa. See Acute Care.

ADMISSION (LTC FACILITY): The number of patients formally admitted to the facility or transferred from a residential care unit of the long-term care facility. Does not include patients returning to the facility under a bed-hold or leave, in which a bed has been held specifically for patient's return. See LTC.

ADMISSION REPORT: The daily hospital or health facility census report, listing patients gained, lost, or changed in their course of care in a particular facility.

ADMISSION SOURCE: The physical site from which the patient was admitted: home, residential care facility, ambulatory surgery facility, skilled nursing/ intermediate care facility, acute hospital care, other hospital care, newborn, prison/jail or other; the licensure of the site: this hospital, another hospital; and the route of admission: hospital's emergency room, or another emergency room, etc.

ADMISSIONS PER 1,000: An indicator calculated by taking the total number of inpatient or outpatient admissions from a specific group (e.g., employer group, HMO population at risk) for a specific period of time (usually 1 year), dividing it by the average number of covered members in that group during the same period, and multiplying the result by 1,000. This indicator can be calculated for behavioral health or any disease in the aggregate and by modality of treatment (e.g., inpatient, residential, and partial hospitalization).

ADMISSION TYPE: The four admission types are: scheduled, unscheduled, infant, and unknown.

ADMISSION WIRE: Formal notification of membership admission or treatment to or by a BC/BS facility or provider.

ADMITS: The number of admissions to a hospital (including outpatient and inpatient facilities). See Admissions, Hospital, Source, and Type.

ADMITTED ASSETS: All insurance company assets that are approved by the state insurance department as existing property in the ownership of the company. Such assets include all funds, securities, property, equipment, rights of action, or resources of any kind owned by the company or held in trust for others. See Assets.

ADMITTED, OR AUTHORIZED COMPANY: An insurance company authorized and licensed to do business in a given state. See Foreign Insurer and Domestic Insurer.

ADMITTING PHYSICIAN: A licensed practitioner who has the necessary privileges at a hospital to admit patients for care or treatment. (In a group practice setting there are often hospital-based physicians.) Internal Medicine usually does all admitting and treatment planning. See Gatekeeper and Internist.

ADULT: A legal determination referring to one who has reached maturity; a person who has reached the age of legal capacity and can enter into insurance contracts.

ADULT DAY CARE: A group program for functionally impaired adults, designed to meet health, social, and functional needs in a setting away from the adult's home.

ADULT FOSTER CARE: Those aged older than 18–21 who do not need daily nursing care but still require assistance in a facility with a home-like environment or atmosphere.

AD VALOREM TAX: A direct tax calculated "according to value" of hospital property. Such tax is based on an assigned valuation (market or assessed) of real hospital property and, in certain cases, on a valuation of tangible or intangible personal property.

ADVANCE CHECK: Payment sent to a health care facility or medical provider that precedes the filing of a health insurance claim.

ADVANCE COVERAGE DECISION: A decision that private fee-for-service plans make on whether or not it will pay for a certain service.

ADVANCED BENEFICIARY NOTICE (ABN): Notice from a medical provider, health care facility, or DME vendors that certain products or medical services may not be covered charges by Medicare. Signature may indicate patient payment responsibility.

ADVANCE DIRECTIVE (HEALTH CARE): A directive that is a written document declaring what medical decisions will be made if the ability to make self-decisions is lost. A health care advance directive may include a living will and a durable power of attorney for health care. See Living Will.

ADVANCED REGISTERED NURSE PRACTITIONER: Nurse with advanced training in a medical specialty that is registered with the state board of nursing to practice in an advanced role. Specialty designations include certified clinical nurse specialists, certified nurse midwives, certified nurse practitioners, and certified registered nurse anesthetists. An ARNP may provide care as an independent practitioner or in collaboration or consultation with a physician.

ADVERSE EVENT: Patient harm or injury as a result of medical intervention.

ADVERSE SELECTION: The tendency of people who are less than standard health insurance risks to seek or continue insurance to a greater extent than other individuals. This so-called "selection against the insurer," or "antiselection," is a form of stacking the deck and is also found in the tendency of policy owners to take advantage of favorable options in health insurance or managed care contracts. Or, a particular health plan, whether indemnity or managed care, is selected against by the enrollee, and thus an inequitable proportion of enrollees requiring more medical services are found in that plan. Example: Low enrollee out-of-pocket costs might lure those individuals requiring more health services into an HMO rather than an indemnity-plan because the former does not have a deductible. Therefore, the HMO would have a greater proportion of less-healthy enrollees, thereby driving up costs and increasing financial risks. Also occurs with one of the following:

- When a premium doesn't cover costs. Some populations, perhaps because of age or health status, have a great potential for high utilization.

- Some population parameter such as age (e.g., a much greater number of 65-year-olds or older to young population) that increases the potential for higher utilization and often increases costs above those covered by a payer's capitation rate. See Risk, Rating, Hazard, and Peril.

ADVISOR: The registered individual or organization that is employed by a hospital or health care entity to give professional advice on its investments and management of its assets or endowment funds. See Agent and Broker.

ADVISORY OPINION: A formal opinion having no legal or presidential force.

ADVOCATE: A person who supports or protects the rights of an insured.

AFFIDAVIT OF CLAIM: A written, signed statement required when a claim is filed with an insurer and containing the facts on which the claim is based.

AFFILIATED CONTRACTOR (Provider): A Medicare carrier, medical professional, or other contractor, such as a durable medical equipment regional carrier (DMERC), which shares some or all of the program safeguard contractor's (PSC's) jurisdiction in which the affiliated contractor performs non-PSC Medicare functions, such as claims processing or education.

AFFILIATED PERSON: Anyone in a position to influence decisions made in a healthcare corporation, including officers, directors, principal stockholders, and members of their immediate families. Their shares are often referred to as "Control Stock."

AFFILIATED PROVIDER: A health care provider or facility that is paid by a health plan to give service to plan members.

AFTERCARE: Services following hospitalization or rehabilitation individualized for each patient's needs, including outpatient facility services and home health care.

AFTERMARKET: A market for a health care security either over the counter or on an exchange after an initial public offering has been made.

AGE: The age in years of an applicant, insured, or beneficiary. Some companies use the age at the last birthday. Other companies use the age at the nearest birthday (last or next).

AGE-ADJUSTED MORTALITY RATE: A mortality rate statistically modified to eliminate the effect of different age distributions in the different populations.

AGE-ATTAINED RATING: A method for establishing health insurance premiums whereby an insurer's premium is based on the current age of the beneficiary. Age-attained-rated premiums increase as the purchaser grows older. See Rating.

AGE BREAK: The grouping of age-related cohorts for medical insurance rating purposes.

AGE CHANGE: The point between natural birthdays at which a client is considered the next age for the purpose of setting insurance premium rates.

AGED ENROLLEE: An individual aged 65 or older, who is enrolled in the small market insurance (SMI) program.

AGE-AT-ISSUANCE RATING: A method for establishing health insurance premiums whereby an insurer's premium is based on the age of individuals when they first purchased health insurance coverage.

AGE AT ISSUE: The age of an insured at the time health insurance coverage goes into effect. Some insurers define issue age as the age at the insured's last birthday. In others, it is defined as the insured's age at the nearest birthday.

AGE LIMITS: Minimum or maximum age limits for the insuring of new applicants or for the renewal of an insurance, HMO, or MCO policy.

AGENCY: The legal relationship empowering one party to act on behalf of another in dealing with third parties. A health or life insurance agent does not generally have the authority to bind the insurance company. See Agent and Broker.

AGENCY AGREEMENT OR CONTRACT: A legal document containing the terms of the contract between the agent and company, signed by both parties.

AGENCY BUILDER: A term used to describe a life or health insurance general agent or agency manager, usually pertaining to some measure of growth in production or gross sales, and usually pertaining to the type of operation in which new agents are recruited and contracted regularly.

AGENCY DEPARTMENT: The home office department of a health insurance company responsible for the appointment and servicing of the agency organization. The agency department is most often responsible for policy sales, conservation of old business, service to policy owners, and various marketing services.

AGENCY DEVELOPMENT: The ongoing building of a life or health insurance agency by a general agent or manager through recruitment of new agents and the continued development of the existing personnel.

AGENCY DIRECTOR: Company director in charge of supervising a territorial division's agencies on a particular type of health insurance sales market.

AGENCY FOR HEALTH CARE POLICY AND RESEARCH (AHCPR): The agency of the Public Health Service responsible for enhancing the quality, appropriateness, and effectiveness of health care services.

AGENCY PLANT: The total force of agents representing a health insurance company. Can also mean the physical facilities of an agency.

AGENCY PROGRAM: Eligible provider of health services other than a facility, practitioner, or supplier. An example is a diabetic rehabilitation education program.

AGENCY SUPERINTENDENT: An officer or other executive of a company in charge of supervising health insurance agencies, either of a territorial division or of the entire company, and usually reporting directly to the agency vice president. Also called superintendent of agencies.

AGENCY SYSTEM: A method of marketing and selling health and life insurance. Entails sales and service by commissioned insurance agents, most often supervised by general agents or agency managers, in contrast to sales by salaried employees or by mail.

AGENT: A person who solicits health insurance or assists in the placing of risks, delivery of policies, or collection of premiums on behalf of an insurer. Typically, a person placing products for a specific insurer is considered the insurer's agent rather than an agent of the policy owner. Or, the role of a broker or dealer firm when it acts as an intermediary, or broker, between its customer (hospital or health care facility, insurance company, HMO, MCO, etc.) and a market maker or contrabroker. For this service, the firm receives a stated commission or fee. See Broker.

AGENT OF RECORD: The agent writing the initial policy application and who is entitled to any and all commissions on the issued insurance contract or the agent assigned by the agency or home office to service a particular policy owner. Also, an agent given written authorization by a present policy owner to seek out and negotiate insurance contracts with companies other than his or her own. Similar to a broker, the agent of record represents the interests of the client in dealings with other insurance companies' agents. The agent of record usually receives a percentage of the commission earned on the new policy. See Agent.

AGENT'S BALANCE: A periodic statement issued by the company of the sums owed to or by a health insurance agent.

AGENT'S COMMISSION: The payment of a percentage of the premium generated from a health or life insurance policy to the agent by a company. See Commission.

AGENT'S LETTER OF RECORD: Written authorization by a policy owner granting the agent authority to act on his or her behalf in negotiating a life or health insurance contract with an insurer other than the agent's own company.

AGENT, SURVEYING: A local agent who submits health insurance business by means of applications but does not actually write policies.

AGE/SEX FACTOR: A measurement used in underwriting. It represents the age and sex risk of medical costs of one population relative to another. A group with an age or sex factor of 1.00 is average. A group with an age or sex factor higher than 1.00 is expected to have higher average medical costs. A group with an age or sex factor less than 1.00 is expected to incur lower than average medical costs.

AGE/SEX RATES (ASR): Also called table rates, they are given group products' set of rates in which each grouping, by age and sex, has its own rates. Rates are used to calculate premiums for group billing and demographic changes are adjusted automatically in the group.

AGE-SPECIFIC MORTALITY RATE: A mortality rate limited to a particular age group. The numerator is the number of deaths in that age group;

the denominator is the number of persons in that age group in the population.

AGGREGATE INDEMNITIES: The sum total that can be collected under all health insurance policies applicable to the covered loss.

AGGREGATE INDEMNITY: Maximum dollar amount collected for a disability or period of disability.

AGGREGATE LIMIT: Maximum dollar amount of coverage in force under a health insurance policy.

AGGREGATE MARGIN: A margin that compares revenues to expenses for a group of hospitals, rather than a single hospital. Computed by subtracting the sum of expenses for all hospitals in the group from the sum of revenues and dividing by the sum of revenues.

AGGREGATE MORTALITY TABLE: A mortality table based on health and life insurance experience in which the rates of mortality at any age are based on all insurance in force at that age, without reference to the duration of insurance.

AGGREGATE PPS OPERATING MARGIN/AGGREGATE TOTAL MARGIN: A prospective payment system operating margin or total margin that compares revenue to expenses for a group of hospitals, rather than a single hospital. Computed by subtracting the sum of expenses for all hospitals in the group from the sum of revenues and dividing by the sum of revenues.

AGGREGATE STOP LOSS: The form of excess health insurance risk coverage that provides protection for the employer against accumulation of claims exceeding a certain level. This is protection against abnormal frequency of claims in total, rather than abnormal severity of a single claim.

AGING SCHEDULE: Method of classifying accounts receivable (ARs) since the amount of time they were recognized. See Accounts Receivable.

AGREEMENT HOSPITAL: Have a set charge that is agreed to with a health fund for the cost of accommodation and other hospital-related charges. These arrangements will vary between funds but provide a higher level of benefit than nonagreement hospitals.

AGREEMENT OF LIMITED PARTNERSHIP: Contractual agreement between the limited partners and the general partner(s).

AHA: American Hospital Association; a trade association for health care facilities.

A&H, A&S (ACCIDENT AND HEALTH INSURANCE, ACCIDENT AND SICKNESS INSURANCE): Once commonly used as generic designation for the entire field now called health insurance.

AID TO FAMILIES WITH DEPENDENT CHILDREN (AFDC) PROGRAM: A program established by the Social Security Act of 1935 and eliminated by welfare reform legislation in 1996. AFDC provided cash payments to needy children (and their caretakers) who lacked support because at least one parent was unavailable. Families had to meet income and resource criteria specified by the state to be eligible. The AFDC program was replaced by a block grant but its standards are retained for use in Medicaid.

AIDS: Acquired Immune Deficiency Syndrome is a life-threatening illness characterized by "opportunistic" (pneumocystosis, candidiasis, cryptococcosis, mycobacterium, herpes, leukoencephalopathy, and Kaposi's sarcoma) infections, immunodeficiency, and tumors caused by the human immuno-deficiency virus I (HIV-I). Patients are usually members of high-risk groups identified as homosexuals, intravenous drug users, hemophiliacs, bisexuals, and prostitutes. By 2005, the disease claimed more than 25 million deaths worldwide and infected more than 60 million people. The ELISA (enzyme linked immunosorbent assay) test is the initial screening serologic tool used to detect the antibody to HIV-I. It has a sensitivity and specificity from 95% to 99%. The Western blot (immunoblot) test is then used to verify the ELISA test although it too may produce conflicting results. The polymerase chain reaction (PCR) test, for viral test loading, is used in cases of conflicting information (amplicor HIV-1 monitor test). It can detect 200 copies of HIV RNA per millimeter of plasma (200–1,000 T-cell count range). It is the "gold standard" viral culture diagnostic test for the disease. Another viral load test is the DNA test, to produce a chemical reaction with HIV RNA, producing measurable light (range: 10,000–1,600,000 eq/ml.). The test is not as precise as the PCR but is more precise over time. Another amplification test is known as the LCx-R (ligase chain reaction) test. Indirect but suggestive traditional laboratory values that may indicate HIV infection include: anemia (of any type), leukopenia, increased erythrocyte sedimentation rate (ESR), decreased cholesterol, and increased serum albumin.

ALEATORY: That which depends on an uncertain event. See Contract of Adhesion.

ALEATORY CONTRACT: Health insurance contract that may or may not provide more in monetary medical benefits than the aggregate amount of premiums paid. See Adhesion Insurance.

ALIEN CARRIER: An insurer whose domicile is a foreign country. See Domestic Carrier.

ALIEN COMPANY: An insurance company incorporated or organized under the laws of any foreign nation, province, or territory.

ALIGNMENT OF INCENTIVES: The economic arrangement between medical providers in health facilities that allow the sharing of fiscal risks and rewards of patient treatment, care, and intervention.

ALL CLAUSE DEDUCTIBLE: A single deductible to cover patient expenses as the result of the same or similar health insurance causes within a given time period.

ALLERGY TREATMENT: A variety of techniques, such as skin testing, immunotherapy ("allergy shots"), and other medications, used to diagnose, prevent, or relieve symptoms of adverse immune responses (allergies).

ALLIANCES (HEALTH INSURANCE PURCHASING COOPERATIVES): Organizations consisting of large groups of purchasers of health care. The buying power of alliances is expected to force competitive marketing among providers.

ALLIED HEALTH PERSONNEL: Specially trained and licensed health workers other than physicians, podiatrists, dentists, osteopaths, optometrists, and nurses.

ALL-INCLUSIVE VISIT RATE: Aggregate costs for any one patient visit based upon annual operating costs divided by patient visits per year. This rate incorporates costs for all health services at the visit.

ALL-OR-NONE OFFERING: A "best-efforts" offering of newly issued hospital securities in which the corporation instructs the investment banker to cancel the entire offering (sold and unsold) if all of it cannot be distributed.

ALL-OR-NONE (AON) ORDER: An order to buy or sell more than one round lot of hospital or other securities at one time and at a designated price or better. It must not be executed until both of these conditions can be satisfied simultaneously.

ALLOCATED BENEFITS: Payments for a specific covered medical purpose, up to a set maximum, such as an x-ray, casts, blood test, etc.

ALLOCATION BASE: Statistic used to allocate health care costs based on a casual relationship.

ALLOGENIC BONE MARROW TRANSPLANT: Bone transplant or marrow from a donor other than the recipient.

ALLOPATHY: Traditional branch of medicine that suggests antagonistic conditions are useful interventions for the illness or condition being treated. See Medical Doctor and MD.

ALLOWABLE CHARGE: The maximum fee that a third party will reimburse a provider for a given service. See UCR.

ALLOWABLE COSTS: Items or elements of an institution's costs that are reimbursable under a payment formula. Allowable costs may exclude, for example, uncovered services, luxury accommodations, costs that are not reasonable, and expenditures that are unnecessary.

ALLOWANCE FOR UNCOLLECTABLE ACCOUNTS: Balance sheet entry that lists the total number of accounts that will not be collected. Also known as bad debt expenses.

ALLOWANCE FOR UNCOLLECTIBLES: Balance sheet account that estimates a medical provider or health care organizations total amount of patient accounts receivable that will not be collected. See Bad Debt Expenses.

ALLOWED AMOUNT: Maximum dollar amount assigned for a procedure based on various pricing mechanisms. Also know as a maximum allowable. See UCR.

ALLOWED CHARGE: The amount Medicare approves for payment to a physician. Typically, Medicare pays 80% of the approved charge and the beneficiary pays the remaining 20%. The allowed charge for a nonparticipating physician is 95% of that for a participating physician. Nonparticipating physicians may bill beneficiaries for an additional amount above the allowed charge.

ALLOWED EXPENSE: The maximum dollar amount for covered health care expenses that a third party will reimburse for a service or item when a claim is made. See Allowed Charge.

ALL-PATIENT DIAGNOSTIC-RELATED GROUPS (APDRG): An enhancement of the original DRGs, designed to apply to a population broader than that of Medicare beneficiaries, who are predominately older individuals. The APDRG set includes groupings for pediatric and maternity cases as well as of services for diabetes, HIV-related conditions, and other special cases.

ALL-PAYER SYSTEM: A system by which all payers of health care bills, such as the government, private insurers, big companies, and individuals. It pays the same rates, set by the government, for the same medical service. This system does not allow for cost shifting.

ALTERNATIVE BIRTH CENTER: Usually a nonhospital facility for giving birth.

ALTERNATIVE DELIVERY SYSTEM: Provision of health services in settings that are more cost-effective than an inpatient, acute-care hospital, such as skilled and intermediary nursing facilities, hospice programs, and in-home services.

ALTERNATIVE DISPUTE RESOLUTION: An unofficial, voluntary, and nonlitigation process to dissolve insurance contract disputes.

ALTERNATIVE FACILITY: A nonhospital health care facility that provides one or more of the following on an outpatient basis: surgical services, emergency health services, rehabilitative services, laboratory or diagnostic services; or provides on an inpatient or outpatient basis: mental health or chemical dependency services. The facility may include an attachment to a hospital but does not include a doctor's office.

ALTERNATIVE HEALTH CARE: (alternative healing, alternative healing therapies, alternative health, alternative medicine, alternative therapeutics, alternative therapies, complementary health care, complementary medicine, extended therapeutics, fringe medicine, holistic healing, holistic health, holistic medicine, innovative medicine, mind body medicine, natural healing, natural health, natural medicine, New Age medicine, new medicine, planet medicine, unconventional medicine, unconventional therapies, unconventional therapy, unorthodox healing, unorthodox therapies, and holistic medicine.)

ALTERNATIVE THERAPIES: Nontraditional health care or medical services and techniques.

- Acupuncture—Treatment of a condition by influencing points on meridians, or lines of energy known as the chi, which interconnect across the body surface and relate to major organs of the body. This is done by the insertion of fine needles.
- Alexander Technique—Movement awareness and the reeducation of that movement to relieve long-term muscular stresses.
- Aromatherapy—Specialized technique, incorporating essential oils that are individually chosen for each treatment.
- Biomagnetics—Electronic magnetic intervention.
- Bowen Technique—A treatment consisting of a specific sequence of gentle, rolling moves done across superficial muscles, tendons, and nerves that realign the body and balance and stimulate energy flow.
- Chinese Medicine or Herbalism—One of the oldest systems of herbal therapy in the world, it treats a wide range of conditions with the use of raw herbs as well as a vast array of prepared or patent medicines available in pill and powder form.
- Dietary—The treatment of disorders and diseases, with specific substances, to correct or prevent an imbalance and to correct daily nutrition. It allows for the biochemical balance to be achieved through supplementation that can be maintained with the daily diet.
- Homoeopathy—A form of natural healing based on the Law of Similars, which states "like cures like." For example, a homoeopathic remedy that could produce symptoms in a healthy person might cure those same symptoms in a sick person.
- Hydrotherapy—Water-based treatment for muscular strains and sprains, muscular fatigue, and backache. Water is also useful in physiotherapy because patients who exercise in a buoyant medium can move weak parts of their bodies without contending with the strong force of gravity.
- Hypnotherapy—A method of lulling the conscious mind to reach the subconscious. When the subconscious is spoken to directly, old patterns and conditioning are reprogrammed and new ideas and positive suggestions are introduced. These positive suggestions are then used to help make the desired changes.
- Kinesiology—The study of body movement that identifies factors that block the body's natural healing process. Dysfunctions are treated at reflex and acupressure points and use of specific body movements.
- Manual Healing—See Massage Therapy
- Massage—Massage is a system of physical treatments aimed at alleviating tissue congestion.
- Mind–Body Control—Suggesting the mind is the center of illness or wellness.

- Myotherapy—A method of relaxing muscle spasm, improving circulation, and alleviating pain. To defuse trigger points, pressure is applied to the muscle for several seconds by means of fingers, knuckles, and elbows.
- Naturopathy—A wide range of diagnostic techniques are employed to assess causative factors, and treatment may involve dietary changes, herbal medicines, homoeopathy, or nutritional supplements.
- Reflexology—A system of manipulation of pressure points in the feet. It is believed that by stimulating these points healing mechanisms can be mobilized.
- Remedial Massage—A blend of approved, scientific massage techniques promoting efficiency in the body's systems that in turn enhances the functioning of the entire person.
- Shiatsu—The traditional Japanese technique of diagnosis and treatment is a method in which the thumbs and the palms of the hand are used to apply pressure to certain points. Deep pressure is used to stimulate these points, clearing blockages and restoring the flow of energy to the body.
- Western Herbalism—Classical herbal medicine uses the Hippocratic principles of treating the person, not the disease. It evaluates the patient's lifestyle and the emotional, circumstantial environment of the patient, not just the physical symptoms. Individually applicable herbal extracts and tinctures are then prescribed.

ALTERNATIVISM: Multifarious accumulation of antiestablishment and nonestablishmentarian movements. Alternativism encompasses alternative health care, apocalypticism, communalism, conspiracy theorizing, the Fortean movement, multilevel marketing (MLM, network marketing), naturism (nudism), organic farming, and parapsychology.

ALTERNATIVIST: A proponent of alternativism (especially medical alternativism) or a division or subgroup thereof. A proponent of a single alternativist method (e.g., the Alexander technique or natural hygiene) is not necessarily an alternativist. Adj., Affirmative of or conforming to alternativism, especially medical alternativism.

AMBAC (AMBAC INDEMNITY CORPORATION): A wholly owned subsidiary of MGIC Investment Corporation which offers noncancelable insurance contracts by which it agrees to pay a security holder all, or any part, of scheduled principal and interest payments on the securities as they become due and payable, in the event that the issuer is unable to pay. Hospital bonds insured by AMBAC are currently granted a Standard & Poor's rating of AAA.

AMBIGUITY: Unclear health insurance policy language subject to different interpretations and usually resolved in favor of the insured. Or, amorphous group of "therapeutic" and "diagnostic" methods chiefly distinguished from establishmentarian (science-oriented) health care by its acceptance of spiritual health as a medical concern. One of its general principles is that a practitioner is a teacher who can empower one. Its purported goal is not to cure, but to effect healing: an experience of physical, mental, and spiritual wholeness.

AMBULANCE: Emergency transportation vehicle used when immediate life saving treatment may be required, as in an emergency or a circumstance, in the opinion of a medical professional, the patient has received significant trauma. Also used for chronic patient transport.

AMBULANCE LEVY: A tax for free emergency ambulance transport between hospitals at the discretion of the ambulance service. See Ambulance.

AMBULANCE SUBSCRIPTION: A subscription from a recognized ambulance provider to cover all ambulance transport. See Ambulance.

AMBULATORY: Movable, revocable, subject to change. Customarily used in discussing wills to denote the power a testator has to change his or her will at any time so desired. See ASC.

AMBULATORY CARE: Health services provided without the patient being admitted (on an outpatient basis). No overnight stay in a hospital is required. The services of ambulatory care centers, hospital outpatient departments, physicians' offices, and home health care services fall under this heading; outpatient medical services. See ASC.

AMBULATORY CARE EVALUATION: Peer review of the need for, or appropriateness of, outpatient medical cares.

AMBULATORY CARE SENSITIVE CONDITIONS: Medical conditions for which physicians broadly concur that a substantial proportion of cases should not advance to the point where hospitalization is needed if they are treated in a timely fashion with adequate primary care and managed properly on an outpatient basis.

AMBULATORY GROUP VISIT: Nonadmitted health care delivery.

AMBULATORY PATIENT CLASSIFICATIONS (APC): A system for classifying outpatient services and procedures for purposes of payment. The APC system classifies some 7,000 services and procedures into about 300 procedure groups. See Ambulatory Surgical Center.

AMBULATORY SURGERY: Surgery performed on a nonhospitalized patient; patient goes home the same day as the surgery. See Ambulatory Surgical Center.

AMBULATORY SURGICAL CENTER (ASC): A freestanding facility certified by Medicare that performs certain types of procedures on an outpatient basis. See Ambulatory Care.

AMBULATORY SURGICAL FACILITY: Provides surgical services on an outpatient basis for patients who do not need to occupy an inpatient, acutecare hospital bed. See ASC.

AMBULATORY VISIT GROUP (AVG): Similar to DRGs (Diagnosis-Related Group), except used for outpatient rather than inpatient hospital care.

AMENDMENT: A description of additional provisions attached to a contract. An amendment is valid only when signed by an officer of a health care insurance company.

AMENDMENTS AND CORRECTIONS: In the final HIPAA privacy rule, an amendment to a record would indicate that the data is in dispute while retaining the original information, whereas a correction to a record would alter or replace the original record.

AMERICAN ACADEMY OF ACTUARIES: A society organized to advance knowledge of actuarial science and concerned with the development of education in the field and the support of high standards within the actuarial profession. See Actuary.

AMERICAN ASSOCIATION FOR HOMECARE: An industry association for the home care industry, including home intravenous therapy, home medical services and manufacturers, and home health providers. AAH was created through the merger of the Health Industry Distributors Association's Home Care Division (HIDA Home Care), the Home Health Services and Staffing Association (HHSSA), and the National Association for Medical Equipment Services (NAMES).

AMERICAN ASSOCIATION OF PREFERRED PROVIDER ORGANIZATIONS (AAPPO): A trade organization for PPOs. See PPOs.

AMERICAN COLLEGE: An education institution located in Bryn Mawr, Pennsylvania, which confers the chartered life underwriter (CLU) and the chartered financial consultant (ChFC) designations and a master of science in Financial Services degree. Concerned with continuing agent training, research, and publication in areas related to the life, health, disability, and other insurance business. Formerly known as the American College of Life Underwriters.

AMERICAN EXPERIENCE TABLE OF MORTALITY: The mortality table published in 1861 by Sheppard Homans, an actuary with the Mutual Life Insurance Company of New York. It was widely used for the calculation of life insurance premiums and reserves and was the basis for the issuing of a large amount of insurance over many years. The Commissioners Standard Ordinary (CSO) Task Force Table has replaced it.

AMERICAN MANAGED CARE AND REVIEW ASSOCIATION (AMCRA): A trade association representing managed care indemnity plans. See Managed Care.

AMERICANS WITH DISABILITIES ACT (ADA): Public Law 336 of the 101st Congress, enacted July 26, 1990. The ADA prohibits discrimination and ensures equal opportunity for persons with disabilities in employment, state and local government services, public accommodations, commercial facilities, and transportation. It also mandates the establishment of telecommunications device for the deaf or TDD/telephone relay services.

AMORTIZATION OF DEBT (LOAN): The process of paying the principal amount of an issue of hospital securities by periodic payments either directly to security holders or to a sinking fund for the benefit of security holders.

AMOUNT BILLED: Value of health care rendered by a facility or provider on a bill or insurance claim.

AMOUNT, DURATION, AND SCOPE: State Medicaid benefit definition of provided health care services.

AMT BOND: Certain private purpose municipal hospital bonds pay tax-exempt interest that is subject to the alternative minimum tax. They are called private purpose rather than public purpose because 10% or more of the proceeds goes to private activities. Examples are bonds used to fund ASCs or private hospitals. The Municipal Securities Rulemaking Board (MSRB) rules require that confirmations indicate if the bond is subject to the AMT.

ANALYTIC EPIDEMIOLOGY: Epidemiology concerned with the search for health-related causes and effects. Uses comparison groups, which provide baseline data, to quantify the association between exposures and outcomes, and test hypotheses about causal relationships.

ANCHOR GROUP: Large medical groups that accept and treat large numbers of managed care patients.

ANCILLARY BENEFITS: Secondary benefits provided in a contract providing insurance coverage, such as benefits provided for miscellaneous hospital charges in a basic room and board hospitalization policy. See Medicare Advantage.

ANCILLARY CARE: Additional health care services performed, such as lab work and X-rays. See Ancillary Services.

ANCILLARY/EXTRAS: These are benefits for health-related services that are not covered by Medicare. Health funds vary considerably in services that they offer as benefits; however, most include services, such as dental, optical, physiotherapy, chiropractic, and naturopathy.

ANCILLARY SERVICES: Professional charges for x-ray, laboratory tests, and other similar patient services. See Ancillary Care.

"AND INTEREST": A hospital bond transaction in which the buyer pays the seller a contract price plus interest accrued since the issuer's last interest payment. Virtually all interest bearing bonds always trade "and interest."

ANESTHESIA: The induced partial or complete loss of painful or other sensation.

ANESTHESIA MINUTE OF SERVICE: The elapsed time of anesthesia services provided to a patient.

ANESTHESIOLOGIST: A doctor who specializes in the administration of anesthesia or other pain management services or interventions.

ANESTHESIOLOGY: The medical science of anesthesia or pain control.

ANESTHETIST: A nonphysician MD/DO who administers anesthesia, such as a certified registered nurse anesthetist (CRNA).

ANNIVERSARY DATE: The beginning of an employer group's benefit year. The first day of effective coverage as contained in the policy group application and subsequent annual anniversaries of that date. An insured has the option to transfer from an indemnity plan (which may have maximum benefit levels) to an HMO.

ANNUAL COMPLETION FACTOR: A math factor that adjusts annual expected health insurance claims to annual incurred claims.

ANNUAL ELECTION PERIOD: The Annual Election Period for Medicare beneficiaries is the month of November each year.

ANNUAL FEES: Predetermined pricing in concierge medicine based on the desired number of patients in a practice. That patient number can range from 100 individuals to upwards of 700 patients.

ANNUAL LIMIT: The maximum amount for a health benefit that will be paid in a continuous 12 month period, either calendar year or membership year. If transferred from another health fund, the calculation may or may not include claims paid by the previous fund.

ANNUAL PREMIUM: The premium amount required on an annual basis under the contractual requirements of a policy to keep a health insurance policy in force. See Premium.

ANNUAL REPORT: A formal statement issued yearly by a hospital, health care corporation, or insurance company to its shareowners. It shows assets, liabilities, equity revenues, expenses, and so forth. It is a reflection of the corporation's condition at the close of the business year (balance sheet) and earnings performance (income statement).

ANNUAL REPORT SUMMARY: A summary of assets and liabilities, receipts and disbursements, current value assets, present value of vested benefits, and any other financial information about an insurance plan and company that must be provided annually to participants. See Annual Report.

ANNUITY: A series of cash payments disbursed at regular time increments.

ANSI: The American National Standards Institute. A national trade group organization founded to develop voluntary business standards in the United States.

ANTIDISCRIMINATORY LAWS: Laws prohibiting insurance companies from offering preferential rates not warranted by the standard rating of the risk.

ANTIREBATE LAWS: State laws that prohibit an insurance agent or company from giving part of the premium back to the insured as an inducement to buy insurance coverage. See Twisting and Churning.

ANTISELECTION: See Adverse Selection and Risk Management.

ANTITRUST: A legal term encompassing a variety of efforts on the part of government to assure that sellers do not conspire to restrain trade or fix prices for their goods or services in the market. See Fraud and Abuse and Stark.

ANY WILLING PROVIDER (AWP): A medical provider who agrees to accept payment in full for services provided. See Any Willing Provider Laws.

ANY WILLING PROVIDER LAWS: Laws that require managed care plans to contract with all health care providers that meet their terms and conditions. See Any Willing Provider.

APPARENT AUTHORITY: The power that is logical for the public to assume an agent has, whether he or she actually has been granted that power by contract or not. An agent can bind the company by acting under apparent authority as well as under actual authority insofar as commitments to the public go. An agent who knowingly commits his or her company under the power of apparent authority is open to a possible civil suit from the company to recover damages. See Implied Authority.

APPEAL: Formal dispute of usually noncovered products or medical services in a health insurance contact. Or, an oral or written request to change a decision regarding a grievance already ruled upon. There are two types of appeals: medical and administrative. See ADR and Mediation.

APPEAL PROCESS: The process to use in a disagreement with any decision about health care or health insurance services. For example, if Medicare does not pay for an item or service, one can have the initial Medicare decision reviewed again. If in a Medicare managed care plan, an appeal can be filed if the plan will not pay for, does not allow, or stops a service that you think should be covered or provided. The Medicare managed care plan must state in writing how to appeal. See ADR. See Mediation.

APPENDIX: An attachment at the end of an insurance contract. It adds to certain provisions of the contract. The appendix is valid only when signed by the party offering the contract.

APPLICANT: The person(s), employee, or entity applying for and signing the written application for a contract of health or managed care insurance or annuity, either on his or her own life or that of another. See Policyholder, and Application and Approval.

APPLICATION: A written form provided by an insurer typically completed by the insurer's agent and, in the case of a health insurance policy, its medical examiner (in most cases) on the basis of personal and verifiable information on the physical condition, occupation, and avocation of the proposed insured. The policy application is signed by the applicant (typically, but not always, the insured) and becomes a legal part of the information for the insurer in deciding whether or not, or on what terms and conditions, a health insurance contract should be issued. See Applicant and Approval.

APPLICATION CARD: An index card statement requesting medical services for which the insured member is eligible.

APPOINTMENT: Agent authorization to act on behalf of a health, life, managed care, or other insurance company. See Application.

APPOINTMENT PAPERS: Documents that the insurance agent compiles and returns to his or her company. These documents are connected with the agent's appointment.

APPROACH TO TAKE: The decision in concierge medicine to be a franchise/affiliate with a premium service plan or remain independent. Although membership in a current practice offers the advantage of experience and expertise, it does require a long-term sharing of revenues. If physicians choose independence, then they must also decide on whether to use outside consultants for transition assistance. The business model of retainer medicine.

APPROPRIATENESS: Appropriate health care is care for which the expected health benefit exceeds the expected negative consequences by a wide enough margin to justify treatment. See Quality of Care.

APPROPRIATIONS: Monies provided by federal agencies for health care and other organizations.

APPROVAL: The primary process of managing health care. Approval usually is used to describe treatments or procedures that have been certified by utilization review. It can also refer to the status of certain hospitals or doctors, as members of a plan. Or, it can describe benefits or services that will be covered under a plan. Generally, approval is either granted by the managed care organization (MCO), third party administrator (TPA), or by the primary care physician (PCP), depending on the circumstances. Approval is also the process of accepting an applicant for a health, disability, long-term care, managed care, or other insurance policy. See Applicant.

APPROVED AMOUNT: Reasonable fee limits sanctioned by Medicare in a given area of covered service. Fee approved by payment by private health plans. Items likely reimbursed by the insurance company. May or may not be the same as the approved charge. See Approved Charge and UCR.

APPROVED CHARGE: Limits of expenses paid by Medicare in a given area of covered service. Charges approved by payment by private health plans. Items likely reimbursed by the insurance company. See UCR.

APPROVED HEALTH CARE FACILITY, HOSPITAL, OR PROGRAM: A facility or program that is authorized to provide health services and allowed by a given health plan to provide services stipulated in contract.

APPROVED SERVICES: Services and supplies covered under an insurance agreement, contract, or certificate within the benefit period.

APPROXIMATE PERCENTAGE COST: Estimated of the annualized interest rate incurred by not taking a health care insurance premium or other discount.

ARBITRATION CLAUSE: A clause within a policy providing that if the policy-owner and the insurer fail to agree on the settlement amount of a claim, they select a neutral arbitrator with the authority to bind both parties to the settlement. See ADR and Mediation.

AREA AGENCY ON AGING (AAA): State and local programs that help older people plan and care for their life-long needs. These needs include adult day care, skilled nursing care/therapy, transportation, personal care, respite care, and meals.

ARREARS: Health insurance membership contributions that have not been paid by the due date.

ARREARS AND ADVANCES: In reference to home service insurance, arrears are the total of premiums due up to and including the current week or month. Advances are the total premiums paid in advance of the current week or month.

ASC-APPROVED PROCEDURE: A procedure that has been approved by Medicare for payment. A procedure may be approved if it can be performed safely in the outpatient setting, if it was performed in the inpatient setting at least 20% of the time when it was approved, and if it is performed in physicians' offices no more than 50% of the time. See Ambulatory Surgery Center.

ASK PRICE: (1) The price at which a health care security or mutual fund's shares can be purchased. The asking or offering price means the net asset value per share plus sales charge. (2) The offer side of a quote.

ASO (Administrative Services Only): A self-insured plan contracts with an insurance company for services, such as claims processing and stop-loss coverage.

ASSESSED VALUATION: The appraised worth of hospital property set by a taxing authority for purposes of ad valorem taxation. It is important to note that the method of establishing assessed valuation varies from state to state, with the method generally specified by state law.

ASSESSMENT: The regular collection, analysis, and sharing of information about health conditions, risks, and resources in a community. The assessment function is needed to identify trends in illness, injury, and death; the factors that may cause these events; available health resources and their application; unmet needs; and community perceptions about health issues.

ASSET-MIX: Percentage of assets relative to the total number of assets, in a health care or other organization.

ASSETS: The resources owned by a healthcare or other organization. Everything of value that a healthcare company owns or has due: (a) fixed assets—cash, investments, money due, materials, inventories (called current assets: buildings and machinery); and (b) intangible assets—patents and good will. See Liability and Net Assets.

ASSETS, INSURANCE COMPANY: Those assets that include all funds, property, goods, securities, rights, or resources of any kind, less such items as are declared nonadmissible by state laws. Nonadmissible items consist mainly of deferred or overdue premiums.

ASSIGN: To transfer an ownership right or risk in a health insurance or other contract to another. See Transfer.

ASSIGNED CLAIM: A health care claim submitted by a medical provider who accepts Medicare. See Assign.

ASSIGNED RISK: A risk that underwriters do not wish to insure, but that must be covered due to state or federal law. See Risk, Risk Pool, and Assign.

ASSIGNEE: The person or party who receives a transferred right or risk when a contract is assigned. See Assign.

ASSIGNMENT: A process under which Medicare pays its share of the allowed charge directly to the physician or supplier. Medicare will do this only if the physician accepts Medicare's allowed charge as payment in full (guarantees not to balance bill). Medicare provides other incentives to physicians who accept assignment for all patients under the Participating Physician and Supplier Program. See Assign.

ASSIGNMENT OF BENEFITS: The payment of medical benefits directly to a provider of care rather than to a member. Generally requires either a contract between the health plan and the provider or a written release from the subscriber to the provider allowing the provider to bill the health plan. See Assign.

ASSIGNOR: A person or business that transfers rights under an insurance policy to another by means of an assignment. See Assign and Assignee.

ASSISTED LIVING: Type of living arrangement in which meals, shelter, transportation, and the activities of daily living are provided in one's own home or another facility.

ASSISTED REPRODUCTIVE SERVICES: Nontraditional methods used to assist conception, such as IVF (In-Vitro Fertilization).

ASSISTIVE TECHNOLOGY: Equipment or systems used to assist patients with functional, physical, or mental impairments and disabilities.

ASSOCIATED MEDICAL CARE PLAN: The formal name for Blue Shield.

ASSOCIATION A&H POLICY: Individual accident and health policies written to cover a member of a trade or professional association. Also called association insurance.

ASSOCIATION OF LIFE INSURANCE MEDICAL DIRECTORS: An organization of doctors and medical directors of insurance companies.

ASSUME: To accept all or part of a company's insurance or reinsurance on a risk.

ASSUMED INTEREST RATE: The rate of interest used by an insurance company to calculate its reserves. Historically, this rate is usually rather low: 2% to 3% for sake of safety.

ASSUMED REINSURANCE: Business accepted for reinsurance from another insurance company.

ASSUMPTION: The amount accepted as reinsurance.

ASSUMPTION OF RISK: Risk retention or self-insurance relative to health, life, disability, auto, home, or other insurance needs. See Peril and Hazard.

ASSURANCE: Making sure that needed health services and functions are available. See insurance. See Insurance.

ASSURED: Same an insured.

ASSURER: Same as insurer.

ATC: Athletic trainer certified.

AT RISK: Subject to some uncertain economic or physical event during the provision of health care services.

ATTAINED AGE: Most insurers base premium rates on the age an insured has attained as of the application for insurance or its issue date (the age and insured has reached on a specific date). Generally, this is the age of the proposed insured based on his or her nearest (or, in some cases, last) birthday, or the insured's age on the policy date plus the number of full years since the policy date.

ATTENDING PHYSICIAN: The physician in charge of a patient's medical, surgical, or health care.

ATTENDING PHYSICIAN STATEMENT: Document requiring addition medical information from a physician for a health, life, disability, or other insurance policy. See Gatekeeper and Internist.

ATTESTATION CLAUSE: The clause of a health policy or MCO/HCO contract to which the officers of the insurance company sign their names to complete the contract. Sometimes used at the end of an application to attest to the truth and completeness of the statements made by an applicant for insurance. Also, that clause in a will in which witnesses certify that the will was signed in their presence by the maker of the will and that it was properly executed.

ATTORNEY IN FACT: The authority granted to an individual to legally act for another. See Power of Attorney.

ATTRITION RATE: Disenrollment expressed as a percentage of total membership. An HMO that begins with 50,000 members and loses 1,000 members per month is experiencing a 2% monthly attrition rate. See Persistency Rate.

AUDIOLOGIST: One who practices audiology.

AUDIOLOGY: The examination, research, and treatment of hearing defects, usually by a nonphysician.

AUDIT: A legally required review of a company, agency's, or individual's financial records. See Fraud and Abuse and Actuary.

AUDITOR: Individual who makes a formal examination and verification of financial and other records. See Actuary and Fraud and Abuse.

AUDIT OF PROVIDER TREATMENT OR CHARGES: A qualitative or quantitative review of services rendered or proposed by a health provider. The review can be carried out in a number of ways: a comparison of patient records and claim form information, a patient questionnaire, a review of hospital and practitioner records, or a pre- or posttreatment clinical examination of a patient. Some audits may involve fee verification. This is usually the first type or "first generation" managed care approach.

AURA: Alleged envelope of invisible vital energy.

AUTHENTICATE: To prove or demonstrate as genuine.

AUTHORIZATION: As it applies to managed care, authorization is the approval of care, such as hospitalization. Preauthorization may be required before admission takes place or care is given by noninsulin diabetes-HMO providers. See Fraud and Abuse.

AUTHORIZATION NUMBER: A number assigned to each authorized referral for service outside the health plan. This number is put on a claim form to allow claims payment.

AUTOADJUDICATION: Those medical and health care claims processed without manual intervention.

AUTOASSIGNMENT: A term used with Medicaid mandatory managed care enrollment plans. Medicaid recipients who do not specify their choice for a contracted plan within a specified time frame are assigned to a plan by the state.

AUTOLOGOUS BONE MARROW TRANSPLANT: The transfer of one's own bone or marrow for the treatment of orthopedic skeletal defects or cancer. See Allogenic Bone Marrow Transplant.

AUTOMATIC PAYMENT PLAN (bank draft): A method of payment where a health insurance premium is deducted directly from an account at a financial institution on a monthly basis.

AUTONOMY: The ethical duty to make correct managed care decisions about individuals, rather than bands, cohorts, or medical groups.

AVAILABILITY: Appropriate health care rendered at the time and place needed and by the appropriate medical provider.

AVAILABLE TIME: The time amount expended in delivery health care.

AVAILS (OF A CONTRACT): The benefit derived from an insurance contract, including death benefit, dividends, waiver of premium, health care cost coverage, etc.

AVERAGE CHARGE PER DAY: The average charge billed by hospitals for 1 day of care, which is Adjusted Total Charges divided by total days of care. Only patients discharged are included in this calculation.

AVERAGE CHARGE PER STAY: The average charge billed by hospitals for an inpatient stay (from the day of admission to the day of discharge), which is Adjusted Total Charges divided by number of discharges. Only patients discharged are included.

AVERAGE DAILY CENSUS (ADC): The average number of patients in a health care facility per day. Derived by dividing the number of patient days for the year by the number of days the facility was open during the year.

AVERAGE DAILY PATIENT LOAD: Number of hospital inpatients, excluding live births, during a reporting period or discharged the same day.

AVERAGE EARNINGS CLAUSE: An optional provision in a disability income policy that permits the company to limit the monthly income disability benefits to the amount of his or her average earnings for the 24 months prior to the disability. Generally found only in guaranteed renewable and noncancellable policies.

AVERAGE HOURLY EXPENSE: Salaries and wages paid to all employees in a specific health care cost center or service and in a given classification for hours worked divided by the total hours worked by those employees.

AVERAGE INDEXED MONTHLY EARNINGS (AIME): The basis used for calculating the primary insurance amount (PIA) for disability and Social Security benefits.

AVERAGE LENGTH OF STAY (ALOS): Using census or discharge days, it is the average number of days of service rendered or period of hospitalization of all inpatients discharged (including deaths) over the reporting period. This average is the result of dividing the patient (census) days by hospital discharges (excluding nursery) for each facility.

AVERAGE MONTHLY WAGE: Figures per week used to determine a worker's Primary Insurance Amount (PIA) for Social Security benefits or worker's compensation.

AVERAGE PAYMENT PERIOD: Ratio that suggests how long it takes for a medical provider or health care organization to pay its bills.

AVERAGE PAYMENT RATE: The amount of money that HCFA (CMS) could conceivably pay an HMO for services to Medicare recipients under a risk contract.

AVERAGE RISK: The basis of all insurance mathematics. A risk in accordance with the conditions called for in the establishment of the basic rate of an insurance company. See Peril and Hazard.

AVERAGE SEMIPRIVATE RATE: Average rate billed for a semiprivate room in a hospital, nursing home, or other health care facility.

AVERAGE WEEKLY BENEFITS: Usually called weekly compensation in workers' compensation insurance. The amount payable per week for disability or death as prescribed by law. This is usually a percentage of the average weekly wage, subject to a minimum and maximum amount.

AVERAGE WEEKLY WAGE: The average rate of employment benefits, salary, or worker's compensation remuneration per week, computed as prescribed by law.

AVERAGE WHOLESALE PRICE (AWP): Commonly used in pharmacy contracting, the AWP is generally determined through reference to a common source of information.

AVOIDABLE FIXED COST: A fixed cost that may no longer be needed if the medical product line, or health care service, is discontinued. See Expense and Cost Driver.

AVOIDABLE HOSPITAL CONDITIONS: Hospitalizations not needed, if appropriate intervention was provided earlier in the course of care and medical treatment.

AVOIDANCE OF RISK: One of four methods to manage risks; taking steps to remove a health or other hazard or engage in another unhealthy or hazardous activity. See Peril and Hazard.

B

BACK-END LOAD: A surrender charge deducted in some life insurance and health insurance products. Most such policies have a decreasing back-end load that generally disappears completely after a certain number of years. See Commissions.

BACK-UP PROVIDER: A designated substitute for a primary care provider who will render treatment in the event the primary care provider is not available. The back-up provider performs the same function as the primary care provider. Doctor.

BAD DEBT EXPENSE: Amount owed to a health care entity that will not be paid. See Accounts Receivable.

BALANCE: In health insurance, the residual amount of money due a company from its agent after all credits and charges are calculated.

BALANCE BILLING: (1) Physician charges in excess of Medicare or contractually allowed amounts, for which Medicare or contractual patients are responsible, subject to a limit. (2) In Medicare and private fee-for-service health insurance, the practice of billing patients in excess of the amount approved by the health plan. In Medicare, a balance bill cannot exceed 15% of the allowed charge for nonparticipating physicians. See Allowed Charge and Nonparticipating Physicians. See Balance.

BALANCED SECURITY: A concept used in needs analysis to determine the amount of income a family would require should the chief wage earner die or become sick, hospitalized, or disabled. It is based on the accounting concept of income versus expenses.

BALANCE SHEET: One of four major financial statements for a health care organization. It presents a summary of assets, liabilities, and net assets for a specific date. A condensed statement showing the nature and amount of a company's assets and liabilities. It shows in dollar amounts what the company owns, what it owes, and the ownership interest (shareholders' equity). See Balance Sheet Reserve.

BALANCE SHEET RESERVE: Amount expressed as a liability on the insurance company's balance sheet for benefits owed to policy owners. See Balance Sheet.

BALANCE SHEET RESERVE PLAN: A funding plan that sets up a bookkeeping entry acknowledging some or all of the liability incurred for the payment of benefits and taking this liability into account in determining profits and the stockholders' equity.

BANDING: Based on the principle of economy of size, life and health insurance premiums are often banded, so that larger size policies are charged a more favorable rate than smaller policies. See Segmentation.

BANK CHECK PLAN: A simplified method of monthly health insurance premium payment. With the prearranged consent of the insured, the insurance company automatically deducts the monthly premium due from the insured's checking account.

BANKRUPT: Unable to pay debts. See Bankruptcy.

BANKRUPTCY: A legal proceeding ordering the distribution of an insolvent person's property among creditors, thus relieving this individual of all liability to these creditors, even though this payment may be less than the full obligation to them. See Bankrupt.

BARE-BONES HEALTH PLANS: Designed mainly for small businesses, these are no-frills, low-cost policies with limited hospitalization, large deductibles and copayments, and low policy limits. Over half of the states have waived mandated health benefits to allow the sale of these plans.

BARRIERS TO ACCESS: Barriers to health insurance coverage access can be financial (insufficient monetary resources), geographic (distance to providers), organizational (lack of available providers), and sociological (discrimination, language barriers).

BASE CAPITATION: Specified amount per person per month to cover health care cost, usually excluding pharmacy and administrative costs as well as optional coverage, such as mental health or substance abuse services. See Capitation and Prospective Payment System.

BASE YEAR COSTS: Medicare term for the amount of money a hospital actually spent to render care in a specific previous annual time period.

BASIC ACCOUNTING EQUATION: Assets equal liabilities plus stockholder's (owner's) equity.

BASIC BENEFITS: A set of "basic health services" specified in the member's certificate and those services required under applicable federal and state laws and regulations.

BASIC BENEFITS PACKAGE: A core set of health benefits everyone would have, either through an employer, a government program, or a risk pool. Most health reform proposals include a basic benefits package.

BASIC COVERAGE: Coverage from Blue Cross/Blue Shield excluding major medical health insurance.

BASIC DRG PAYMENT RATE: The payment rate a hospital will receive for a Medicare patient in a particular diagnosis-related group (DRG). The payment rate is calculated by adjusting the standardized amount to reflect wage rates in the hospital's geographic area (and cost of living differences unrelated to wages) and the costliness of the DRG.

BASIC HEALTH PLAN (BHP): State-sponsored health insurance plan for children and adults not eligible for the standard Medicaid program or who do not otherwise receive employment-based coverage. The plan pays all costs for children in families with incomes up to 200% of the federal poverty level and part of insurance costs for adults up to 200% of the federal poverty level. Individuals or families above the income cutoff can purchase BHP coverage at unsubsidized rates.

BASIC HOSPITALIZATION POLICY: A medical expense health plan that provides payment for hospital expenses only. Pays first-dollar benefits, but has relatively low limits.

BASIC HOSPITAL PLAN: Minimum payments under a health insurance policy.

BASIC LIFE INSURANCE: An insurance policy that provides a health benefit when an insured dies.

BASIC PREMIUM: A percentage of the standard premium used to determine the premium for a workers' compensation risk, utilizing the retrospective rating plan that permits adjustment of the final premium for a risk on the basis of the loss experience of the insured during the period of protection, subject to maximum and minimum limits. See Premium.

BASIC RATE: The manual or experience rate from which are taken discounts or to which are added charges to compensate for the individual circumstances of risk.

BASIC AND STANDARD: Basic and Standard health plans provide comprehensive major medical coverage with benefits for fundamental health care needs. Basic is available to individuals or small employer groups who have been without employer-sponsored health care coverage for the past 12 months.

BASIS: Property basis is the original cost adjusted by charges (such as deductions for depreciation) or credits (such as capitalized expenditures for improvements); it sets the basis for calculating depreciation and assists in establishing the gain or loss on sale of the property.

BASIS POINT: One tenth, of 1% of yield. If a yield increases from 8.25% to 8.50%, the difference is referred to as a 25 basis point increase. The exchange rate where one percentage point equals 100 basis points (bps).

BASSINET DAY: A live birth that occupies a newborn nursery bassinet at the time a census was taken.

BATCH: A collection of health insurance claims or payments in or on a computer system or health care information technology network.

BATCH BALANCING: Health insurance claims or other items processed against a control group to avoid duplication fraud or loss.

BATCH NUMBERING: A serial number applied to each health insurance claim or payment for identification purposes.

BED: Literally, a cot or overnight sleeping chamber, room, or place in a health care facility or hospital.

BED AVAILABLE: Fully functioning health care facility bed that is available for patient use.

BED CAPACITY: The number of licensed beds in a hospital or health care facility.

BED DAYS: A measurement used by managed care plans to indicate the total number of days of hospital care provided to a member of a health or managed care plan.

BED HOLD: The holding of a patient's bed while the patient is on temporary leave or is admitted to an acute hospital for an expected short stay.

BED LICENSE: The number of beds a hospital or health care facility is approved to have and maintain for patient care.

BED SET-UP: The bed inside a hospital or health care facility that is ready and available in all ways to receive a patient.

BED SIZE: The average number of licensed beds for a hospital or long-term care facility.

BED SIZE GROUP: Based on the number of hospital or long-term care facility beds licensed.

BEFORE-AND-AFTER DESIGN (EVALUATION): A design in which only a few before-intervention and after-intervention health care measures are taken.

BEFORE-TAX EARNINGS: A person's gross income from salary, commissions, fees, etc., before deductions for federal, state, or other income taxes.

BEGINNING INVENTORY: The amount of health care inventory on hand at the start of an account period. See Ending Inventory.

BEHAVIORAL HEALTH CARE: The diagnosis, care, treatment, and research directed toward mental, drug abuse, and psychotic diseases and disorders.

BEHAVIORAL OFFSET: This is the change in the number and type of services that is projected to occur in response to a change in fees. A 50% behavioral offset suggests that 50% of the savings from fee reductions will be offset by increased volume and intensity of services. See Volume Offset.

BEHAVIORAL RISK FACTOR SURVEILLANCE SYSTEM: Annual telephone survey of state residents aged 18 and older that measures a variety of behaviors that affect health, such as diet, smoking, and use of preventive health services.

BENCHMARKING: The identification of best practices in the health care, health insurance, or other industry that shows superior performance.

BENEFICIAL INTEREST: A financial or other valuable interest arising from an insurance policy.

BENEFICIARY (eligible, enrollee, member): Any person eligible as either a subscriber or a dependent for a managed care service in accordance with a contract. Someone who is eligible for or receiving benefits under an insurance policy or plan. The term is commonly applied to people receiving benefits under the Medicare or Medicaid programs. The person to whom the proceeds of a life or health insurance policy are payable when the insured dies. There are three types of beneficiaries: Primary beneficiaries are those first entitled to the proceeds; secondary beneficiaries are entitled to proceeds only if no primary beneficiary is living when the insured dies; tertiary beneficiaries are those entitled to proceeds if no primary or secondary beneficiaries are alive when the insured dies. Secondary and tertiary beneficiaries are also referred to as alternate or contingent beneficiaries, because their claims are contingent on the deaths of the primary beneficiaries.

BENEFICIARY CHANGE: The replacement of one beneficiary in a policy with another. The beneficiary may be changed only if the policy gives such right to the policy owner and if the law permits.

BENEFICIARY ENCRYPTED FILE: A restricted public use file. An Agreement for Release of the Centers for Medicare & Medicaid (CMS) Beneficiary Encrypted Files data use agreement is required.

BENEFICIARY LIABILITY: The amount beneficiaries must pay providers for Medicare-covered services. Liabilities include copayments and coinsurance amounts, deductibles, and balance billing amounts. See Exclusions.

BENEFICIARY, PRIMARY: The principal beneficiary who is first entitled to the proceeds of a policy upon the death of the insured.

BENEFIT: Monetary sums payable to a recipient, contingent upon the occurrence of the conditions set out in the policy. Not synonymous with indemnity.

BENEFIT FOR CHILD OF RETIRED WORKER: Under Social Security, a monthly benefit provided for a natural, adopted, or step child or, in some cases, for a grandchild of a person receiving old-age benefits. The benefit is paid until the child is 18 years (or beyond, if the child is totally and permanently disabled), or until 22 years, if he or she is a full-time student in a public or accredited school or college, unless the child marries.

BENEFIT CLAUSE: A provision in health policies that describes the payments and the services provided under the contract.

BENEFIT DAYS: The number of days that a health or managed care company will provide benefits for within a given time period.

BENEFIT DEPARTMENT: The home office department in a life insurance company that processes all claims under life, health, group, or disability benefit policies. It handles the distributions of benefits of the company's policies.

BENEFIT FOR DISABLED CHILD OF DECEASED, DISABLED, OR RETIRED WORKER: Under Social Security, a monthly benefit provided for an eligible disabled child or grandchild (although older than 18 years) of a deceased, disabled, or retired worker.

BENEFIT FOR DISABLED WIDOW OR WIDOWER AGED 50–62: Under Social Security, a monthly benefit paid to an eligible disabled widow or widower of a covered worker; in some cases, paid as early as age 50. The amount of the benefit depends on the Primary Insurance Amount (PIA) of the deceased covered worker and the widow or widower's age when benefits begin.

BENEFIT EXHAUSTED DATA: A Medicare term for the date a beneficiary has used maximum benefits for the current benefit or enrollment period.

BENEFIT LEVELS: The entitlement limitations based on a health or managed medical care contract or insurance policy.

BENEFIT LIMITATIONS: Any provision, other than an exclusion, that restricts coverage in the evidence of coverage, regardless of medical necessity. See Evidence of Coverage.

BENEFIT PAYMENT SCHEDULE: List of amounts an insurance plan will pay for covered health care services.

BENEFIT PERIOD: In reference to health insurance, the maximum length of time benefits will be paid for any one accident, illness, or hospital stay.

BENEFIT PERIOD MAXIMUM: The total dollar amount, number of days, or number of visits allowed during a benefit period for each person covered under health care insurance certificate.

BENEFITS: Benefits are specific areas of Plan coverage's (i.e., outpatient visits, hospitalization, and so forth) that make up the range of medical services that a payer markets to its subscribers. Also, a contractual agreement, specified in an Evidence-of-Coverage determining covered services provided by insurers to members. See Exclusions.

BENEFITS ADMINISTRATOR: The person responsible for administering an insurance program for a group. Benefits administrators maintain employee insurance information, submit membership changes, and pay group premiums.

BENEFITS-TO-COSTS RATIO: The total discounted benefits divided by the total discounted costs.

BENEFIT OF SELECTION: The desirable advantage employed by an insurance company through the careful selection of insurance risks.

BENEFITS (EVALUATION): Net health insurance project outcomes, usually translated into monetary terms. Benefits may include both direct and indirect effects.

BENEFITS EXPLORATION: Net project outcomes, usually translated into monetary terms. Health care insurance coverage benefits may include both direct and indirect effects.

BENEFITS PACKAGE: Services covered by a health insurance plan and the financial terms of such coverage, including cost sharing and limitations on amounts of services. See Cost Sharing.

BENEFITS PERCENTAGE: Disability insurance benefit payable and determined as a percentage of the insured's predisability income up to an overall maximum benefit amount.

BENEFITS PLAN: The terms, conditions, and scope of a long-term care, disability, managed care, or other health insurance policy.

BIG I: See National Association of Insurance Agents.

BILATERAL CONTRACT: One that both parties have enforceable commitments, as in a contract of sale, one party promises to deliver the item sold and the other party promises to pay the stated price. Health insurance contracts are not bilateral. They are unilateral because only one party, the insurer, makes an enforceable promise to pay; the insured can not be required to pay the premium. See Alleatory. See Adhesion.

BILLED CLAIMS: The fees or billed charges for health care services provided to a covered person that have been submitted by a health care provider to a payer.

BILLING CODE OF 1992 (UB-92): A Federal code billing form that requires hospitals follow a specific billing procedures. Similar to (CMS) HCFA 1500, but reserved for the inpatient component of health services.

BILLING, COLLECTIONS, AND DISBURSEMENT POLICY: Tools that health and managed care organizations use to increase the amount of cash available by increasing cash premium receipts and slowing cash disbursements for benefits.

BILLING CYCLE: The exact date on which certain medical services are billed.

BILLING FLOAT: Time delayed between medical services provision and invoicing the third party or patient.

BINDER: A temporary or preliminary agreement that provides insurance coverage until a policy can be written or delivered.

BINDING RECEIPT: The receipt for payment of the first premium that assures the applicant that if he or she dies before receiving the policy, the company will pay the full claim if the policy is issued (or would have been issued) as applied for.

BIOFEEDBACK: Any method that involves electronic monitors wherewith one tries to influence autonomic activities, such as the beating of the heart. Forms of biofeedback include electromyographic biofeedback, which measures muscle tension, and thermal biofeedback, which measures skin temperature.

BIOLOGICALS: Usually a vaccine or drug used for a medical condition.

BIOMETRIC IDENTIFIER: An identifier based on some physical characteristic, such as fingerprints, DNA, or iris-scan.

BIOTERRORISM (BIOLOGICAL WARFARE): The unlawful use, wartime use, or threatened use, of microorganisms or toxins to produce death or disease in humans. Often viewed as the preferred choice of warfare of less powerful groups of people in attempt to wage war or protect themselves from more powerful groups or nations. However, biological agents could be used by individuals or by powerful nations as well.

BIRTH RATE: The number of births related to the total population in a given group during a given period of time.

BLACKOUT PERIOD: The period of years during which no Social Security benefit is payable to the surviving spouse of a deceased, fully insured worker, between the time the youngest child of the worker (in the spouse's case) attains the age of 18 years and the spouse's age of 60 years. See Blackout Period Income.

BLACKOUT PERIOD INCOME: Income to help meet expenses during the blackout period. See Blackout Period.

BLANKET ACCIDENT MEDICAL EXPENSE: A reimbursement health policy that entitles insured that suffer an accidental bodily injury to collect up to the maximum policy benefits for all hospital and medical expenses incurred, without any limitations on individual types of medical expenses. Some included expenses are: treatment by doctors, surgeons, nurses, hospital room and board, drugs, x-rays, and lab fees.

BLANKET EXPENSE POLICY: One that pays all charges or costs for a designated illness or injury, up to a maximum figure, as compared with a health care policy that pays only specified amounts for designated allowable charges or costs.

BLANKET INSURANCE: A contract of health insurance that covers all of a class of persons not individually identified in the contract. A group health insurance policy covering a number of individuals who are not individually named but are exposed to the same hazards, such as members of an athletic team, company officials who are passengers in the same company plane, etc.

BLANKET MEDICAL EXPENSE: A policy or provision in a health insurance contract that pays all medical costs, including hospitalization, drugs, and treatments, without limitation on any item except possibly for a maximum aggregate benefit under the policy. It is often written with an initial deductible amount. See Expense and Blanket Insurance.

BLANKET POLICY: A health insurance contract that protects all members of a certain group against a specific hazard. See Blank Insurance.

BLEND RATE: Forecasting new insurance premiums based on group and insurance entity experience.

BLOCK GRANT: Federal funds made to a state for the delivery of a specific group of related services, such as drug abuse-related services.

BLUECARD: A teleprocessing system that allows any Blue Cross and Blue Shield Plan to make available to other Blue Cross and Blue Shield Plans (in or out of state) the same discounts they have negotiated with providers for their own customers.

BLUE CARD PROGRAM: The Blue Cross and Blue Shield Association (BCBSA) program that permits members of any Blue Plan to have access to health care services from participating providers throughout the United States.

BLUE CROSS: Blue Cross plans are nonprofit hospital expense prepayment plans designed primarily to provide benefits for hospitalization coverage, with certain restrictions on the type of accommodations to be used.

BLUE CROSS/BLUE SHIELD: Service organizations providing hospital and medical expense coverage under which payments are made directly to the health care providers rather than to the individual. Blue Cross pays hospital expenses and Blue Shield pays physicians' and other medical expenses.

BLUE CROSS/BLUE SHIELD ASSOCIATION NATIONAL TRANSPLANT NETWORK FACILITY: A facility that contracts with the Blue Cross and Blue Shield Association to perform specific organ transplants.

BLUE CROSS COMMISSION: The national Blue Cross organization that coordinates the various local and state Blue Cross plans, but has no authority except to establish standards and provide guidance to any hospital service plan it recognizes.

BLUE PLAN: A generic designation for those companies, usually writing a service rather than a reimbursement contract, that are authorized to use the designation Blue Cross or Blue Shield and the insignia of either.

BLUE SHIELD: Blue Shield plans are prepayment plans offered by voluntary nonprofit organizations covering medical and surgical expenses.

BOARD: A type of assisted living arrangement, usually outside the home.

BOARD CERTIFICATION (Boarded, Diplomate): A doctor who is board certified has pursued advanced training in his or her specialty and has passed a qualifying examination; a doctor who is board eligible has received the training but has not taken or passed the exam. See Board Eligible.

BOARD ELIGIBLE: Describes a physician who is eligible to take the specialty board examination by virtue of being graduated from an approved medical school, completing a specific type and length of training, and practicing for a specified amount of time. Some HMOs and other health facilities accept board eligibility as equivalent to board certification, significant in that many managed care companies restrict referrals to physicians without certification. See Board Certification.

BOARDS OF HEALTH: The various States Board of Health have members who are experienced in matters of health and sanitation, perhaps an elected city official who is a member of a local board of health, a local health officer, and several people representing consumers of health care. Local boards of health are governing bodies that supervise matters pertaining to the preservation of the life and health of the people within their jurisdiction. Each local board of health enforces public health statutes and rules, supervises the maintenance of all health and sanitary measures, enacts local rules and regulations, and provides for the control and prevention of any dangerous, contagious, or infectious disease.

BOARD OF TRUSTEES: A Board established by the Social Security Act to oversee the financial operations of the Federal Supplementary Medical Insurance Trust Fund. The Board is composed of six members, four of whom serve automatically by virtue of their positions in the federal government: the Secretary of the Treasury, who is the Managing Trustee; the Secretary of Labor; the Secretary of Health and Human Services; and the Commissioner of Social Security. The other two members are appointed by the President and confirmed by the Senate to serve as public representatives.

BODILY INJURY: Any physical injury to a person. Refers to injury to the body of a person and is usually specifically defined in the policy. See Accident, Disease, and Illness.

BODY-CENTERED PSYCHOTHERAPY (body-oriented psychotherapy, body psychotherapy, direct body-contact psychotherapy, humanistic body psychotherapy): Any combination of: (a) psychotherapy and (b) massage therapy, touch therapy, or movement techniques.

BOND: A loan certificate representing credit in an issuer, and issued to raise long-term funds. The issuer pays interest, usually semiannually, plus principal when due. See Debt.

BOND RATING: The likelihood of loan default.

BOND-RATING AGENCY: Firms that assess the credit worthiness of companies, health care providers, clinics, hospitals insurers, and facilities or managed care plans.

BONUS PAYMENT: An additional amount paid by Medicare for services provided by physicians in health professional shortage areas. Varies with Medicare's share of allowed charges.

BOOK VALUE: Cost of capital assets minus accumulated depreciation for a health care, managed care, or other organization. The net asset value of a health care or insurance company's common stock. This is calculated by dividing the net tangible assets of the company (minus the par value of any preferred stock the company has) by the number of common shares outstanding.

BORDERLINE RISK: In health insurance, a risk (usually the insured) that is questionable and on the border between being acceptable and unacceptable to the insurer. See Adverse Selection.

BOREN AMENDMENT: To OBRA-80 that repealed the amendment that states follow Medicare principles in health insurance coverage or reimbursement policies.

BOUTIQUE MEDICAL PRACTICE: Noncovered, nonparticipating, fee-for-service private medical practice that is electively reimbursed by an annual fee or retainer. See Concierge Medicine.

BRACES: Rigid and semirigid appliances and devices commonly used to support a weak body part or to restrict or restrain motion in a diseased or injured part of the body. Braces do not include elastic stockings, elastic bandages, garter belts, arch supports, orthodontic devices, or other similar items.

BRANCH MANAGER: A life or health insurance company employee who manages one of the company's branch offices. The branch manager is in charge of all activities of the branch office and is responsible for hiring and training agents.

BRANCH OFFICE: A life or health insurance company field office established to supervise business within a certain territory. It is the sole representative agency of the company in a given area. Essentially, it is an agency under the management of a salaried branch manager employed by the insurer. See Branch Manager.

BRANCH OFFICE SYSTEM: A system of providing insurance services through branch offices of the insurer. See Branch Manager.

BRAND-NAME DRUG: A drug manufactured by a pharmaceutical company that has chosen to patent the drug's formula and register its brand name. See Generic Drug.

BREACH OF CONTRACT: The violation of, or failure to perform, the terms of a contract. Breaking of a legally binding agreement. A health insurance policy is a legal contract, and failure to comply with terms incorporated in the policy constitutes a breach of contract. Because health insurance policies are unilateral contracts, only the insurer can be held liable for breach of contract. See Breach of Warranty and Policy.

BREACH OF WARRANTY: When used in reference to a health insurance applicant or policy owner, the result of making fraudulent statements or withholding information that causes an insurance company to assume a risk it would not otherwise insure. Misrepresentation by an insurance policy owner as to a condition precedent to the issuance of the policy is illegal. See Breach of Contract.

BREAK-EVEN ANALYSIS: Approach to analyze health care revenue, costs, and volume. It is based on production or medical service costs between those that are variable (change when output changes) and those that are fixed (not directly related to volume). See Break-Even Point.

BREAK-EVEN POINT: The HMO membership level at which total revenues and total costs are equal and therefore produces neither a net gain nor loss from operations.

BROADBANDING: The grouping of jobs and roles into fewer but wider pay ranges to encourage incentives, such as health care management development, career ladders, and skill- and competency-based pay.

BROKER: A broker differs from a health insurance agent because the broker legally represents the customer rather than the insurer. Brokers may purchase policies on behalf of their clients through almost any MCO, HMO, or health insurer. See Agent.

BROKERAGE BUSINESS: Business a company receives from insurance brokers. Also business directed to the company by full-time (career) agents of other companies. See Broker.

BROKERAGE DEPARTMENT: The department of an insurance company designated to assist agents in handling insurance outside of their territory and to help brokers place insurance.

BROKER AGENCY: A health insurance general agency servicing business of brokers other than full-time (career) agents of the company represented by the agency. See Broker.

BROKER-AGENT: An individual who represents one or more health insurers but may also serve as a broker by searching the market to place an applicant's policy to maximize protection and minimize cost.

BUDGET: Document of the financial planning control cycle, using the cash conversion cycle for a healthcare organization.

BUDGET NEUTRAL: For the Medicare program, adjustment of payment rates when policies change so that total spending under the new rules is expected to be the same as it would have been under the previous payment rules. See Budget.

BUDGET PLAN: A plan whereby large policies of health insurance are divided into smaller policies, to expire and be renewed on consecutive years, the policies being written at pro rata of the long-term rates so that the premium payment is spread over several years. See Budget.

BUDGET VARIANCES: Differences between budgets plans and that which was achieved. See Budget.

BUNDLED BILLING: All-inclusive global fee or packaged price for medical services for a specific procedure, treatment, or intervention. See Unbundled Billing.

BUNDLED PAYMENT: A single comprehensive payment for a group of related services. See Unbundled Billing.

BUNDLED SERVICE: Combines related specialty and ancillary services for an enrolled group or insured population by a group of associated providers. See Bundled Payment.

BUNDLING: The use of a single payment for a group of related services. See Unbundling.

BURIAL INSURANCE: A slang term usually referring to a small policy of life or health ($1,000 to $5,000) intended to pay the funeral costs of the deceased insured.

BUSINESS ASSOCIATE: A person or organization that performs a function or activity on behalf of a covered entity, but is not part of the covered entity's workforce. A business associate can also be a covered entity in its own right. See HIPAA.

BUSINESS COALITION: An employer community or co-operative to purchase health care services at a low cost for employees.

BUSINESS HEALTH INSURANCE: Health insurance coverage issued primarily to indemnify a business for the loss of services of a key employee or a partner or an active close corporation stockholder; or, in a partnership or close corporation, to buy out the interest of a partner or stockholder who becomes permanently disabled.

BUSINESS RELATIONSHIPS: The term is often used to describe a formal contract for the provision of healthcare, insurance, business, or other services or goods.

BUY-IN: Arrangements the states may make for paying Medicare premiums on behalf of those they are required or choose to cover.

C

CA: Certified acupuncturist.

CAFETERIA PLAN (SECTION 125 PLAN): In the health care context, an employee benefit plan in which the employee has the option to select among various types of health care plans, such as traditional indemnity, catastrophic coverage, or managed care benefits plan. Usually, there is some type of cost sharing between the employee and their employer. Other insurance and benefit options are also available. See Flexible Spending Account.

CALENDAR YEAR: January 1 through December 31 of any given year.

CALENDAR YEAR MAJOR MEDICAL PLAN: A major medical insurance plan that provides reimbursement of covered expenses, with a deductible amount to be applied only once during the period from January 1 of any year through December 31 of the same year.

CALIFORNIA RELATIVE VALUE STUDIES (CRVS): A coded listing of physician services with unit values to indicate the relativity of charges to the median. See RBRVUs.

CALL: To the life or health insurance agent, any bona fide effort made to contact a prospect to arrange an insurance sales interview.

CALLABLE LOANS: Loans (debt certificates) that may be redeemed prior to maturity.

CANCELLATION: In insurance, it is the termination of a contract by either the insured or the insurer prior to the end of the policy period. In life and noncancelable health insurance, the company generally may not cancel a policy, except under certain conditions, for nonpayment of premiums.

CANCELLATION PROVISION: A provision in a health policy that allows the insurance company to cancel the contract at any time, providing the insured is notified in writing.

CANNIBALIZATION: Occurs when one health care service, organizations, providers, or product negatively impacts a similar entity.

CAP (Competitive Allowance Program): The reimbursement agreement between a health insurance company and providers of health care services for traditional benefit programs. Providers are paid predetermined maximum allowances for covered health care services and agree to file claims on behalf of members.

CAP: A limit placed on the number of dollars that a health plan will pay in a specified period of time.

CAPACITY: The ability to perform the core public health functions of assessment, policy development, and assurance on a continuous, consistent basis, made possible by maintenance of the basic infrastructure of the public health system, including human, capital, and technology resources.

CAPACITY STANDARDS: Statements of what public health agencies and other state and local partners must do as a part of ongoing, daily operations to adequately protect and promote health and prevent disease and injury.

CAPITAL: The source of funds to finance noncurrent assets of a health care organization. The total worth of an individual, a partnership, or all shares of company stock. The assets and principal as contrasted with income (which may or may not result from ownership or use of those assets or that principal).

CAPITAL APPRECIATION: The increase in value of an investment over time.

CAPITAL ASSET: An item not ordinarily bought and sold in the course of one's business, but having monetary value and often the source of income or used in the production thereof. See Assets.

CAPITAL BUDGET: A method used to forecast and justify capital expenses. See Fixed Costs, Variable Costs, and Budget.

CAPITAL CHARGES: The funds necessary to cover interest upon and amortization of monies invested in an enterprise. The costs of borrowed money, business or personal. See Expenses.

CAPITAL CONSERVATION METHOD: A method of determining the amount of money needed to satisfy projected income needs that employs only the earnings on principal (not the principal itself) to satisfy those needs.

CAPITAL COSTS: Depreciation, interest, leases and rentals, and taxes and insurance on tangible medical or health care assets like physical plant and equipment. See Costs.

CAPITAL EXPENDITURES: Outlays of cash or other property or the creation of liability in exchange for property to remain permanently in the business; usually land, buildings, machinery, and equipment.

CAPITAL FINANCING: Financing of noncurrent assets. See Capital Structure.

CAPITAL GAIN (OR LOSS): The gain (or loss) resulting from the sale of a capital asset in relation to its purchase price or value at the time of acquisition.

CAPITAL GAINS DISTRIBUTIONS: Payments to mutual fund shareholders of gains realized on the sale of the fund's portfolio securities. These amounts, if any, are paid once a year.

CAPITAL GAINS TAX: A provision in the federal income tax law that previously subjected profits from the sale of capital assets to less tax than would be required for ordinary income.

CAPITAL GOODS: The means of production, such as factory buildings, equipment, etc., used to produce wealth. Also goods used in the production of other goods.

CAPITAL, GROSS WORKING: See Current Assets.

CAPITALIZATION: The act or process of converting (obtaining the present worth of) future incomes into current equivalent capital value. The monetary total of the securities (bonds, preferred stocks, and common stocks) issued or authorized by a hospital or health care corporation. Total capitalization also includes retained earnings.

CAPITALIZATION OF INTEREST: The process of automatically adding the unpaid interest to the principal of a policy loan. See Capitalization.

CAPITALIZATION OF POLICY LOANS: The process of increasing the policy loan principal to take into account the unpaid loan interest.

CAPITALIZATION RATE: The rate of interest or return used in the process of capitalization, ordinarily assumed to reflect the factor or risk to capital so invested. See Capitalization.

CAPITALIZED VALUE: The money valuation of a business arrived at by dividing the annual profits by an assumed rate of earning that is usually the current capitalization rate for similar risks. See Capitalization.

CAPITAL LEASE: The renting of a health care or other asset for almost all of its economic, but not always useful, life.

CAPITAL MARKET: The market for equity securities (stocks) and debt obligations with maturities in excess of one year. The market for long-term investment funds, involving primarily investment bankers, savings banks, insurance companies, pension funds, and trust companies. See Money Markets.

CAPITAL NET WORTH: A business's total assets, less its liabilities. See Capitalization.

CAPITAL STOCK: The shares of ownership in a corporation.

CAPITAL STOCK INSURANCE COMPANY: An insurance company owned by its stockholders, much as any other corporation, contrasted with a mutual insurance company that is owned by its policy owners and operated for their own benefit. See Capital Stock.

CAPITAL STRUCTURE: The relative amounts of debt and equity in a health care or other organization.

CAPITAL STRUCTURE RATIOS: The relationship and structure of a health care or other organization's assets and whether the company can assume new debt. See Capitalization.

CAPITAL SUM: In health insurance, the amount provided for the loss of life, of two bodily members (such as arms or legs), the sight of both eyes, or of any two members and eyes. Indemnities for loss of one member of the sight of one eye are usually percentages of the capital sum. Often used interchangeably with principal sum or accidental death benefit. See Capitalization.

CAPITAL UTILIZATION METHOD: A method of determining the amount of money needed to satisfy future income needs, based on the projection that both the earnings and principal will be spent at the end of the period during which the income will be needed.

CAPITATED CONTRACT: Health insurance contract that pays a fixed fee per each patient it covers. See Capitation.

CAPITATION: (1) Method of payment for health services in which a physician or hospital is paid a fixed amount for each person served regardless of the actual number or nature of services provided. (2) A method of paying health care providers or insurers in which a fixed amount is paid per enrollee to cover a defined set of services over a specified period, regardless of actual services provided. (3) A health insurance payment mechanism that pays a fixed amount per person to cover services. Capitation may be used by purchasers to pay health plans or by plans to pay providers. See Prospective Payment System.

CAPPED RENTAL ITEM: Health insurance/Medicare/managed care-covered durable medical equipment and related supplies with payment or reimbursement limits.

CAPTIVE AGENT: In insurance, an agent who has agreed to sell insurance for only one company or group. See Agent and Broker.

CARDIOLOGY: The Branch of medicine dealing with the diagnosis and treatment of heart ailments. See Cardiologist.

CAREER PATH: A step-by-step systematized approach to the continuing development of a health or life insurance agent's education and career training.

CARE GIVER: One, like a nurse, who renders medical care for a sick, injured, disabled, or elderly patient.

CARE MAPS: Guidelines for suggested medical care and treatment. Similar to clinical or critical care algorithms or best clinical practices. See Clinical Guidelines.

CARE NETWORK: A family of primary care clinics, physicians, specialists, hospitals, and other health care professionals who provide a full range of health care services to members. Care networks decide whether members need referrals to see specialists within the care network. See MCO, PPO, and HMO.

CARE PLAN: Usually a written outline of care for a specific patient, produced by a nurse, in a hospital or health care facility.

CARRIER: An insurer; an underwriter of risk. (1) An organization, typically an insurance company, that has a contract with the CMS (formerly Health Care Financing Administration) to administer claims processing and make Medicare payments to health care providers for most Medicare Part B benefits. (2) A private contractor that administers claims processing and payment for Medicare Part B services.

CARRIER: A person or animal without apparent disease that harbors a specific infectious agent and is capable of transmitting the agent to others. The carrier state may occur in an individual with an infection that is not apparent throughout its course or during the incubation period, convalescence, and post convalescence of an individual with a clinically recognizable disease.

CARRYOVER DEDUCTIBLE: Allows any amount applied toward the deductible during the last quarter of the calendar year to apply also toward the next year's deductible. For example, expenses incurred during October, November, or December will apply toward the next year's deductible amount. See Corridor Deductible and Deductible.

CARVE-IN: A managed care or health insurance strategy in which a payer includes ("carves-in") a portion of the benefit as a total package and hires an MCO or HMO to provide these benefits. See Inclusions.

CARVE-OUT: A payer strategy in which a payer separates (carves out) a portion of the benefit and hires an MCO to provide these benefits. This permits the payer to create a health benefits package, get to market quicker with such a package, and maintain greater control of their costs. Many HMOs and insurance companies adopt this strategy because they do not have in-house expertise related to the services carved out. See Exclusions.

CARVE-OUT COVERAGE: Carve out refers to an arrangement in which some benefits (e.g., mental health) are removed from coverage provided by an insurance plan, but are provided through a contract with a separate set of providers. Also, carve out may refer to a population subgroup when separate health care arrangements are made.

CARVE-OUT SERVICE: A carve out is typically a service provided within a standard benefit. See Exclusions.

CASE: An insurance-covered illness, accident, injury, disease, or situation.

CASE-FATALITY RATE: The proportion of persons with a particular condition who die from that condition. The denominator is the number of incident cases; the numerator is the number of cause-specific deaths among those cases.

CASE MANAGEMENT: The process by which all health-related matters of a case are managed by a physician or nurse or designated health professional. Physician case managers coordinate designated components of health care, such as appropriate referral to consultants, specialists, hospitals, ancillary providers, and services. Case management is intended to ensure continuity of services and accessibility to overcome rigidity, fragmented services, and the misutilization of facilities and resources. It also attempts to match the appropriate intensity of services with the patient's needs over time. See Quality Assurance.

CASE MANAGER: The leader of health-related matters for a specific patient, who may or may not be a registered nurse or other designated health professional. See Case Management.

CASE MIX: The types of inpatients a hospital or postacute facility treats. The more complex the patients' needs, the greater the amount spent for patient care.

CASE-MIX INDEX: A measure of the relative costliness of treating in an inpatient setting. An index of 1.05, for example, means that the facility's patients are 5% more costly than average.

CASE RATE: Flat fee paid for a client's treatment based on their diagnosis or presenting problem. For this fee the provider covers all of the services the client requires for a specific period of time. Also bundled rate, or flat fee-per-case. Very often used as an intervening step prior to capitation. In this model, the provider is accepting some significant risk, but does have considerable flexibility in how it meets the client's needs. Keys to success in this mode: (1) properly pricing case rate, if provider has control over it; and (2) securing a large volume of eligible clients. See Flat Fee.

CASH: Coins, currency, or other liquid marketable securities used to finance a health insurance, managed care, or other organization's daily operations.

CASH ASSETS: Assets consisting of cash or cash equivalents that can be quickly converted to cash. See Money Markets.

CASH BASIS ACCOUNTING: Accounting systems that recognizes revenues when cash received and expenses when paid. See Accrual Accounting.

CASH BUDGET: A projection of cash inflows and outflows. See Budget.

CASH EQUIVALENTS: Assets that can be readily converted into cash.

CASH FLOW: Reported net income of a corporation plus amounts charged off for depreciation, depletion, amortization, and extraordinary charges to reserve accounts for the particular year under consideration. All of these additional items are bookkeeping deductions and are not paid out in actual dollars and cents. The cash flow may be from operations, financing, or investing activities. See Balance Sheet. See Annual Report.

CASH INDEMNITY BENEFITS: Monetary sums paid to a patient for health insurance incurred services or covered claims.

CATASTROPHE: A sudden, unexpected, unavoidable, and severe calamity or disaster. With respect to health insurance, an event that causes a medical loss of extraordinary amount.

CATASTROPHE HAZARD: The hazard of loss as a result of a simultaneous medical peril to which all in a particular group, or a large number of health insureds, are subject. See Catastrophic Illness.

CATASTROPHE INSURANCE: See comprehensive major medical insurance and major medical expense insurance. See Catastrophic Hazard or Illness.

CATASTROPHIC CASE: Any medical condition where total cost of treatment (regardless of payment source) is expected to exceed an amount designated by the HMO contract with the medical group. See Catastrophe.

CATASTROPHIC HEALTH INSURANCE: Health insurance that provides protection against the high cost of treating severe or lengthy illnesses or disability. Generally such policies cover all, or a specified percentage of, medical expenses above an amount that is the responsibility of another insurance policy up to a maximum limit of liability.

CATASTROPHIC ILLNESS: A sudden, unexpected, unavoidable, and severe illness, disease, disability, or injury. Catastrophic Hazard.

CATASTROPHIC LIMIT: The highest amount of money paid out of pocket during a certain period of time for certain covered charges. Setting a maximum amount you will have to pay protects you. See Catastrophe.

CATASTROPHIC LOSS: Large loss that does not lend itself to prediction. See Catastrophic Insurance.

CATASTROPHIC REINSURANCE: An agreement whereby a reinsuring health care company assumes defined losses above a stated aggregate amount that may result from a catastrophe. See Catastrophe.

CATCHMENT AREA: The geographic area from which an MCO, HMO, or health plan draws its patients.

CATEGORICALLY NEEDY: Medicaid eligibility based on defined and variable indicators of financial need by families with children, pregnant women, and persons who are aged, blind, or disabled. Persons not falling into these categories cannot qualify, no matter how low their income. The Medicaid statute defines over 50 distinct population groups as potentially eligible, including those for which coverage is mandatory in all states and those that may be covered at a state's option. The scope of covered services that states must provide to the categorically needy is much broader than the minimum scope of services for other groups receiving Medicaid benefits.

CATEGORICAL PROGRAMS: Public health insurance for a given category of patients.

CAUSE OF DISEASE: A factor (characteristic, behavior, event, etc.) that directly influences the occurrence of disease. A reduction of the factor in the population should lead to a reduction in the occurrence of disease. See Death.

CAUSE OF LOSS: Health, disability, or other insurance perils that produces a loss. See Perils.

CAUSE-SPECIFIC MORTALITY RATE: The mortality rate from a specified cause for a population. The numerator is the number of deaths attributed to a specific cause during a specified time interval; the denominator is the size of the population at the midpoint of the time interval.

CAVEAT EMPTOR: Latin expression for "let the buyer beware," meaning an insured buys any insurance policy at his or her own risk.

CEDE: Transfer risk from an insurance company to a reinsurance company.

CEDING COMPANY: The insurance company that transfers all or part of the insurance or reinsurance it has written to another insurer (i.e., to a reinsuring company). See Cede.

CENSUS: The enumeration of an entire population, usually with details being recorded on residence, age, sex, occupation, ethnic group, marital status, birth history, and relationship to head of household. A census also is the population of a hospital, department, nursing home, or other health care facility.

CENSUS DAYS: Patient days in a hospital or similar facility. See Patient Census Days.

CENTER OF INFLUENCE: In life or health insurance prospecting, an individual with outstanding prestige or influence within a group, who can provide the agent with qualified referrals and may be helpful in the agent's dealings with those prospects.

CENTERS OF EXCELLENCE: A medical center that has been identified by a health insurer as particularly expert in performing a costly or complex medical procedure. See Census.

CENTERS FOR MEDICAID AND MEDICARE SERVICES (CMS): Former Health Care Financing Administration (HCFA), Department of Health and Human Services (DHHS). See CMS. See HCFA.

CENTRALIZATION: The degree to which power and authority is concentrated in a health care organization.

CERTAINTY: The absence of risk in an investment, decision, or insurance policy.

CERTIFICATE OF AUTHORITY (COA): Issued by state governments, it gives an HMO or insurance company its license to operate within the state. See Certificate of Need (CON).

CERTIFICATE OF COVERAGE (CC): A legal description of the benefits included under, and to be provided by, a health plan when a certificate of coverage is required by law.

CERTIFICATE OF DEPOSIT (CD): Negotiable securities issued by commercial banks against money deposited with them for a specified period of time. They vary in size according to amount of deposit and maturity period and may be redeemed before maturity only by sale in a secondary market. Sometimes called *Jumbo CDs*, the usual minimum size may vary. These are unsecured by any specific bank asset. See Cash.

CERTIFICATE OF INCORPORATION (CHARTER): A state-validated certificate recognizing a health care business organized as a legal corporate entity.

CERTIFICATE OF INSURANCE (COI): Health insurance document issued to a group insurance plan demonstrating participation in insurance coverage. See COA, CC, and CON.

CERTIFICATE OF LIMITED PARTNERSHIP: The legal document used to form the limited partnership, usually filed with the appropriate state government, for ambulatory surgical centers, medical equipment facilities, or outpatient treatment centers. Two or more persons must sign the certificate, although as a practical matter, the limited partners often execute a power of attorney authorizing the general partner to act on their behalf in filing the certificate. See COA and CC.

CERTIFICATE OF NEED (CON): A legal description of the benefits included under, and to be provided by, a health plan when a certificate-of-coverage is required by law. A state agency must review and approve certain proposed capital expenditures, changes in health services provided, and purchases of expensive medical equipment. Before the request goes to the state, a local review panel (the health systems agency or hospital administration services) must evaluate the proposal and make a recommendation. SEE COA.

CERTIFIED: Approval, usually from the state or other agency.

CERTIFIED HEALTH CONSULTANT: Financial educational program for health insurance consultants.

CERTIFIED HEALTH PLAN: A managed health care plan certified by the Health Services Commission and the Office of the Insurance Commissioner to provide coverage for the Uniform Benefits Package to state residents.

CERTIFIED MEDICAL PLANNER©: Professional designation, first charted in 2000 that integrates personal financial planning process for physicians with specific knowledge of contemporaneous managed care business principles, health insurance fundamentals, and medical practice business concepts, as accredited by the Institute of Medical Business Advisors, Inc., Atlanta, Georgia (www.MedicalBusinessAdvisors.com). This program responds to the growing need of medical providers and physicians for help in their financial and professional lives.

CERTIFIED NURSE MIDWIFE: An individual who has passed the requirements of the American College of Nurse Midwifery (ACNM).

CERTIFIED NURSING ASSISTANT (CNA): One who helps a registered nurse (RN) with feeding, bathing, toileting, and other duties of in- or outpatient care, but is not an RN.

CERTIFIED REGISTERED NURSE ANESTHETIST (CRN): A registered nurse specially trained to administer anesthesia during operations and surgical procedures.

CESTUI QUE VIE: An insured. See Insured.

CHAIN FACILITY: A hospital or long-term care facility owned by a parent organization that owns other such facilities.

CHAIN ORGANIZATION: Several health care organizations leased, owned, or controlled by patent organizations.

CHAMPUS: Civilian Health and Medical Program of the Uniformed Services. The federal program providing health care coverage to families of military personnel, military retirees, certain spouses, and dependents of such personnel. See Tricare.

CHANGE OF COVER: Upgraded level of coverage that may result in a lower level of benefits applies during any waiting periods for preexisting ailments.

CHANGE OF OCCUPATION PROVISION: An optional health insurance provision that states that if the insured changes occupations, the insurance company must be notified so that premium rates can be adjusted. If the insured fails to notify the company, coverage on a claim will be based on what the insured's premium payment would have purchased under the current occupation classification.

CHANNELING: A hospital insurance policy that provides malpractice liability insurance to nonemployed physicians of a hospital or health care facility.

CHARGE: The posted prices of provider services.

CHARGEBACK: The amount of money reimbursed to the health maintenance organization. Usually, the difference between the average discount price and the price bid to the pharmaceutical manufacturer. See Rebate.

CHARGE-BASED SYSTEM: A system in which medical providers set the rates for health care services.

CHARGE DOCUMENT: A health care bill or invoice.

CHARGE MASTER: A comprehensive review of a physician, clinic, facility, medical provider, or hospital's charges to ensure Medicare billing compliance through complete and accurate HCPCS/CPT and UB-92 revenue code assignments for all items including supplies and pharmaceuticals.

CHARITY CARE: Free or reduced fee care provided due to financial situation of patients. The difference between full charges for services rendered to patients who are not able to pay for all or part of the services provided and the amount paid by or on behalf of the patient, if any. Previously included care provided to medically indigent for which counties are responsible with fee health and medical services to the needy and indigent. See Pro-Bone Care and Charity Hill-Burton Act.

CHARITY HILL-BURTON: The amount of charity care rendered by the hospital to satisfy, or partially satisfy, its obligations to uncompensated services as required under the federal Hill-Burton Program of 1947. Previously included care provided to medically indigent patients for which counties are responsible. See Health Maintenance Organization Act.

CHARTERED FINANCIAL CONSULTANT (ChFC): A designation awarded by the American College in Bryn Mawr, Pennsylvania, to financial services agents who complete 10 fundamental financial planning courses. This program answers the growing needs of individuals seeking proficient help in their personal financial planning process. See CFP© and CMP©.

CHARTERED LIFE UNDERWRITER (CLU): A designation conferred by the American College in Bryn Mawr, Pennsylvania. Recipients must pass examinations in business courses, including insurance, investments, and taxation and must have professional experience in life insurance planning. See CFP© and CMP©.

CHEMICAL DEPENDENCY: Any condition resulting from dependency on or abuse of a psychoactive substance as described in the *Diagnostic and Statistical Manual of Mental Disorders*, 4th Ed. Rev. (*DSM-IV-R*), or subsequent revisions, published by the American Psychiatric Association.

CHEMICAL DEPENDENCY RECOVERY HOSPITAL: A health facility that provides 24-hr inpatient care for persons who have a dependency on alcohol or drugs. Care includes patient counseling, group and family therapy, physical conditioning, outpatient services, and dietetic services. The facility must have a medical director who is a physician and surgeon licensed in its state. See CDRS.

CHEMICAL DEPENDENCY RECOVERY HOSPITAL BEDS: Beds in a chemical dependency recovery hospital or a general acute-care hospital classified by the Division of Licensing and Certification, as chemical dependency recovery beds and used for the same services as those in a chemical dependency recovery hospital. See CDRS.

CHEMICAL DEPENDENCY RECOVERY SERVICES (CDRS): Services provided as a supplemental service in general acute-care beds or acute psychiatric beds. The services must be provided in a distinct part of the facility. The services are similar to those provided in hospitals licensed as chemical dependency recovery hospitals or in chemical dependency recovery beds in general acute-care hospitals.

CHEMOTHERAPY: The use of medical chemicals and drugs to diagnosis and treat disease.

CHERRY PICKING: Screening out unhealthy patients for a health insurance plan.

CHILD CONVERSION CODE: A schedule of covered dependency under covered insurance benefits.

CHILD'S BENEFIT: In reference to Social Security, a benefit payable to an unmarried child of a retired, disabled, or deceased worker until the child is aged 18 years (or until aged 22 if a full-time student or indefinitely if totally disabled) in an amount equal to a portion of the worker's Primary Insurance Amount.

CHIROPODIST (OLD TERM): See DPM, Doctor, Foot Doctor, and Doctor of Podiatric Medicine.

CHIROPRACTIC CARE: An alternative medicine therapy that involves adjusting the spine and joints to treat pain. This care is provided by a licensed chiropractor. See Doctor of Chiropractic and Doctor.

CHPDAC: California Health Policy and Data Advisory Commission. The appointed body that represents California health providers and health consumers, reviews office policies and procedures, and provides recommendations and guidance on long-range office direction.

CHRONIC CARE: Long-term care of individuals with long-standing, persistent diseases or conditions. It includes care specific to the problem as well as other measures to encourage self-care, to promote health, and to prevent loss of function. See Long-Term Care (LTC).

CHRONIC ILLNESS: An illness marked by long duration or frequent reoccurrence, such as arthritis, diabetes, heart disease, asthma, and hypertension.

CHURNING: The practice of a provider seeing a patient more often than is medically necessary, primarily to increase revenue through an increased number of visits. A practice, in violation of the Security and Exchange Commission's rules, in which a salesperson effects a series of transactions in a customer's account which are excessive in size or frequency in relation to the size and investment objectives of the account. An insurance agent who is churning an account is normally seeking to maximize the income (in commissions, sales credits, or mark ups) derived from the account. See Churning, Twisting, and Rebating.

CIRCUMVENTION: Any possible prohibited Stark Bill arrangement in which medical providers or the three cover entities of HIPAA in different locales cross-refer patients and transfer health care entity ownership; for monetary gain. See Fraud and Abuse.

CIRCUMVENTION SCHEME: A Stark prohibited arrangement in which physicians located in different cities transfer ownership and cross-refer patients, for monetary gain. See Fraud and Abuse.

CIVIL EXCLUSION: The act prohibiting medical providers from receiving federal health care funds. See Fraud and Abuse and Circumvention.

CLAIM: Request for payment made to the insurance company by medical facilities, members, or practitioners for health services provided to plan members. A claim may be approved (cleared for payment, rejected [not approved for payment], pended, or suspended [put aside for further investigation]).

CLAIM AGENT: An individual authorized by an insurance company to pay a loss. See Claim.

CLAIMANT: One who submits a claim for payment of benefits for a suffered loss, according to the provisions of an insurance policy. See Claim.

CLAIMS CLEARINGHOUSE: Organizations that examine and format claims for adherence to insurer requirements before the claim is actually submitted to the insurance company for payment.

CLAIMS DEPARTMENT: Department of a health care insurance company that administers and pays claims by their insureds. See Claimant.

CLAIMS EXAMINATION: The process of judging whether the claim submitted by the medical facility meets the insurer's requirements.

CLAIMS EXPENSE: Cost incurred to adjust an insurance claim. See Claimant.

CLAIMS FORMS PROVISION: In health insurance policies, a provision that requires the insurance company to provide claim forms to a policy, owner usually within 15 days after the insurer receives notice of a claim.

CLAIMS LIMIT: Time limit on health care claims that usually must be made within 2 years of the service, or they will not be reimbursed.

CLAIMS RESERVE: Within a life or health insurance company, those amounts set aside to cover future payments or claims already incurred.

CLAIMS REVIEW: The method by which an enrollee's health care service claims are reviewed prior to reimbursement. The purpose is to validate the medical necessity of the provided services and to be sure the cost of the service is not excessive. See UR.

CLAIMS SETTLED: Amount of provider bill that is discharged when a claim is processed.

CLAIMS STATUS: Current classification of a health care claim awaiting disposition.

CLASS: Group of insureds with the same characteristics, established for health insurance rate-making purposes.

CLASSIFICATION: The systematic organized arrangement of defined classes or risks of patients to determine an underwriting rating into which a risk is placed.

CLASSIFIED INSURANCE: In life or health insurance, coverage on impaired risks.

CLASSIFIED RISK: In life and health insurance policies, the scaling of premiums to compensate for substandard health or other risks, more commonly called substandard risks.

CLASS RATE: The health insurance premium rate applicable to a specified class or risk.

CLAUSE: Portion in a written health or other insurance policy that explains coverage, exclusions, premiums, duties, etc. See Contract and Policy.

CLAYTON ACT: Law that forbids actions believed to lead to monopolies, including: (a) charging different prices to different purchasers of the same product without justifying the price difference; and (b) giving a distributor the right to sell a product only if the distributor agrees not to sell competitors' products. The Clayton Act applies to managed care and health insurance companies only to the extent that state laws do not regulate such activities.

CLEAN CLAIM: A claim that meets all insurer requirements and is submitted before the filing limit.

CLEAN-UP FUND: A reserve intended to cover the medical costs of a last illness, burial expenses, probate charges, miscellaneous outstanding bills, etc. Also, Clearance Fund.

CLEARANCE FUND: See Clean-up Fund.

CLIENT: In insurance, a person or company on whose behalf the agent or broker acts. The term usually infers that a well-developed business relationship exists between the insured and the agent or broker, with more than one purchase of insurance having been made or contemplated. See Patient.

CLINIC: A facility for outpatient medical services.

CLINICAL AUDIT: Health review of medical care for quality improvement purposes.

CLINICAL COST CENTERS: Health care units responsible for providing medical care with associated costs.

CLINICAL OR CRITICAL PATHWAYS: A map or algorithm of preferred treatment or intervention activities. Outlines the types of information needed to make decisions, the timelines for applying that information, and the actions needed to be taken by whom. Provides a way to monitor care "in real time." These pathways were developed for specific diseases or events. Proactive providers are working now to develop these pathways for the majority of their interventions and developing the software capacity to distribute and store this information. See Care Maps.

CLINICAL DATA REPOSITORY: The component of a computer-based patient record (CPR) that accepts, files, and stores clinical data over time from a variety of supplemental treatment and intervention systems for such purposes as practice guidelines, outcomes management, and clinical research. May also be called a data warehouse.

CLINICAL DECISION SUPPORT (CDS): The capability of a data system to provide key data to physicians and other clinicians in response to flags or triggers that are functions of embedded, provider-created rules. A system that would alert case managers that a client's eligibility for a certain service is about to be exhausted would be one example of this type of capacity. CDS is a key functional requirement to support clinical or critical pathways. See Critical Path and Care Maps.

CLINICAL LABORATORY IMPROVEMENT AMENDMENT (CLIA): Used by the Centers for Medicare and Medicaid Services to regulate all laboratory testing (except research) performed on humans in the United States. In total, CLIA covers approximately 175,000 laboratory entities. The Division of Laboratory Services, within the Survey and Certification Group, under the Center for Medicaid and State Operations has the responsibility for implementing the CLIA Program. The objective of the CLIA program is to ensure quality laboratory testing. Although all clinical laboratories must be properly certified to receive Medicare or Medicaid payments, CLIA has no direct Medicare or Medicaid program responsibilities.

CLINICAL PERSONAL HEALTH SERVICES: Health services generally provided one on one in a medical clinical setting.

CLINICAL PRACTICE GUIDELINES: Treatment schedules written by experts on the most effective and cost-efficient ways to treat a disease, injury, or illness. See Care Maps and Disease Management.

CLINICAL PREVENTIVE SERVICES: Health care services delivered to individuals in clinical settings for the purpose of preventing the onset or progression of a health condition or illness.

CLINICAL PRIVILEGES: Permission to provide medical services at a given institution.

CLINICAL PROTOCOLS: Guidelines for treating specific injuries and condi-tions. Medical professionals develop guidelines to evaluate the appropriateness of specific procedures. See Clinical Decision Support and Care Maps.

CLINICAL TEACHING SUPPORT FUNDS: Cover the cost of treating certain cases that provide educational benefit as well as the exploration of current medical technology and techniques. Patients are typically unable to pay for all or part of these services. These funds are not considered compensation for bad debts. Also known as CTS funds.

CLINICAL TRIALS: Long and carefully supervised and documented procedures, treatments, surgery, medical interventions, drugs used in new ways or new to the world existence to determine safety and efficacy.

CLINICIAN: A medical doctor, nurse, psychologist, optometrist, podiatrist, dentist, or other allied health care provider that treats patients.

CLINIC WITHOUT WALLS (CWW): Similar to an independent practice association and identical to a practice without walls (PWW). Practitioners form CWWs and PWWs for bargaining power offered by centralizing some administrative functions, but still choosing to practice separately. Many of these were formed to allow practitioners the ability to effectively contract with managed care entities.

CLOSE: That part of a health insurance sales interview designed to motivate the prospect to arrive at a buying decision regarding the plan being presented by the agent. A trial close is an attempt by the agent to move a prospect closer to a decision-making position.

CLOSED ACCESS: A managed health care arrangement in which covered persons are required to select providers only from the health plans participating providers. See Managed Care and HMO.

CLOSED CONTRACT OF INSURANCE: An insurance contract wherein rates and policy provisions cannot be changed. Fraternal insurance companies are not permitted to write this type of insurance.

CLOSED FORMULARY: The finite list of drugs available to beneficiaries of a health care plan.

CLOSED-PANEL HEALTH MAINTENANCE ORGANIZATION/PREFERRED PROVIDER ORGANIZATION (HMO/PPO): A type of HMO/PPO in which physicians must either belong to a special group of physicians that has contracted with the HMO/PPO or must be employees of the HMO/PPO. Generally, medical services are delivered in an HMO/PPO-owned health center. This term usually refers to a group or staff HMO/PPO models. See Managed Care.

CLOSE RATIO: Percentage or ratio of health insurance policies sold per one hundred prospect sales presentations.

CLUSTER: An aggregation of cases of a disease or other health-related condition, particularly cancer and birth defects, which are closely grouped in time and place. The number of cases may or may not exceed the expected number; frequently the expected number is not known.

CME UNITS: Continuing Medical Education Units.

CMS: Centers for Medicare and Medicaid Services. Formerly known as the Health Care Financing Administration (HCFA). See HCFA.

CMS-DIRECTED IMPROVEMENT PROCESS: Any project where the Centers for Medicare and Medicaid Services (See CMS, formerly HCFA) specifies the subject, size, pace, data source, analytic techniques, educational intervention techniques, or impact measurement model. These projects may be developed by CMS in consultation with Networks, the health care community, and other interested people. See HCFA.

COB (coordination of benefits): See Non-Duplication of Benefits.

COBRA (Consolidated Omnibus Budget Reconciliation Act): Federal law under which group health plans sponsored by employers with 20 or more employees must offer continuation of coverage to employees who leave their jobs, voluntarily or otherwise, and their dependents. See OBRA. See ERISA.

CODE OF FEDERAL REGULATIONS: The official compilation of federal rules and requirements.

CODE SET: Under HIPAA, this is any set of codes used to encode data elements, such as tables of terms, medical concepts, medical diagnostic codes, or medical procedure codes. This includes both the codes and their EDI descriptions. See HIPAA.

CODE SET MAINTAINING ORGANIZATION: Under HIPAA, this is an organization that creates and maintains the code sets adopted by the Secretary of the Department of Health and Human Services (DHHS) for use in the electronic transactions for which standards are adopted. See HIPAA.

CODICIL: An addendum or supplementary document making an addition to or change in a will. It is subject to the same legal formalities of execution (e.g., witnesses) as the will.

CODING: A mechanism for identifying and defining physicians' services. See Billing.

COGNITIVE IMPAIRMENT: A breakdown in a person's mental state.

COHORT: A well-defined group of people who have had a common experience or exposure, who are then followed up for the incidence of new diseases or events, as in a cohort or prospective study. A group of people who die during a particular period or year is called a death cohort.

COHORT STUDY: A type of observational analytic study. Enrollment into the study is based on exposure characteristics or membership in a group. Disease, death, or other health-related outcomes are then ascertained and compared. See Cohort.

COINSURANCE: The percentage of costs of medical care that a patient pays himself. Coinsurance rates generally hover in the 10% to 20% range.

Coinsurance and deductibles are most commonly found in indemnity, fee-for-service insurance, and the PPO market. Their absence in the HMO arena is one of the strong marketing appeals of HMOs.

COINSURANCE (PERCENTAGE PARTICIPATION): A health insurance principle under which the company insures only part of the potential loss, with the insured paying the other part. For instance, in a major medical policy, the company may agree to pay 75% of the insured's expenses, the insured to pay the other 25%. Most commonly used as synonymous with risk sharing or loss sharing. The coinsurance provision states that the insurance company and the policy owner will share covered losses.

COINSURER: One who shares the risk under an insurance policy or policies.

COLD CANVASSING (CALLING): A prospecting method whereby a health or life insurance agent, without any prior introduction, contacts prospects about whom he or she has little or no qualifying information.

COLLECTION FLOAT: Time lag between medical bill submission and ultimate payment.

COLLECTION POLICIES AND PROCEDURES: Instructions that address when and how to collect health care revenue.

COLLECTIVE UNCONSCIOUS (universal consciousness): Alleged inborn psychological concept common to all humans, but varying with the particular society, people, or race, that enables telepathy.

COLLEGE OF HEALTH CARE INFORMATION MANAGEMENT EXECUTIVES: A professional organization for health care chief information officers (CIOs).

COLLEGE OF INSURANCE, THE AMERICAN: The older term for an academic institution endorsed and supported by insurance business leaders and life insurance companies, providing a complete curriculum leading to a Bachelor of Business Administration degree. Various certificate courses are offered, as well as preparation for licenses, designations, and fellowship examinations. See American College. See CLU and ChFC.

COLLUSION: A secret agreement between two or more competitive parties for fraudulent or illegal purposes. See Fraud and Abuse.

COMMAND-CONTROL HMO: A strictly physician-controlled HMO, MCO, or other health plan. See Managed Care, HMO, and EHO.

COMMERCIAL HEALTH INSURANCE: Health insurance that provides both disability insurance and medical insurance. See Insurance.

COMMERCIAL INSURANCE: The most prevalent form of life and health insurance coverage, the most distinguishing features of which are that the insurer need not accept the premium and renew the coverage from one premium due date to the next and that rates may be adjusted at the company's option.

COMMERCIAL MCO: A health maintenance organization, an eligible organization with a contract under the HMO Act, a Medicare-Choice organization; a provider-sponsored organization or any other private or public organization that meets the requirements of the HMO Act. These MCOs provide comprehensive services to commercial or Medicare enrollees, as well as Medicaid enrollees. See HMO and EHO.

COMMERCIAL PAPER: A short-term debt (negotiable promissory note) for health care companies, issued at a discount and usually without collateral.

COMMERCIAL PARTNERSHIP: A partnership, either general or limited, that usually has some substantial inventory or fixed assets representing the capital investment of the partners.

COMMERCIAL PLAN: Refers to the benefit package an insurance company/ HMO/PPO offers to employers. This is distinguished from a senior plan that is offered to Medicare beneficiaries.

COMMISSION: The percentage of the premium paid to a health insurance agent or broker by the insurer as compensation. The fee for handling transactions for a client in an agency capacity. See Twisting, Churning, and Rebating.

COMMISSION BROKER: A member of the New York Stock Exchange executing orders on behalf of his own organization and its customers.

COMMISSION, CONTINGENT: A commission, the amount of which is dependent upon the profitableness or some other characteristic of the business, written by an insurance agent or reinsurer.

COMMISSIONER: The head of a state insurance department. The public officer charged with the supervision of the insurance business in the state and the administration of insurance laws. Called superintendent or director in some jurisdictions.

COMMISSIONERS DISABILITY TABLE: A table of morbidity approved in 1964 by the National Association of Insurance Commissioners.

COMMISSIONERS STANDARD ORDINARY MORTALITY TABLE (CSO): A standard mortality table prepared by the National Association of Insurance Commissioners used in the life and disability insurance rate calculations.

COMMITMENTS: A guarantee by an insurance company to accept certain risks.

COMMON ACCIDENT PROVISION: An optional provision in a life insurance contract that states that the primary beneficiary must outlive the insured a specified amount of time (usually 30 or 60 days) to receive policy proceeds. Otherwise, the contingent beneficiary receives the proceeds. This provision protects the interests of the contingent beneficiary in the event that the insured and the primary beneficiary die as a result of the same accident (or within a certain period of time, regardless of the causes).

COMMON COSTS: Costs that are shared by a number of common health care services or departments such as operating room, emergency room, and radiology.

COMMON DISASTER CLAUSE: See Common Accident Provision.

COMMUNITY-BASED CARE: The blend of health and social services provided to an individual or family in their place of residence for the purpose of promoting, maintaining, or restoring health or minimizing the effects of illness and disability.

COMMUNITY CARE NETWORK (CCN): This vehicle provides coordinated, organized, and comprehensive care to a community's population. Hospitals, primary care physicians, and specialists link preventive and treatment services through contractual and financial arrangements, producing a network that provides coordinated care with continuous monitoring of quality and accountability to the public. Although the term Community Care Network (CCN) is often used interchangeably with Integrated Delivery System (IDS), the CCN tends to be community based and nonprofit. See CHC.

COMMUNITY HEALTH CENTER (CHC): An ambulatory health care program (defined under §330 of the Public Health Service Act) usually serving a catchment area that has scarce or nonexistent health services or a population with special health needs; sometimes known as the neighborhood health center. Community health centers attempt to coordinate federal, state, and local resources into a single organization capable of delivering both health and related social services to a defined population. Although such a center may not directly provide all types of health care, it usually takes responsibility to arrange all medical services needed by its patient population. See CCN.

COMMUNITY HEALTH INFORMATION NETWORK (CHIN): An integrated collection of computer and telecommunication capabilities that permit multiple providers, payers, employers, and related health care entities within a geographic area to share and communicate client, clinical, and payment information. Also known as community health management information system.

COMMUNITY HEALTH MANAGEMENT INFORMATION SYSTEM (CHMIS): Iowa statewide program, established by the legislature, that uses uniform electronic claims forms and processing to reduce administrative costs and improve health system data and information.

COMMUNITY MENTAL HEALTH CENTER: An integrated collection of mental health care providers, facilities, and durable medical equipment vendors located within a geographic area or solitary location.

COMMUNITY RATING: Under the HMO Act, community rating is defined as a system of fixing rates of payment for health services that may be determined on a per person or per family basis and may vary with the number of persons in a family but must be equivalent for all individuals and for all families of similar composition. With community rating, premiums do not vary for different groups of subscribers or with such variables as the group's claims experience, age, sex, or health status. Although there are certain exceptions, in general, federally qualified HMOs must community rate. The intent of community rating is to spread the cost of illness evenly over all subscribers rather than charging the sick more than the healthy for coverage.

COMMUNITY RATING BY CLASS (CRC; CLASS RATING): For federally qualified HMOs, the community rating by class (i.e., adjustment of community-rated premiums on the basis of such factors as age, sex, family size, marital status, and industry classification). These health plan premiums reflect the experience of all enrollees of a given class within a specific geographic area, rather than the experience of any employer group.

COMORBID CONDITION: A medical condition that, along with the principal diagnosis, exists at admission and is expected to increase hospital length of stay by at least 1 day for most patients.

COMPANY-IMPOSED WAITING PERIODS: The predetermined length of time employed to be eligible for health and dental insurance.

COMPANY SERVICE AREA: The geographical area covered by a network of health care providers. See Demographic.

COMPARABLE HOSPITALS: These are all nonfederal licensed hospitals in other than prepaid health plans, state, Shriner's, specialty hospitals, and psychiatric health facilities.

COMPENDIUM: A list of information about drugs, their interactions, and their side effects.

COMPENSABLE INJURIES: In workers' compensation coverage, injuries that arise out of and in the course of the individual's employment and are therefore eligible for compensation.

COMPETENCY-BASED PAY: Medical or health care plan compensation based on the development of those attributes that distinguish exceptional performers, such as customer orientation, team commitment, and conflict resolution.

COMPETITIVE ADVANTAGE: Any factor that promotes marketplace acceptance of an insurance product.

COMPETITIVE BIDDING: A pricing method that elicits information on costs through a bidding process to establish payment rates that reflect the costs of an efficient health plan or health care provider.

COMPETITIVE MEDICAL PLAN: (1) A health plan that is eligible for a Medicare risk contract (although it is not a federally qualified HMO) because it meets specified requirements for service provision, payment, and financial solvency. (2) Some form of alternative healthcare delivery plan, like a Medical Savings Account (MSA) or Health Savings Account (HAS).

COMPLAINT: An oral or written statement of dissatisfaction with a health plan or with health services provided through the health plan.

COMPLETION FACTOR: Month factory to adjust incurred claims to medical claims paid.

COMPLICATION: A medical condition that arises during a course of treatment and is expected to increase the length of stay by at least 1 day for most patients.

COMPOSITE RATE: A group billing rate that applies to all subscribers within a specified group, regardless of whether they are controlled for single or family coverage.

COMPOUND INTEREST: Interest earned on interest. Interest earned on principal over a given period that is then added to the original principal to become the new principal upon which interest is earned during the new period, and so on, from period to period. See Simple Interest.

COMPREHENSIVE COVERAGE: Protection under one insurance agreement that covers all hazards within the general scope of the contract, except those specifically excluded.

COMPREHENSIVE HEALTH INSURANCE: A health insurance policy that incorporates the coverage of major medical and basic medical expense policies into one policy.

COMPREHENSIVE MAJOR MEDICAL INSURANCE: A medical expense policy designed to give the protection offered by both a basic and a major medical health insurance policy. It is characterized by a high maximum benefit, a coinsurance clause, and a low, corridor deductible. Also sometimes known as catastrophe insurance or major medical expense insurance. See Corridor Deductible.

COMPREHENSIVE OUTPATIENT REHABILITATION CENTER: A health care facility that provides medical, social, and psychological services for patient recovery.

COMPTROLLER: The financial officer in charge of funds for a health plan, insurance company, or managed care entity.

COMPULSORY HEALTH INSURANCE: Plans of insurance under the supervision of a state or federal government, providing protection for medical, hospital, surgical, and disability benefits to all who qualify.

COMPUTER-BASED PATIENT RECORD (CPR): A term for the process of replacing the traditional paper-based chart through automated electronic means; generally includes the collection of patient-specific information from various supplemental treatment systems (i.e., a day program and a personal care provider); its display in graphical format; and its storage for individual and aggregate purposes. Also called an electronic medical record, online medical record, or paperless patient chart.

CONCEALMENT: In insurance, failure of the insured to disclose a material fact to the insurance company at the time application is made. Telling only part of the truth or hiding the truth altogether. See Misrepresentation.

CONCEPTUAL UTILIZATION: Long-term, indirect utilization of the ideas and findings of an evaluation. See Utilization Review.

CONCIERGE MEDICINE: Noncovered, nonparticipating, fee for top-tier service private medical practice that is electively reimbursed by an annual fee or retainer. May be used with traditional insurance to cover allowable expenses. See Boutique Medical Practice.

CONCURRENT AUTHORIZATION: Health care services delivery approval prior to the administration of those services.

CONCURRENT CARE: Medical care administration by two or more doctors or medical, surgical, mental, or health care services, administered at the same time.

CONCURRENT REVIEW: A method of reviewing patient care, during hospital confinement, to validate the necessity of current care and to explore alternatives to inpatient care. Usually done by a nurse or other than the one providing the care. See Utilization Review.

CONDITION: Actions an insured must take to keep a policy in force (i.e., pay health or disability insurance premiums). A provision in a contract that has the effect of modifying, suspending, or revoking the principal obligation if a future, uncertain event happens or fails to happen.

CONDITIONAL BINDING RECEIPT: See Binding Receipt.

CONDITIONAL COVERAGE: Insurance coverage applied for and paid for at the same time, but not yet issued.

CONDITIONALLY RENEWABLE CONTRACT: A contract of health insurance that provides that the insured may renew the contract from period to period or continue the contract to a stated date or an advanced age, subject to the right of the insurance company to decline renewal, but only under conditions specified in the contract.

CONDITIONAL PAYMENT: A payment made by Medicare in certain circumstances if the insurance company or other payer does not pay the bill within a proscribed number of days. See Premium.

CONDITIONAL RECEIPT: Evidence of a temporary health insurance contract pending an acceptable policy contract and premium payments. See Binding receipt.

CONDITIONAL RENEWAL: A health insurance contract that provides renewal to a stated date or advanced age to the right of the insurance company to decline renewal only under conditions defined in the contract. See Renewal.

CONFIDENTIALITY: Right to speak confidentially with a health care provider without anyone else finding out what was said.

CONFIDENTIAL RISK REPORT: A report on the suitability of an insurance risk based on an investigation of physical and moral hazards.

CONFINEMENT CLAUSE: A clause in some health insurance policies that specifies that disability income benefits are payable as long as the insured is confined at home, in a hospital, or in a sanitarium.

CONFINEMENT/CONFINED: Referring to inpatient care, it is an uninterrupted stay following formal admission to any hospital, skilled nursing facility, or alternative facility.

CONFINING CONDITION: Illness, sickness, disability, or condition that confines the insured to home. See Injury.

CONFINING SICKNESS: An illness that confines the insured to his or her home, a hospital, or a sanitarium.

CONFLICT OF INTEREST: A conflict between self-interest and the best interests of a managed care or health insurance plan.

CONGREGATE LIVING HEALTH FACILITY (CLHF): As licensed by the Department of Health Services' Licensing and Certification Division, CLHFs provide care to patients with terminal or life-threatening illness or with catastrophic and severe injury. CLHFs provide care in a noninstitutional, homelike setting.

CONSENT: To give approval. In life and health insurance, a policy may not be taken out on a person without that person's approval. Consent is given when the insured signs the application.

CONSIDERATION: The exchange of value, for a promise, upon which an insurance contract is based. Consideration is an essential element of a binding contract. In a health insurance contract, the policy owner's consideration is the first premium payment and the application; the health insurance company's consideration is the promise(s) contained in the contract. Future premiums are not consideration but rather a condition precedent to the insurer's obligation.

CONSIDERATION CLAUSE: That part of an insurance contract that sets forth the amount of initial and renewal premiums and the frequency of future payments.

CONSOLIDATED LICENSE: A general acute-care hospital with more than one physical plant on a single license, under specified circumstances. The second physical plant may be another hospital or a long-term care facility.

CONSOLIDATION: The concentration of health care plans, providers, or services in the hands of a few companies, doctors, or facilities.

CONSULTANT: An independent or company dedicated adviser specializing in healthcare economics or finance, health insurance, or business management. Usually, it is a health insurance agent, Financial Advisor, Certified Financial Planner©, or Certified Medical Planner©.

CONSULTANT, MEDICAL: A doctor who is an expert in a specific branch of medicine.

CONSULTATION: The act of seeking another medical opinion.

CONSUMER ASSESSMENT OF HEALTH PLAN SATISFACTION (CAHPS): A consumer assessment of health plan performance on measures, such as customer service, access to health services, and claims processing.

CONSUMER-DRIVEN HEALTH PLANS (DEFINED BENEFIT CONTRIBUTION PLANS): Health insurance programs that raise the employee's share of health care costs and place health care cost management directly in the employee's hands. See MSA and HSA.

CONSUMER HEALTH ALLIANCE: Regional cooperatives between government and the public that oversee new payment systems. Once known as Health Insurance Purchasing Cooperatives (HIPCs), the alliances would make sure health plans within a region conformed to federal coverage and quality standards and oversee costs within any mandated budget.

CONSUMER PRICE INDEX (CPI): A measure of the core rate of inflation, according to a diverse market basket of goods and services.

CONSUMER PRICE MEDICAL INDEX (CPMI): A measure of the core rate of medical and health care services inflation, according to a diverse market basket of health care goods and medical services.

CONTACT: Exposure to a source of an infection or a person so exposed. See Policy.

CONTAGIOUS: Capable of being transmitted from one person to another by contact or close proximity. See Illness. See Disease.

CONTEMPLATION OF DEATH: A phrase used to describe the apprehension or expectation of approaching and impending death that arises from some presently existing sickness or physical condition or from some impending danger. As applied to transfers of property, the phrase means that thought of death is the impelling cause of transfer, and the motive that induces transfer is a thought that leads to testamentary disposition.

CONTINGENCIES: Unknown and uncontrollable changes in the health care or managed care insurance space that may affect financial solvency of an organization or medical provider.

CONTINGENCY FEES: Remuneration based on future occurrences, as when an attorney accepts a medical malpractice case on a contingent basis, to be paid by future settlements, if won.

CONTINGENCY RESERVE: A managed care or health insurance company's assigned fund for future settlements or claims.

CONTINGENT BENEFICIARY: Person named to receive insurance benefits if the primary beneficiary is not alive.

CONTINUATION OF ENROLLMENT: Allows MCOs to offer enrollees the option of continued enrollment in the MEDICARE + CHOICE plan when enrollees leave the plan. CMS has interpreted this to be on a permanent basis. MEDICARE + CHOICE organizations that choose the continuation of enrollment option must explain it in marketing materials and make it available to all enrollees in the service area. Enrollees may choose to exercise this option when they move or they may choose to disenroll.

CONTINUED STAY REVIEW: A review or hospital audit conducted by an internal or external auditor to determine if the current place of service is still the most appropriate to provide the level of care required by the client.

CONTINUING CARE RETIREMENT COMMUNITY (CCRC): Housing community for mental and physical care needs over time.

CONTINUITY OF CARE: Uninterrupted medical care from initial diagnosis, through testing and treatments and until discharge. May also be known as the continuum of care.

CONTINUOUS CARE: Around the clock, 24-hr, nursing care at home.

CONTINUOUS COVERGE: Transfer from one health insurance plan to another, without interruption in medical benefits.

CONTINUUM OF CARE: A range of medical, nursing treatments, and social services in a variety of settings that provides services most appropriate to the level of care required. For example, a hospital may offer services ranging from nursery to a hospice.

CONTRA ASSET: The asset value increase that decreases the value of a related asset. See Asset: See Liability.

CONTRACEPTION: The intentional prevention of pregnancy through various means, such as drugs, devices, or surgery. May or may not be covered in a health insurance or managed care plan.

CONTRACT: A legal agreement between a payer and a subscribing group or individual that specifies rates, performance covenants, the relationship among the parties, schedule of benefits, and other pertinent conditions. The contract usually is limited to a 12-month period and is subject to renewal thereafter. Contracts are not required by statute or regulation, and less formal agreements may be made. See Policy.

CONTRACT: In insurance, the policy is a legal contract. The chief requirements for the formation of a valid contract are (a) parties having legal capacity to enter into a contract; (b) mutual assent of the parties to a promise or set of promises, generally consisting of an offer made by one party and an acceptance thereof by the other; (c) a valuable consideration; (d) the absence of any statute or other rule making the contract void; and (e) the absence of fraud or misrepresentation by either party. A life or health insurance policy meeting these requirements qualifies as a contract. (See also: contract of insurance.)

CONTRACT OF DECEDENT: An agreement entered into before the death of a deceased person.

CONTRACT HOSPITAL: A covered hospital contracted by a health insurance company to admit members of the plan.

CONTRACT OF INSURANCE: A legal and binding contract whereby an insurer agrees to pay or indemnify an insured for losses, provide other benefits, or render service to, or on behalf of, an insured. The contract of insurance is often called an insurance policy, but the policy is merely the evidence of the agreement. In life and health insurance, the contract of insurance consists of the policy, the application, and any attached supplements, riders, or endorsements.

CONTRACT LIMITATIONS: Any amounts a covered person is responsible for paying, based on his or her contract with the insurer. See Terms, Conditions, and Exclusions.

CONTRACT MANAGEMENT: The computerized modeling, forecasting, trend analysis, and data banking of health insurance information on a large group scale.

CONTRACT MIX: The distribution of members in a health insurance or managed care plan, usually by dependency.

CONTRACT MONTH: One calendar month within the contract period of a health care insurance plan.

CONTRACT PROVIDER: Any hospital, skilled-nursing facility, extended-care facility, individual, organization, or licensed agency that has a contractual arrangement with an insurer for the provision of services under an insurance contract. See Doctor.

CONTRACT RATES: Contractual agreement from a payer, to a medical provider, with set reimbursement rates, usually at a discount.

CONTRACT YEAR: A period of 12 consecutive months, commencing with each anniversary date. May or may not coincide with a calendar year.

CONTRA PREFERENDUM: A legal concept that any ambiguity in a contract must be interpreted against the person who drew the contract, because he or she had the opportunity to make it clear. Because the insurance company writes insurance contracts, any ambiguity would be interpreted in favor of the insured. See Contract and Policyholder.

CONTRIBUTION MARGIN: Amount remaining after subtracting variable costs from revenues. It is the profit of each new medical service unit available to cover all health care costs.

CONTRIBUTORY PROGRAM: Program in which the cost of group coverage is shared by the employee and the employer or insureds.

CONVALESCENT CARE: Ambulatory care that is rendered or partially self-administered by the patient with an emphasis on recovery.

CONVERSION: In group health insurance, the opportunity given the insured and any covered dependents to change their group insurance to some form of individual insurance, without medical evaluation upon termination of the group insurance.

CONVERSION CLAUSE: Health insurance policy contract provision that allows changeover to an individual health plan after termination of the group policy.

CONVERSION FACTOR: A dollar amount for one base unit in the relative value scale (RVS). The price paid to the provider for a given service equals the relative value of the service multiplied by the dollar amount of the conversion factor. For example, a blood sugar determination might have a relative value of 4.0, and the conversion factor might be $4.00. The price of the blood sugar determination would therefore be $16.00.

CONVERSION FACTOR UPDATE: Annual percentage change to the conversion factor. For Medicare, the update is set by a formula to reflect medical inflation, changes in enrollment, growth in the economy, and changes in spending as a result of other changes in law.

CONVERSION PLAN: A member's group plan is canceled; the member opts to continue coverage under an individual health or life insurance plan.

CONVERSION PRIVILEGE: Option that allows employees who are terminating employment to continue some or all of their long-term disability coverage at their own expense without submitting evidence of insurability. See Long-Term Disability.

CO-OPERATING PROVIDER: A medical provider who has entered into an agreement to provide health care to plan members.

COORDINATED BENEFITS: A process wherein if an individual has two group health plans, the amount payable is divided between the plans so that the combined coverage amounts to, but does not exceed, 100% of the charges. The procedures set forth in a subscription agreement to determine which coverage is primary for payment of benefits to members with duplicate coverage.

CO-ORDINATED CARE: Another term for managed medical care.

COORDINATED COVERAGE: Method of integrating benefits payable under more than one health insurance plan (for example, Medicare and retiree health benefits). Coordinated coverage is typically orchestrated so that the insured's benefits from all sources do not exceed 100% of allowable medical expenses. Coordinated coverage may require beneficiaries to pay some deductibles or coinsurance.

COORDINATION PERIOD: Occurs when private health insurance is the first payer, and Medicare is the secondary payer.

COPAYMENT (COPAY): A cost-sharing arrangement in which the HMO enrollee pays a specified flat amount for a specific service (such as $30.00 for an office visit or $18.00 for each prescription drug). The amount paid must be nominal to avoid becoming a barrier to care. It does not vary with the cost of the service, unlike coinsurance that is based on some percentage of cost. Supplemental cost-sharing arrangement in which an HMO enrollee pays a specified amount for a specific service.

CORE FUNCTIONS: Three basic functions of the public health system: (a) assessment; (b) policy development; and (c) assurance. State and local public health agencies must perform these functions in order to protect and promote health, and prevent disease and injury.

CORPORATE PRACTICE OF MEDICINE: The various state and federal laws that prohibit the layman from directly or indirectly practicing medicine.

CORPORATION: An association of stockholders created as an entity under law and regarded as an artificial person by courts, offering limited liability to stockholders, continuity in existence, and easy transferability of ownership interests.

CORRIDOR DEDUCTIBLE: The name for the deductible that lies between the benefits paid by the basic plan and the beginning of the major medical benefits when a major medical plan is superimposed over a basic health plan.

COSMETIC PROCEDURE: Any medical or surgical procedure that improves physical appearance without being medically necessary or without correcting a physical function.

COSMETIC SURGERY: Any surgical intervention aimed at improving appearance and form over function.

COST: Inputs or expenses, both direct and indirect, required to produce an intervention, medical goods, or services. See Expense.

COST-APPROACH: Costing method that adds a marginal charge of the price of an item, like a laboratory test or drug.

COST (+) APPROACH: Method of determining medical costs with a margin added for profit.

COST-AVOIDANCE: Ability of a health care organization to obviate the need for costs by operating in new ways.

COST-BASED REIMBURSEMEMT: Medical care payment method based on provider costs or those delivering the services.

COST-BASED SYSTEM: A method of medical payments that starts with the provider's costs, as opposed to fees, as the starting point for reimbursement.

COST-BENEFIT ANALYSIS: Analytical procedure for determining the economic efficiency of a program, expressed as the relationship between costs and outcomes, usually measured in monetary terms.

COST CENTER: An organizational division, department, or unit performing functional activities within a facility; for each such center, cost accountability is maintained for revenues produced and for controllable expenses incurred. See Expense and Profit Center.

COST-TO-CHARGE RATIO: The quotient of cost (total operating expenses minus other operating revenue) divided by charges (gross patient revenue) expressed as a decimal.

COST-CONTAINMENT: Actions that control or reduce health care costs. Control or reduction of inefficiencies in the consumption, allocation, or production of health care services that contribute to higher than necessary costs. (Inefficiencies in consumption can occur when health services are inappropriately used; inefficiencies in allocation exist when health services could be delivered in less costly settings without loss of quality; and inefficiencies in production exist when the costs of producing health services could be reduced by using a different combination of resources.) See UCR.

COST-CONTRACT: An arrangement between a managed health care plan and (CMS) HCFA under Section 1876 and/or 1833 of the Social Security Act, under which the health plan provides health services and is reimbursed its costs. The beneficiary can use providers outside the plan's provider network.

COST DRIVER: Medical or health care events or service activities that cause a cost to be incurred.

COST EFFECTIVENESS: The efficacy of a program in achieving given intervention outcomes in relation to the program costs. See Efficiency.

COST OF GOODS USED: Amount or cost of supplies used to produce a medical service. May be determined by the product of the numbers of relative value units and relative value unit cost.

COST OF ILLNESS ANALYSIS (COI): An assessment of the economic impact of an illness or condition, including treatment costs.

COST OF INSURANCE: The cost or value of the actual net insurance protection in any year (face amount less reserve), according to the yearly renewable term rate used by a company on government published term rates.

COST OF LIVING ADJUSTMENT (COLA): A rider available with some health insurance and managed care policies that provides for an automatic increase in benefits, offsetting the effects of inflation.

COST MINIMIZATION ANALYSIS (CMA): An assessment of the least costly medical interventions among available alternatives that produce equivalent outcomes.

COST-MINIMIZING ACTIVITY: Any method used in managed care to reduce health care expenses while not jeopardizing patient care, diagnosis, or treatment.

COST OBJECT: Any medical product or service for which a cost is determined (patient exam, visit, test, or intervention).

COST OUTLIER: A medical case that is more costly to treat compared with other patients in a particular diagnosis-related group. Outliers also refer to any unusual occurrence of cost, cases that skew average costs, or unusual procedures.

COST PLUS APPROACH: Medical or health care service or product price determination that includes a margin for the cost of that medical product or service.

COST OF RISK (COR): A measurement of the total costs associated with providing health or managed medical care insurance, for the payer or underwriter.

COST SHARING: Paying a portion of health care or disability costs, such as premiums, deductibles, or copayments, etc. Payment method where a person is required to pay some health costs to receive medical care. The general set of financing arrangements whereby the consumer must pay out-of-pocket to receive care, either at the time of initiating care, or during the provision of health care services, or both. Cost sharing can also occur when an insured pays a portion of the monthly premium for health care insurance.

COST SHIFTING: Charging one group of patients more to make up for underpayment by others. Most commonly, charging some privately insured patients more to make up for underpayment by Medicaid.

COUNSEL: Legal advice; also, a lawyer or lawyers engaged to give such advice or to conduct a case in court.

COUNTER AGENT: In health insurance, an underwriting employee who accepts and acts upon applications submitted by buyers and brokers over the counter in an agency of an insurance company.

COUNTERSIGNATURE LAW: Statute regulating the countersigning of health and life insurance policies in a particular state. A law requiring that all insurance contracts covering property or persons in a state be countersigned by an insurance company representative located in that state; usually a licensed resident insurance agent.

COUNTY INDIGENT PROGRAMS: Atypical payer category includes indigent patients paid for in whole or part by various state realignment funds, the County Medical Services Program (CMSP), California Health Care for Indigent Program (CHIP), specified tobacco tax funds, and other funding sources for which the hospital renders a bill or other claim for payment to a county. This category also includes indigent patients who are provided care in county hospitals or in certain noncounty hospitals whether or not a bill is rendered.

COUNTY INDIGENT PROGRAMS NET PATIENT REVENUE: County Indigent Programs gross patient revenue minus County Indigent Programs deductions from revenue.

COUPON RATE: Rate of interest charged on a bond that is fixed.

COVENANT: The legal provisions in a life, health, or managed care insurance contract. See Policy, Terms, Conditions, and Contracts.

COVENANTS OR BOND COVENANTS: The issuer's enforceable promise to perform or refrain from performing certain actions. With respect to hospital municipal securities, covenants are generally stated in the bond contract. Covenants commonly made in connection with a bond issue include covenants to charge fees sufficient to provide required pledged revenues (called a *rate covenant*); to maintain casualty insurance on the project; to complete, maintain, and operate the project; not to sell or encumber the project; not to issue parity bonds unless certain earnings tests are met (called an *additional bonds covenant*); and, not to take actions that would cause the bonds to be arbitrage bonds. See Policy, Terms, Conditions, and Contracts.

COVER: The act of offering health insurance coverage; to include within the coverage of an insurance contract. See Benefits and Exclusions.

COVERAGE: Health care services provided to an insured person as a member and as an individual, family, or group, and paid by the insurance company according to the terms, conditions, limitations, and exclusions of the contract. Payment will occur provided that the services are rendered when that contract is in effect. Health care services provided or authorized by the payer's Medical Staff or payment for health care services.

COVERAGE APPROACH: A method of setting medical service or insurance premium charges to cover their costs.

COVERAGE BASIS: The maximum dollar coverage for medical services in a Medicare + Choice program.

COVERAGE CRITERIA: Objective and consistent medical standards that are used by a health plan medical director to determine whether a given service will be covered.

COVERAGE DECISION: An insurance coverage decision to pay for or provide a medical service or technology for particular clinical indications.

COVERED BENEFIT: A medically necessary service that is specifically provided for under the provisions of an evidence of coverage. A covered benefit must always be medically necessary, but not every medically necessary service is a covered benefit. For example, some elements of custodial or maintenance care, which are excluded from coverage, may be medically necessary, but are not covered. See Exclusions.

COVERED EXPENSES: In an insurance contract, those costs for which benefits are payable or which may be applied against a deductible amount. For example, under a medical expense contract, those expenses, such as hospital, medical, and miscellaneous health care, incurred by the insured and for which he or she is entitled to receive benefits.

COVERED PERSON OR MEMBER: In reference to either a subscriber or an enrolled dependent, a covered person is one who both meets the eligibility requirements of the contract and is enrolled for coverage under the contract.

COVERED WORKER: A person who has earnings creditable for Social Security purposes on the basis of services for wages in covered employment or on the basis of income from covered self-employment. The number of hospital insurance-covered workers is slightly larger than the number of old-age, survivor's, and disability insurance-covered workers because of different coverage status for federal employment. See Worker's Compensation.

COVER NOTE: Written statement by a life or health insurance agent informing the insured that coverage is in effect; used in lieu of a binder but differing because the insurance company prepares the insurance binder, while the broker or agent prepares the cover note.

CPT (Current Procedural Terminology): A list of physician or provider services or procedures that are represented by a five-digit code. These codes have become a nationwide dialect for services and procedures within the health care industry.

CREDENTIALING: The process of determining physician or medical provider eligibility for hospitals, physician hospital organizations (PHOs), outpatient clinics and centers, or other medical staff memberships and privileges to be granted to those physicians or medical providers. Credentials and performance are periodically reviewed, which could result in a doctor's privileges being denied, modified, or withdrawn. The process of reviewing a provider's qualifications to be sure they meet the criteria established by a managed care organization.

CREDENTIALS: Professional qualifications or those qualifications of a health care facility or entity.

CREDIBILITY: The extent to which health insurance claims experiences are expected to repeat.

CREDITABLE COVERAGE: Atypical health insurance coverage through an individual or employer-sponsored health plan with benefits equal to or greater than the basic plan, Medicare, or Medicaid, TriCare (formerly CHAMPUS), Indian Health Service (or tribal organization) state health benefits risk pool, federal employee program, a public health or church plan, or a college plan that is not a limited benefit plan. Creditable coverage does not include limited benefit plans, dread disease plans, or short-term major medical if it is the coverage immediately prior to the effective date of the basic or standard coverage.

CREDIT HEALTH INSURANCE: Insurance coverage issued to a creditor, on the life of a debtor.

CREDITOR: An entity or third party that is owed money.

CRITICAL ACCESS HOSPITAL: Usually a small health care facility that provides acute inpatient health and medical care services.

CRITICAL ILLNESS INSURANCE: Health insurance policy that pays a lump sum or face amount if the insured is diagnosed with a specific critical condition.

CRITICAL PATHWAY: Focus on a patient and document essential steps in the diagnosis and treatment of a condition or the performance of a condition. They document a standard pattern of care to be followed for each patient and are developed primarily as a nursing tool specific to a health care organization and its unique system. Synonyms for care paths: critical paths; practice guidelines or parameters; clinical guidelines, protocols, or algorithms; care tracks; care maps; care process models; case care coordination; collaborative case management plans; collaborative care tracks; collaborative paths; coordinated care; minimum standards; patient pathways; quality assurance triggers; reference guidelines; service strategies; recovery routes; target tracks; standards of care; standard treatment guidelines; total quality management; key processes; and anticipated recovery paths. See Care Maps.

CRITICAL PREMIUM: The first premium an insured pays after the policy is in force, the initial premium having been collected by the agent at the time of policy application or delivery. It is considered critical in terms of high lapse potential, with the greatest number of policy lapses occurring at this time.

CRUDE DEATH RATE: The ratio of total deaths to total population during a given period of time, such as a year.

CRUDE MORTALITY RATE: The mortality rate from all causes of death for a population.

CUMULATIVE TRAUMA: Injury that continues from a physical or physic wound.

CURE PROVISION: A time bomb or statute of limitations to remedy a health care dispute and avoid contract termination.

CURRENT ASSETS: Assets used or consumed within 12 months. Cash plus any other assets that will be sold, converted into cash, or used during a hospital's cash conversion cycle, or the cycle of cash to medical services, to third-party insurance payer, and back to cash, again. Most commonly included with cash are marketable securities, patient accounts receivable, and inventory. See Liabilities and Net Assets.

CURRENT COMPENSATION: That compensation that provides an employee with an immediate benefit, the most obvious example of which is his or her current base pay.

CURRENT DEBT: See Current Liabilities.

CURRENT INTEREST RATE: General term used to describe the interest rate of earnings credited to variable and universal life products (versus the fixed rate of traditional life insurance policies).

CURRENT LIABILITIES: As a rule, debts or obligations that must be met within a year. On a stock, the annual dividend divided by the current ask price; on a bond, the annual interest dividend by the current market value. In other words, "What you get, divided by what you pay." See Assets, Liabilities, and Net Liabilities.

CURRENTLY INSURED: Under Social Security, a status of limited eligibility that provides only death benefits to widows or widowers and children; does not provide old-age or disability benefits. To qualify as currently insured, a worker must have at least 6 quarters of coverage in the 13-quarter period ending with the quarter in which he or she dies or becomes eligible for old-age or disability benefits.

CURRENT POPULATION SURVEY: U.S. Bureau of the Census survey conducted nationally to measure employment, health insurance status, income, and other variables.

CURRENT PROCEDURAL TERMINOLOGY (CPT): A standardized mechanism of reporting services using numeric codes as established and updated annually; first produced, owned, and copyrighted in 1961 by the American Medical Association.

CURRENT RATIO: A measure to determine how easily current debt may be paid (current assets: current liabilities). See Current Assets and Current Liabilities.

CURRENT YEAR: The present health insurance contract or policy year.

CUSTODIAL CARE: Care provided primarily to assist a patient in meeting the activities of daily living, but not care requiring skilled-nursing services. In a medical context, the care necessary to meet personal needs, such as walking, bathing, dressing, and eating. Medical training is not required, but this care must be provided on a doctor's order.

CUSTOMARY CHARGE: One of the screens previously used to determine a physician's payment for a service under Medicare's customary, prevailing, and reasonable payment system. Customary charges are calculated as the physician's median charge for a given service over a prior 12-month period. Also known as usual, customary, and reasonable (UCR) charge.

CUSTOMARY, PREVAILING, AND REASONABLE (CPR): The method of paying physicians under Medicare from 1965 until implementation of the Medicare Fee Schedule in January 1992. Payment for a service was limited to the lowest of: (a) the physician's billed charge for the service; (b) the physician's customary charge for the service; or (c) the prevailing charge for that service in the community. Similar to the usual, customary, and reasonable system used by private insurers. See Medicare Fee Schedule and Usual, Customary, and Reasonable.

CUSTOMARY AND REASONABLE CHARGES: In health insurance, the basic concept used in determining the benefit package in a major medical plan: to pay all reasonable and necessary medical costs, but not to pay excessive or unnecessary costs. Insurance companies and government providers may refuse to cover excessive expenses if they determine that charges made were not within customary and reasonable limits.

CUT-OFF PROVISION: A provision in health insurance that regulates the period during which benefits are payable under major medical and comprehensive medical expense insurance.

CUT RATE: An insurance premium charge that is below a scheduled rate.

CYCLE BILLING: The time period in which acknowledged receipts, invoices, premiums, or other bills are periodically repeated and sent.

D

DAc: doctor of acupuncture.

DAILY HOSPITAL BENEFIT: In medical expense health policies, benefit coverage for hospital charges, such as room, board, nurses, and other routine services, provided on a per diem (daily) basis. Sometimes referred to as DBR (daily board and room).

DAILY OPERATIONS: The common and usual activities of a health or medical care organization.

DATABASE MANAGEMENT SYSTEM (DBMS): The separation of data from the computer application that allows entry or editing of data.

DATA INTERVIEW: In life or health insurance selling, a meeting during which the agent and prospect learn more about each other, and the prospect learns more about his or her own insurance needs.

DATA USE AGREEMENT (DUA): HIPAA regulation states that a health care entity may use or disclose a limited data set if that entity obtains a data use agreement from the potential recipient and can only be used for research, public health, or health care operations. Relates to privacy rules of HIPAA.

DATE OF EMPLOYMENT: The first day of work, often related to heath insurance coverage.

DATE OF INCEPTION: See Date of Policy and Date of Issue.

DATE OF ISSUE: The date that an initial health care insurance contract premium is received and the contract owner information is approved.

DATE OF POLICY: The date appearing on the front page of a health insurance policy indicating when the policy went into effect.

DATE OF SERVICE: The date when a covered person is provided with a health care service. See DOS.

DATE OF TERMINATION: The exact ending date, if any, of a health insurance policy.

DAY OUTLIER: A patient with an atypically long length of stay compared with other patients in a particular diagnosis-related group.

DAYS IN ACCOUNTS RECEIVABLE: Net accounts receivable divided by average revenue per day (gross patient revenue divided by days in the reporting period). This ratio indicates the time necessary to convert receivables into cash.

DAYS CASH ON HAND: The number of days that a health care organization can cover with its most liquid assets (cash and marketable securities or operating expenses minus depreciation/365 days).

DAYS (OR VISITS) PER 1,000: An indicator calculated by taking the total number of days (for inpatient, residential, or partial hospitalization) or visits (for outpatient) received by a specific group for a specific period of time (usually 1 year). This number is then divided by the average number of covered members or lives in that group during the same period and multiplied by 1,000. A measure used to evaluate utilization management performance. See Days Per Thousand.

DAYS PER THOUSAND: The number of hospital care days, used in a year, per 1,000 HMO members. See Days (or Visits) per 1,000.

DAY TREATMENT CENTER: A psychiatric facility that is licensed to provide outpatient care and treatment of mental or nervous disorders or substance abuse under the supervision of physicians.

DEATH: Termination of life.

DEATH BENEFIT: Policy proceeds to be paid upon the death of the insured. In life and accidental death and dismemberment health policies, the face amount to be paid to a beneficiary upon proof of death of the insured. The sum payable as the result of the death of the insured. In a pension plan, the benefit payable to the beneficiary on the death of a participating employee.

DEATH BENEFIT FOR PARENTS: Under Social Security, a monthly death benefit beginning at age 62, payable to each natural or adoptive parent or stepparent of a deceased, fully insured individual, if the parent or stepparent was dependent upon the insured for at least one half of his or her support and has not remarried since the individual's death (unless to a person also eligible for certain Social Security benefits).

DEATH-TO-CASE RATIO: The number of deaths attributed to a particular disease during a specified time period divided by the number of new cases of that disease identified during the same time period.

DEATH, CONTEMPLATION OF: See Contemplation of Death.

DEATHS, DISCOUNTS FOR: A reduction in the anticipated cost of providing benefits that results from assuming that a certain number of participants in a group pension plan will die before retirement. A recognized mortality table is used as the basis for these assumptions—the greater the number of deaths, the greater the discount for death for survivors.

DEATH SPIRAL: An insurance term that refers to a vicious spiral of high premium rates and adverse selection, generally in a free-choice environment.

DEATH TRAUMA COVERAGE: A few health insurance funds have this coverage as an add-on benefit to some of their hospital or extras cover. Conditions and benefits vary widely between fund policies.

DEBENTURE: An unsecured long-term debt offering by a health care corporation, promising only the general assets ("full faith and credit") as protection for these creditors.

DEBIT: A combination insurance agent's group of policy owners from whom premiums are regularly collected. A debit book is the agent's list of active policy owners. The term also applies to the territory in which an agent collects premiums.

DEBT FINANCING: Borrowing money or capital at current interest rate costs.

DEBT RATIOS: Comparative statistics showing the relationship between the issuer's outstanding debt and such factors as its tax base, income, or population. Such ratios are often used in the process of determining credit quality of an issue, primarily on general obligation or hospital revenue bonds. Some of the more commonly used ratios are: (a) net overall debt to assessed valuation; (b) net overall debt to estimated full valuation; and (c) net overall debt per capita.

DEBT SERVICE: The amount of money necessary to pay interest on an outstanding debt, the principal of maturing serial hospital revenue bonds, and the required contributions to a sinking fund for term bonds. Debt service on bonds may be calculated on a calendar year, fiscal year, or bond fiscal year basis.

DEBT SERVICE RESERVE FUND: The fund in which moneys are placed which may be used to pay debt service if pledged revenues are insufficient to satisfy the debt service requirements. The debt service reserve fund may be entirely funded with bond proceeds, or it may only be partly funded at the time of issuance and allowed to reach its full funding requirement over time, because of the accumulation of pledged revenues. If the debt service reserve fund is used in whole or part to pay debt service, the issuer usually is required to replenish the funds from the first available funds or revenues.

DECEDENT: A dead insured.

DECLARATION: In insurance, a statement made by the applicant at the time of policy application, usually relative to underwriting information that the insurer deems vital, and to which the applicant is probably the one best able to supply accurate information. In life and health insurance policies, the declaration is copied into the policy. See Dec Sheet.

DECLARE A DIVIDEND: To announce or approve a cash payment (dividend) to a corporation's shareowners out of the company's earnings or surplus.

DECLINE: A company refuses to accept the request for health insurance coverage.

DEC SHEET: See Declaration.

DEDUCTIBLE: Provision or clause in an insurance contract that the first given number of dollars, or percentage, or expenses will not be reimbursed or covered. (1) The amount paid by the patient for medical care prior to insurance covering the balance. (2) A type of cost sharing where the insured party pays a specified amount of approved charges for covered medical services before the insurer will assume liability for all or part of the remaining covered services. (3) Cumulative amount a member of a health plan has to pay for services before that person's plan begins to cover the costs of care. See Corridor Deductible.

DEDUCTIBLE AGGREGATE: Total annual deductible for a health insurance policy.

DEDUCTIBLE CARRY-OVER: A policy feature whereby covered expenses in the last three months of the year may carry over to be counted toward the next year's deductible.

DEDUCTIBLE CARRY-OVER CREDIT: Last quarter deductible that may be used for the next year.

DEDUCTIBLE CLAUSE: An insurance policy provision that specifies an amount to be deducted from any loss, leaving the company liable only for the excess of that stated amount.

DEDUCTIBLE COVERAGE: An insurance policy provision stipulating that only the loss in excess of a minimum figure is covered.

DEDUCTIBLE COVERAGE CLAUSE: A provision in an insurance policy that states that, in return for a reduced rate, the insured will assume losses below a specified amount. In a health insurance policy, for example, that portion of covered hospital and medical charges that an insured person must pay before the policy's benefits begin.

DEEMED: An agreement by medical providers, durable medical equipment vendors, or health care facilities to follow the terms and condition of a health insurance, Medicare, or managed care plan.

DEFAMATION: The act of harming someone's character, fame, or reputation by false and malicious words, including libel and slander. Many state insurance laws provide penalties for verbal or printed circulation of derogatory information calculated to injure the business or reputation of any life or health insurance company or agent, or for aiding in such activities.

DEFAULT: In health insurance, the policy owner's failure to make a premium payment by a policy's final due date or by the end of its grace period. Or, breach of some covenant, promise to duty imposed by a hospital or other contract. The most serious default occurs when the issuer fails to pay principal, interest, or both, when due. Other technical defaults result when specifically defined events occur, such as failure to perform covenants. Technical defaults may include failing to charge rates sufficient to meet rate covenants or failing to maintain insurance on the project. If the issuer defaults in the payment of principal, interest, or both, or if a technical default is not cured within a specified period of time, the bondholders or trustee may exercise legally available rights and remedies for enforcement of the bond contract.

DEFEASANCE: A clause included in some health insurance policies which provides that performance of certain specified acts will nullify the contract agreement.

DEFENSIVE MEDICINE: Medical exams, procedures, or interventions performed to reduce the risk of medical negligence claims. Prescribing additional tests or procedures to justify medical care and strengthen support for medical decisions or to corroborate diagnosis. This defensiveness is a result of lawsuits, malpractice claims, and the onslaught of external utilization review entities questioning care decisions. Defensive medicine is said to be one of the primary causes of the increasing cost of health care. Many physicians and the AMA fight for tort reform to reduce the need for defensive medicine.

DEFERRED COMPENSATION ADMINISTRATOR: A company that provides services through retirement planning administration, third-party administration, self-insured plans, compensation planning, salary survey, and workers' compensation claims administration.

DEFERRED NONEMERGENCY CARE: Medical intervention that can be postponed without patient injury.

DEFERRED PREMIUM: Delayed monthly health insurance premium to transfer incurred but not reported expenses.

DEFERRED REVENUE: Money received but not yet earned, as in some capitated health insurance contracts.

DEFICIENCY: Serious finding of inadequacy with a health care provider, medical treatment, durable medical equipment vendor, drug, surgical intervention, or health care facility.

DEFICIT REDUCTION ACT: 1984 law that states that Medicare becomes the secondary payer for those aged 65–69 years who have a working spouse aged younger than 65 years.

DEFINED CONTRIBUTION COVERAGE: A funding mechanism for health benefits whereby employers make a specific dollar contribution toward the cost of health insurance coverage for employees, but make no promises about specific benefits to be covered.

DEFINITION: The meaning of important words in a health, life, or other insurance policy.

DEFINITION OF PARTIAL OR RESIDUAL DISABILITY: Applies when an insured is able to return to work part-time or even full time (with a loss of earnings). If the employee is working in this limited capacity and is earning less than a certain level of income, he or she will still be eligible for limited benefits under the plan. Not all disability insurance carriers use this terminology to describe a part-time work situation, but most provide some type of benefit to encourage employees to return to work.

DEFINITION OF TOTAL DISABILITY: Probably the most important provision in a disability contract is the definition of disability that will be used to determine an employee's eligibility for benefits.

- Own Occupation (Own Occ): Under this definition, an insured is considered disabled only if unable to perform the duties of his or her occupation.
- Any Occupation (Any Occ): Under this definition, an insured is considered disabled only if unable to work in any occupation for which he or she is qualified by education, training, or experience. This is closely related to the definition that the Social Security Administration uses in determining disability.

DEFLATION: A sustained period of falling interest rates, prices, and economics. See Inflation.

DEGREE OF RISK: In insurance, the probable deviation of actual experience from expected experience. See Peril and Risk.

DEINSTITUTIONALIZATION: Policy that calls for the provision of supportive care and treatment for medically and socially dependent individuals in the community rather than in an institutional setting.

DEMAND MANAGEMENT: Promoting and reducing the need for medical services through such strategies as prevention, risk identification, risk management, and empowering consumers and providers to make appropriate choices about care through education and informed decision-making tools.

DEMAND RATIONING: Barrier to health insurance access as a result of financial constraints.

DEMISE: To die; death; to convey an estate to another by will or lease; to transfer by descent or bequest.

DEMOGRAPHIC: Information about health plan member's names, addresses, dates of birth, and phone numbers.

DEMOGRAPHIC INFORMATION: Characteristics, such as age, sex, race, and occupation, of descriptive epidemiology used to characterize the populations at risk.

DEMOGRAPHIC RATING: Modified community insurance rating that considers important characteristics and parameters of individuals.

DEMOGRAPHY: The study of populations from the standpoint of their vital statistics.

DENIAL CODE: Classification system and identification number used to deny health insurance claims.

DENTAL CARE: All services provided by or under the direction of a dentist. Such services include: the care of teeth and the surrounding tissues; correction of an overbite or underbite; and any surgical procedure that involves the hard or soft tissues of the mouth. See Dentist, Doctor of Dental Surgery (DDS), and Doctor of Medical Dentistry (DMD).

DENTAL EXPENSE INSURANCE: A form of medical expense health insurance covering the cost of treatment and care of dental disease and injury to the insured's teeth. This coverage is more commonly included in group-health insurance policies than in individual health policies.

DENTIST: Any doctor of dental surgery, DDS or DMD, who is licensed and qualified to provide dental care under the law of jurisdiction in which treatment is received.

DEPARTMENT OF HEALTH INSURANCE (DOHI): State government agency usually charged with health and other insurance regulations.

DEPARTMENT OF JUSTICE (DOJ): The federal agency that enforces the law and handles criminal investigations. As the nation's largest law firm, the DOJ protects citizens through effective law enforcement, crime prevention, and crime detection. It is the agency that prosecutes those in the health care system guilty of proven fraudulent activity. See Fraud.

DEPENDENCY PERIOD: For life insurance purposes, the years when children are dependent upon parents. This usually is considered to be until the youngest is 18 years old because that is the period during which Social Security benefits are payable to eligible spouses caring for eligible children of deceased, disabled, or retired workers.

DEPENDENCY PERIOD INCOME: One of the basic uses for life insurance. Income for the family during the years until the youngest child reaches maturity (usually ages 18–21).

DEPENDENT: The lawful spouse and each unmarried child who is not employed on a regular full-time basis and who is dependent upon the declaring individual for support and maintenance. The term includes stepchildren, adopted children, and foster children. One who relies on a spouse, parent, grandparent, legal guardian, or one with whom they reside for health care insurance. The definition of dependent is subject to differing conditions and limitations between health care plans.

DEPENDENT COVERAGE: Health insurance coverage for a dependent person. Coverage is usually at a far cheaper rate than if independent or primary coverage is used. See Dependent.

DEPOSIT PREMIUM: A premium deposit required by an insurance company on those forms of health insurance subject to premium adjustment. Also called provisional premium. See Premium.

DEPRECIATION: Decreasing value or wasting away, over time. Or, the continuous decline in the value of a health care company's buildings and equipment in the course of its operations. It is an item of expense through which the money paid for the plant and equipment is shown as having been spent in installments over the productive lifetime of the plant or equipment. See Accumulated Depreciation.

DEPRECIATION TAX SHIELD: The inflow of funds that provide tax reduction in the amount of taxes owed.

DERMATOLOGY: Diagnosis, treatment, and research on skin disease and the integument system of hair and nails.

DESIGNATED HEALTH SERVICES: The eleven types of medial services prohibited by Stark II laws, from physician referrals for those with financial ties to another health care entity, doctor, provider, or facility: (a) physical therapy; (b) clinical laboratory; (c) radiology; (d) occupational therapy; (e) radiation; (f) durable medical equipment; (g) home health care; (h) parenteral and enteral care; (i) outpatient drugs; (j) inpatient and outpatient hospital services; and (k) orthotic and prosthetic devices.

DESIGNATED HOSPITAL: Hospital or facility under contract to your health care plan.

DESIGNATED MENTAL HEALTH PROVIDER: Person or place authorized by a health plan to provide or suggest appropriate mental health and substance abuse care.

DESIGNATED TRANSPLANT FACILITY: A hospital or alternative facility that has entered an agreement either with or on behalf of a health plan to provide health services for covered transplants.

DEVELOPMENTAL DISABILITY (DD): A severe, chronic disability that is attributable to a mental or physical impairment or combination of mental and physical impairments; is manifested before the person attains age 22; is likely to continue indefinitely; results in substantial functional limitations in three or more of the following areas of major life activity: self-care, receptive and expressive language, learning, mobility, self-direction, capacity of independent living, economic self-sufficiency; and reflects the person's needs for a combination and sequence of special, interdisciplinary, or generic care treatments of services that are of lifelong or extended duration and are individually planned and coordinated.

DEVELOPMENTALLY DISABLED (DD): A person with a disability attributable to mental retardation, cerebral palsy, epilepsy, or other neurologically handicapping conditions found to be closely related to mental retardation or to require similar treatment. This term is also used to describe the nursing care given to such persons.

DHM: Doctor of homeopathic medicine. See Doctor.

DIABETES (TYPE I): A person is insulin dependent and requires insulin treatment for his or her lifetime.

DIABETES (TYPE II): A person is not insulin dependent but may manage his or her condition by diet, exercise, weight control, and in some instances, oral medications or insulin.

DIABETES EDUCATION PROGRAM: Self-managed outpatient education program. The program helps those with Type I or Type II diabetes understand the process of the disease and its daily management.

DIABETIC DURABLE MEDICAL EQUIPMENT: Purchased or rented ambulatory items, such as glucose meters and insulin-infusion pumps, prescribed by a health care provider for use in managing a patient's diabetes as covered by Medicare.

DIAGNOSIS: The specific or provisional name of a mental or physical disease, illness, disability, condition, or injury.

DIAGNOSIS-RELATED GROUPS (DRGs): (1) System of classifying patients on the basis of diagnoses for purposes of payment to hospitals. (2) A system for determining case mix, used for payment under Medicare's prospective payment system (PPS) and by some other payers. The DRG system classifies patients into groups based on the principal diagnosis, type of surgical procedure, presence or absence of significant comorbidities or complications, and other relevant criteria. DRGs are intended to categorize patients into groups that are clinically meaningful and homogeneous with respect to resource use. Medicare's PPS currently uses almost 500 mutually exclusive DRGs, each of which is assigned a relative weight that compares its costliness to the average for all DRGs.

DIAGNOSIS AND STATISTICAL MANUAL OF MENTAL DISORDERS, **3RD ED., REV.** *(DSMIII-R)*: American Psychiatric Association manual of diagnostic criteria and terminology.

DIAGNOSTIC ADMISSION: Entrance into a health care facility for tests and explorative interventions to establish a cause of illness.

DIAGNOSTIC COVERAGE: Medical insurance that pays expenses up to a stated amount for such diagnostic services as x-ray examination or other laboratory tests.

DIAGNOSTICIAN: A physician who determines the nature of an ailment. See Doctor.

DIAGNOSTIC AND TREATMENT CODES: See DRGs.

DIALYSIS: A process by which dissolved substances are removed from a patient's body by diffusion from one fluid compartment to another across a semipermeable membrane. The two types of dialysis that are currently commonly in use are hemodialysis and peritoneal dialysis.

DIALYSIS CENTER (RENAL): A hospital unit that is approved to furnish the full spectrum of diagnostic, therapeutic, and rehabilitative services required for the care of end-state renal disease patients (including inpatient dialysis) furnished directly or under arrangement.

DIALYSIS FACILITY (RENAL): A unit (hospital based or freestanding) that is approved to furnish dialysis services directly to end-stage renal disease patients.

DIALYSIS STATION: A portion of the dialysis patient treatment area that accommodates the equipment necessary to provide a hemodialysis or peritoneal dialysis treatment. This station must have sufficient area to house a chair or bed, the dialysis equipment, and emergency equipment if needed. Provision for privacy is ordinarily supplied by drapes or screens. See Dialysis Center.

DIFFERENCE IN CONDITIONS: In life or health insurance, a rider that expands coverage written on a named period basis, whereby all risks subject to exclusion are incorporated into the coverage.

DIGITAL IMAGING AND COMMUNICATIONS IN MEDICINE: A standard for communicating images, such as x-rays, in a digitized form. This standard could become part of the HIPAA claim attachments standards.

DIRECT CONTRACT HMO: A health plan contracting directly with individual physicians, rather than a group of doctors. Similar to an independent physician, or individual practice association (IPA) model health plan.

DIRECT CONTRACTING: Direct contracting usually refers to a service (e.g., substance abuse treatment) that an employer contracts directly to save money on its employees' health plan, leaving employees free to choose among other eligible providers for their primary, obstetric, pediatric, and other medical care needs.

DIRECT COST: The cost of a medical service that can be directly traced to a specific patient or medical service; the opposite of an indirect cost. See Expense.

DIRECT DEBT: The sum of the total bonded debt and any short-term debt of the hospital issuer. Direct debt may be incurred in the issuer's own name or assumed through the annexation of territory or consolidation with another governmental unit.

DIRECT ENROLLED: A nongroup member who pays his or her insurance premium directly to the health insurer.

DIRECT PAY: Payment for health insurance premiums by a member, not the employer.

DIRECT PAYMENT SUBSCRIBER: A person enrolled in a prepayment plan who makes individual premium payments directly to the plan rather than through a group. Rates of payment are generally higher, and benefits may not be as extensive as for the subscriber enrolled and paying as a member of the group.

DIRECT SELLING: See Direct Contracting.

DIRECT UTILIZATION: Explicit utilization of specific ideas and findings of an evaluation by decision makers and other stakeholders.

DIRECT WRITER: An exclusive insurance sales agency system.

DISABILITY: A physical or mental impairment caused by accident or illness that partially or totally limits one's ability to perform duties of his or her own occupation or any occupation for which the individual is reasonably suited by education, training, or experience. In life and health insurance policies or government benefit programs, definitions of disability may vary. See Long-Term Care Insurance.

DISABILITY BENEFIT: Provision in a life insurance policy that states that, in the event of an insured's total disability, the insurance company will waive payment of premiums falling due during the disability period and, in some cases, will also pay an income during disability. Also, the benefits payable under a disability income policy.

DISABILITY BENEFITS INSURANCE: Insurance providing benefits to employees for accident or sickness that is not covered by workers' compensation laws.

DISABILITY BENEFITS LAW: A disability benefits system, established by statute, under which employees, temporarily out of work because of nonoccupational disability caused by either illness or injury, receive certain benefits, provided they meet minimum specified requirements.

DISABILITY BUYOUT: Agreement in disability insurance to buy out the interest of a disabled member.

DISABILITY BUY-OUT INSURANCE: A type of disability insurance coverage, issued in connection with a buy-sell agreement that, in the event of a business partner's (or stockholder's) total disability, pays a stated benefit for the purpose of buying out the business interest of the disabled associate.

DISABILITY, CONTINUOUS: See Continuous Disability.

DISABILITY FREEZE: Under Social Security, a provision that preserves the insured status and benefit level of those who become disabled. Thus, in any later calculation of benefits, the disability period is excluded in determining the average monthly wage or average indexed monthly earnings, as appropriate, on computing the worker's Primary Insurance Amount.

DISABILITY INCOME: A disability benefit provided by a specific health insurance contract that pays a regular monthly income if the insured is disabled by sickness or accident. Also, under certain life insurance contracts, a limited disability income may be provided under a rider in the event of total and permanent disability of the insured.

DISABILITY INCOME BENEFIT FOR WORKER: Under Social Security, a monthly benefit, equal to the worker's Primary Insurance Amount, paid to a disabled worker who meets stipulated requirements.

DISABILITY INCOME BENEFITS FOR WORKER'S DEPENDENTS: Under Social Security, a monthly benefit paid to dependents of persons drawing disability benefits. Eligible dependents, and their benefit amounts, are the same as though the worker had retired at the time of disability.

DISABILITY INCOME CHECKUP: In insurance, an analysis of the prospect's disability income situation. It is designed to help the prospect determine how much of a reduced income would be required in the event of disability, how much of that income would be provided under the prospect's present plans, and how to supplement and increase the coverage, if necessary.

DISABILITY INCOME INSURANCE: A form of health insurance that provides specific periodic payments to replace income that is actually or presumptively lost, when the insured is unable to work as a result of sickness or injury. Important clauses to consider include: (a) benefit amount; (b) total versus partial disability; (c) elimination period; (d) duration of benefits; (e) physician's care; (f) recurrent disability; (g) preexisting conditions; and (h) residual disability.

DISABILITY INCOME INSURANCE RECORDS SYSTEM (DIIRS): A Medical Information Bureau (MIB) recording system for nonmedical information concerning prospects for disability insurance coverage.

DISABILITY INCOME RIDER: Addition to a life or health insurance policy stating that when the policyholder becomes disabled for 6 months, the premiums for enforcement may be waived pending certain policy provisions.

DISABILITY INSURANCE, GROUP: See Group Disability Insurance.

DISABILITY INSURANCE, MORTGAGE: See Mortgage Disability Insurance.

DISABILITY INSURANCE TRAINING COUNCIL: An organization established by the International Accident and Health Association for the promotion of health insurance education on an institutional level, primarily through adult or continuing education divisions of colleges and universities.

DISABILITY, PARTIAL: Inability to perform one or more important duties of a member's occupation. The exact degree of such inability that must exist to constitute partial disability depends upon the terms of the individual policy. See Disability Income Insurance.

DISABILITY, PENSION: A pension payable in the event that an employee becomes totally and permanently disabled before normal retirement age.

DISABILITY, PERMANENT-TOTAL: Disability equivalent to a complete and permanent loss of earning power. Different health insurance policies define permanent-total disability in various ways and often specify that certain injuries (such as total loss of sight, loss of both hands or both legs) constitute permanent and total disability, regardless of the injured's ability to undertake gainful employment.

DISABILITY PREMIUM WAIVER INSURANCE: A provision (sometimes included automatically, sometimes optional and requiring an additional premium) in a life insurance contract or rider that provides that no further premiums will be due during a period of disability, providing the disability (as defined in the contract) extends beyond the stated period (usually six months).

DISABILITY PROVISION: A provision in an insurance policy that explains the term and benefits provided in the event the insured becomes disabled and defines what is meant by disability.

DISABILITY, RECURRENT: Usually considered a recurrent disability if there has not been an interval of at least 6 months between the new disability and the current disability. See Disability Income Insurance.

DISABILITY RETIREMENT BENEFITS: Pension benefits paid because of retirement a result of disability.

DISABILITY, TEMPORARY-PARTIAL: A disability causing a partial loss of earning power, but from which full recovery can be expected.

DISABILITY, TEMPORARY-TOTAL: A disability that prohibits the insured from performing any of his or her duties, but from which complete or partial recovery can be expected.

DISABILITY, TOTAL: There are various definitions of total disability in health insurance. The two most common state that the totally disabled individual is incapable of: (a) performing any of the duties of his or her occupation commensurate with education and training; or (b) performing any income-earning job, without regard to education and training. The actual definition will depend upon the wording in the policy. See Partial Disability.

DISABLED (HOSPITAL): The bed classification (and facility classification) for providing a special treatment program for persons who are developmentally disabled. Intermediate care facility for the developmentally disabled as defined by § 1250(g) of the Health and Safety Code.

DISABLED (PERSONAL): A permanent or temporary, physical or mental, partial or total condition precluding normal life or job functions. See Disability Income Insurance.

DISALLOWANCE: The amount of medical care reimbursement over and above the provider's usual amount; fee ceiling or maximum allowable amount that is not recognized for payment.

DISBURSEMENT FLOAT: The amount of time between medical services provided, and payment, in a health care organization.

DISCHARGE: A patient who was formally admitted to a hospital as an inpatient for observation, diagnosis, or treatment, with the expectation of remaining overnight or longer, and who is discharged under one of the following circumstances: (a) is formally discharged from care of the hospital and leaves the hospital; (b) transfers within the hospital from one type of care to another type of care; or (c) has expired.

DISCHARGE DAYS: The total number of days between the admission and discharge dates for each patient (length of stay). The day of admission but not the day of discharge is counted as a discharge day (except for admission and discharge on the same day, which is counted as one discharge day). Discharge days include any days from previous years for those patients admitted prior to the year of discharge and excludes days in the current year for patients not discharged by December 31. The two patient day's statistics are discharge days and census days (i.e., the cumulative census for a specific time period). Census days are necessary to calculate occupancy rates, whereas discharge days are more appropriate to calculate average lengths of stay.

DISCHARGE PLANNING: The evaluation of a patient's medical needs to arrange for appropriate care after discharge from an inpatient setting.

DISCLAIMER: An insurance company statement that a claim has been denied because a policy provision or clause had been breached.

DISCOUNT: A reduction in premium payments or medical product or service costs.

DISCOUNT DRUG LIST: Certain drugs available for a reduced price from a drug manufacturer.

DISCOUNTED CASH FLOWS: Adjusted cash flow to reflect present value for cost of capital, over time.

DISCOUNTED FEE-FOR-SERVICE: Agreement between a provider and payer that is less than the medical provider's full fee. This may be a fixed amount per service or a percentage discount. Providers generally accept such contracts because they represent a means to increase their volume or reduce their chances of losing volume.

DISCOUNTING: The treatment of time in valuing costs and benefits (i.e., the adjustment of costs and benefits to their present values), requiring a choice of discount rate and time frame.

DISCOVERY PERIOD: Time period allowed to change policy terms, conditions, or cancel completely.

DISCREPANCY NOTICE: Billing record inconsistency that may or may not be economic, secretarial, or administrative in nature.

DISCRIMINATION: Treating certain groups of people unfairly in the sale or pricing of policies. It also refers to the favoring of certain insurance agents or agencies by handling of like risks in different ways. Actually, the nature of underwriting is based upon discrimination of the good risk from the poor risk. What is prohibited is treating any of a given class of risk differently from other like risks.

DISEASE: A sickness or illness covered under a health or managed care insurance policy, as described in the terms and conditions of the policy. See Illness and Injury.

DISEASE MANAGEMENT: A type of product or service now being offered by many large pharmaceutical companies to get them into broader health care services. Bundles use of prescription drugs with physician and allied professionals, linked to large databases created by the pharmaceutical companies, to treat people with specific diseases. The claim is that this type of service provides higher quality of care at more reasonable price than alternative, presumably more fragmented, care. The development of such products by more capitalized companies should be the indicator necessary to convince a provider of how the health care market is changing. Competition is coming from every direction: other providers of all types, payers, employers (who are developing their own in-house service systems), and the drug companies.

DISENROLL: To end health plan insurance coverage. See Disenrollment.

DISENROLLMENT: The process of terminating the benefits or coverage of persons or groups. See Cancellation and Disenroll.

DISMEMBERMENT: Loss of, or inability to use specific members (arms and legs) of the body. See Disability Income Insurance.

DISMEMBERMENT BENEFIT: Income paid under health or life insurance coverage for the loss of various arms or legs, bodily parts, or extremity combinations. See Disability Income Insurance.

DISMEMBERMENT INSURANCE: Accidental death insurance. See Disability Income Insurance.

DISPENSING FEE: A fee charge for filling a drug prescription.

DISPOSITION: The consequent arrangement or event ending a patient's stay in the hospital. The following dispositions are usually reported: Routine Discharge, Acute Care Within This Hospital, Other Type of Hospital Care Within This Hospital, Skilled Nursing/Intermediate Care Within This Hospital, Acute Care at Another Hospital, Another Type of Hospital Care at Another Hospital, Skilled Nursing/Intermediate Care Elsewhere, Residential Care Facility, Prison/Jail, Against Medical Advise, Died, Home Health Service, or Other Institution.

DISPROPORTIONATE SHARE ADJUSTMENT: A payment adjustment made under Medicare's prospective payment system, or under the Medicaid system, for hospitals that serve a relatively large volume of low-income patients.

DISPROPORTIONATE SHARE HOSPITAL: Any hospital or health care facility that serves a high percentage of Medicaid or other low-income patients.

DISPROPORTIONATE SHARE PAYMENTS: State supplemental payments paid to disproportionate share hospitals for each paid patient day. In California, for example, the payments are made to hospitals serving a high percentage of Medi-Cal and other low-income patients.

DISTRIBUTIONAL EFFECTS: Effects of health care insurance programs that result in a redistribution of resources in the general population.

DISTRIBUTION CHANNELS: The physical method in which health care is delivered.

DIVIDEND: Partial premium return when insurance earnings exceed costs.

DIVIDENDS: Distributions to stockholders earned and declared by a corporate healthcare or hospital board of directors.

DME: durable medical equipment.

DN: doctor of naprapathy, doctor of nutripathy, or doctor of naturology. See Doctor.

DOCTOR: Any doctor of medicine (MD) or doctor of osteopathy (DO), who has a valid unlimited medical license and is qualified under the law of jurisdiction in which treatment is received. May also include limited licensed practitioners, such as podiatrists (doctor of podiatric medicine [DPM]), dentists (DDS/DMD), or doctor of optometry (OD), etc.

DOCTOR OF CHIROPRACTIC: Any doctor of chiropractic (DC) who has a valid chiropractic license and is qualified under the law of jurisdiction in which treatment is received. See Doctor.

DOCTOR OF DENTAL MEDICINE: Any doctor of dental medicine (DMD) who has a valid limited medical license and is qualified under the law of jurisdiction in which treatment is received. See Doctor. See DMD.

DOCTOR OF DENTAL SURGERY: A dentist or doctor of dentistry (DDS/DMD) who has a valid limited dental license and is qualified under the law of jurisdiction in which treatment is received. See Doctor and DDS.

DOCTOR OF MEDICINE: Any doctor of allopathic medicine (MD) who has a valid unlimited medical license and is qualified under the law of jurisdiction in which treatment is received. See Doctor.

DOCTOR OF OPTOMETRY: Any eye doctor of optometry (OD) who has a valid limited optometric license and is qualified under the law of jurisdiction in which treatment is received. See Doctor.

DOCTOR OF OSTEOPATHY: Any doctor of osteopathic medicine (DO). A doctor of osteopathic medicine with valid unlimited osteopathic medical license and is qualified under the law of jurisdiction in which treatment is received. See Doctor.

DOCTOR OF PODIATRIC MEDICINE: A podiatrist. Any doctor of podiatric medicine (DPM) who has a valid limited medical license to treat medical and surgical conditions of the foot, ankle, and leg (in some jurisdictions) and is qualified under the law of jurisdiction in which medical and surgical treatment is received. See Doctor and Foot Doctor.

DOH: Department of Health.

DOI: Department of Insurance.

DOMC: Department of Managed Care (California).

DOMESTIC COMPANY: A company is a domestic company in the state or province in which it is incorporated or chartered.

DOMESTIC PARTNERS: Unmarried couples who are eligible as spouses for coverage under one partner's health or life insurance plan.

DOMICILIARY CARE: Nonmedical treatment, such as personal assistance, showering, and dressing, that is not covered under home nursing.

DONATIONS/SUBSIDIES FOR INDIGENT CARE: Donations, grants, or subsidies voluntarily provided for the care of medically indigent patients. Includes discretionary tobacco tax funds provided by a county to a noncounty hospital.

DONOR: A person who gives organs and body fluids or parts to help others in need.

DOS: The date(s) on which a medical service was rendered to a patient. Dates of service can also refer to dates during which a patient was hospitalized. See Date of Service.

DOUBLE DISMEMBERMENT: Loss of any two limbs, the sight of both eyes, or the loss of one limb and sight of one eye.

DOUBLE INDEMNITY: A provision in a life or health insurance policy, subject to specified conditions and exclusions, under which double the face amount of the policy is payable if the insured dies as a result of an accident. Generally, the insured's death must occur prior to a specified age and result from accidental bodily injury caused solely through external, violent, and accidental means, independently and exclusively of all other causes, and within 60 or 90 days after such injury.

DOWNCODING: An invalid insurance codes that requires a physical description of the medical intervention for payment.

DREAD DISEASE INSURANCE: A health insurance policy that protects against medical expenses resulting from a certain dreaded disease, such as cancer.

DROP AT (DATE): An order for nonrenewal of an insurance policy as of a certain date.

DROP-INS (DUMP-INS): Refers to lump sum or large single premium health insurance payments.

DRUG FORMULARY: A list of prescription drugs that are approved for use and covered by an insurance plan. These prescriptions may be dispensed to covered persons at participating pharmacies. The formulary is subject to review and change. See Trade Name Drug and Generic Drug.

DRUGIST LIABILITY INSURANCE: Errors and omissions and negligence and malpractice insurance for a pharmacist or druggist.

DRUG PRICE REVIEW: A weekly average wholesale price review of drug prices.

DRUG PROVIDER: Physician, pharmacist, or other health care provider licensed to dispense medical drugs and pharmaceuticals.

DRUG TIERS: Drug tiers are definable by a health plan. Pharmacy health benefits programs (PBPs) introduced the optional tier to give health care plans the ability to group different drug types together (i.e., Generic, Brand, Preferred Brand). In this regard, tiers could be used to describe drug groups that are based on classes of drugs. If the tier option is used, plans should provide further clarification on the drug type(s) covered under the tier in the PBP notes section(s). This option was designed to afford users additional flexibility in defining the prescription drug benefit. See Trade Name Drug and Generic Drug.

DRUG UTILIZATION REVIEW (DUR): The methodology used by HMOs and PPOs to monitor prescription usage. Typically, a DUR committee examines the number of prescriptions, per member, per month, and average cost per prescription. Utilization and costs are reviewed according to individual physician, physician group, specialty, retail pharmacy, employee group, and member. See Trade Name Drug and Generic Drug.

DSM: The Diagnostic and Statistical Manual of Mental Disorders.

DTC: Direct to consumer drug advertisements on TV or radio or in electronic or print media. See Trade Name Drug. See Generic Drug.

DUAL CHOICE (MULTIPLE CHOICE, DUAL OPTION): The opportunity for an individual within an employed group to choose from two or more types of health care coverage, such as an HMO and a traditional insurance plan. Section 1310 of the HMO Act provides for dual choice.

DUAL ELIGIBILITY: A Medicare beneficiary who also receives the full range of Medicaid benefits offered in his or her state.

DUE DATE: The date a health insurance premium is required to be received.

DUE PROCESS: The right to appeal termination of a health care insurance contract.

DUMMY APPLICATION: An unsigned application for health insurance provided by an employer for an employee until coverage is accepted.

DUPLICATE COVERAGE INQUIRY: When one insurance company or medical plan contacts another to ask if a covered person has other insurance coverage in place. If the covered person does, then the insurance companies must coordinate their benefits.

DUPLICATION OF BENEFITS: Duplication of benefits is overlapping or identical coverage of the same insured under more than one policy, usually the result of contracts of different insurance companies, service organizations, or prepayment plans.

DURABLE MEDICAL EQUIPMENT (DME): Defined as medical equipment that meets the following criteria: (a) can withstand repeated use, (b) is primarily and customarily used to serve a medical purpose, (c) generally is not useful to a person in the absence of illness or injury, (d) is appropriate for home use, (e) MS-1450: The uniform institutional DME claim form, and (f) MS-1500: The uniform professional DME claim form.

DURABLE MEDICAL EQUIPMENT REGIONAL CARRIER (DMERC): A private firm that helps pay covered DME bills for covered Medicare patients.

E

EARLY AND PERIODIC SCREENING, DIAGNOSIS, AND TREATMENT (EPSDT): A health program that covers screening and diagnostic services to determine physical or mental defects in recipients the age of majority, as well as health care and other measures to correct or ameliorate any defects and chronic conditions discovered.

EARNED INCOME: Gross salary, wages, commissions, and fees, derived from active employment. Contrast to unearned income that includes income from investments, rents, annuities, and insurance policies. Funds received from any other source are not included.

EARNED PREMIUM: The amount of premium that would compensate the insurance company for its loss experience, expenses, and profit year to date. Premium portion of an insurance policy that has been rendered. See Premium.

EARNINGS: Money derived from personal services (i.e., salary, wages, and commissions). See Earned Income.

EARNINGS LIMITATION: The limitation on the amount of income a person who is receiving Social Security benefits can earn before those benefits are reduced. Both the earnings limitation amount and the benefit reduction are subject to escalation.

E-CODES: External cause of injury; *International Classification of Diseases* (9th Rev.) code for poisoning.

ECONOMIC CREDENTIALING: Evaluating a physician's economic behavior (i.e., tests ordered, hospital bed days, outcomes) in deciding upon medical staff appointment or reappointment.

EDITS: Kick-out or nonpayment health care claims criteria that preclude reimbursement. A dirty claim.

EFFECTIVE DATE: The date a health insurance plan agreement becomes effective.

EFFECTIVENESS: The net health benefits provided by a medical service or technology for typical patients in community practice settings.

EFFICACY: The net health benefits achieved or achievable under ideal conditions for carefully selected patients.

EFFICIENCY: Benchmarking and measuring inputs against medical outputs.

EGRESS: The act of leaving a managed care or other health insurance plan.

EIANOI: Ancient Greek society that was influential in developing the idea of insurance and risk coverage.

ELDERCARE: Public, private, formal, and informal programs and support systems, and government laws to meet the needs of the elderly, including: housing, home care, pensions, Social Security, long-term care, health insurance, and elder law. See Elder Law.

ELDERLAW: The group of laws about rights and issues of the health and finances of elderly persons. See Elder Care.

ELECTION: The buy or make decision to acquire insurance coverage.

ELECTION (MEDICARE): The decision to join or leave the original Medicare plan or a Medicare + Choice plan. There are four types of election periods in which you may join and leave Medicare health plans: (a) annual election period, (b) initial coverage election period, (c) special election period, and (d) open enrollment period. See Annual Election Period.

ELECTION PERIODS: The period of eligibility to buy or make a decision to acquire insurance. See Election.

ELECTIVE CARE: Medical care that could be performed at another place or time without patient jeopardy and which may or may not be covered by usually health insurance policies.

ELECTIVE SURGERY: Surgery that does not need to be performed on an urgent or emergent basis. See Cosmetic Surgery.

ELECTRONIC BILLING: Medical, durable medical equipment, and related health insurance bills or premiums submitted though electronic data interchange (nonpaper claims) systems. See EDI and HIPAA.

ELECTRONIC CLAIM: The digital representation of a medical bill or invoice.

ELECTRONIC DATA INTERCHANGE (EDI): Method used to link health care administrative duties by computer networks, to increase speed, decrease costs, and improve confidentiality and efficiency. Also used to reduce health insurance and worker's compensation insurance costs by using a single, or several, linked databases for administrators, medical claims, and related vendor services. See HIPAA.

ELECTRONIC MEDIA QUESTIONNAIRE: A process that large employers can use to complete their requirements for supplying IRS/SSA/HCFA Data Match information electronically.

ELECTRONIC MEDICAL CLAIMS (EMC): This term usually refers to a flat file format used to transmit or transport medical claims, such as the 192-byte UB-92 Institutional EMC format and the 320-byte Professional EMC NSF (national standard format). See Electronic Data Interchange (EDI) and HIPAA.

ELECTRONIC MEDICAL RECORD (EMR): Digital file or representation of a private medical record.

ELECTRONIC REMITTANCE ADVICE: Any of several electronic formats for explaining the payments of health care claims.

ELIGIBILITY GUARANTEE: Assurance of reimbursement to the medical group for services or goods provided to a member who subsequently is found to be ineligible for benefits.

ELIGIBILITY PERIOD: The period of time in contributory plans (usually 31 days), during which a new employee may apply for group life and or health insurance coverage.

ELIGIBILITY REQUIREMENTS: Rules in group life, health, or disability insurance to determine which employees may enter into the plan.

ELIGIBILITY VERIFICATION: The insurance confirmation of active membership coverage and policy.

ELIGIBLE DEPENDENTS: Persons able to receive health insurance benefits because of family orientation.

ELIGIBLE EXPENSES: Reasonable and customary charges for health care services incurred while coverage is in effect. See Expenses and Exclusions.

ELIGIBLE PERSON: A person eligible for benefits under a health care plan and meets the eligibility requirements specified in the health insurance contract.

ELIMINATION PERIOD: The period of time before insurance benefits begin.

EMERGENCY: Sudden unexpected onset of illness or injury that requires the immediate care and attention of a qualified physician, and which, if not treated immediately, would jeopardize or impair the health of the member, as determined by the payer's medical staff. Significant in that emergency may be the only acceptable reason for admission without precertification. See Accident and Ambulance.

EMERGENCY ACCIDENT BENEFIT: In health insurance, a hospital benefit payable for outpatient emergency treatment of an injury. A group medical benefit that reimburses the insured for expenses incurred for emergency treatment of accidents.

EMERGENCY CARE: Medical care rendered for a condition for which the patient believes acute life-threatening attention is required. See Emergency.

EMERGENCY CENTER: Short-term care facility for medical problems requiring immediate attention. See Urgent Care Center.

EMERGENCY DEPARTMENT: See ER.

EMERGENCY EXPENSE BENEFITS: See Funeral or Emergency Expense Benefits.

EMERGENCY HEALTH SERVICES: Any health service used in the treatment of an emergency. See Ambulance and ER.

EMERGENCY MEDICAL SERVICE SYSTEM: Emergency system that uses ambulances and technicians to bring rapid medical help to people with injuries or severe illnesses. See ER and EMT.

EMERGENCY MEDICAL TECHNICIANS: Trained volunteers or professionals who deliver emergency care from and on an ambulance. See Ambulance and EMT.

EMERGENCY MEDICAL TRANSPORTATION: Nonemergency medical transportation to doctors' offices, clinics, hospitals, or for therapy, rehabilitation, or other medical services or treatments, etc.

EMERGENCY MEDICAL TREATMENT AND ACTIVE LABOR ACT (EMTALA): The Emergency Medical Treatment and Active Labor Act, codified at 42 U.S.C. §1395dd. EMTALA requires any Medicare-participating hospital that operates a hospital emergency department to provide an appropriate medical screening examination to any patient that requests such an examination. If the hospital determines that the patient has an emergency medical condition, it must either stabilize the patient's condition or arrange for a transfer; however, the hospital may only transfer the patient if the medical benefits of the transfer outweigh the risks or if the patient requests the transfer. Centers for Medicare and Medicaid regulations at 42 C.F.R. § 489.24(b) and §413.65(g) further clarify the statutory language.

EMERGENCY MEDICINE: Branch of medicine that deals with situation requiring immediate care and usually provided in an emergency room or through the operating room.

EMERGENCY ROOM: The ambulatory services cost center in a hospital that provides emergency treatment to the ill and injured requiring immediate medical or surgical care on an unscheduled basis, including occasional care for conditions that would not be considered emergencies.

EMERGENCY SERVICES: Services provided in connection with an unforeseen acute illness or injury requiring immediate medical attention: (a) Level 1: Requires one emergency room (ER) physician with additional specialty coverage available within 30 min; (b) Level 2: Requires one ER physician with additional specialty coverage available within 30 min, with provisions for patient transfer to another facility; and (c) Level 3: Requires one ER physician available within the facility through immediate two-way voice communication, with specialist available upon request and provisions for patient transfer to another facility.

EMERGENT CONDITIONS: Any medical situation of immediate life or limb threat to the patient.

EMERGI-CENTER: See Freestanding Emergency Medical Services Center.

EMERGING HEALTH CARE ORGANIZATIONS (EHO): Physicians, hospitals, health care systems, and payers who are integrating or merging because of the constant competitive influx of the health care industrial complex and in response to managed care. See Clinic, Hospital, and ASC.

EMPIRICAL: Resulting from experimentation. See Empirical Probability.

EMPIRICAL PROBABILITY: Mathematical relationship resulting from experimentation and used to determine health care insurance premiums or rate settings. See Empirical.

EMPLOYEE ASSISTANCE PROGRAM (EAP): A service, plan, or set of benefits that are designed for personal or family problems, including mental health, substance abuse, gambling addiction, marital problems, parenting problems, emotional problems, or financial pressures.

EMPLOYEE BENEFIT INSURANCE PLAN: Employer provisions for the social and economic welfare of its employees; usually consisting of the following nontaxable benefits: (a) life insurance; (b) health insurance; (c) pension plans; (d) disability insurance; and (e) accidental death or dismemberment insurance.

EMPLOYEE BENEFIT PROGRAMS: Programs that offers benefits to employees by an employer, covering such contingencies as medical expenses, disability, retirement, and death, usually paid for wholly or in part by the employer. Sometimes called fringe benefits because they are usually separate from wages and salaries.

EMPLOYEE BENEFITS: Expenses incurred for vacation pay, sick leave pay, holiday pay, Federal Insurance Contributions Act (FICA), state unemployment insurance, federal unemployment insurance, workers' compensation insurance, group health insurance, group life insurance, pension, and retirement costs, etc.

EMPLOYEE BENEFIT SURVEY: Survey of employers administered by the U.S. Bureau of Labor Statistics to measure the number of employees receiving particular benefits, such as health insurance, paid sick leave, and paid vacations.

EMPLOYEE CERTIFICATE OF INSURANCE: The employee's evidence of participation in a group health insurance plan, consisting of a brief summary of plan benefits. The employee is provided with a certificate of insurance rather than the actual insurance policy. See CON and CIO.

EMPLOYEE AND CHILD(REN) COVERAGE: Benefit coverage allowable for the plan enrollee and eligible dependent child(ren).

EMPLOYEE CONTRIBUTION: The employee's share of the health premium costs.

EMPLOYEE RETIREMENT INCOME SECURITY ACT (ERISA) OF 1974: Also called the Pension Reform Act. The act regulates the majority of private pension and welfare group benefit plans in the United States. It sets forth requirements governing, among many areas, participation, crediting of service, vesting, communication and disclosure, funding, and fiduciary conduct. A key legislative battleground because ERISA exempts most large self-funded plans from state regulation and, hence, from any reform activities undertaken at state level that is the arena for much health care reform.

EMPLOYEE AND SPOUSE COVERAGE: Benefits allowable for the plan enrollee and spouse.

EMPLOYEE WELFARE BENEFIT PLAN: Any plan or program that is established or maintained by an employer or an employee organization for the purpose of providing its participants or their beneficiaries with medical, surgical or hospital care, or benefits in the event of sickness, accident, disability, death or unemployment, or vacation benefits or training programs or similarly related programs (other than pension or retirement programs).

EMPLOYER: Any person acting directly as an employer or indirectly in the interest of an employer. This includes a group or association of employers acting for their respective employer members.

EMPLOYER CONTRIBUTION: The portion of the cost of a health insurance plan that is borne by the employer. See ERISA.

EMPLOYER GROUP HEALTH PLAN: Health, life, disability, or long-term care insurance coverage offered as a fringe benefit of the workplace.

EMPLOYER MANDATE: Under the Federal HMO Act, describes conditions when federally qualified HMOs can mandate or require an employer to offer at least one federally qualified HMO plan of each type (independent physician association/network or group/staff).

EMPLOYMENT BENEFIT PLAN: Any employee life, health, retirement, or other benefit plan (such as parental leave or day care facilities) provided totally or partly by an employer.

EMPLOYMENT MODEL IDS: An integrated delivery system (IDS) that owns or operates physician practices or other health care entities. See IDS.

EMPOWERED HMO: A HMO or health plan giving physicians much independence and latitude in their decision making and medical treatment services.

EMS LEVEL: The Emergency Medical Services level a facility is licensed by the Division of Licensing and Certification, Department of Health Services. Only a general acute-care hospital (GAC) can be licensed for emergency medical services. Licensed levels are:

1. Standby—the provision of emergency medical care in a specifically designated area of the hospital that is equipped and maintained at all times to receive patients with urgent medical problems and capable of providing physician services within a reasonable time.
2. Basic—the provision of emergency medical care in a specifically designated area of the hospital that is staffed and equipped at all times to provide prompt care for any patient presenting urgent medical problems.
3. Comprehensive—the provision of diagnostic and therapeutic services for unforeseen physical and mental disorders that, if not properly treated, would lead to marked suffering, disability, or death. The scope of services is comprehensive, with in-house capability for managing all medical situations on a definitive and continuing basis.

EMS STATION: An Emergency Medical Services (EMS) treatment station. This is a specific place within the EMS department adequate to treat one patient at a time. Holding or observation beds are not included. See ER and Ambulance.

EMS VISITS: Visits made during the year to the Emergency Medical Service (EMS) Department. These visits are classified in the following three categories: (a) Nonurgent—a patient with a nonemergent injury, illness, or condition; sometimes chronic, that can be treated in a nonemergency setting and not necessarily on the same day they are seen in the EMS department; (b) Urgent—a patient with an acute injury or illness where loss of life or limb is not an immediate threat to their life, or a patient who needs a timely evaluation; and (c) Critical—a patient presents an acute injury or illness that could result in permanent damage, injury, or death. See ER.

EMS VISITS RESULTING IN ADMISSIONS: Emergency medical services visits that result in hospital admissions.

EMT: emergency medical technician.

EMT-BASIC: The EMT-basic has the knowledge and skills of the first responder but is also qualified to function as minimum staff for an ambulance. Example: At the scene of a cardiac arrest, the EMT-basic would be expected to defibrillate and ventilate the patient with a manually operated device and supplemental oxygen.

EMT-INTERMEDIATE: The EMT-intermediate has the knowledge and skills of the first responder and EMT-basic, but in addition can perform essential advanced techniques and administer a limited number of medications.

EMT-PARAMEDIC: The EMT-Paramedic has demonstrated the skill expected of a Level 3 (EMT-Intermediate) provider, but can administer additional interventions and medications. See ENT, ER, and Ambulance.

ENABLING SERVICE: Any method to ease patient access into the health care system.

ENCOUNTER: The face-to-face contact between a patient and a health care provider. A member visits to the medical group with the intent of seeing a health care provider. There may be a variety of services performed at an encounter: a brief office visit, EKG, lab test, and an immunization. See Visit.

ENCOUNTER DATA: Description of the diagnosis made and services provided when a patient visits a health care provider under a managed care plan. Encounter data provide much of the same information available on the bills submitted by fee-for-service providers. See HCFA 1500.

ENCOUNTER FEE: The bill for a health care encounter.

ENCOUNTER FORM: The physical paperwork that documents a physical encounter (interview) for medical care. See HCFA 1500.

ENCOUNTERS PER MEMBER PER YEAR: The total number of encounters for the year divided by the number of members.

ENDEMIC DISEASE: The constant presence of a disease or infectious agent within a given geographic area or population group; may also refer to the usual prevalence of a given disease within such area or group. See Illness.

ENDING INVENTORY: The amount of durable medical equipment or other health care-related inventory on hand at the end of an accounting period.

ENDOCRINOLOGY: Branch of medicine dealing with the ductless glands, like thyroid, pituitary, adrenals, ovaries, and testes.

ENDORSEMENT: Amendment to the policy used to add or delete coverage. Also referred to as a *rider*. A form to change the terms and conditions of an insurance policy. It is the written modification to an insurance policy. An endorsement may also be in the form of a rider. No endorsement is valid unless signed by an executive officer of the company and attached to and made a part of the policy. See Rider.

END-STAGE RENAL DISEASE: Permanent kidney failure.

END-STAGE RENAL DISEASE TREATMENT FACILITY: A facility, other than a hospital, that provides dialysis treatment, maintenance, or training to patients or caregivers on an ambulatory or home-care basis. See End State Renal Disease.

ENHANCED BENEFITS: Additional or optional benefits of any insurance package or policy, usually for an additional premium fee.

ENROLL: To join a health plan, usually at work.

ENROLLED DEPENDENT: A dependent that is enrolled for coverage under the health plan's contract.

ENROLLED GROUP: Persons with the same employer or with membership in an organization in common, who are enrolled collectively in a health plan. Often, there are stipulations regarding the minimum size of the group and the minimum percentage of the group that must enroll before the coverage is available.

ENROLLEE: A member of a prepaid health care, governmental, or other health insurance plan. A person who is directly or independently eligible for coverage of health services provided under a health plan contract on their own behalf and not as a dependent.

ENROLLEE HOTLINES: Toll-free telephone lines usually staffed by the state or enrollment broker that beneficiaries call when they encounter a problem with their insurance policies. The people who staff hotlines are knowledgeable about program policies and may play an intake and triage role or may assist in resolving the problem.

ENROLLING GROUP: An employer or other group with whom an insurer has made a health plan contract.

ENROLLMENT: The number of members in an HMO or health insurance plan. The number of members assigned to a physician or medical group providing care under contract with an HMO. Also, can be the process by which a health plan signs up individuals or groups as subscribers.

ENROLLMENT APPLICATION: A form that new members complete and send to Membership for entry into the membership computer system.

ENROLLMENT AREA: The geographic area within a designated radius of the PMG (Primary Medical Group) selected by the subscriber.

ENROLLMENT BROKER: A third-party organization that enrolls and educates Medicaid members and provides services to encourage the appropriate use of Medicaid managed care services.

ENROLLMENT FEE: The charge to enroll in a health care plan.

ENROLLMENT PERIOD: A period of time certain to join Medicare or some other private health insurance, or managed care plan, either on an individual or group basis.

ENROLLMENT PROTECTION: The practice of a managed care organization or HMO to protect its contracted medical groups against part or all losses incurred for physician services above a specified dollar amount while caring for the HMO's enrollees. Also referred to as stop loss or reinsurance.

ENTERPRISE SCHEDULING: Computerized patient scheduling for maximum whole system efficiency.

ENTIRE CONTRACT CLAUSE: Health or other insurance contract clause that stipulates the policy represents the entire agreement without other outstanding agreements. See Contract and Policy.

ENVIRONMENTAL HEALTH: An organized community effort to minimize the public's exposure to environmental hazards by identifying the disease or injury agent, preventing the agent's transmission through the environment, and protecting people from the exposure to contaminated and hazardous environments.

ENVIRONMENTAL SERVICES: Health care inpatient facility services like house-cleaning, laundry, sanitary, and trash removal.

EPIDEMIC: The occurrence of more cases of disease than expected in a given area or among a specific group of people over a particular period of time.

EPIDEMIOLOGY: The study of the distribution and determinants of health-related states or events in specified populations, and the application of this study to the control of health problems.

EPISODE: 60-day unit of payment for prospective payment systems.

EPISODE OF CARE: The health care services given during a certain period of time, usually during a hospital stay. Health, disability, medical, or long-term care (LTC) services that are provided during the normal course of insurance coverage and during a time period certain. See Episode.

EQRO ORGANIZATION: Federal law and regulations require states to use an external quality review organization (EQRO or QRO) to review the care provided by capitated managed care entities. EQROs may be peer review organizations (PROs), another entity that meets PRO requirements, or a private accreditation body.

EQUITY: The ownership interest of common and preferred stockholders in a health care company. The term also refers to the excess of value of securities over the debit balance in a margin (general) account. The money value of property or interest in property, after all claims have been deducted. In connection with cash values and policy loan indebtedness, the policy owner's equity is the portion of cash value remaining to the policy owner after deduction of all indebtedness on account of loans or liens secured by the policy. As a principle of insurance, fair and impartial treatment—the principle that insurance premiums shall be set according to the degree of risk assumed and the benefits granted. In insurance law, equity is the name given to the rules and decisions that originated with equity courts from those that were handed down by law courts dealing with the common law and statute law. The importance of equity in cases concerning insurance lies in the fact that equitable remedies may be available when the legal remedy may not be adequate for the injured party. Also used to indicate a risk or ownership right in property or a business, etc., as shares of stock.

EQUITY FINANCING: The purchase of an asset with internally generated funds, such as cash or stock. See Equity.

EQUIVALENCY REVIEW: The process that the Centers for Medicare and Medicaid Services (CMS) employ to compare an accreditation organization's standards, processes, and enforcement activities to the comparable CMS requirements, processes, and enforcement activities.

ERISA: The Employee Retirement Income Security Act of 1974. ERISA exempts self-insured health plans from state laws governing health insurance, including contribution to risk pools, prohibitions against disease discrimination, and other state health reforms.

ERROR (active): An incorrect or inappropriate act of commission or omission.

ERROR (latent): Incorrect action that implies a predisposing circumstance or condition.

ESRD: End-stage renal disease.

ESRD ELIGIBILITY REQUIREMENTS: To qualify for Medicare under the renal provision, a person must have end-stage renal disease and either be entitled to a monthly insurance benefit under Title II of the Act (or an annuity under the Railroad Retirement Act), be fully or currently insured under Social Security (railroad work may count), or be the spouse or dependent child of a person who meets at least one of the two last requirements. There is no minimum age for eligibility under the renal disease provision.

ESRD FACILITY: A facility that is approved to furnish at least one specific end-stage renal disease service. These services may be performed in a renal transplantation center, a renal dialysis facility, self-dialysis unit, or special purpose renal dialysis facility.

ESRD NETWORK: All Medicare-approved end-stage renal disease facilities in a designated geographic area specified by the Centers for Medicare and Medicaid Services (CMS).

ESRD NETWORK ORGANIZATION: The administrative governing body of the end-stage renal disease network and liaison to the federal government.

ESRD PATIENT: A person with irreversible and permanent kidney failure who requires a regular course of dialysis or kidney transplantation to maintain life.

ESRD SERVICES: The type of care or service furnished to an end-stage renal disease patient. Such types of care are transplantation, dialysis, outpatient dialysis, staff-assisted dialysis, home dialysis, and self-dialysis and home dialysis training.

ESSENTIAL COMMUNITY PROVIDERS: Providers such as community health centers that have traditionally served low-income populations.

ESTABLISHED PATIENT: One who had received professional services from the physician, or another physician (health care provider) of the same specialty who belongs to the group practice, within the past 3 years. See Patient.

ESTIMATED PREMIUM: Health insurance premium setting method based on expectations of projected loss experiences. The remained is due at the end of the year to reflect actual loss experiences and costs.

ESTIMATED THIRD-PARTY PAYER SETTLEMENTS: Monies due or from third-party payers for advances or overpayments from third-party administrators and medical insurance payers.

ESTOPPEL: To bar statements upon which another party must rely, as when the misleading words and actions of a health, managed care, or disability insurance agent are stopped from having to perform according to the provision of the contract.

ETHICS IN PATIENT REFERRALS ACT: Federal act and its amendments, commonly called the Stark laws, that prohibit a physician from referring patients to laboratories, radiology services, diagnostic services, physical therapy services, home health services, pharmacies, occupational therapy services, and suppliers of durable medical equipment in which the physician has a financial interest.

EVALUATION: The historical review and physical examination of a patient. See H&P.

EVALUATION AND MANAGEMENT (EM) SERVICE: A nonprocedural service, such as a visit or consultation, provided by physicians to diagnose and treat diseases and counsel patients.

EVERGREEN CONTRACTS: Managed care contracts that automatically renew themselves.

EVIDENCE: Signs that something is true or not true. Doctors can use published studies as evidence that a treatment works or does not work.

EVIDENCE-BASED MEDICINE: The medical practice that unites clinical expertise and best processes for enhanced medical care decision making.

EVIDENCE OF COVERAGE: See evidence of insurability.

EVIDENCE OR EXPLANATION OF COVERAGE (EOC) OR EXPLANATION OF BENEFITS (EOB): A booklet provided by the carrier to the insured summarizing benefits under an insurance plan.

EVIDENCE OF INSURABILITY: The information obtained through medical examinations or written statements about a person's health for the underwriting of an insurance policy. This information may determine insurance coverage rates by identifying existing health conditions. Also, the information or proof of health is usually a requirement for those that apply for excess life insurance.

EXAMINATION: The medical examination of an applicant for life or health insurance.

EXAMINATION UNDER OATH: A clause in some insurance policies that permits the insurance company to obtain statements on claims and related facts from an insured under oath. Perjury charges may result from false claims.

EXAMINED BUSINESS: Health or life insurance coverage written on an applicant who has been examined and who has signed the application but has paid no premium.

EXAMINER: A physician appointed by the medical director of a life or health insurer to examine applicants. See Doctor.

EX-ANTE EFFICIENCY ANALYSIS: An efficiency analysis undertaken prior to a health care program implementation, usually as part of program planning, to estimate net outcome in relation to costs.

EXCESS CHARGES: The difference between a medical provider's actual charge (which may be limited by Medicare or the state) and the Medicare-approved payment amount.

EXCESS COVER FOR CATASTROPHE: A type of health reinsurance that takes effect in the event of loss above a stated amount.

EXCESS INSURANCE: Health coverage against loss in excess of a stated amount or in excess of coverage provided under another insurance contract.

EXCESS LINE BROKER: In insurance, a person licensed to place coverage not available in his or her state (or not available in sufficient amount) through insurers not licensed to do business in the state where the broker operates. Sometimes called surplus line broker. See Broker.

EXCESS RISK: Aggregate or specific, stop-loss health, or other insurance coverage.

EXCLUDED HOSPITALS AND DISTINCT-PART UNITS: Specialty hospitals (rehabilitation, psychiatric, long-term care, children's, and cancer) that are excluded from Medicare's hospital inpatient prospective payment system (PPS). Hospitals located in U.S. territories, federal hospitals, and Christian Science Sanatoria are also excluded from PPS. Excluded facilities are paid under cost-reimbursement, subject to rate of increase limits. Rehabilitation facilities moved into a prospective payment system and Congress HCFA/CMS to develop a legislative proposal for a prospective payment system for long-term care facilities.

EXCLUDED PERILS: Exclusions of medical benefits from health or disability insurance coverage. See Hazards.

EXCLUDED PERIOD: See Probationary Period.

EXCLUSION: A provision in an insurance policy excluding certain risks or otherwise limiting the scope of coverage. Certain causes and conditions listed in the policy that are not covered.

EXCLUSION CLAUSE: In insurance, a policy provision that excludes certain risks from coverage, such as aviation, war, or preexisting conditions.

EXCLUSION COVERAGE: Method of integrating payment for health benefits provided by Medicare and an employer. Medicare payments are subtracted from actual claims and the employer-sponsored plan's benefits are applied to the balance. Such coverage generally leaves the beneficiary responsible for the employer's plan's cost sharing and deductibles.

EXCLUSION MEDICAL BENEFITS: Exclusions listed under most group health insurance plans usually include: (a) worker's compensation; (b) convalescent or rest homes; (c) cosmetic and dental procedures; (d) misdemeanor- or felony-related medical expenses; (e) self-inflicted injuries or attempted suicide; (f) unreasonable medical expense charges; and (g) phone, fax, computer, or Internet access-related hospital expenses.

EXCLUSIONS: (1) Specific provisions in group disability plans that exclude coverage in certain situations. Typically, a plan will not pay benefits for disabilities arising from war, participation in a riot, commission of a felony, or self-inflicted injury. Populations or services can be excluded from a mainstream managed care plan and reimbursed on a fee-for-service basis. An exclusion is generally employed if mainstream plans are unwilling to enroll high cost individuals or if a system of care does not exist to serve this population because either their disease is rare or their rural or remote location prohibits the formation of a managed care network. (2) Specified hazards, listed in an insurance policy, for which benefits will not be paid.

(3) Clauses in an insurance contract that deny coverage for select individuals, groups, locations, properties, or risks; or health services not covered under an insurance plan. See Benefits, Exclusion, and Benefits.

EXCLUSIONS FROM MEDICAL BENEFITS: Exceptions section in many health and managed care insurance policies that exclude coverage for certain abortions, cosmetic surgery, orthopedic shoes, speech therapy, durable medical equipment, and other products and services.

EXCLUSIONS (MEDICARE): Items or services that Medicare does not cover, such as most prescription drugs, long-term care, and custodial care in a nursing or private home. See Exclusions.

EXCLUSIVE AGENCY SYSTEM: An insurance marketing approach whereby agents sell and service insurance under contracts that limit representation to one or more insurers under common management and that reserve to the insurer the ownership, use, and control of policy records and the expiration data.

EXCLUSIVE AGENT: In insurance, an agent granted the sole rights to sell a company's products within a given market or territory. See Agent or Broker.

EXCLUSIVE PROVIDER ARRANGEMENT (EPA): An indemnity or service plan that provides benefits only if care is rendered by providers with which it contracts (with some exceptions for emergency and out-of-area services).

EXCLUSIVE PROVIDER ORGANIZATION (EPO): A health plan with reduced choice for its health care insureds. It is a plan in which patients must go to a participating provider or receive no benefit. This is a cross between an HMO and a PPO. Like a PPO, doctors typically are paid on a fee-for-service basis and are not at risk. However, patients have less freedom to go out of network than with a PPO. Also, it is a managed care organization usually made up of a group of physicians, one or more hospitals, and other providers who contract with an insurer, employer, or other sponsoring group to provide discounted medical services to enrollees. It is similar to a PPO in that it allows the patient to go out of network for care; however, the patient will not be reimbursed if they do so. See HMO, IPO, and PPO.

EXCLUSIVE REMEDY: The inability to sue an employer in cases of worker's compensation injuries.

EXCLUSIVITY CLAUSE: A part of a contract that prohibits physicians from contracting with more than one managed care organization. See HMO, PPO, and IPA.

EXECUTED CONTRACT: A legal agreement that has been carried out by two or more parties.

EXECUTIVE DIRECTOR: The chief medical director or operating officer of a managed care or health insurance plan.

EX GRATIA PAYMENT: Settlement of a claim by an insurer, even though the company does not feel it is legally obligated to pay. Settlement is made to prevent an even larger expense to the company as a result of having to defend itself in court or for goodwill purposes.

EXPANSION: Growth of a health insurance plan. Some HMOs compute plan expansion as part of the capitation rate to provide the necessary capital for growth.

EXPANSION DECISION: Capital investments to increase the operational capacity, and hence profits, of a health care organization.

EXPECTANCY POLICY: A special type of health policy, providing term insurance coverage during pregnancy.

EXPECTATION OF LIFE: In life and health insurance, the mean number of years, based on mortality table figures, that a large group of persons of a given age will live.

EXPECTED CLAIMS: The estimated claims for a person or group for a contract year based usually on actuarial statistics.

EXPECTED EXPENSE RATIO: Ratio of expected incurred health or disability insurance costs and written premiums received.

EXPECTED EXPENSES: Expected health insurance-related costs, exclusive, or managed care claims-related costs.

EXPECTED INCURRED CLAIMS: Monetary amount of insurance claims for a particular time period that are still expected to be paid.

EXPECTED MORBIDITY: The expected incidence of sickness or injury within a given age group during a given period of time.

EXPECTED MORTALITY: The number of deaths that should occur among a group of persons during a given period, based on the mortality table being used. See Mortality and Morbidity.

EXPECTED SOURCE OF PAYMENT: These payer categories are used to indicate the type of entity or organization expected to pay or did pay the greatest share of the patient's bill:

- Medicare—A federally administered third-party reimbursement program authorized by Title XVIII of the Social Security Act. Includes crossovers to secondary payers.
- Medi-Cal—A state-administered third-party reimbursement program authorized by Title XIX of the Social Security Act.
- Private Coverage—Payment covered by private, nonprofit, or commercial health plans (whether insurance or other coverage) or organizations. Included are payments by local or organized charities, such as the Cerebral Palsy Foundation, Easter Seals, March of Dimes and Shriners, etc.
- Workers' Compensation—Payment from workers' compensation insurance, government or privately sponsored.
- County Indigent Programs—Patients covered under Welfare and Institutions Code Section 17000. Includes programs funded in whole or in part by County Medical Services Program (CMSP), California Health Care for Indigent Program (CHIP), or Realignment Funds whether or not a bill is rendered.

- Other Government—Any form of payment from American government agencies, whether local, state, federal, or foreign, except those included in the Medicare, Medi-Cal, Workers' Compensation, or County Indigent Programs categories listed above. Includes California Children Services (CCS), the Civilian Health and Medical Program of the Uniformed Services (TRICARE), and the Veterans Administration.
- Other Indigent—Patients receiving care pursuant to Hill-Burton obligations or who meet the standards for charity care pursuant to the hospital's established charity care policy. Includes indigent patients, except those described in the County Indigent Programs.
- Self-Pay—Payment directly by the patient, personal guarantor, relatives, or friends. The greatest share of a patient's bill is not paid by insurance or health plan.
- Other Payer—Any third-party payment not included in the other categories. Included are cases where no payment will be required by the facility, such as special research or courtesy patients.

EXPEDITED APPEAL: A Medicare + Choice or managed care organization's second look at whether it will provide a health service. A beneficiary may receive a fast decision within 72 hr when life, health, or ability to regain function may be jeopardized.

EXPEDITED ORGANIZATION DETERMINATION: A fast decision from the Medicare + Choice organization about whether it will provide a health service. A beneficiary may receive a fast decision within 72 hr when life, health, or ability to regain function may be jeopardized.

EXPEDITED REINSTATEMENT OF BENEFITS: Disability benefits reinstated immediately as Social Security Insurance (SSI) or Social Security Disability Insurance (SSDI) is received, which ended due to employment. This provision may be available for up to 5 years after Social Security work incentives have been exhausted.

EXPENDITURE: The issuance of checks, disbursement of cash, or electronic transfer of funds made to liquidate an expense regardless of the fiscal year the medical service was provided or the expense was incurred. When used in the discussion of the Medicaid program, expenditures refer to funds spent as reported by the States.

EXPENDITURE, CAPITAL: The amount of money paid for a fixed asset.

EXPENSE: Funds actually spent or incurred providing goods, rendering medical services, or carrying out other health mission-related activities during a period. Expenses are computed using accrual accounting techniques that recognize costs when incurred and revenues when earned and include the effect of accounts receivables and accounts payable on determining annual income. The costs of doing business for a health insurance or managed medical care insurance company. The overhead cost involved in running the business, aside from losses of claims.

EXPENSE ALLOWANCE: In insurance, compensation, or reimbursement in excess of prescribed commissions. Money paid by an insurer to an agent or agency head for incurred expenses.

EXPENSE BUDGET: The proforma budget used to forecast health care operational expenses.

EXPENSE CHARGE: In variable insurance and universal life insurance policies, all costs are individually deducted and accounted for within the policies. These expense charges are fixed amounts or percentages deducted from gross premiums paid and cash value, as specified in the policy.

EXPENSE CONSTANT: A flat health insurance charge added in the computation of the premium in which the pure premium is so low that the cost of issuing and servicing the policy cannot be recovered.

EXPENSE PER DAY: Total health care expenses of the facility exclusive of ancillary expenses divided by patient days.

EXPENSE PER DISCHARGE (HOSPITAL): Adjusted inpatient expenses divided by discharges (excluding nursery).

EXPENSE FACTOR: See Load.

EXPENSE INCURRED: Health insurance expenses paid and expenses to be paid. See IBNR.

EXPENSE LIABILITIES: Taxes and expenses incurred by a health insurance company as a result of normal business operating activities.

EXPENSE LOADING: The amount added to a health insurance premium during the rate-making process to cover the expenses of maintaining the business, commissions, administration, and overhead.

EXPENSE OF MANAGEMENT: See Load.

EXPENSE PAID: Money paid out by a health insurance company related to normal operating expenses, but not the cost of health care claims payments. Money disbursed by the health insurance company for conducting business other than for the purpose of paying claims.

EXPENSE RATIO: In insurance, that part or percentage of the premium devoted to paying the acquisition and service costs of insurance written. Incurred health insurance minus related expenses, divided by written premiums.

EXPENSE RESERVE: A fund set aside to pay future expenses. A health insurance company's responsibility for incurred but unpaid expenses. See Incurred but Not Reported.

EXPENSE RISK: The liability of a managed care or health insurance company for higher costs than charged for in the policy premiums.

EXPENSE PER UNIT OF SERVICE: The average cost to the hospital of providing one unit of service.

EXPERIENCE: (1) A record of predicting future health insurance claims losses and used in premium-setting calculations. (2) The loss record of an insured or of a type of insurance written. This record is used in adjusting premium rates and predicting future losses. (3) Also, a statistical compilation relating premiums to losses.

EXPERIENCED MORBIDITY: The actual morbidity experience of a health insurance company. See Morbidity.

EXPERIENCED MORTALITY: The actual mortality experience of a health insurance company. See Mortality.

EXPERIENCE MODIFICATION: The adjustment of health insurance premiums as a result of the application of experience rating, usually expressed as a percentage.

EXPERIENCE MORTALITY OR MORBIDITY: The actual mortality or morbidity experience of an indicated group of insured's, as compared to the expected mortality or morbidity.

EXPERIENCE, POLICY YEAR: In insurance, experience measured during 12-month periods beginning with a policy's date of issue.

EXPERIENCE-RATED PREMIUM: A premium that is based on the anticipated claims experience of, or utilization of service by, a contract group according to its age, sex, constitution, and any other attributes expected to affect its health service utilization and that is subject to periodic adjustment in line with actual claims or utilization experience.

EXPERIENCE RATING: (1) The rating system by which the plan determines the capitation rate by the experience of the individual group enrolled. Each group will have a different capitation rate based on utilization. This system tends to penalize small groups with high utilization. (2) A method of determining the premium based on a group's claims experience, age, sex, or health status. Experience rating is not allowed for federally qualified HMOs. (3) Health insurance premium-establishing method based on the average cost of anticipated or actual health care costs, using demographics and other variables in the proforma calculation. See Rating.

EXPERIENCE REFUND: In health reinsurance, a predetermined percentage of the net reinsurance profit that the reinsurer returns to the ceding company as a form of profit sharing at year end.

EXPERIMENTAL DRUGS, DEVICES, OR PROCEDURES: Drugs, devices, or procedures that are limited primarily to laboratory research. See Investigational Procedures and Promising Therapy.

EXPERIMENTAL, INVESTIGATIONAL, OR UNPROVEN: Any health care services, products, or procedures considered by a health plan or government agency to be ineffective, unreasonable, unnecessary, or not proven effective through scientific research.

EXPERIMENTAL OR UNPROVEN PROCEDURES: Any health care services, supplies, procedures, therapies, or devices that the health plan determines regarding coverage for a particular case to be either: (a) not proven by scientific evidence to be effective; or (b) not accepted by health care professionals as being effective.

EXPIRATION: The date on a health insurance policy indicating termination of coverage.

EXPIRATION DATE: The date on a health insurance policy that indicates when coverage ends.

EXPIRATION FILE: A record often kept by insurance agents indicating the expiration dates of the policies written or servicing.

EXPIRATION NOTICE: Written notification to an insured showing the termination date of an insurance contract.

EXPIRY: Termination of a health insurance policy at the end of its period of coverage.

EXPLANATION OF BENEFITS (EOB): A statement of coverage that lists any health services that have been provided as well as the amount billed and payment made by the health plan for those services.

EXPLANATION OF COVERAGE: A statement or booklet of coverage that lists any health services that will be provided, as needed, for covered medial services.

EXPLANATION OF MEDICARE BENEFITS: A statement of Medicare Part B coverage that lists assignments available, and if not physician accepted, with a benefit check payable to the recipient for them.

EX-POST EFFICIENCY ANALYSIS: An efficiency analysis undertaken subsequent to knowing a program's net outcome effects.

EXPOSURE: The possibility of insurance loss. In mortality or morbidity studies, the total number included in the study.

EXPRESS COVENANTS: Those parts of a contract created by specific words of the parties and that state their intention. See Contract and Policy.

EXPRESSED AUTHORITY: The specific authority given in writing to the agent in the agency agreement. See Agent.

EXTENDED BENEFITS: Coverage in excess of basic health insurance benefit or for a longer time period than normally expected.

EXTENDED CARE FACILITY (ECF): A nursing or convalescent home offering skilled-nursing care and rehabilitation services. See Hospice and LTC.

EXTENDED COVERAGE: An additional agreement or rider broadening an insurance contract. A provision in certain health policies (usually group) to allow the insured to receive benefits for specific losses sustained after termination of coverage, such as maternity expense benefits incurred in a pregnancy in progress at the time of termination.

EXTENDED PERIOD OF ELIGIBILITY (EPE): The 36 consecutive months that starts at the end of the tail work period. During the extended period of eligibility, any month in which gross earnings (income before taxes) are $810 or more (for 2004), an individual's wages are considered substantial gainful activity (SGA). When an individual's earnings first reach SGA, a 3-month grace period begins, allowing a beneficiary to continue receiving Social Security Disability Insurance (SSDI) payments regardless of wages.

However, after the 3-month grace period, an individual will not receive SSDI income benefits if wages are at or above SGA. If wages fall below SGA, SSDI payments will resume. Beneficiaries that continue to earn SGA income, after the EPE, will no longer be eligible for SSDI payments. The SGA earnings for blind beneficiaries are different. In 2004, SGA for the blind was $1,340.

EXTERNAL AUDIT: Health care audit program performed by an outside and unbiased third party, to ensure medical services were rendered and proper insurance claims made.

EXTERNALITIES: Effects of a program that impose costs on persons or groups who are not targets.

EXTERNAL QUALITY REVIEW ORGANIZATION (EQRO): Is the organization with which the state contracts to evaluate the care provided to Medicaid-managed patients. Typically, the EQRO is a peer-review organization. It may conduct focused medical record reviews (i.e., reviews targeted at a particular clinical condition) or broader analyses on quality. Although most EQRO contractors rely on medical records as the primary source of information, they may also use eligibility data and claims or encounter data to conduct specific analyses.

EXTERNAL QUALITY REVIEW PROGRAM: A health insurance, managed care, or HMO initiative for determining the quality of medical care provided to plan members, by outside review organizations.

EXTRAORDINARY ITEM: Rare and infrequent health care budget line item expense.

EXTRA TERRITORIALITY: The worker's compensation insurance provision that allows a worker injured in one state to come under the law auspices of his home state.

E-Z CLAIM: A 3-part health insurance claim form that represents a charge and receipt form as well as an insurance bill.

F

5-YEAR REVIEW: A review of the accuracy of Medicare's relative value scale that the Health Care Financing Administration (now Centers for Medicare and Medicaid Services) is required to conduct every 5 years.

5-YEAR WINDOW: Includes the 5 years (60 consecutive months) immediately proceeding the onset date of disability established by Social Security. Every month the 5-year window rolls forward regardless of work activity. This window stays open until all nine trial work months have been used. If an individual does not work all nine trial work months within 5 years, the window rolls or moves forward until all nine trial work months are used. Once an individual's trial work period expires, the extended period of eligibility automatically begins.

FACE: First page of an insurance policy. See Declaration.

FACE VALUE: See Face Amount.

FACILITY: A licensed, certified, or accredited facility that provides inpatient and outpatient services. Examples of facilities are hospitals, nursing facilities, and ambulatory surgical facilities.

FACILITY CHARGE: Service fee submitted for payment by a health care facility, such as a clinic, hospital, or ambulatory care center.

FACILITY NAME: The name under which the health facility is doing business.

FACILITY TO TREAT CHEMICAL DEPENDENCY: A licensed, freestanding facility that is approved by an insurer to provide treatment for chemical dependency conditions.

FACTORING: The sale of medical accounts receivable at a discount.

FACTUAL EXPECTATION: Expectation of an occurrence resulting in monetary interest that gives rise to an insurable interest, as when a family has an interest in the health or welfare of its bread winner.

FACULTATIVE: Ability of a reinsurance company to accept or reject the risk of a ceding company.

FACULTY PRACTICE PLAN (FPP): A form of group practice organized around a teaching program. It may be a single group encompassing all the physicians providing services to patients at the teaching hospital and facilities, or it may be multiple groups drawn along specialty lines.

FAIL-SAFE BUDGET MECHANISM: An overall limit on Medicare proposed spending based on economic assumptions of the Congressional Budget Office that provide a safeguard against unrestrained growth in Medicare spending.

FAIR MARKET VALUE: A legal term variously interpreted by the courts, but generally meaning the price at which a willing buyer will buy and a willing seller will sell an asset.

FAIR VALUE: Value that is reasonable and consistent with all of the known facts.

FALSE CLAIM: Incorrect or fraudulent medical insurance claim. See Fraud and Abuse.

FALSE NEGATIVES: (1) Occur when the medical record contains evidence of a service that does not exist in the encounter data. This is the most common problem in partially or fully capitated plans because the provider does not need to submit an encounter to receive payment for the service, and therefore may have a weaker incentive to conform to data collection standards. (2) Also, a term used in the clinical laboratory when referring to medical test results.

FALSE POSITIVES: (1) Occurs when the encounter data contain evidence of a service that is not documented in the patient's medical record. If we assume that the medical record contains complete information on the patient's medical history, a false positive may be considered a fraudulent service.

In a fully capitated environment, however, the provider would receive no additional reimbursement for the submission of a false positive encounter. (2) Also, a term used in the clinical laboratory when referring to medical test results.

FAMILY CARE EXPENSES: A disabled employee with family care responsibilities may need extra help when trying to return to work. This type of benefit provides an incentive to the employee who is taking part in a rehabilitation program by allowing credit or partial reimbursement for certain expenses incurred for family care. An optional benefit under most long-term disability plans.

FAMILY COVERAGE: Benefits are allowed for the plan enrollee and eligible family members.

FAMILY DEPENDENCY PERIOD: In insurance, a term referring to the years when the spouse of a deceased wage earner is caring for dependent children, generally considered to continue until the youngest child is 18–21 years old.

FAMILY DEPENDENT: A person entitled to coverage because he or she is the enrollee's spouse, single dependent child of either the enrollee or the enrollee's spouse (including stepchildren or legally adopted children), or resident of the enrollee's home.

FAMILY EXPENSE POLICY: A health insurance policy that covers the medical expenses of the policy owner and his or her immediate dependents (usually spouse and children).

FAMILY HISTORY: Background information and history used by health, life, and disability and managed care insurance companies.

FAMILY INCOME: The total income earned by a family unit and used for family maintenance. Income earned by more than one family member, such as when both spouses are employed.

FAMILY MEDICAL LEAVE ACT (FMLA): Law passed in 1993 that requires employers with more than 50 people to give them 12 weeks of leave per birth, or to care for a sick family member or adopted child.

FAMILY PHYSICIAN: Physician who provides primary care in a manner that considers patients in relation to their families and social environments as factors in the diagnosis and treatment of disease. See Gatekeeper and Internist.

FAMILY SITUATION: For life, disability, and health insurance purposes, any group having at least two people, including at least one income provider upon whose earnings the family depends for its financial support. Generally, the family must also include one or more dependent children.

FAUX HMO: False health-plan with an intermediary attempt to negotiate health care reimbursement down, with resale to another HMO. Also known as a mirror or silent HMO.

FAVORABLE SELECTION: The result of enrolling in a health plan a disproportionate share of healthy individuals compared with the population from which the share is drawn. See Adverse Selection, Risk Adjustment, and Risk Selection.

FAVORABLE VARIANCE: Actual revenues that surpass expected revenues.

FAVORED NATIONS DISCOUNT: A contractual agreement between a provider and a payer stating that the provider will automatically provide the payer with the best discount it provides anyone else.

FDA: The Food and Drug Administration.

FEDERAL DEFICIT: Federal government spending in excess of revenues.

FEDERAL EMPLOYEE HEALTH BENEFIT ACQUISITION REGULATIONS (FEHBAR): The regulations applied to the Office of Personnel Management's purchase of health care benefits programs for federal employees.

FEDERAL EMPLOYEES HEALTH BENEFITS PROGRAM (FEHBP): The health benefits program for federal employees that is administered through the U.S. Office of Personnel Management.

FEDERAL INSURANCE CONTRIBUTION ACT PAYROLL TAX: Medicare's share of FICA is used to fund the Health Insurance Trust Fund (HITF). In FY 2005, employers and employees each contributed 1.45% of taxable wages, with no limitations, to the HITF.

FEDERAL INSURANCE CONTRIBUTIONS ACT: Provision authorizing taxes on the wages of employed persons to provide for the Old-Age, Survivor's, and Disability Insurance (OASDI) and Health Insurance (HI) programs. Covered workers and their employers pay the tax in equal amounts.

FEDERALLY QUALIFIED HEALTH CENTER (FQHC): A facility located in a medically underserved area that provides Medicare beneficiaries preventive primary medical care under the general supervision of a physician. Health centers that have been approved by the government (Department of Health and Human Services) for a program to give low cost health care. Medicare pays for some health services in FQHCs that are not usually covered, like preventive care. FQHCs include community health centers, tribal health clinics, migrant health services, and health centers for the homeless.

FEDERALLY QUALIFIED HMO: An HMO that meets certain federally stipulated provisions aimed at protecting consumers (e.g., providing a broad range of basic health services, assuring financial solvency, and monitoring the quality of care). HMOs must apply to the federal government for qualification. Administered by the Office of Prepaid Health Care of the Health Care Financing Administration (HCFA), Department of Health and Human Services (DHHS), and the Centers for Medicaid and Medicare Services (CMS).

FEDERAL MANAGERS' FINANCIAL INTEGRITY ACT: A program to identify management inefficiencies and areas vulnerable to fraud and abuse and to correct such weaknesses with improved internal controls.

FEDERAL MEDICAID MANAGED CARE WAIVER PROGRAM: The process used by states to receive permission to implement managed care programs for Medicaid or other categorically eligible beneficiaries.

FEDERAL MEDICAL ASSISTANCE PERCENTAGE (FMAP): The portion of the Medicaid program that is paid by the Federal government.

FEDERAL POVERTY LEVEL (FPL): The amount of income determined by the federal Department of Health and Human Services to provide a minimum for food, clothing, transportation, shelter, and other necessities.

FEDERAL QUALIFICATION: A status defined by the HMO Act, conferred by Health Care Financing Administration (Centers for Medicare and Medicaid Services) after conducting an extensive evaluation of the HMO's organization and operations. An organization must be federally qualified or be designated as a competitive medical plan to be eligible to participate in Medicare cost and risk contracts. Likewise, an HMO must be federally qualified or state plan defined to participate in the Medicaid managed care program.

FEDERAL TRADE COMMISSION (FTC) ACT: The empowering of the FTC to work with the DOJ to enforce health care antitrust statutes and laws. See DOJ.

FEE: A charge or price for professional services.

FEE ALLOWANCE: See Fee Schedule.

FEE DISCLOSURE: Physicians and caregivers discussing their charges with patients prior to treatment.

FEE SCHEDULE: A listing of accepted fees or established allowances for specified medical procedures. As used in medical care plans, it usually represents the maximum amounts the program will pay for the specified procedures. See UCR.

FEE SCHEDULE PAYMENT AREA: A geographic area within which payment for a given service under the Medicare Fee Schedule does not vary. See Geographic Adjustment Factor.

FEE-SCREEN YEAR: A specified period of time in which small market insurance recognized fees pertain.

FEE-FOR-SERVICE: (1) Method of reimbursement based on payment for medical services rendered by practitioners. The payment may be by an insurance company, patient, or government program, such as Medicare or Medicaid. (2) Refers to payment in specific amounts for specific services rendered—as opposed to retainer, salary, or other contract arrangements. In relation to the patient, it refers to payment in specific amounts for specific services received, in contrast to the advance payment of an insurance premium or membership fee for coverage, through which the services or payment to the supplier are provided. See Prospective Payment System.

FEE STRUCTURE AND PANEL SIZE: A physicians' target income level, the number of patients to be served, and the services offered in a concierge medical practice.

FELLOW OF THE INSTITUTE OF ACTUARIES: A designation for an individual who has been examined by and becomes a member of the Institute of Actuaries. See Actuary.

FELLOW, LIFE MANAGEMENT INSTITUTE (FLMI): A professional management designation in the life and health insurance industry.

FELLOW OF THE SOCIETY OF ACTUARIES (FSA): A designation given to members of the Society of Actuaries, earned by the completion of 10 examinations in mathematics, statistics, insurance, actuarial science, accounting, finance, and employee benefits.

FHA PROGRAM LOAN: Federal Housing Administration (FHA) mortgage insurance that guarantees the interest and principal on a loan for a medical or health care provider.

FICA CONTRIBUTIONS FOR SSI: Social Security Insurance requires a worker to pay Federal Insurance Contributions Act (FICA) taxes for specified lengths of time, called credits. One Social Security Death Index (SSDI) credit equals one quarter of the year or 3 months. Four SSDI credits are available in a 12 month-period. The number of work credits needed to qualify for Social Security Insurance depends on the age of disability onset. Generally, an individual will need 40 credits (10 years), 20 of which were earned in the last 10 years before becoming disabled: (a) Before age 24: an individual may qualify if they have credits for $1^1/_2$ years of work (6 credits) within the past 3 years; (b) aged 24–31: an individual may qualify if they have credit for 3 years of work (12 credits) out of the past 6 years; and (c) aged 31 or older: In general, an individual needs to have the number of work credits shown in Table 1. Unless an individual

Table 1. Work Credits Required for Social Security Disability Insurance Eligibility for Those Born After 1929

Became Disabled At Age:	Number of Credits Needed
31 through 42	20
44	22
46	24
48	26
50	28
52	30
54	32
56	34
58	36
60	38
62 or older	40

is blind, he or she must have earned at least 20 of the credits in the last 10 years before an individual became disabled.

FIDUCIARY: Relating to, or founded upon, a trust or confidence. A fiduciary relationship exists when an individual or organization has an explicit or implicit obligation to act on behalf of another person or organization's interests in matters that affect the other person or organization. This fiduciary is also obligated to act in the other person's best interest with total disregard for any interests of the fiduciary. Traditionally, it was generally believed that a physician had a fiduciary relationship with patients. This is being questioned in the era of managed care as the public becomes aware of the other influences that are affecting physician decisions. Doctors are provided incentives by managed care companies to provide less care, by pharmaceutical companies to order certain drugs, and by hospitals to refer to their hospitals. With the pervasive monetary incentives influencing doctor decisions, consumer advocates are concerned because the patient no longer has an unencumbered fiduciary.

FIDUCIARY BOND: A bond that guarantees the faithful performance in life and health insurance matters, among others.

FIELD UNDERWRITING: The initial screening of prospective buyers of health insurance, performed by sales personnel in the field. May also include quoting of premium rates.

FILING LIMIT: The amount of time allowed by an insurer for claim submittal.

FINANCE: The sources, timing, and channels of public health funds, and the authority to raise and distribute those funds.

FINANCE COMMITTEE: Committee of the board of directors for managed care whose duty it is to review financial results, approve budgets, set and approve spending authorities, review the annual audit, and review and approve outside funding sources.

FINANCIAL DATA: Data regarding the financial status of managed care entities.

FINANCIAL INTERCHANGE: Provisions of the Railroad Retirement Act (RRA) providing for transfers between the trust funds and the Social Security Equivalent Benefit Account (SSEBA) of the Railroad Retirement program to place each trust fund in the same position as if railroad employment had always been covered under Social Security Insurance (SSI).

FINANCIAL RATIOS: Financial ratios, with ratio analysis, are the calculation and comparison of mathematic ratios derived from the information in a managed care company's financial statements. The level and historical trends of these ratios can be used to make inferences about a company's financial condition, premiums and payouts, operations, and attractiveness as an investment or insurance policy.

FINANCING MIX: The methods in which a health care organization provides for its daily working capital and operating needs.

FIRST-DOLLAR COVERAGE: Insurance coverage without a front-end deductible so that coverage begins with the first dollar of expense incurred by the insured for any covered benefit.

FIRST PASS: A health insurance claim that has been adjudicated from submission to payment or rejection.

FIRST RESPONDER: The first responder uses a limited amount of equipment to perform initial assessment and intervention and is trained to assist other emergency medical services.

FISCAL AGENT: Contracted claims agency that processes Medicaid health insurance claims.

FISCAL INTERMEDIARY: The agent (e.g., Blue Cross) that has contracted with providers of service to process claims for reimbursement under health care coverage. In addition to handling financial matters, it may perform other functions, such as providing consultative services or serving as a center for communication with providers and making audits of providers' needs.

FISCAL SERVICES: The nonrevenue producing costs centers for those services generally associated with the accounting, credit, collection, and admitting operations of a facility.

FISCAL SOUNDNESS: The required amount of funds that a managed care organization must keep on reserve because of financial risk, as regulated by the Department of Insurance.

FISCAL YEAR: (1) A 12-month period for which an organization plans the use of its funds, such as the Federal government's fiscal year (October 1 to September 30). Fiscal years are referred to by the calendar year in which they end; for example, the Federal fiscal year 2007 begins October 1, 2006. Hospitals can designate their own fiscal years, and this is reflected in differences in time periods covered by the Medicare Cost Reports. (2) A 12-month period over which a health care company balances its books. The term is ordinarily used only when the 12-month period is not a regular calendar year.

FIVE ELEMENTS: Earth, metal, water, wood, and fire as manifestations (phases or transformations) of chi. The expression *five elements* derives from two Chinese words: *wu* (five) and *xing* (move or walk). Its implicit meaning is five processes. According to ancient Chinese cosmology, the five elements compose everything. In Chinese medicine, each of the five elements symbolizes a group of physiologic functions: Earth (soil) represents balance or neutrality; metal (coal, fossils, and inorganic matter) represents decay; water (moisture) represents a state of maximum rest leading to a change of functional direction; wood (organic matter) represents a growth phase; and fire (gases) represents maximum activity.

FIXED ASSETS: Nonmovable health care entity assets. See Assets.

FIXED ASSET TURNOVER: Ratio of dollars generated for each dollar reinvested in a health care organization's plant and equipment.

FIXED COSTS: Costs that do not change with fluctuations in census or in utilization of services. See Variable Costs.

FIXED-INCOME SECURITY: A preferred stock or a debt security with a stated percentage or dollar income return.

FIXED LABOR BUDGET: A series of income and outflow revenue projections for human labor costs.

FLAT CANCELLATION: Cancellation of a health insurance policy as of the date of its start with no premium charge.

FLAT FEE PER CASE: Flat fee paid for a client's treatment based on their diagnosis or presenting problem. For this fee, the provider covers all of the services the client requires for a specific period of time. Often characterizes second generation managed care systems. After the managed care organizations squeeze out costs by discounting fees, they often come to this method. If the provider is still standing after a discount blitz, this approach can be good for the provider and clients because it permits a lot of flexibility for the provider in meeting client needs.

FLAT MATERNITY BENEFIT: A stipulated benefit in a hospital reimbursement policy that is paid for maternity confinement, regardless of the actual cost of the confinement.

FLEXIBLE BENEFIT PLAN: Employee choice among several employer benefits. May be contributory or noncontributory in nature.

FLEXIBLE BUDGET: An estimate of revenues and expenses over time and a range of health care services. See Budget.

FLEXIBLE SPENDING ACCOUNT (FSA): A way for covered persons to use pretax dollars; money set aside from their salary that may be reimbursed to pay for any health care services not covered under the terms and conditions of their contract. Use-it or lose-it funding. See FSA, HC, DCE, HAS, and HRA.

FLEXIBLE SPENDING ACCOUNT/HEALTH CARE/DEPENDENT CARE EXPENSES: An employee plan that permits the deferral of pretax earnings, for various purposes, such as unreimbursed medical expenses. Use it or lose it. See FSA.

FLOATER: A colloquial term for a security with a floating or variable interest rate.

FLOATING RATE or VARIABLE RATE: An interest rate on a security that changes at intervals according to an index or a formula or other standard of measurement as stated in the hospital revenue bond contract. One common method is to calculate the interest rate as a percentage of the rate paid on selected issues of treasury securities on specified dates.

FLOW OF FUNDS: The order and priority of handling, depositing, and disbursing pledged revenues, as set forth in a hospital revenue bond contract. Generally, the revenues are deposited, as received, into a general collection account or revenue fund for disbursement into the other accounts established by the bond contract. Such other accounts generally provide for payment of the costs of debt service, operation and maintenance costs, debt service reserve deposits, redemption, renewal and replacement, and other requirements.

FMLA: Family Medical Leave Act.

FOCUSED STUDIES: State-required studies that examine a specific aspect of health care (such as prenatal care) for a defined point in time. These projects are usually based on information extracted from medical records or managed care organization or prepaid health plan (MCO/PHP) administrative data, such as enrollment files and encounter or claims data. State staff, external quality review organization staff, MCO/PHP staff, or more than one of these entities may perform such studies at the discretion of the state.

FOOT DOCTOR: A podiatrist. Any doctor of podiatric medicine (DPM) who has a valid limited medical license and is qualified under the law of jurisdiction in which medical and surgical treatment is received. See Doctor, Podiatrist.

FORM: An insurance policy itself or the riders, endorsements, and attachments connected to it.

FORMAT: HIPAA data elements that provide or control the enveloping or hierarchical structure or assist in identifying data content of a transaction.

FORMATIVE EVALUATION: Formative evaluation, including pretesting, is designed to assess the strengths and weaknesses of materials or campaigning strategies before implementation. It permits necessary revisions before the full effort goes forward. Its basic purpose is to maximize the chance for program success before the communication activity starts.

FORMATTING AND PROTOCOL STANDARDS: Data base and electronic health care information submission standards developed and mandated by HIPAA and other legislation.

FORMULARY: A list containing the names of certain prescription drugs that an HMO covers when dispensed to its members who have drug coverage.

FORMULARY DRUGS: Those drugs listed on a formulary.

FOR PROFIT: A health care organization where financial profits, if any, can be distributed outside the company. See Not for Profit.

FORTUITIOUS EVENT: Unforeseen accident, illness, or adverse occurrence.

FOUNDATION MODEL: Organization of physicians that is a separate and autonomous corporation with its own Board of Directors. The foundation may operate as a prepaid group practice or as an individual practice association for an HMO.

FRACTIONAL PREMIUM: Health, disability, life, or other insurance premium paid on a proportional basis, such as daily, weekly, biweekly, or monthly.

FRANCHISE DISABILITY INCOME: A collectively renewable form of disability income protection. Similar to individual insurance because each insured receives his or her own policy and chooses the elimination period, benefit period, and amount of indemnity.

FRATERNAL: In insurance, refers to a fraternal benefit society that generally writes fraternal insurance, like health, long-term care, life, or disability insurance on its members.

FRAUD: A deception that could result in an insured unnecessarily paying for medical services. For example, if a provider files a claim for a service that was not provided. See Abuse and Over Utilization.

FRAUD AND ABUSE: Federal and state, Medicare and Medicaid, violations of the Internal Revenue Code, Stark I and II laws, or other codes that proscribe patient referrals to entities in which a family member has a financial interest. Abuse is unneeded, harmful, or poor-quality health care delivery or services. See Over Utilization.

FRAUD ALERT: Warning from the Office of the Inspector General (OIG) to medical providers that warns of possible fraud and abuse law violations.

FREEDOM OF CHOICE: A principle of Medicaid that allows a recipient the freedom to choose among participating medical providers.

FREEDOM OF INFORMATION ACT (FOIA): U.S. law requiring the disclosure of certain medical information upon written request of the patient.

FREE-LOOK PERIOD: Time frame to evaluate a health or other insurance policy and return it to the insurer for a full refund. A time period (usually 10 days) in which a new policy holder may examine an individual health, life, or disability insurance policy and exchange it for a full refund, if not satisfied in any way. See Free-Look Provision.

FREE-LOOK PROVISION: A provision in life and health insurance policies that gives the policy owner a stated amount of time (usually 10 days) to review a new policy. It can be returned within this time for a 100% refund of premiums paid, but cancellation of coverage is effective from date of issue.

FREESTANDING EMERGENCY MEDICAL SERVICE CENTER: A health care facility whose primary purpose is the provision of care for emergency medical conditions.

FREESTANDING FACILITY: Ambulatory care facility without a physical connection to a hospital.

FREESTANDING OUTPATIENT SURGICAL CENTER: A facility that only provides outpatient surgical services.

FREQUENCY: The number of times a health service is provided over a given time period.

FRINGE BENEFITS: Refers generally to benefits, formal or informal, other than salary or wages, provided for employees by employers.

FSA: flexible sending account.

FULL CAPITATION: The plan or primary care case manager is paid for providing services to enrollees through a combination of capitation and fee-for-service reimbursements. See Capitation.

FULL DISABILITY: The loss of full capacity for earned income.

FULL OLD-AGE BENEFIT FOR WORKER: Under Social Security, a monthly benefit paid for life to a worker who is fully insured and has reached age 65.

FULL-RISK CAPITATION: The complete acceptance of all fiscal risk by a health care plan, facility, or provider for the plans members.

FULL-TIME EMPLOYEE (EQUIVALENT) (FTE): Generally, employees of an employer who work for 1,000 or more hours in a 12-month period, as defined for pension plan purposes in the Employees Retirement Income Security Act (ERISA).

FULL-TIME STUDENT: Any person enrolled in a study program, in high school, college, or a vocational school that is considered a full-time attendant by that institution. Age limit restrictions may apply.

FULLY ALLOCATED COSTS: Medical service costs after considering all directed and fair share costs.

FULLY FUNDED PLAN: A health plan under which an insurer or managed care organization bears the financial responsibility of guaranteeing claim payments and paying for all incurred covered benefits and administration costs.

FULLY INSURED: Under Social Security, an individual's status of complete eligibility for benefits. Provides retirement benefits as well as survivor benefits. A fully insured individual has also met one of the requirements for disability benefits. A group health care plan funding arrangement in which the group policy holder makes monthly premium payments to the organization that provides the health care coverage and the insurer bears the responsibility of guaranteeing claims payments.

FULLY LOADED: All marketing, sales, and administrative fees of a health insurance or managed care contract, including agent commissions. See Load.

FUNCTIONAL COSTS: Operating costs classified by function or purpose.

FUNCTIONAL INDEPENDENCE MEASURE (FUNCTION-RELATED GROUP): A patient classification system developed for medical rehabilitation patients.

FUNCTIONAL STATUS: The ability to perform activities of daily living. See ADLs.

FUNDING LEVEL: Amount of revenue required to finance a medical care program.

FUNDING METHOD: System for employers to pay for a health benefit plan. Most common methods are prospective or retrospective premium payment, shared risk arrangement, self-funded, or refunding products. See also Self-insured, Risk, and Premium.

FUNDING VEHICLE: The fully funded account into which the money that an employer and employees would have paid in premiums to an insurer or managed care organization is deposited until the money is paid out.

FUTURE VALUE (FV): The amount of money that an invested lump sum or series of payments will be worth, at some point in the future.

FUTURE VALUE FACTOR (FVF): A multiplier for an invested lump sum of money or payment stream used to estimate its future value.

G

GAG CLAUSE: A provision of a contract between a managed care organization and a health care provider that restricts the amount of information a provider may share with a beneficiary or that limits the circumstances under which a provider may recommend a specific treatment option.

GAIN/LOSS: Difference between the amounts of money received when selling an asset, and its books value, or, the difference between sale and purchase price of a security.

GAINSHARING: An incentive health care program focused on improving operating results, typically implemented at a group or organizational level.

GAMING: Any attempted scheme, system, or method to defraud or bill the health care insurance system by not paying for services rendered.

GAP FILLING: Used when no comparable, existing test is available. Carrier specific amounts are used to establish a national limitation amount for the following year.

GAPS: The costs or services that are not covered under the original Medicare plan.

GASTROENTEROLOGY: Medical specialty of the stomach and intestines.

GATEKEEPER: One role of a primary care doctor in an HMO or other managed care network that requires its members to have their care provided, arranged, or authorized by member's primary care physicians. See Doctor and Internist.

GENERAL ACUTE CARE: Services provided to patients (on the basis of physicians' orders and approved nursing care plans) who are in an acute phase of illness but not to the degree that requires the concentrated and continuous observation and care provided in the intensive care centers.

GENERAL ADMINISTRATIVE EXPENSES: Health care operating expenses that are not within the supply or labor budgets.

GENERAL AGENCY: An independently owned life and health insurance agency under the control of a general agent, who has a contractual agreement with an insurance company, is paid primarily by commission, and pays all or most of his or her own expenses. See Agent.

GENERAL AGENCY SYSTEM: The marketing of life and health insurance through general agents rather than through branch offices. See Agent.

GENERAL AGENT: An individual appointed by the insurer to administer its business in a given territory. The general agent is responsible for building his or her own agency and service force and is compensated on a commission basis, although usually with some expense allowances. See Agent.

GENERAL AGENTS AND MANAGERS ASSOCIATION: An organization of local general agents and managers in a community that generally is affiliated with the General Agents and Managers Conference. The association works to advance common interests of its members and the general public through efforts to raise the level of competence of the life and health insurance field operations by educational means.

GENERAL AGENTS AND MANAGERS CONFERENCE: A national association of life and health insurance general agents and managers, affiliated with the National Association of Life Underwriters. Their goal is to find solutions to managerial problems and to provide a forum for exchanging ideas.

GENERAL CARE FLOOR: A hospital or health care facility floor not designated as a critical, cardiac, or step-down care floor.

GENERAL ENROLLMENT PERIOD: Usually the open time period certain for Medicare or other private insurance company application submissions and processing.

GENERAL FUND OF THE TREASURY: Funds held by the Treasury of the United States, other than revenue collected for a specific trust fund (such as supplemental medical insurance) and maintained in a separate account for that purpose. The majority of this fund is derived from individual and business income taxes.

GENERALIST: Physicians who are distinguished by their training as not limiting their practice by health condition or organ system, who provide comprehensive and continuous services, and who make decisions about treatment for patients presenting with undifferentiated symptoms. Typically include family practitioners, general internists, and general pediatricians. See Gatekeeper, Hospitalist, and Internist.

GENERAL MARKET: A broad category of people or businesses having something in common as potential buyers of insurance, such as medical people in general. This compares with specific markets, such as high school teachers, accountants, lawyers, etc.

GENERAL OBLIGATION BOND: A hospital bond that is secured by the full faith and credit of a state issuer with taxing power. General obligation bonds issued by local units of government are typically secured by a pledge of the issuer's ad valorem taxing power; general obligation bonds issued by states are generally based upon appropriations made by the state legislature for the purposes specified.

GENERAL OPERATING EXPENSES: Expenses of an insurance company other than commissions and taxes; the administrative costs of running a business.

GENERAL PARTNERSHIP: A partnership in which each partner contributes to the business, either in the form of money or services, and also shares in the control and management of the business. Each partner in a general partnership is personally liable for the full amount of partnership indebtedness.

GENERAL PRACTITIONER: A family practitioner that provides medical care to people of all ages.

GENERAL REVENUE: Income to the supplemental medical insurance (SMI) trust fund from the general fund of the U.S. Treasury. Only a very small percentage of total SMI trust fund income each year is attributable to general revenue. See Revenue.

GENERAL SERVICES: The non-revenue-producing cost centers for those services related to the operation and maintenance of a facility, such as food services, housekeeping, etc.

GENERIC DRUG: A prescription drug that has the same active-ingredient formula as a brand-name drug. A generic drug is known only by its formula name and its formula is available to any pharmaceutical company. Generic drugs are rated by the Food and Drug Administration (FDA) to be as safe and as effective as brand-name drugs and are typically less costly. See Trade Drug.

GENERIC DRUG LIST: A list of prescription medications that are sold at a generic product level and are covered by a health plan. This list varies according to the insurer and is subject to review and change. See Trade Drug.

GENERIC SUBSTITUTION: Stocking a limited number (usually one) of brands of a multisource product and automatically dispensing the equivalent product when a different brand of the same therapeutic entity is ordered. See Trade Drug.

GENETIC SCREENING OR TESTING: Any laboratory test that is used to directly detect abnormalities, defects, or deficiencies in human genes or chromosomes.

GEOGRAPHIC ADJUSTMENT FACTOR (GAF): The average of an area's three geographic practice cost indexes weighted by the share of the service's total relative value units accounted for by the work, practice expense, and malpractice expense components of the Medicare Fee Schedule. See Geographic Practice Cost Index and Relative Value Units.

GEOGRAPHIC PRACTICE COST INDEX (GPCI): An index summarizing the prices of resources required to provide physicians' services in each payment area relative to national average prices. There is a GPCI for each component of the Medicare Fee Schedule: physician work, practice expense, and malpractice expense. The indexes are used to adjust relative value units to determine the correct payment in each fee schedule payment area. See Fee-Schedule Payment Area and Medicare Fee Schedule.

GERONTOLOGY: The study of, and learning about, older people and the process of aging.

GIMMICKS: A negative reference to certain clauses or coverage found in some life and health insurance policies. The inference is that the policy owner is not receiving the same value of coverage that he or she may think is provided by a policy.

GLOBAL BUDGETING: Limits placed on categories of health spending. A method of hospital cost containment in which participating hospitals must share a prospectively set budget. Method for allocating funds among hospitals may vary but the key is that the participating hospitals agree to an aggregate cap on revenues that they will receive each year. Global budgeting may also be mandated under a universal health insurance system. See Budget.

GLOBAL CAPITATION: Providers are paid a single per-member-per-month rate to cover all care (professional, facilities, and technical services) for a population of people.

GLOBAL CASE RATES: Providers are paid a lump sum upon referral to cover all care (professionals, facilities, and technical services) specific to a defined episode. See Flat Fee and Fee Schedule.

GLOBAL FEE: A total charge for a specific set of services, such as obstetrical services that encompass prenatal, delivery, and postnatal care. Managed care organizations will often seek contracts with hospitals that contain set global fees for certain sets of services. Outliers and carve outs will be those services not included in the global negotiated rates. See UCR and Capitation.

GLOBAL SURGERY: Health Care Financing Adminstration-designed payment package for specific procedures without complication and for a given aftercare time period.

GOODWILL: An intangible and often major business asset that generally includes such things as the reputations of the owners, the number of satisfied clients, customers, patients, and the continuing influx of new business.

GOVERNANCE: The legal authority and responsibility for the public health system.

GRACE PERIOD: Most life insurance contracts provide that premiums may be paid at any time within a period of generally 30 or 31 days following the premium due date, the policy remaining in full force in the meantime. If death occurs during the grace period, the premium is deducted from the proceeds payable. As a general rule, no interest is charged on overdue premiums if paid during the grace period. In health policies, a period of time (usually 30 days) after the premium due date, the policy remaining in force and without penalty for past due payment.

GRADUATE MEDICAL EDUCATION (GME): The period of medical training that follows graduation from medical school; commonly referred to as internship, residency, and fellowship training. See Undergraduate Medical Education, Doctor, and Physician.

GRANDFATHER CLAUSE: A legal theory or contract clause that allows continued coverage after a contract for health, managed care, or other insurance has changed, based on the original agreement.

GRANTS: The funds given to a health care entity for a special project, and usually for a certain time period, along with various other terms and conditions.

GRIEVANCE: Any complaint or request for change made by a covered person regarding a decision made by an insurance company.

GRIEVANCE PROCEDURES: The process by which an insured can air complaints and seek remedies.

GROSS BENEFIT AMOUNT: The total benefit amount an insurance company pays before deductions. Deductions are made for an individual's disability income and for earnings he or she is receiving.

GROSS CHARGES PER 1,000: An indicator calculated by taking the gross charges incurred by a specific group for a specific period of time, dividing it by the average number of covered members or lives in that group during the same period, and multiplying the result by 1,000. This is calculated in the aggregate and by modality of treatment (e.g., inpatient, residential, partial hospitalization, and outpatient). A measure used to evaluate utilization management performance.

GROSS COSTS PER 1,000: An indicator calculated by taking the gross costs incurred for services received by a specific group for a specific period of time, dividing it by the average number of covered members or lives in that group during the same period, and multiplying the result by 1,000. This is calculated in the aggregate and by modality of treatment (e.g. inpatient, residential, partial hospitalization, and outpatient). A measure used to evaluate utilization management performance.

GROSS DOMESTIC PRODUCT (GDP): The total current market value of all goods and services produced domestically during a given period; differs from the Gross National Product (GNP) by excluding net income that residents earn abroad.

GROSS EARNINGS: Total earnings before deduction of taxes and expenses.

GROSS EXPENSE PER DISCHARGE: The average expense incurred by hospitals to provide inpatient care, including room and board, patient care services, and goods sold, from admission to discharge. Gross inpatient expenses divided by discharges, excluding nursery discharges. See Expense.

GROSS EXPENSE PER VISIT: The average expense incurred by hospitals to provide care for one outpatient visit. Gross outpatient expenses divided by outpatient visits.

GROSS INCOME: Income before taxes are deducted. See Revenue and Before-Tax Earnings.

GROSS INPATIENT EXPENSES: Operating expenses related to providing inpatient services. Excludes nonoperating expenses and income taxes but includes physician professional component expenses. Gross inpatient expenses are determined by allocating total operating expenses using the ratio of gross inpatient revenue to the total gross patient revenue.

GROSS INPATIENT REVENUE: Total inpatient charges at the hospital's full established rates for services rendered and goods sold, including revenue from daily hospital services, inpatient ambulatory services, and inpatient ancillary services. Also includes charges related to hospital-based physician professional services. Other operating revenue and nonoperating revenue are excluded.

GROSS NET PREMIUMS: In insurance, gross premiums minus return premiums, but not less reinsurance premiums.

GROSS OUTPATIENT EXPENSES: Total operating expenses relating to outpatient services. Excludes nonoperating expenses and income taxes, but includes physician professional component expenses. Gross outpatient expenses are determined by allocating total operating expenses using the ratio of gross outpatient revenue to total gross revenue.

GROSS OUTPATIENT REVENUE: Total outpatient charges at the hospital's established rates for outpatient ambulatory and outpatient ancillary services rendered and goods sold. Also includes charges related to hospital-based physician professional services. Other operating revenue and nonoperating revenue are excluded.

GROSS PATIENT REVENUE: The total charges at a hospital's established rates for the provision of patient care services before deductions from revenue are applied. Includes charges related to hospital-based physician professional services. Other operating revenue and nonoperating revenue are excluded: (a) Gross Inpatient Revenue—Gross revenue for daily hospital services and inpatient ancillary services before deductions from revenue are applied; (b) Gross Outpatient Revenue—Gross revenue for outpatient ancillary services before deductions from revenue are applied.

GROSS PATIENT SERVICE REVENUE: The total charges at the facility's established rates for the provision of patient care before deductions from revenue are applied. The total amount of monies a health care organization earns, at full retail price, for its medical services.

GROSS PREDISABILITY SALARY (INCOME): The total pretax income paid to an individual by the employer while covered by disability insurance prior to the start of the disability.

GROSS PREMIUM: The net premium (risk factor), plus the expense of operation (loading), less the interest factor (credit); the premium for participating life insurance shown in the rate book. The total amount of premium paid by the policy owner.

GROSS PREMIUM VALUATION: The present value of future insurance gross premiums, minus the present value of future policy benefits and expenses.

GROSS RATES: The rates listed in an insurance company's rate book. The gross rate is the net or pure premium, plus a loading for expenses and contingencies.

GROSS REVENUE PER DAY: The average amount charged by a hospital for one day of inpatient care (gross inpatient revenue divided by patient-census days). See Revenue.

GROSS REVENUE PER DISCHARGE: The average amount charged by a hospital to treat an inpatient from admission to discharge (gross inpatient revenue divided by discharges).

GROSS REVENUE PER VISIT: The average amount charged by a hospital for an outpatient visit (gross outpatient revenue divided by outpatient visits).

GROSS WORKING CAPITAL: See Current Assets.

GROUP: The business organization or legal entity that has entered into the contract with a health insurance company or HMO for the provision of medical and hospital services. A number of people classed together by some common factor: sex, age, place of employment, occupation, location, etc. In group insurance, the collective individuals covered by a master policy.

GROUP ACCIDENT AND HEALTH INSURANCE: See Group Insurance.

GROUP APPLICATION: In group insurance plans, a form signed by the employer that includes schedules of insurance, eligibility requirements, method of premium payment, etc. It becomes part of the group insurance contract.

GROUP CERTIFICATE: Under a group insurance plan, the document provided to each member of the group, showing the benefits provided under the group contract. See Certificate of Insurance.

GROUP CONTRACT: A contract of insurance made with an employer or other entity that covers a group of persons identified in reference to their relationship to the entity. These identified individuals may include dependents or other family members. Premiums may be paid entirely by the employer or other entity, entirely by identified individuals, or jointly. Group eligibility for such insurance may be defined or limited by state laws or by insurer underwriting. The group contractual arrangement is used most generally to cover employees of a common employer, employees of the employer-members of a trade association or trusteeship, members of a welfare or employee-benefit association, members of a labor union, members of professional or other association not formed for the purpose of obtaining insurance or debtors. This definition applies to life and health insurance, to annuities, and to some contracts in property or liability insurance.

GROUP CONVERSION: The options of a group managed care members to take on nongroup health coverage without continued evidence of good health.

GROUP CREDIT LIFE AND HEALTH INSURANCE: Credit insurance written on a group basis.

GROUP DISABILITY INSURANCE: A health insurance contract issued to cover designated groups having the same employer or common affiliation of interest, and that offers benefits primarily for loss of time and income, although there may be some individual hospital or medical expense coverage as well.

GROUPER PROGRAM: A software program that groups discharges to major diagnostic categories (MDCs) and diagnostic-related groups (DRGs) based on the logic of *DRGs: Diagnostic-Related Groups Definitions Manual.*

GROUP HEALTH INSURANCE: Health insurance provided to members of a group of persons, as employees of one or more employers or members of associations or labor unions. The term is usually used to distinguish this type of health insurance from individual health insurance. One master contract is written to cover the group.

GROUP HEALTH INSURANCE POLICY: Health insurance provided to members of a group of persons, as employees of one or more employers or members of associations or labor unions. The term is usually used to distinguish this type of health insurance from individual health insurance. One master contract is written to cover the group. Characteristics include: (a) benefits schedule; (b) eligible expenses; (c) coordination of medical benefits; (d) exclusions; and (e) primary plan.

GROUP INSURANCE: Insurance protecting a group of persons, usually employees of the same firm. It is based on the principle that the selection process may be applied directly to groups of people, as well as to individuals. If certain general requirements are met, the insurance principles can be applied to groups of nonselected persons. As a rule, the group must have been formed for a purpose other than to obtain insurance; the members must either all be insured or, if premiums are paid in part by the individuals, at least 75% must become insured; the amount of insurance for each member of the group must be determined by a formula precluding individual selection or choice by the individuals insured.

GROUP INSURANCE, MASTER CONTRACT: An insurance agreement between the employer (or any principal recognized by the laws of the various states as eligible to effect a group insurance contract) and the insurance company. This is the agreement that insures the designated employees or group members.

GROUP MODEL: A managed care organization that contracts with providers of an existing medical group.

GROUP MODEL HMO: (a) An HMO model in which the HMO contracts with one or more medical groups to provide services to members. As with the staff model, all services except hospital care are generally provided under one-roof. Both group and staff models are known collectively as prepaid group practice plans. (b) (Also direct service plan, group practice prepayment plan; prepaid health care): A plan which provides health services to persons covered by a prepayment program through a group of physicians usually working in a group clinic or center. See HMO, PPO, and Managed Care.

GROUP NETWORK HMO: An HMO that contracts with one or more independent group practice to provide services to its members in one or more locations.

GROUP PRACTICE: A group of persons licensed to practice medicine in the state, that as their principal professional activity, and as a group responsibility, engage or undertake to engage in the coordinated practice of their profession primarily in one or more group practice facilities, and who (in their connection) share common overhead expenses (if and to the extent such expenses are paid by members of the group), medical and other records, and substantial portions of the equipment and the professional, technical, and administrative staffs.

GROUP PRACTICE HMO: HMO with a restricted number of medical providers that are usually employed exclusively by the health insurance or managed care company.

GROUP PRACTICE WITHOUT WALLS (GPWW): A legal entity formed by a network of physicians who maintain their individual practices.

GROUP SPONSOR: One that sponsors a cohort for health insurance benefits that is usually an employer or fraternal organization.

GROUP UNDERWRITING: Automatic issuance of predetermined amounts of life or health insurance to all members of a group.

GUARANTEED INSURABILITY: Health and disability insurance contract options that permit the purchase of additional proscribed amounts without evidence of insurability.

GUARANTEED ISSUE: The requirement that each insurer and health plan accept everyone who applies for coverage and guarantee the renewal of that coverage as long as the applicant pays the premium.

GUARANTEED ISSUE RIGHTS (ALSO CALLED *MEDIGAP PROTECTIONS*): Medical rights in certain situations when insurance companies are required by law to sell or offer a Medigap policy. In these situations, an insurance company cannot deny insurance coverage or place conditions or charge more for a policy because of past or present health problems.

GUARANTEED RENEWABLE: The requirement that each insurer and health plan continue to renew health policies purchased by individuals as long as the person continues to pay the premium for the policy.

GUARANTY FUND: A state-required pool of funds covering benefits of insolvent insurers and designed to protect providers and consumers.

GUIDELINES: May be referred to as practice parameters, clinical practice guidelines, or protocols. These are statements by authoritative bodies as to the procedures appropriate for the physician to employ in making a diagnosis and treating it. The goal of guidelines is to change practice styles, reduce inappropriate and unnecessary care, and cut costs. See Care Maps.

GUIDELINES, PRACTICE PARAMETERS, AND PRACTICE PATTERNS: Rules and regulations intended to set a standard of practice and treatment for health care providers.

GYNECOLOGY: Branch of medicine dealing with the female reproductive tract.

H

HAIR ANALYSIS (HAIR ELEMENT ANALYSIS, HAIR MINERAL ANALYSIS, HAIR-SHAFT ANALYSIS): Diagnostic technique that involves laboratory analysis of a sample of hair. It allegedly can be a useful guide to determining bodily well-being.

HANDICAPPED: As defined by §504 of the Rehabilitation Act of 1973, any person who has a physical or mental impairment that substantially limits one or more major life activities, has a record of such impairment, or is regarded as having such an impairment.

HANDICAPPED DEPENDENT: Unmarried dependent children who are not capable of self-support.

HAZARD: A specific insurance or risk management situation that introduces or increases the probability of a loss-incurring event, as contrasted with the broader term for the cause of possible loss, peril. For example, accident, sickness, fire, flood, burglary, and explosion are perils. Slippery floors, unsanitary conditions, shingle roofs, congested traffic, unguarded premises, and uninspected boilers are hazards. See Perils.

HAZARD, MORAL: See Moral Hazard.

HCFA: Health Care Financing Administration (older term; now CMS).

HCFA-1450: The Health Care Finance Administration's (older term, now CMS) name for the institutional uniform claim form, or UB-92. See EDI Section.

HCFA 1500: The Health Care Finance Administration's (older term, now CMS) standard form for submitting physician service claims to third-party (insurance) companies.

HCFA COMMON PROCEDURE CODING SYSTEM (HCPCS): A Medicare coding system based on the American Medical Association's *Current Procedural Terminology* (CPT) expanded to accommodate additional services covered by Medicare. See Coding, *Current Procedural Terminology*, ICD-9, and CMS.

HEAD OF HOUSEHOLD: For income tax purposes, an unmarried person who has dependent children or other dependents (related by blood or marriage) who can be claimed as exemptions. Tax rates for heads of households are generally lower than for single taxpayers.

HEALTH: The state of complete physical, mental, and social well-being and not merely the absence of disease or infirmity. It is recognized, however, that health has many dimensions (anatomical, physiological, and mental) and is largely culturally defined. The relative importance of various disabilities will differ depending upon the cultural milieu and the role of the affected individual in that culture. Most attempts at measurement have been assessed in terms of morbidity and mortality.

HEALTH AND ACCIDENT UNDERWRITERS CONFERENCE: Association of Life Insurance Companies now merged into Health Insurance Association of America (HIAA) that conducted research in rating accident and health risks.

HEALTH CARE AUTHORITY (HCA): State agencies that manage various state-sponsored health plans, including the Basic Health Plan and programs for public employees and retirees.

HEALTH CARE CLEARINGHOUSE: A public or private entity that does either of the following, including but not limited to, billing services, repricing companies, community health management information systems or community health information systems, and value-added networks, and switches and performs these functions: (a) processes or facilitates the processing of information received from another entity in a nonstandard format or containing nonstandard data content into standard data elements or a standard transaction; and (b) receives a standard transaction from another entity and processes or facilitates the processing of information into nonstandard format or nonstandard data content for a receiving entity.

HEALTH CARE CODE MAINTENANCE COMMITTEE: An organization administered by the Blue Cross/Blue Shield Association that is responsible for maintaining certain coding schemes used in the X12 transactions and elsewhere. These include the Claim Adjustment Reason Codes, the Claim Status Category Codes, and the Claim Status Codes.

HEALTH CARE FINANCING ADMINISTRATION (HCFA): The former agency within the Department of Health and Human Services that administered federal health financing and related regulatory programs, principally the Medicare, Medicaid, and Peer Review Organization. See Centers for Medicaid and Medicare Services (CMS).

HEALTH CARE POWER OF ATTORNEY: Legal instrument of authority whereby one person makes a medical decision for another person (patient) who is permanently or temporarily incapacitated. Usually couples with a living will.

HEALTH CARE PREPAYMENT PLAN (HCPP): (1) Plans that receive payment for their reasonable costs of providing Medicare Part B services to Medicare enrollees. See Cost Contract and Risk Contract. (2) A health plan with a Medicare cost contract to provide only Medicare Part B benefits. Some administrative requirements for these plans are less stringent than those of risk contracts or other cost contracts. See Medicare Cost Contract and Medicare Risk Contract.

HEALTH CARE PROVIDER: An individual or institution that provides medical services (e.g., a physician, hospital, laboratory). This term should not be confused with an insurance company that provides insurance. See Doctor, Physician, and Nurse.

HEALTH CARE PROVIDER TAXONOMY CODES: An administrative code set that classifies health care providers by type and area of specialization. The code set will be used in certain adopted transactions.

HEALTH CARE QUALITY IMPROVEMENT ACT (HCQIA): This federal act, passed in 1996, provides liability protection for physicians and hospitals that participate in peer review and established a national clearinghouse to collect physician disciplinary and malpractice information.

HEALTH CARE QUALITY IMPROVEMENT INITIATIVE (HCQII): Designed by the Health Care Financing Administration to reshape the approach to improve the quality of care delivered to Medicare enrollees. See Quality Improvement.

HEALTH CERTIFICATE: In life insurance, a signed statement declaring that the health of the insured is not impaired. This must be filed with a request for reinstatement of a lapsed policy. See CON.

HEALTH FACILITY PLANNING AREA (HFPA): A geographic area that is a subdivision of a health service area (Defined by the California only). Office of Statewide Health Planning and Development (OSHPD).

HEALTH AND HUMAN SERVICES (HHS): The Department of Health and Human Services that is responsible for health-related programs and issues. Formerly, it was the Department of Health, Education, and Welfare. The Office of Health Maintenance Organizations (OHMO) is part of HHS and detailed information on most companies is available there through the Freedom of Information Act (FIA).

HEALTH IMPACT ASSESSMENT: Any combination of procedures or methods by which a proposed policy or program may be judged as to the effect(s) it may have on the health of a population.

HEALTH INDICATOR: A measure that reflects, or indicates, the state of health of persons in a defined population (e.g., the infant mortality rate).

HEALTH INDIVIDUAL RETIREMENT ACCOUNTS (IRAs): Proposed tax-preferred plans to encourage saving for future medical expenses. Funds in health IRAs could be later cashed out for medical expenses.

HEALTH INFORMATION SYSTEM: A combination of health statistics from various sources, used to derive information about health status, health care, provision and use of services, and impact on health.

HEALTH INSURANCE: Coverage that provides for the payments of benefits as a result of sickness or injury. Includes insurance for losses from accident, medical expense, disability, or accidental death and dismemberment.

HEALTH INSURANCE ASSOCIATION OF AMERICA (HIAA): An inter-company organization of health insurers headquartered in Washington, DC.

HEALTH INSURANCE BENEFITS: In health insurance, policy benefits payable as a result of disability from covered sickness or accident. Sickness coverage is rarely written separately, unless the insured also carries an amount of accident insurance with the same company.

HEALTH INSURANCE, CLASSIFICATIONS: (a) Cancelable; (b) optionally renewable; (c) franchise; (d) industrial; (e) group; (f) limited; (g) guaranteed renewable; and (h) noncancelable and guaranteed renewable. Health policies that are renewable at the option of the insured, as contrasted with guaranteed renewable policies, are often referred to as commercial policies.

HEALTH INSURANCE FUTURES: One-year futures contract (traded on the CBOT [Chicago Board of Trade]) that allows health insurance companies and self-insurers to hedge possible losses.

HEALTH INSURANCE INSTITUTE: The public relations arm of the Health Insurance Association of America. It provides for a flow of information from health insurers to the public and from the public to the insurers.

HEALTH INSURANCE ORGANIZATIONS (HIOs): Public or private entities that contract on a prepaid capitated risk basis to provide a comprehensive set of services to Medicaid enrollees.

HEALTH INSURANCE PORTABILITY AND ACCOUNTABILITY ACT OF 1996 (HIPAA): Sometimes referred to as the Kennedy-Kassebaum bill, this legislation sets a precedent for Federal involvement in insurance regulation. It sets minimum standards for regulation of the small group insurance market and for a set group in the individual insurance market in the area of portability and availability of health insurance. As a result of this law, hospitals, doctors, and insurance companies are now required to share patient medical records and personal information on a wider basis. This wide-based sharing of medical records has led to privacy rules, greater computerization of records, and consumer concerns about confidentiality.

HEALTH INSURANCE PURCHASING COOPERATIVE (HIPC): A group of several employers pooled together to increase their bargaining power and thereby ensuring the most cost effective insurance rates. A local board created under managed competition to enroll individuals, collect and distribute premiums, and enforce the rules that manage the competition.

HEALTH INSURANCE QUALITY AWARD: An annual award sponsored by the International Association of Health Underwriters and the National Association of Life Underwriters for equaling or exceeding certain favorable percentages of persistency of health insurance policies written by agents.

HEALTH-LEVEL SEVEN (HL7): A data interchange protocol for health care computer applications that simplifies the ability of different vendor-supplied information systems to interconnect. Although not a software program in itself, HL7 requires that each health care software vendor program HL7 interfaces for its products. See HIPAA and EDI.

HEALTH MAINTENANCE ORGANIZATION (HMO): A legal corporation that offers health insurance and medical care. HMOs typically offer a range of health care services at a fixed price (see capitation). Types of HMOs: (a) Staff Model—Organization owns its clinics and employs its docs; (b) Group Model—Contract with medical groups for services; (c) IPA Model—Contract with an Independent Physician Association (IPA); (d) Direct Contract Model—Contracts directly with individual physicians; and (e) Mixed Model—Members get options ranging from staff to IPA models.

HEALTH OUTCOMES INSTITUTE (HOI): A nonprofit organization dedicated to promoting the development of managed care through education, collection of data, and outcomes research.

HEALTH PLAN: A generic term to refer to a specific benefit package offered by an insurer. Also used to pertain to the insurer (e.g., "I signed up for the Golden Rule health plan today.").

HEALTH PLAN EMPLOYER DATA AND INFORMATION SET (HEDIS): A set of standardized performance measures designed to ensure that purchasers and consumers have the information they need to reliably compare the performance of managed health care plans. The performance measures in HEDIS are related to many significant public health issues such as cancer, heart disease, smoking, asthma, and diabetes. HEDIS also includes a standardized survey of consumers' experiences that evaluates plan performance in areas such as customer service, access to care, and claims possessing. HEDIS is sponsored, supported, and maintained by the National Committee for Quality Assurance. There are two parts to HEDIS: Effectiveness of Care Measures (ECM) and the Consumer Assessment of Health Plan Study (CAHPS).

HEALTH PLAN FLEXIBLE SPENDING ACCOUNT (HPFSA): A fund to which employees contribute pretax money to pay for health insurance premiums or unreimbursed medical costs. Exclusions exists on a use-it or lose-it basis.

HEALTH PLAN PARTICIPATION: The decision of a potential concierge medical practice to be a preferred provider or disenroll in health plans opting for retainer medicine.

HEALTH PLAN PURCHASING COOPERATIVE (HPPC): A health insurance purchasing entity advanced by some health system reform proposals to enroll individuals, collect premiums, purchase enrollees' insurance from participating health plans, and enforce the rules that manage health plan competition.

HEALTH POLICY: An insurance policy that indemnifies for loss (income or expenses) resulting from bodily injury or sickness.

HEALTH PROFESSIONAL SHORTAGE AREA (HPSA): (1) An urban or rural geographic area, a population group, or a public or nonprofit private medical facility that the Secretary of Health and Human Services determines to be served by too few health professionals. Physicians who provide services in HPSAs qualify for the Medicare bonus payment. Replaces Health Manpower Shortage Area. (2) Federally designated areas within a state that have fewer than a specified number of physicians per unit of population.

HEALTH PROFILE: Single instrument measuring different aspects of quality of life (QOL); individual score may be aggregated into an index.

HEALTH PROMOTION: Health promotion is the science and art of helping people change their lifestyle to move toward a state of optimal health. Optimal health is defined as a balance of physical, emotional, social, spiritual, and intellectual health.

HEALTH REIMBURSEMENT ARRANGEMENTS (HRA): A type of health insurance plan that reimburses employees for qualified medical expenses. These accounts consist of funds set aside by employers to reimburse employees for qualified medical expenses, just as an insurance plan will reimburse covered individuals for the cost of services incurred. HRAs provide first-dollar medical coverage until funds are exhausted. Under a health reimbursement account, the employer provides funds, not the employee. All unused funds are rolled over at the end of the year. Former employees, including retirees, can have continued access to unused reimbursement amounts. Health reimbursement accounts remain with the originating employer and do not follow an employee to new employment.

HEALTH RISK BEHAVIORS: Behaviors, such as smoking, lack of exercise, and overeating, that increase the potential for an individual to experience disease or injury. See Risk and Perils.

HEALTH RISK FACTORS: In addition to health risk behaviors, risk factors include genetic factors, such as a family history of heart disease, or environmental factors, such as living in a polluted area. See Perils and Risk.

HEALTH SAVINGS ACCOUNT: Tax-free accounts that are paired with a variety of high-deductible health insurance plans (traditional, managed care, HMO, PPO, etc.) that empower patients to have greater control over their health care and treatment decisions. See MSA and FSA.

HEALTH SERVICE AGREEMENT: The detailed procedure and benefit description given to each enrolled employer.

HEALTH SERVICE AREA (HSA): A geographic area consisting of one or more contiguous counties designated by the United States Department of Health and Human Services for health planning on a regional basis.

HEALTH SERVICES RESEARCH: Health services research is the study of the scientific basis and management of health services and their effect on access, quality, and cost of health care.

HEALTH STATEMENT: A form that contains information about a prospective member's health status. These forms are completed by prospective members and reviewed by underwriting to decide if the person will be allowed to enroll based on an assessment of risk.

HEALTH STATUS: An overall evaluation of an individual's degree of wellness or illness with a number of indicators, including quality of life and functionality. See Illness, Disease, and Injury.

HEALTH STATUS INDEX: A weighting scheme for calculating the total number of quality adjusted life years.

HEALTH SYSTEMS AGENCY (HSA): A health agency created under the National Health Planning and Resources Development Act of 1974. HSAs were usually nonprofit private organizations and served defined health service areas as designated by the states.

HEARING: A procedure that gives a dissatisfied claimant an opportunity to present reasons for the dissatisfaction and to receive a new determination based on the record developed at the hearing.

HEARING SERVICES: Routine hearing exams, as well as other medically necessary tests and treatments related to auditory problems.

HEDIS MEASURES FROM ENCOUNTER DATA: Measures from encounter data as opposed to having the plans generate HEDIS measures. See HEDIS.

HEMATOLOGY/ONCOLOGY: Branch of medicine dealing with the blood and blood forming tissues and their diagnosis and treatment.

HERBALISM (MEDICAL HERBALISM): Ancient approach to healing characterized by using plants, or substances derived from plants, to treat a range of illnesses or to improve the functioning of bodily systems.

HERBOLOGY: Purported science and art of using plants for healing. See Alternative Healthcare.

HHS: The Department of Health and Human Services that is responsible for health-related programs and issues. Formerly, the Department of Health, Education, and Welfare (HEW). The Office of Health Maintenance Organizations (OHMO) is part of HHS and detailed information on most companies is available there through the Freedom of Information Act (FIA).

HIERARCHICAL COEXISTING CONDITIONS MODEL (HCC): A risk-adjusted model that groups beneficiaries based on their diagnoses.

HIGH-PRESSURE SELLING: In insurance sales, encouraging the buyer to purchase any insurance without full consideration of needs for insurance and his or her ability to continue payments on the policy or using tactics that embarrass or deceive people into buying against their wishes.

HIGH-RISK GROUP: A group in the community with an elevated risk of disease. See Risk and Rating.

HIGH-RISK POOL FOR THE MEDICALLY UNINSURED: State health plans that provide insurance for the medically uninsured. See Risk and Rating.

HILL-BURTON: Coined from the names of the principal sponsors of the Public Law 79-725 (the Hospital Survey and Construction Act of 1946). This program provided Federal support for the construction and modernization of hospitals and other health facilities. Hospitals that receive Hill-Burton funds incur an obligation to provide a certain amount of charity care.

HIO (HEALTH INSURANCE ORGANIZATION): An entity that contracts on a prepaid, capitated risk basis to provide comprehensive health services to recipients.

HIPAA DATA DICTIONARY OR HIPAA DD: A data dictionary that defines and cross-references the contents of all X12 transactions included in the HIPAA mandate. It is maintained by X12N/TG3.

HIQA: Health Insurance Quality Award granted annually by the International Association of Health Underwriters or the National Association of Life Underwriters for high persistency of health insurance policies written by agents. See Quality Improvement and HEDIS.

HISTORICAL MARKET PAYER: Economic payment method that determines medical charges based on some combination of traditional, comparable, and marketplace charges.

HISTORIC MARKET APPROACH: See UCR charges and Historical Market Payer.

HIV/AIDS: Disability Form 4814 for Social Security recognizes and defines 41 opportunistic infections affecting individuals living with HIV/AIDS, in the Blue Book's "Listing Level of Impairment." A disabling condition is recognized if it is one of the 41 opportunistic infections listed on SSA Form 4814. If an individual disabled by HIV/AIDS does not qualify under "Listing Level of Impairments" in the 4814, they may still qualify under Social Security's definition of disability if medical records demonstrate they are disabled as a result of repeated manifestations. The repeated manifestations (symptoms of the condition) must be so disabling that the individual is unable to perform any work for which he or she is reasonably educated, and the disabling condition will continue for at least 1 year.

HMO ACT OF 1973: Federal legislation requiring all employers with traditional health insurance benefits to offer HMO benefits.

HMO REGULATORY ACT: A state agency empowered to grant or rescind an HMO's authority to transact business, to license its solicitors, and to regulate its affairs in the best interest of the consuming public. In nearly all states, these powers are vested in insurance departments. See PPO and IPA.

HOLDBACK: An amount, usually a set fee or percentage of billed charges, kept by the preferred provider organization or third-party administrator to cover losses. See With-hold.

HOLD HARMLESS CLAUSE: A clause frequently found in managed care contracts whereby the HMO and the physician hold each other not liable for malpractice or corporate malfeasance if either of the parties is found to be liable. Many insurance carriers exclude this type of liability from coverage. It may also refer to language that prohibits the provider from billing patients if their managed care company becomes insolvent. State and federal regulations may require this language. See Indemnification.

HOLISTIC HEALTH: Health emphasizing the whole person.

HOLISTIC MEDICINE: Care and treatment of every aspect of the entire whole person.

HOME: Location, other than a hospital or other facility, where the patient receives care in a private residence.

HOME BOUND: Normally unable to leave home. Leaving home takes considerable and taxing effort. A person may leave home for medical treatment or short, infrequent absences for nonmedical reasons, such as a trip to the barber or to attend religious services. See Hospice. See Long-Term Care and ADLs.

HOME AND COMMUNITY-BASED SERVICE WAIVER: Medicaid coverage exception allowing for medical care rendered in the home setting. Typically for health, physically, or mentally disabled adults.

HOME HEALTH AGENCY: A program or facility that is lawfully authorized and certified to provide health care services in the home. See Hospice and ADLs.

HOME HEALTH CARE: Full range of medical and other health-related services, such as physical therapy, nursing, wound care management, counseling, and social services that are delivered in the home of a patient, by a provider.

HOME INFUSION THERAPY: In-home administration of nutrients, antibiotics, or other drugs and fluids intravenously or through a feeding tube.

HOME MEDICAL EQUIPMENT: Item that meets the following criteria: (a) it is durable enough to withstand repeated use; (b) it is primarily and customarily manufactured to serve a medical purpose; and (c) it is not useful in the absence of illness or injury. Examples include wheelchairs, walkers, and crutches. See DME.

HOMEOPATHY: Medicine form that emphasizes minute quantities of drugs to produce the same symptoms and fight disease.

HOME PATIENTS: Able individuals, who have their own dialysis equipment at home, and after proper training, perform their own dialysis treatment alone or with the assistance of a helper.

HOME STYLE BIRTHING: A nontraditional birthing unit, in which labor, delivery, and recovery, as well as nursery services, are provided in a single room for each delivery.

HOMOGENOUS: The same or similar insurable risk.

HOMOGENOUS EXPOSURES: A similar group or cohort of people with the same expectations of health care loss, as in a group of diabetic patents.

HORIZONTAL ANALYSIS: Economic look at the percentage changes in a health care organization's line items from one year to the next.

HORIZONTAL INTEGRATION: Merging of two or more firms at the same level of production in some formal, legal relationship. In hospital networks, this may refer to the grouping of several hospitals, the grouping of outpatient clinics with the hospital, or a geographic network of various health care services. Integrated systems seek to integrate both vertically with some organization and horizontally with others. See Vertical Integration.

HOSPICE: A facility or program which provides palliative and supportive care for terminally ill patients and their families, either directly or on a consulting basis with the patient's physician or another community agency. The whole family is considered the unit of care, and care extends through their period of mourning. See LTC and ADL.

HOSPICE CARE: Medical or mental healthcare rendered in a hospice setting. Care provided for the purpose of easing the physical and emotional suffering of a sick individual, rather than of curing the illness. This care is available at a hospice facility or at the individual's home. See Hospice.

HOSPICE SERVICES: Services to provide care to the terminally ill and their families.

HOSPITAL: Any institution duly licensed, certified, and operated as a hospital. In no event shall the term hospital include a convalescent facility, nursing home, or any institution or part thereof which is used principally as a convalescence facility, rest facility, nursing facility, or facility for the aged. An institution for the care and treatment of ill, injured, infirm, mentally abnormal, or deformed persons, with organized facilities for diagnosis and surgery and providing 24-hr nursing service and medical supervision. In some hospital policies, institutions for the treatment of mentally ill persons are expressly excluded from the definition of hospital. See EHO and ASC.

HOSPITAL AFFILIATION: A contractual agreement between an HMO and one or more hospitals whereby the hospital provides the inpatient benefits offered by the HMO.

HOSPITAL ALLIANCES: Groups of hospitals joined together to share services and group purchasing programs to reduce costs. May also refer to a spectrum of contracts, agreements, or handshake arrangements for hospitals to work together in developing programs, serving covered lives, or contracting with payers or health plans. See also Network, Integrated Delivery System, PHO, and Provider Health Plan.

HOSPITAL ASSUMPTIONS: These include differentials between hospital labor and nonlabor indices compared with general economy labor and nonlabor indices; rates of admission incidence; the trend toward treating less complicated cases in outpatient settings; and continued improvement in diagnosis-related groups coding.

HOSPITAL AUDIT COMPANIES: Retrospective audit providers that typically achieve a 14–20% savings of billed claims.

HOSPITAL BENEFITS: Benefits payable when an insured is hospitalized. Health insurance benefits payable for charges incurred while the insured is confined to, or treated in, a hospital, as defined in the policy.

HOSPITAL CONFINEMENT INSURANCE: Pays a fixed dollar amount for each day the insured is confined to a hospital.

HOSPITAL DAY: A term to describe any 24 hr period commencing at 12:00 a.m., or 12:00 p.m., whichever is used by a hospital to determine a hospital day, during which a patient receives hospital services at the hospital.

HOSPITAL DAYS (PER 1,000): A measurement of the number of days of hospital care HMO members use in a year. It is calculated as follows: Total number of days spent in a hospital by members divided by total members. This information is available through Department of Health and Human Services, Office of Health Maintenance Organizations, and a variety of sources.

HOSPITAL DBA NAME: The name under which the hospital is doing business as, which may be different from its legal name.

HOSPITAL EXPENSE INSURANCE: Basic medical expense insurance that provides benefits subject to a specified daily maximum for hospital room and board charges, plus lab, ambulance, and operating room costs. Also referred to as hospitalization insurance or basic hospital insurance.

HOSPITAL INCOME INSURANCE: A form of insurance that provides a stated weekly or monthly payment while the insured is hospitalized, regardless of expenses incurred and regardless of whether or not other insurance is in force. The insured can use the weekly or monthly benefit as he chooses, for hospital or other expenses.

HOSPITAL INDEMNITIES: In health insurance, additional benefits provided under the terms of a policy if the insured is confined in a hospital.

HOSPITAL INPATIENT PROSPECTIVE PAYMENT SYSTEM (PPS): Medicare's method of paying acute care hospitals for inpatient care. Prospective per case payment rates are set at a level intended to cover operating costs for treating a typical inpatient in a given diagnosis-related group (DRG). Payments for each hospital are adjusted for wages, teaching activity, care to the poor, and other factors. Hospitals may also receive additional payments to cover extra costs associated with atypical patients (outliers) in each DRG. Capital costs, originally excluded from PPS, are being phased into the system. By FY 2001, capital payments were made on almost fully prospective, per case basis. Prospective payment systems were also developed for Medicare payments for home health services, outpatient hospital services, skilled-nursing facilities, and rehabilitation facilities.

HOSPITAL INPUT PRICE INDEX: An alternative name for hospital market basket.

HOSPITAL INSURANCE (HI): The part of the Medicare program that covers the cost of hospital and related posthospital services. Eligibility is normally based on prior payment of payroll taxes. Beneficiaries are responsible for an initial deductible per spell of illness and copayments for some services. Also called Part A coverage or benefits.

HOSPITALIST: A hospital-based physician stationed primarily in the hospital to handle all admissions from a specific practice or group. A doctor responsible for treatments and processes during a patient's hospital stay. See Doctor.

HOSPITALIZATION POLICY: A limited health insurance policy that provides payment only in the event hospital expenses are incurred. If such a policy pays first-dollar benefits but has relatively low limits, it is called a basic hospitalization policy or plan.

HOSPITAL LIABILITY INSURANCE: Insurance that covers the following incidents or perils in a hospital, or similar health care facility: (a) Malpractice or liability errors or mistake; (b) patient to patient injuries; (c) ambulance injury; (d) food or other item injury; and (e) costs to defend the hospital in a lawsuit, even if baseless.

HOSPITAL MARKET BASKET: The hospital market basket index is one component Medicare relies upon to set payment levels for various hospital services. The market basket reflects the broad array of operating and capital costs, categorized for measurement purposes that hospitals incur to provide medical care. The market basket index has been periodically reviewed and the relative cost measures, or weights, recalibrated so that changes in costs are appropriately reflected in Medicare payment adjustments.

HOSPITAL MISCELLANEOUS BENEFITS: Under a health insurance plan, benefits payable up to a stated maximum for reimbursement of expenses incurred during a period of hospital confinement for such services as x-ray examination, laboratory service, drugs, anesthesia, ambulance service, oxygen, and use of the operating room, etc.

HOSPITAL OUTSHOPPING: The bypassing of local hospitals by patients in favor of other hospitals (usually because the patients believe the quality of care is better in the other hospital).

HOSPITAL ROOM BENEFITS: In health insurance, benefits payable up to a specified daily maximum for the purpose of paying hospital room and board charges.

HOSPITAL SURGICAL EXPENSE INSURANCE: Medical expense health insurance that combines basic hospital coverage and basic surgical coverage into one policy.

HOUSE CONFINEMENT: A provision in some health insurance contracts that requires an insured to be confined to the house to be eligible for benefits. This provision is most commonly found in policies providing loss of income benefits.

HOUSE CONFINEMENT CLAUSE: A health insurance optional provision requiring that the disabled insured is confined to a house to be eligible for benefits. House is expanded to include a hospital, sanitarium, visit to a hospital or office of a physician, or certain activities made at the direction of a doctor for therapeutic purposes. See House Confinement.

HUMAN CAPITAL METHOD: Calculation of health insurance benefits in terms of reduced treatment costs and reduced productivity. May now be largely discredited.

HUMAN DEPRECIATION CONCEPT: The concept that people, like machines, wear out and die, thus needing health and life insurance.

HUNTER DISABILITY TABLES: Tables that show the probability of total and permanent disability.

HURDLE RATE: The interest rate or cost of capital.

HYDROTHERAPY: (1) Hydrotherapeutics—Scientific external use of water to treat certain diseases (e.g., hot baths to relieve pain). (2) Water therapy—A variety of methods whose categories are: (a) external hydrotherapies (e.g., whirlpool baths); and (b) internal hydrotherapy (e.g., colonic irrigation). Some alternativists depict water as a universal remedy provided by nature.

HYPNOTHERAPY: The induction of a sleeplike state to treat chronic pain or to facilitate changes in behavior or disposition.

I

IBNR (INCURRED BUT NOT REPORTED): Potential accounting liabilities resulting from medical services not currently reported. Usually occurs in a capitated or prospective health insurance payment system. See Accounts Receivable and Bad Debt Expense.

ICD: International Classification of Diseases of the United States Department of Health and Human Services.

IC/DD (ICF/DD): intermediate care/developmentally disabled.

ICF: Intermediate care facility (ICF) is the lower of two levels of long-term care.

ICU/CCU: Intensive Care Unit/Coronary Care Unit. The daily hospital services cost centers that provide nursing care of the most concentrated and exhaustive nature. This unit is staffed with specially trained nursing personnel and contains monitoring and specialized support equipment for patients who (because of shock, trauma, or threatening conditions) require intensified, comprehensive, observation and care. See Hospitalist and Intensivist.

IDENTIFICATION OF BENEFITS: A provisional list of health insurance benefits that are reimbursed, usually up to a maximum amount.

IDENTIFICATION (ID) CARD: A card given to each person covered under a health plan that identifies an insured as being eligible for benefits.

IDENTIFICATION CLAUSE: A clause, formerly included in some health insurance policies that provided that if the insured is physically unable to communicate with relatives and friends, the company will notify them and pay necessary expenses (up to a specified amount) to put the insured in their care. See Policy and Contract.

IDS (INTEGRATED DELIVERY SYSTEM): A network of hospitals, physicians, and other medical services, along with an HMO or insurance plan, formed to cost-effectively provide a population with a full continuum of care (i.e., from prevention through check-ups, tests, surgery, rehabilitation, long-term, and home care) that is accountable for costs, quality of care, and customer satisfaction. See IPA and HMO.

ILLEGAL HOLDING OF PREMIUMS: In insurance, an agent's handling of collected premium other than as specified by state laws. Consequently, the agent may be accused of embezzlement or of fraudulently converting funds for personal use. See Fraud and Abuse.

ILLEGAL OCCUPATION PROVISION: An optional health insurance provision that states that if the insured is injured while engaging in an illegal occupation, the insurance company is not obligated to pay the claim. See Fraud and Abuse.

ILLNESS FREQUENCY RATE: The number of illnesses suffered by employees per 1,000,000 employee-hours of work on an annual basis.

ILLNESS OR INJURY: Any bodily disorder, bodily injury, disease, or mental health condition, including pregnancy and complications of pregnancy.

ILLNESS SEVERITY RATE: The number of days lost as a result of disabling illnesses or death per 1,000 employee-hours, with 6,000 days charged for death.

IMMEDIATE (NON-EMERGENCY) CARE: Medical intervention on a non-emergency basis but needed for the benefit of the patient. See Urgent Care.

IMMEDIATE FAMILY MEMBER: Child, spouse, or parent.

IMMUNIZATION: Injection with a specific antigen to promote antibody formation, to create immunity to a disease, or to make a person less susceptible to a contagious disease.

IMPACT EVALUATION: Impact evaluation focuses on the long-range results of an insurance or managed care program and changes or improvements in health status as a result. Impact evaluations are rarely possible because they are frequently costly, involve extended commitment, and may depend upon other strategies in addition to communication. Also, the results often cannot be directly related to the effects of an activity or program because of other (external) influences on the target audience that will occur over time.

IMPACT PROGRAM: A medical cost management program that shifts medical intervention to the most efficient but least expensive venue.

IMPAIRED CAPITAL: When insurance company liabilities and claims consume a company's surplus, the capital is impaired. Suspension of the right to do business normally follows.

IMPAIRED RISK: A person who has an unfavorable health condition or is exposed to a dangerous occupational hazard that makes them a substandard insurance risk. A risk that is substandard, below average, or less desirable.

IMPAIRMENT: An injury, physical ailment, condition, or disability that negatively affects a person's insurance risk rating and possibly insurability. See Disability and ADLs.

IMPAIRMENT OF CAPITAL: A condition to which the surplus account of an insurance stock company has been exhausted, so that it must invade the capital account to meet liabilities.

IMPAIRMENT RIDER: A rider attached to a health insurance contract that waives the insurance company's liability for all future claims on a preexisting condition.

IMPLEMENTATION SPECIFICATION: Specific instructions for implementing a HIPAA standard.

IMPLIED AUTHORITY: Authority that, while not specifically granted to the agent in the agency agreement, the agent can assume he or she has through common sense. Authority that is apparently necessary for an agent's ability to carry out day-to-day or routine responsibilities. See Agent and Agency Risk.

IMPLIED CONSENT: In the selling situation, the concept that unless a prospect explicitly disagrees with what is presented or said, his or her agreement may be assumed.

IMPLIED CONTRACT: A legally binding contractual agreement in which the parties speak by their actions rather than by their oral or written words.

An insurance contract is not an implied contract because every condition is included in the policy.

IMPLIED TRUST: A trust raised or created by implication of law; a trust implied or presumed from circumstances.

IMPROVEMENT PLAN: A plan for measuring health care processes for outcome improvement. Medical providers and the insurance network usually develop the plan.

INACTIVE: A health or life insurance plan that has been cancelled, no longer in force or effective.

INAPPROPRIATE UTILIZATION: Utilization of services that are in excess of a beneficiary's medical needs and condition (over utilization) or receiving a capitated Medicare payment and failing to provide services to meet a beneficiary's medical needs and condition (underutilization or misutilization with wrong services). See Fraud and Abuse and Quality Improvement.

IN-AREA EMERGENCY SERVICE: The use of a local, rather than remote hospital or health care facility, in the case of a medical emergency.

IN-BEFORE SERVICE: Medical care rendered prior to the date of health plan membership.

INCENTIVE: Economic and financial motivators to health care entities and medical providers to deliver cost-effective and appropriate care.

INCEPTION DATE: Date that a health care insurance policy becomes effective.

INCHOATE: Not yet completed. A health insurance contract is inchoate until executed by all parties.

INCIDENCE: The number of cases of disease, infection, or some other event having their onset during a prescribed period of time in relation to the unit of population in which they occur. Incidence measures morbidity or other events as they happen over a period of time. Examples include the number of accidents occurring in a manufacturing plant during a year in relation to the number of employees in the plant or the number of cases of mumps occurring in a school during a month in relation to the number of pupils enrolled in the school. It usually refers only to the number of new cases, particularly of chronic diseases. Hospitals also track certain risk management or quality problems with a system called incidence reporting.

INCIDENCE RATE: The mathematical statistics of a medical or health care occurrence. See Incidence.

INCIDENTAL MALPRACTICE: Medical negligence that is the responsibility of a person or organization not in the medical profession.

INCIDENTAL PROCEDURE: Procedures that are a part of another procedure and not allowed as a separately reimbursable benefit.

INCIDENTS OF OWNERSHIP: The right to exercise any of the privileges in the insurance policy (change beneficiary, withdraw cash values, make loans on the policy, make assignment, etc.).

INCOME: The money a person or company has coming in from any source. Income is made up of the amount received from both personal and investment earnings, as well as realized capital gains.

INCOME-EARNING ABILITY: The ability of an individual to earn an income or wage. The three major threats to income-earning ability are death, disability, and old age, all of which may be protected against by life and health insurance.

INCOME, GROSS: See Before-Tax Earnings.

INCOME LOSS FROM HEALTH CARE OPERATIONS: Gross patient service revenue plus other operating revenue minus deductions from revenue and total health care expenses. See Revenues.

INCOME STATEMENT: One of four major kinds of financial statements used by businesses. It is primarily a flow report that lists a company's income or revenues and its expenses for a certain period of time to summarize a company's financial operations. See Balance sheet, Statement of Changes in Financial Position (Cash Flow Statements), and Changes in Operations.

INCOMPETENT: One who is incapable of managing his or her legal and financial affairs because of mental deficiency or failure to have yet attained legal age.

INCOMPLETE: For insurance purposes, the status of an application lacking certain information necessary for underwriting or classifying the risk.

INCONTESTABILITY: An insurance policy provision whereby the insurer, after the policy has been in effect for a specified period, gives up the right to dispute a claim. Ordinary policies are usually incontestable after having been in effect for 2 years; weekly premium, usually after 1 year.

INCONTESTABLE CLAUSE: A life and health insurance policy provision that states that the insurance company may not contest payment of benefits (assuming premiums have been paid) after a specified period, usually 1–3 years after issue. This, in effect, gives the insurance company time to determine if there have been any misrepresentations made on the application.

INCORPORATION BY REFERENCE: Producing a contract from a document, by reference in a contract.

INCUBATION PERIOD: See Probationary Period.

INCURRED BUT NOT REPORTED (IBNR): Refers to health claims that reflect services already delivered, but, for whatever reason have not yet been reimbursed, reported, or captured as a liability by the insurance company. These are bills "in the pipeline." This is a crucial concept for proactive providers who are beginning to explore arrangements that put them in the role of adjudicating claims—as the result, perhaps, of operating in a subcapitated system. Failure to account for these potential claims could lead to some very bad decisions because of liability underestimation. Good administrative operations have fairly sophisticated mathematical models to estimate this amount at any given time. See Accounts Receivable.

INCURRED CLAIM: A situation where insurance premium payment may be demanded under the provisions of the policy or all claims with dates of service within a specified period.

INCURRED CLAIMS LOSS RATIO: Incurred claims divided by premiums. Medical expenses not yet paid by the managed care or health insurance company. See Expenses and Claims.

INCURRED EXPENSES: Expenses paid or to be paid.

INCURRED LOSS: Managed care or health insurance losses occurring within a fixed period, whether or not adjusted, and paid during the same period. Obtained by adding to losses paid during a given year those losses still outstanding at the end of the year, less losses outstanding at the beginning of the year. See Incurred Loss Ratio.

INCURRED LOSS RATIO: The ratio, fraction, or percentage of losses incurred to premiums earned. Relationship of incurred losses to health insurance premiums, experienced by the insuring entity. See Incurred Loss.

INDEMNIFY: To restore to the victim of a loss, in whole or in part, by payment, repair, or replacement to his or her original financial condition; to make an insured financially whole again, but not to an extent that there is profit from the loss.

INDEMNITY: Payment of an amount to offset all or part of an insured loss. The insured is indemnified for a specified loss or part thereof. Not synonymous with benefits. A benefit plan where a covered person is reimbursed dollars spent, according to a contract for any covered health care services rendered, or makes good or whole a loss.

INDEMNITY BENEFITS: Medical reimbursement method allowing a number of health care dollars for medical services. See UCR and Health Insurance.

INDEMNITY CARRIER: An insurer that offers coverage under contract and, after the review of claims, reimburses its covered persons for money spent on health care services.

INDEMNITY DISABILITY POLICY: An insurance policy used to fund buy-sell business agreements for a disabled partner's interest. See Disability and Long-Term Care.

INDEMNITY INSURANCE: The traditional form of health insurance where the physician bills the patient rather than their insurer for reimbursement or payment to the physician. See HMO.

INDEMNITY PERIOD: The time during which a loss is totally or partially covered. In a health insurance plan, for example, disability income payments are ordinarily limited to a specified indemnity period that may be relatively brief or it may be as long as the insured's lifetime. See Waiting Period.

INDEMNITY PLAN (INDEMNITY HEALTH INSURANCE): A plan that reimburses physicians for services performed or beneficiaries for medical expenses incurred. Such plans are contrasted with group health plans, which provide service benefits through group medical practice. See HMO.

INDEMNITY REINSURANCE: A type of reinsurance contract characterized by a series of independent transactions in which the ceding insurer transfers its liability with respect to individual policies, in whole or in part, to the reinsurer.

INDENTURE: The legal conditions and terms of a hospital or other bond or note.

INDEPENDENT PHYSICIAN ASSOCIATION (IPA): Contracts with individual physicians who see HMO members, as well as their own patients, in their own private offices. It is the ability of IPA physicians to see both IPA and private patients in their own offices that principally distinguishes an IPA from a group or staff HMO. Physicians in an IPA are paid either on a capitation or a modified fee-for-service basis. See Independent Practice Association.

INDEPENDENT PRACTICE ASSOCIATION (IPA): An HMO that contracts with individual physicians or small physician groups to provide services to HMO enrollees at a negotiated per capita or fee-for-service rate. Physicians maintain their own offices and can contract with other HMOs and see other fee-for-service patients. See Group-Model HMO, Health Maintenance Organization, Network-Model HMO, Staff-Model HMO, and Independent Physician Association.

INDETERMINATE PREMIUM: Refers to term policies where the actual premium charged may be lower than the guaranteed premium stated in the policy. Policies with indeterminate premiums generally make reference to the guaranteed (or maximum) premium that can be charged, and the current (or lower) premium, based on the current and projected mortality or investment experience.

INDEXING: Designed to provide some protection against inflation. After the first year of disability, a disabled employee's predisability earnings are usually increased (or indexed) by a certain percentage on an annual basis.

INDICATOR: A measure of a specific component of a health improvement strategy. An indicator can reflect an activity implemented to address a particular health issue, such as the number of children aged 2 years who have received all appropriate immunizations, or it might reflect outcomes from activities already implemented, such as a decline in the number of cases of childhood measles in any given year.

INDIRECT COST: Health care cost not traced to specific patient or medical service; the opposite of a direct cost. See Fixed Cost, Variable Cost, and Expense.

INDIRECT INSURANCE PAYMENTS: Insurance payment sent to the patient, rather than medical provider.

INDIRECT MEDICAL EDUCATION (IME) ADJUSTMENT: A payment adjustment applied to diagnosis-related groups and outlier payments under a prospective payment system for hospitals that operate an approved graduate medical education program. For operating costs, the adjustment is based on the hospital's ratio of the number of interns and residents to the number of beds. For capital costs, it is based on the hospital's ratio of interns and residents to average daily occupancy.

INDIVIDUAL CASE MANAGEMENT: Provision that emphasizes the specialized care needs of patients with severe illnesses or injuries. Arrangements may be made to waive standard certificate limitations to provide a more appropriate and comfortable setting for continued treatment. See Disease Management and Clinical Path Method.

INDIVIDUAL CONSIDERATION: A unique medical claim that must be personally examined because of variances of the diagnosis or medical treatment rendered.

INDIVIDUAL CONTRACT HEALTH INSURANCE: A contract of health insurance, made with an individual, that covers the insured and, in medical expense policies, may cover specified members of his or her family. In general, any health insurance contracts except group or blanket contracts. See HSA and MSA.

INDIVIDUAL INSURANCE: Health policies purchased by individuals directly from an insurance company, not through the auspices of another organization, such as an employer or association. See Health Insurance.

INDIVIDUAL PLANS: A type of insurance plan for individuals and their dependents that are not eligible for coverage through an employer group (group coverage).

INDIVIDUAL PRACTICE ASSOCIATION (IPA): An HMO model in which the HMO contracts with a physician organization that in turn contracts with individual physicians. The IPA physicians provide care to HMO members from their private offices and continue to see their fee-for-service patients. A managed-care model that contracts with individual practitioners or an association of individual practices to provide health care services in return for a negotiated fee. The individual practice association, in turn, compensates its physicians on a per capita, fee schedule, or other agreed basis. A cohort of medical providers who agree to treat a named population under a per-member/per-month capitation reimbursement agreement model. See HMO and MCO.

INDIVIDUAL STOP-LOSS: Excessive claims, above a specific amount, not charged against a group health insurance policy provider.

INDUCEMENT BY MISREPRESENTATION: See Twisting.

INDUSTRIAL HEALTH INSURANCE: Health insurance providing small amounts of benefits, with premiums due weekly or monthly, and collected by a home service agent.

INEVITABLE ACCIDENT: An accident that can neither be foreseen nor prevented.

INFANT: A person under legal age. Contracts made by infants are not enforceable against them and may be repudiated later. Special state statutes alter the above generalization and provide that certain infants may contract for life, health or other insurance.

INFERTILITY: A condition whereby an otherwise healthy person is documented as unable to conceive after 1 year of unprotected sexual intercourse.

INFLATION: The gradual rise in health care prices over time.

INFLATION FACTOR: A premium loading to provide for future increases in medical costs and loss payments resulting from inflation. A loading to provide for future increases resulting from inflation in medical costs and loss payments.

INFLATION PROTECTION: Provisions in a health insurance policy that increase benefit levels to account for anticipated increases in the cost of covered services.

IN-FORCE BUSINESS: Life or health insurance for which premiums are being paid or for which premiums have been fully paid. The term refers to the total face amount of a life insurer's portfolio of business. In health insurance, it refers to the total premium volume of an insurer's portfolio of business.

IN-FORCE REQUIREMENT: Long-term care insurance policy clause that mandates a specific number of years prior to the reception of benefits.

INFORMED CONSENT: Oral or written consent in which the patient agrees to undergo medical procedures during the course of treatment.

INFUSI-CENTER: Non-hospital-based ambulatory center offering intravenous and related infusion services.

INITIAL COVERAGE ELECTION PERIOD: The time immediately prior to entitlement to Medicare Part A and enrolled in Part B. This time period and coverage limit is usually approved by the Centers for Medicare and Medicaid Services (CMS).

INITIAL ELIGIBILITY PERIOD: The time period during which prospective members can apply for coverage without providing evidence of insurability.

INITIAL ENROLLMENT QUESTIONNAIRE (IEQ): Data gathering sheet sent to Medicare eligible patients regarding the priority of payment mechanisms.

INITIAL OPEN ENROLLMENT PERIOD: The first time that eligible people may enroll themselves and any dependents under a contract for insurance benefits.

INITIAL PREMIUM: The first health, life, disability, long-term care, or other insurance premium paid at the time the policy goes into effect. See Premium.

INJURY: Damage or hurt done or suffered. In health insurance, an injury refers to bodily damage sustained by accident. See Illness and Accident.

INJURY INDEPENDENT OF ALL OTHER MEANS: An injury resulting from an accident and not from an illness.

INLIER: Health care diagnosis and treatment statistics that fall within accepted norms for the same or similar diagnosis.

IN-NETWORK: Medical providers or facilities within the same health insurance, managed care, or other health care plan.

INPATIENT: A patient who has been admitted, at least overnight, to a hospital or other health facility for the purpose of receiving diagnostic treatment or other health services. The person is registered as a bed patient in a hospital and receives physician services for at least 24 consecutive hours. Services provided by a hospital or health benefits payable when a patient is legally admitted to a hospital facility. See Patient.

INPATIENT CARE: Care given a registered bed patient in a hospital, nursing home, or other medical or postacute institution.

INPATIENT HOSPITAL SERVICES: These services include bed and board, nursing services, diagnostic or therapeutic services, and medical or surgical services.

INPATIENT PSYCHIATRIC FACILITY: A facility that provides inpatient psychiatric services for the diagnosis and treatment of mental illness on a 24-hr basis, by or under the supervision of a physician.

INPUT: The labor capital and other resources hospitals use to produce goods and services.

INQUIRY BLANK: An insurance form submitted to the company by an agent for the purpose of determining whether or not the company will give authority to have an applicant medically examined. A form used by agents to query the underwriting department to determine the general attitude respecting a specific impaired risk.

INSIDE LIMITS: Limits placed on hospital expense benefits that modify benefits from the overall maximums listed in the policy. An inside limit when applied to room and board, limits the benefit to not only a maximum amount payable but also limits the number of days the benefit will be paid. In health insurance, the upper benefit limit that is intended to impose reasonable limits on covered expenses for them to be considered customary and reasonable. A major medical plan, for instance, may limit the daily hospital room benefit to $125, or x-rays to $750 per claim.

INSIDER TRADING: The act, in violation of the Securities and Exchange Commission's Rule 10b-5 and the Insiders Trading Act of 1988, of purchasing or selling securities (or derivative instruments based on those securities) based on information known to the party purchasing or selling the securities in his capacity as an insider (i.e., as an employee of the issuer of the securities) or as a result of information illicitly provided to him by an insider.

INSOLVENCY: A legal determination occurring when a managed care plan no longer has the financial reserves or other arrangements to meet its contractual obligations to patients and subcontractors.

INSOLVENCY CLAUSE: In reinsurance, a clause that holds the reinsurer liable for its share of loss assumed under the treaty, even though the primary insurer is insolvent.

INSPECTION: The independent checking on facts about an insurance applicant or claimant, usually by a commercial inspection agency.

INSPECTION BUREAU: A private organization in the business of investigating risks for insurance companies.

INSPECTION RECEIPT: A receipt obtained from an insurance applicant when a policy (upon which the first premium has not been paid) is left with him or her for further inspection. It states that the insurance is not in effect and that the policy has been delivered for inspection only.

INSPECTION REPORT: The report of an investigator containing facts required for the insurance company to make a decision on an application for new insurance or for reinstatement of an existing policy. See Commercial Inspection Report.

INSTITUTIONAL PROVIDERS: Health care facility providers, as opposed to individual medical practitioners.

INSTITUTIONAL SALES: Sales of securities to hospitals, banks, financial institutions, mutual funds, insurance companies, or other business organizations (institutional investors) that possess or control considerable assets for large scale investing.

INSTRUMENTAL ACTIVITIES OF DAILY LIVING (IADL): An index or scale that measures a patient's degree of independence in aspects of cognitive and social functioning including shopping, cooking, doing housework, managing money, and using the telephone. See Activities of Daily Living and ADLs.

INSURABILITY: All conditions pertaining to an individual that affect his or her health, susceptibility to injury, as well as life expectancy and thus insurability. These factors are considered in determining the amount of risk. If the risk is too high, the insurance company will refuse coverage, as the individual is considered to be uninsurable by that company's underwriting standards.

INSURABLE INTEREST: The interest arising when one person has a reasonable expectation of benefiting from the continuance of another person's life or of suffering a loss at his or her death. A person generally is considered to have an unlimited insurable interest in him or herself. However, a person must have an insurable interest in another person at the time of application to insure the other's life. Where no insurable interest exists, policies obtained by one person on the life of another are not enforceable by law because they are considered contrary to the public policy.

INSURABLE RISK: Insured or peril with acceptable requirements to an insurance company. See Risk and Peril.

INSURANCE: Protection, through specified money compensation or reimbursement for loss, provided by written contract against the happening of specified chance or unexpected events. The transfer of risk that results when one party, for a consideration, agrees to indemnify or reimburse another a specified amount for loss caused by designated contingencies. The first party is called the insurance company; the second, the insured; the contract, the insurance policy; the consideration, the premium; the property in question, the risk; and the contingency in question, the hazard or peril. The term assurance, common in England, is ordinarily considered identical to, and synonymous with, insurance. Insurance is a method of social risk transfer to another party (insurance company) for various perils and hazards of the insured. See Managed Care.

INSURANCE AGENT: The representative of an insurance company who sells its products. An employee. See Broker.

INSURANCE BROKER: The representative of an insured who searches the marketplace on behalf of finding the best products for his or her client. See Agent.

INSURANCE CARRIER: A workers' compensation carrier, property, and casualty carrier and other insurance carriers who protect against risk and losses in exchange for a prepaid premium.

INSURANCE COMMISSIONER: A key executive in life and health insurance industry regulation for each state.

INSURANCE COMPANY: A corporation, association, or fraternal benefit society engaged primarily in the business of furnishing insurance protection to the public. Accepts various perils, hazards, and risks of an insured in return for premium payments, and in return, promises to indemnify for losses, provide other pecuniary benefits, or render a service. Selection is based on: financial stability, reputation, and state insurance capacity.

INSURANCE CONTRACT: The legal and written policy with list of benefits, responsibilities, clauses, terms, and condition of an insurance policy. A legally binding unilateral agreement between insurance company and policy owner. See Insurance Policy.

INSURANCE DEPARTMENT: A division of the state government that has supervisory responsibility over insurance matters and the regulation of insurance companies and agents doing business within its borders.

INSURANCE ECONOMIC SOCIETY OF AMERICA: An organization established for the study of all forms of social insurance and to disseminate information to enlighten the public. Members strive to bring about a unified opinion and cooperative effort of all men and women in the insurance business, maintain insurance as a free enterprise, and develop research work involving studies of the insurance business and certain phases of compulsory social insurance.

INSURANCE EXAMINER: The representative of a state insurance department assigned to audit and examine the financial affairs and records of an insurance company.

INSURANCE IN-FORCE: The annual premium payable on current contracts of insurance.

INSURANCE INSTITUTE OF AMERICA: A society of individuals interested in improving education in the area of insurance.

INSURANCE INTEREST: Any interest in an individual, for insurance purposes, of such a nature that his or her death might cause monetary loss to the beneficiary or some other party. See Insurable Interest.

INSURANCE WITH OTHER INSURERS PROVISION: An optional provision in individual medical expense health insurance policies that limits double payment of benefits when the insured has more than one policy covering the same loss. The insured is to receive one settlement for each claim, so as not to profit from the loss.

INSURANCE POLICY: The printed form prepared by an insurance company to serve as the legal contract between the policy owner and the company with list of benefits, responsibilities, clauses, terms, and conditions. See Insurance Contract.

INSURANCE POOR: A belief held or comment often made when an insured carries so much insurance and pays so much in premiums that there is not enough money left to live on comfortably.

INSURANCE PREMIUM: The designated amount of money payable by the insured to the insurance company that is required to keep the contract in force.

INSURANCE PROGRAM: A unified life or health insurance plan that coordinates the needs, policies, and settlement options available to carry out the aims and objectives of a client.

INSURANCE RATE: The ratio of the premium to the total amount of insurance carried, usually expressed in dollars per $100 or per $1,000 of coverage.

INSURANCE REGISTER: A policy owner's personal record or file of important data about insurance carried: dates of purchase, amounts of premiums, expiration, companies, etc.

INSURANCE REGULATION: Government requirements and restrictions imposed on insurance companies. Because insurance is a business that can affect the financial security of vast numbers of people, government regulation (setting of rates, standards, operating and licensing requirements, etc.) is deemed essential. It is a primary function of insurance regulation to maintain the financial solvency of all insurance companies. In the United States, the role of regulation is assumed by the states.

INSURANCE RESERVES: The present value of future claims, minus the present value of future premiums. Reserves are balance sheet accounts set up to reflect actual and potential liabilities under outstanding insurance contracts. There are two main types of insurance reserves: (a) premium reserves; and (b) loss (or claim) reserves.

INSURANCE RISK: A general term denoting the hazard involved in insuring a person or group. The premium or cost of insurance is based upon the relative risk or hazard involved. A term denoting the hazard involved in insuring a person or group. The premium or cost of insurance is based upon the relative risk or hazard involved. See Risk and Peril.

INSURANCE RISK, PURE: See Mortality Risk.

INSURANCE SALESPERSON: See Agent.

INSURANCE SERVICE ASSOCIATION OF AMERICA: A society of insurance agents whose goal is the exchange of information and interchange of business.

INSURANCE SUPERINTENDENT: See Commissioner.

INSURED: The party or plan member to an insurance contract, covering health or other insurance, to whom, or on behalf of whom, the insurer agrees to indemnify for losses, provide benefits, or render services. The individual or group covered by the contract of insurance. See Policy Holder.

INSURED ADDITIONAL: A person, other than the original named insured, who is protected under a life or health insurance contract.

INSURED NAMED: The person identified as the insured in a life or health insurance policy.

INSURED STATUS: When determining Social Security benefits, an eligible worker is either fully insured or currently insured or both, depending on his or her year of birth and the quarters of coverage with which he or she has been credited. Insured status determines the benefits the worker or dependents can receive.

INSURER: The company underwriting the insurance and assuming the risk. The party to an insurance contract that undertakes to indemnify for losses, provide other pecuniary benefits, or render services.

INSURING AGREEMENT: See Insuring Clause.

INSURING CLAUSE: An essential written portion or policy clause of an insurance contract, defining and describing its features, responsibilities, perils, covered and excluded items, date of coverage, and date of termination, etc. The insuring clause states the policy's intent and contains the insurance company's promises. See Terms, Conditions, Contract, and Policy.

INTEGRATED DEDUCTIBLE: In superimposed major medical plans, a deductible amount between the benefits paid by the basic health insurance plan and those paid by major medical. All or part of the integrated deductible may be absorbed by the basic plan.

INTEGRATED DELIVERY SYSTEM (IDS): A single organization or entity that usually includes a hospital, a large medical group, and an insurance vehicle, such as an HMO or PPO, that provides ambulatory and tertiary care for its enrollees. Typically, all provider revenues flow through the organization.

INTEGRATED HEALTH CARE SYSTEM: A single health care organization that provides ambulatory and tertiary care to its enrollees.

INTEGRATED SERVICE NETWORK (ISN): Integrated Service Networks are organizations that are accountable for the costs and outcomes associated with delivering a full continuum of health care services to a defined population. Under an ISN arrangement, a network of hospitals, physicians, and other health care providers furnish all needed health services for a fixed payment.

INTEGRATIVE MEDICINE: A combination of traditional, alternative, or holistic health care.

INTENSITY OF SERVICES: The number and complexity of resources used in producing a patient care service, such as a hospital admission or home health visit. Intensity of services reflects, for example, the amount of nursing care, diagnostic procedures, and supplies.

INTENSIVE CARE: Medical care for complex illness and to patients who are unable to maintain vital functions.

INTENSIVE CARE FOR NEWBORN NURSERY (ICNN): An ICNN service is a critical care unit for newborn infants (neonates). It is licensed as ICNN, rather than as ICU, and has different standards of care. These units are for the provision of comprehensive and intensive care for all contingencies of the newborn infant including infant transport service. ICNN beds are certified for two levels of care: (a) the NICU (Neonatal Intensive Care Unit) meets all ICNN standards and is sometimes referred to as the tertiary level; and (b) INICU (Intermediate Newborn Intensive Care Unit) meets all ICNN licensing standards except for the provision of neonatal cardiovascular surgery and transport service.

INTENSIVIST: A physician employee of a hospital who usually remains on site to treat patients in the intensive care, critical care, or other special units. See Hospitalist.

INTENTIONAL INJURY: An injury resulting from an intentional act. Self-inflicted injuries are not covered under the terms of an accident policy.

INTERCOMPANY ADVANCES: The total amount due the health facility from related organizations more than 1 year after the balance sheet date.

INTEREST: The rent paid for borrowed money or received for loaned money. A person's share of ownership in property or a business, etc.

INTEREST ACCRUED: Interest earned but not yet payable.

INTEREST-ADJUSTED COST METHOD: An insurance method of comparing costs of similar policies by using an index that takes into account the time value of money due at different times through interest adjustments to the annual premiums, dividends, and cash value increases at an assumed interest rate.

INTEREST, EXACT: The interest that is computed on the basis of 365 days of the year.

INTEREST FACTOR: One of three factors taken into consideration by an insurance company when calculating premium rates. This is an estimate of the overall average interest that will be earned by the insurer on invested premium payments.

INTEREST RATE: That percentage of a principal sum earned from investment or charged upon a loan.

INTERFACE: A means of communication between two computer systems, two software applications, or two modules. Real-time interface is a key element in health care information systems because of the need to access patient care information and financial information instantaneously and comprehensively. Such real-time communication is the key to managing health care in a cost-effective manner because it provides the necessary decision-making information for clinicians, providers, and payers.

INTERFUND BORROWING: The borrowing of assets by a trust fund (OASI, DI, HI, or SMI) from another of the trust funds when one of the funds is in danger of exhaustion.

INTERMEDIARY: A company that pays some expenses of Medicare Part A and Medicare Part B bills.

INTERMEDIATE: A type of disability insurance that is less than total or a notice of the condition of a continuing disability. See Partial Disability.

INTERMEDIATE CARE (IC): Occasional nursing and rehabilitative care under a doctor's order and performed under the supervision of skilled medical personnel. A level of nursing care service that provides long-term care for patients who are ambulatory or semiambulatory and have a recurring need for skilled nursing supervision and supportive care but who do not require continuous skilled nursing care.

INTERMEDIATE CARE FACILITY (ICF): An institution, such as a home for the aged or rest home, that is licensed under state law to provide on a regular basis, health-related care and services to individuals who do not require the degree of care or treatment that a hospital or skilled-nursing facility is designed to provide. Public institutions for care of the mentally retarded.

INTERMEDIATE DISABILITY: See Partial Disability.

INTERMEDIATE NOTICE: In disability insurance, a report, required by many insurance companies, informing the company regarding the progress of a continuing disability. Also called second preliminary notice.

INTERMEDIATE NURSING FACILITY: A health facility licensed by the state and often certified by Medicare or Medicaid to provide intermediate care.

INTERMEDIATE REPORT: A claim report on the condition of a continuing disability.

INTERNAL CLAIMS PROCESSING: Reviewing medical claims to ensure appropriateness of care.

INTERNAL MEDICINE: Generally, that branch of medicine that is concerned with diseases that do not require surgery, specifically, the study and treatment of internal organs and body systems; it encompasses many subspecialties. Internists, the doctors who practice internal medicine, often serve as family physicians to supervise general medical care. See Hospitalist and Gatekeeper.

INTERNAL RATE OF RETURN: (1) The percentage return on an investment. (2) The calculated value for the discount rate necessary for total discounted program benefit to equal total discounted program costs.

INTERNATIONAL ASSOCIATION OF HEALTH UNDERWRITERS: An association of agents and related personnel of the health insurance business.

***INTERNATIONAL CLASSIFICATION OF DISEASES, 10TH REV., CLINICAL MODIFICATION* (ICD-10-CM):** A coding scheme used to document the incidence of disease, injury, mortality, and illness.

INTERVENTION STRATEGY: Generic term used in public health to describe a program, method or policy designed to have an impact on an illness or disease or prevent illness or injury, as in a smoking prevention clinic.

INTRAHOSPITAL TRANSFER: An in-house discharge from one level of care to another level of care, usually from intensive care to medical or surgical acute care. The patient is moved to another care unit, but not discharged from the hospital. These are also called Service Discharges.

INTRINSIC VALUE: A call option is said to have intrinsic value when the market price of the underlying health care security is greater than the exercise price. A put option is said to have intrinsic value when the market price of the underlying health care security falls below the exercise price.

INVALIDITY: Sickness. See Injury and Accident.

INVESTIGATIONAL DRUG, DEVICE, OR PROCEDURE: A medical drug, device, or procedure that lacks reliable evidence permitting conclusions about its safety, effectiveness, or effect on health outcomes. See Experimental Drug, Device, or Procedure and Promising Therapy.

INVESTIGATIONAL TREATMENT: Treatment is considered investigational when the service, procedure, drug, or treatment modality has progressed to limited human application but has not achieved recognition as being proven and effective in clinical medicine.

INVESTMENT ADVISOR: A person in the business of rendering advice or analysis regarding securities for compensation. Persons meeting this definition must register as advisers with the Securities and Exchange Commission under the Investment Adviser's Act of 1940. The term does not include attorneys and accountants giving advice as an incidental part of their professional practice.

INVESTMENT BANKER: A broker or dealer organization that provides a service to industry through counseling and underwriting of hospital securities.

INVESTMENT COMPANY: An institution engaged primarily in the business of investing and trading in hospital or other securities for others including face amount certificate companies, unit trust companies, and management companies, both open-end and closed-end.

INVESTMENT GRADE: The broad credit designation given to hospital or other bonds that have a high probability of being paid and minor, if any, speculative features. Bonds rated BBB or higher by Standard and Poor's Corporation, or Baa or higher by Moody's Investors Service, Inc., are deemed by those agencies to be investment grade.

INVESTOR: One giving capital to another with the expectation of financial return.

INVESTOR-OWNED: An ownership group that includes health facilities that are partnerships, sole proprietorships, and corporations or divisions of corporations that issue stock.

IPA (INDEPENDENT PRACTICE ASSOCIATION): A confederation of physicians and other providers assembled for the purpose of contracting with payers. HMOs and participating providers accept the fee schedules negotiated by the IPA, but typically may continue to see patients covered by other plans. See HMO.

IPA MODEL HMO: A type of open-panel HMO that typically includes large numbers of individual private practice physicians. Under this structure, physicians practice in their own offices. See Group Staff Model.

IPO: Initial public offering. The first time securities are sold to the public.

ISSUE: Any of a health care company's class of securities or the act of distributing them.

ISSUED AND OUTSTANDING STOCK: That portion of authorized stock distributed among investors by a health care corporation.

ISSUE LIMITS: The maximum disability benefit an insurer will pay any one individual.

ISSUER: A health care corporation, municipality, state, trust, or association engaged in the distribution of its securities.

ITEMIZED BILL: A bill or invoice for medical services rendered and the charge for each.

J

JACKET: Outer covering of a health, life, disability, long-term care, or other insurance policy.

JOB-LOCK: The inability of individuals to change jobs because they would lose crucial health benefits.

JOINT COMMISSION ON THE ACCREDITATION OF HEALTHCARE ORGANIZATIONS (JCAHO): Formerly called JCAH, or Joint Commission on Accreditation of Hospitals, this is the peer review organization that provides the primary review of hospitals and health care providers. Many insurance companies require providers to have this accreditation to seek third-party payment, although many small hospitals cannot afford the cost of accreditation. JCAHO usually surveys organizations once every 3 years, sending in a medical and administrative team to review policies, patient records, professional credentialing procedures, governance, and quality improvement programs. JCAHO revises its standards annually.

JOINT COST: Common health care costs.

JOINT VENTURE: Hybrid business structure where two entities unite for a common purpose, but remain as independent entities.

JUNIOR SECURITIES: Common stocks and other issues whose claims to assets and earnings are contingent upon the satisfaction of the claims of prior obligations.

JUNK BOND: A speculative security with a rating of BB or lower. Sometimes called a high yield security.

K

KENNEDY-KASSEBAUM ACT: This act established the federal law that group insurance plans must not discriminate based on health status and insurance renewability. Part I is for privacy, and Part II is for EDI. See HIPPA and EDI.

KERR-MILLS ACT: See Medicaid.

KICKBACK: The federal antikickback statute makes it a crime to knowingly and willfully offer, pay, solicit, or receive *any remuneration* to induce a person to: (a) refer an individual to a person for the furnishing of any item or service covered under a federal health care program; or (b) to purchase, lease, order, arrange for, or recommend any good, facility, service, or item covered under a federal health care program. The term *any remuneration* encompasses any bribe or rebate, direct or indirect, overt or covert, cash or in kind, and any ownership interest or compensation interest.

KIT, SALES: Manuals, forms, applications, and various other sales aids (such as advertising, charts, diagrams, estate plans, and other related material) to help an insurance agent make a more efficient sales presentation.

KNOWLEDGE-BASED SYSTEM: A computerized decision support system to assist medical providers in the care and treatment of patients.

KNOX-KEENE ACT: California legislation (1975) amending the Health and Safety Code that licenses HMOs separately from insurance companies. Provides for regulation by the department of corporations commissioner.

L

LABOR BUDGET: An expense projection of a health care entity's fixed, variable, and other costs of its labor pool. See Budget.

LABOR-DELIVERY-RECOVERY (LDR): A program, formerly approved as ABC (Alternative Birthing Center), for low-risk mothers, with equipment and supplies for uncomplicated deliveries, in a home-like setting, with stays of less than 24 hr that has been approved by the Division of Licensing and Certification, Department of Health Services (the beds do not have to be licensed beds).

LABOR-DELIVERY-RECOVERY-POSTPARTUM (LDRP): A program for all mothers, with equipment and supplies for complicated deliveries, in a home-like setting, with stays that can exceed 24 hr, which has been approved by the Division of Licensing and Certification, Department of Health Services (and provided in licensed perinatal beds).

LAc: licensed acupuncturist.

LAG STUDY: A report that tells managers how old the health claims are that are being processed and how much is paid out each month and compares it to the amount of money that was accrued for expenses each month.

LAPSE: Termination of a health insurance, long-term care, disability, or other insurance policy because of nonpayment of premiums.

LAPSE POLICY: A health, life, or other insurance policy whose coverage terminated.

LAPSE RATE: The rate at which insurance policies terminate through failure of insureds to continue paying either scheduled or minimum premiums, usually expressed as a ratio of lapses during a given period of time to the total number of policies of that type issued.

LAPSE RATIO: The ratio of the number of life and health insurance contracts lapsed without value or surrendered for cash within a given period to the number in force at the beginning of the period. See Liquidity Ratio.

LARGE CLAIM: The total sum of covered expenses that exceeds a specific health plan's claim limit.

LARGE CLAIM POOLING: System that isolated claims above a certain level and charges them to a pool funded by charges of all groups who share the pool. Designed to help stabilize significant premium fluctuations.

LARGE GROUP: State definition usually greater than 100 health insurance plan members.

LARGE GROUP HEALTH PLAN: Employer-sponsored health plan for usually more than 100 members.

LARGE URBAN AREA: An urban statistical region with population of 1 million or more.

LATE ENROLLEE: An employee who did not enroll at the first opportunity or following a qualifying event must wait until open enrollment to enroll. Open enrollment is defined as the month preceding the employer group health plan anniversary date. The request for application must be completed and received by Blue Cross and Blue Shield of Kansas in the month preceding the employer group health plan anniversary date.

LAUNDRY AND LINEN: The cost center that provides laundry and linen services for facility use and personal laundry services.

LAW OF LARGE NUMBERS: The theory of probability that is the basis of insurance; the larger the number of risks or exposures, the more closely will the actual results obtained approach the probable results expected from an infinite number of exposures.

LAYING ON OF HANDS: Contact healing.

LEADING PRODUCERS ROUND TABLE (LPRT): An organization of insurance agents who qualify for membership annually or on a lifetime basis by producing (selling) certain high levels of health insurance premium volume in a year; sponsored by the International Association of Health Underwriters.

LEGACY SYSTEMS: Computer applications, both hardware and software, that have been inherited through previous acquisition and installation. Most often new systems that stress open design and distributed processing capacity are gradually replacing such older systems.

LEGAL ACTION PROVISION: A mandatory health provision that states that the policy owner must allow 60 days after submitting the proof of loss forms before taking legal action, and if the policy owner sues, such action must occur within 3 years.

LEGAL CAPACITY: The ability to enter into a legal contract (i.e., being of legal age, sane, not a convict, or enemy alien). Only such an individual is considered a legally competent party.

LEGAL GUARDIAN: An adult charged with administering the legal affairs of a minor person.

LEGEND DRUG: Drug that the law says can only be obtained by prescription.

LENGTH OF STAY (LOS): The number of consecutive days a patient is hospitalized.

LETTER OF INTENT: A written understanding between health plan and a physician to provide medical services to its members.

LETTER OF REQUEST: A formal request from the requestor on organizational letterhead detailing their data needs and purposes. In addition, if this project is federally funded, a letter of support is required from the federal project officer on their organizational letterhead.

LETTER OF SUPPORT: A letter from the federal project officer justifying the need for Centers for Medicare and Medicaid data and supporting the requestor's use of such data.

LEVEL COMMISSION: Same insurance agent commission, annually.

LEVEL DEBT SERVICE: A maturity schedule in which the combined annual amount of principal and interest payments remains relatively constant over the life of the issue.

LEVERAGE: A financial condition brought about by the assumption of a high percentage of debt in relation to the equity in a health care corporation's capital structure. Leverage is the use of borrowed money.

LIABILITIES: A health care organization's legal obligations to pay a creditor. All the outstanding claims for money against a health care corporation: (a) accounts payable; (b) wages and salaries; (c) dividends declared or payable; (d) accrued taxes; and (e) fixed or long-term liabilities as mortgage bonds, debentures, and bank loans. See Assets.

LIABILITY: An unclaimed insurance obligation.

LIABILITY INSURANCE: Liability insurance is insurance that protects against claims based on negligence or inappropriate action or inaction, which results in bodily injury or damage to property.

LICENSE: With respect to insurance, certification issued by the appropriate state department of insurance policies that an individual is qualified to sell insurance for the period stated (usually 1–2 years) and renewable upon application without the necessity of the applicants undergoing the original qualifying requirements.

LICENSED BED DAYS: The sum of the number of days each bed was licensed during the calendar year. Takes into account any changes in the licensed number of beds that occurred during the year. If there were no license changes, licensed bed days would equal the number of licensed beds times the number of days in the year.

LICENSED BEDS: (a) Average: The average number of beds licensed by the Licensing and Certification Division of the Department of Health Services, less those beds in suspense, during the reporting period. (b) End of Period: The number of beds licensed by the Department of Health Services, less those beds in suspense, as of the last day of the reporting period.

LICENSED VOCATIONAL NURSE: Similar to a licensed practical nurse.

LICENSEE: The holder of a health facility license issued under Chapter 2 (commencing with §250) of the Health and Safety Code or Chapter 8.6 (commencing with §760) of the Health and Safety Code.

LICENSING: A process most states employ, which involves the review and approval of applications from HMOs prior to beginning operation in certain areas of the state. Areas examined by the licensing authority include: (a) fiscal soundness; (b) network capacity; (c) medical management information system; and (d) quality assurance. The applicant must demonstrate it can meet all existing statutory and regulatory requirements prior to beginning operations.

LIEN: Interest usually granted to lender in a secured loan situation.

LIFECARE: A signed contractual agreement between a residential care patient and a residential care facility with a distinct part being a skilled-nursing facility (SNF), stating a set fee covering the remainder of the patient's life (the fee can be paid in a lump sum or monthly payments). There is no extra cost to the resident when transferred to the distinct SNF.

LIFE ENERGY: See vital force.

LIFE EXPECTANCY: Average expected length of life for a group of people, of a particular age, chosen at a particular time.

LIFETIME MAXIMUM: Maximum dollar amount paid toward a medical insurance clam.

LIFETIME RESERVE DAYS: In health insurance, each beneficiary has 60 lifetime reserve days that he or she may opt to use when regular inpatient hospital benefits are exhausted. The beneficiary pays one-half of the inpatient hospital deductible for each lifetime reserve day used.

LIFETIME RESERVE DAYS (MEDICARE): The 60 days that Medicare will pay in a hospital for more than 90 days. These 60 reserve days can be used only once during a lifetime. For each lifetime reserve day, Medicare pays all covered costs except for a daily coinsurance.

LIMITATIONS: There may be specific provisions included in group disability insurance plans that limit coverage in certain situations. Often only limited benefits are payable for specific conditions or under specific circumstances (e.g., mental illness and preexisting conditions).

LIMITED PARTNERSHIP: Association of two or more persons, including one or more general partners (each of whom has unlimited liability), and one or more limited partners (whose individual liability is limited).

LIMITING CHARGE: The maximum amount that a nonparticipating physician is permitted to charge a Medicare beneficiary for a service; in effect, a limit on balance billing. Starting in 1993 the limiting charge has been set at 115% of the Medicare-allowed charge.

LINE OF BUSINESS: A health plan, HMO, exclusive provider organization, managed care organization, or PPO set up as a line of business within another, larger organization, usually an insurance company. This legally differentiates it from a freestanding company or a company set up as a subsidiary.

LINE ITEM: Service or item-specific detail of claim.

LIQUIDATION: Refers to the sequence of payouts when health care corporations go bankrupt. The order is as follows: (a) Internal Revenue Service; (b) secured creditors, including senior bondholders; (c) unsecured creditors, including junior bonds (debentures); (d) preferred stockholders; and (e) common stockholders.

LIQUIDITY: The speed at which an asset can be converted to cash. (1) The ability of the market in a particular security to absorb a reasonable amount of trading at reasonable price changes. Liquidity is one of the most important characteristics of a good market. (2) The easy ability of investors to convert their securities holdings into cash and vice versa.

LIQUIDITY RATIOS: Relationships of short-term obligation payment abilities.

LIVING WILL: An advanced directive document for life-sustaining treatment, when death is imminent or the patient no longer has control of his or her faculties.

LLOYDS BROKER: One who has authority to negotiate insurance contracts with the underwriters on the floor at Lloyds.

LLOYDS OF LONDON: An English institution within which individual underwriters accept insurance risks. Lloyds provides the support facilities for such activity but is not in itself an insurance company.

LMT: licensed massage therapist.

LOAD: The amount added to net premiums (risk factor minus interest factor) to cover the company's operating expenses and contingencies. The loading includes the cost of securing new business, collecting premiums, and general management expenses. Precisely, it is the excess of the gross health insurance premiums over net premiums. See Commissions.

LOADING CHARGE: The additional charge for overhead costs added to the health insurance net premium. See Commissions.

LOAN AMORTIZATION: To payback or extinguish a loan, bond, or debt.

LOCAL ACCESS TRANSPORT AREA (LATA): A defined region in which a telephone and long distance carrier operates—an important concept for those community health information networks that depend on phone lines. When creating communications networks, organizations try to avoid crossing boundaries of these, if possible, because costs escalate dramatically when there is a need to communicate over more than one Local Access Transport Area. See CHINS.

LOCAL CODES: A generic term for code values defined for a state or other political subdivision or for a specific payer. This term is most commonly used to describe the HCFA (Centers for Medicare and Medicaid Services) Common Procedure Coding System.

LOCALITY: A specific Medicare geographic boundary for establishing payment levels.

LOCATION: The place where medical services are rendered.

LOCATION CODE: A numeric designation on the billing form of a medical provider or health care entity.

LOCK-BOX: A bank accessible mailbox for the deposit receipts of a medical care provider.

LOCK-IN: A contractual provision by which members, except in cases of urgent or emergency need, are required to receive all their care from the network health care providers.

LOGICAL OBSERVATION IDENTIFIERS, NAMES, AND CODES: A set of universal names and ID codes that identify laboratory and clinical observations. These codes, which are maintained by the Regenstrief Institute, are expected to be used in the HIPAA claim attachments standard.

LONGER TERM CARE MINIMUM DATA SET: The core set of screening and assessment elements of the Resident Assessment Instrument (RAI). This assessment system provides a comprehensive, accurate, standardized, reproducible assessment of each long-term care facility resident's functional capabilities and helps staff to identify health problems. This assessment is performed on every resident in a Medicare or Medicaid-certified long-term care facility, including private pay.

LONGITUDINAL DATA: Medical or health care information that covers multiple time periods and is used in ratio analysis and economic benchmarking. See Horizontal Data.

LONG RANGE: The next 75–100 years.

LONG-TERM CARE: Ongoing health and social services provided for individuals who need assistance on a continuing basis because of physical or mental disability. Services can be provided in an institution, the home, or the community and include informal services provided by family or friends, as well as formal services provided by professionals or agencies. See Hospice, Long-Term Care Insurance, and Activities of Daily Living.

LONG-TERM CARE HOSPITAL: Medicare term for a hospital whose average length of stay is more than 25 days and not otherwise a mental health or rehabilitation hospital.

LONG-TERM CARE (LTC) INSURANCE: Day-to-day care policy for those aged older than 65, consisting of residential or institutional assistance for those unable to perform two of five basic activities of daily living: walking, dressing, eating, toileting, and mobility. There are three insurance plan types: Skilled-Nursing Care, Intermediate Care, and Custodial Care. Important considerations of LTC insurance include these characteristics: (a) waiting period; (b) renewability; (c) age eligibility; (d) benefits period length; (e) inflation guard; (f) premium waiver; (g) no aged indexed premium increases; and (h) no preexisting condition clause. See ADLs.

LONG-TERM CARE OMBUDSMAN: An advocate for assisted living or nursing home patients.

LONG-TERM DISABILITY INCOME INSURANCE: Disability income insurance that typically provides disability income benefits that begin at the end of a specified waiting period and that continue until the earlier of the date when the insured person returns to work, dies, or becomes eligible for pension benefits. See LTC and Hospice.

LONG-TERM INSURANCE: See Long-Term Care Insurance. See ADLs.

LOSS PAYABLE CLAUSE: The policy provision that provides for payment of a loss by the health insurance company to someone other than the insured.

LOSS RATE: The timing and number of insurance loses within a given time period.

LOSS RATIO: The percentage of health insurance losses in relation to premiums. See Loss, Medical Loss, and Medical Loss Ratios.

LOSS RATIO, WRITTEN-PAID: The ratio of losses paid to premiums written by the insurance company during a specific time interval.

LOSS REPORT: The document detailing the facts of the claim filed by the agent, or a claim report.

LOSS RESERVE: Estimated liability for unpaid insurance claims or losses that have occurred as of any given valuation date. Usually includes losses incurred but not reported, losses due but not yet paid, and amounts not yet due.

LOSS RETENTION: See Deductible.

LUMP-SUM DEATH BENEFIT: Under Social Security, a benefit designed to help defray funeral expenses and paid at the death of all covered individuals who are either fully insured or currently insured. The payment is made to the surviving widow or widower of the deceased. If there is no surviving widow or widower, payment is made to the funeral director or to the person who paid the funeral expenses. The lump-sum death benefit equals three times the PIA (Primary Insurance Amount) of the deceased individual, up to a certain maximum amount.

M

MAC: See Maximum Allowable Costs.

MAIL FLOAT: Time lag between health care payer invoicing and ultimate receipt of payment for medical service rendered.

MAIL ORDER PHARMACY PROGRAM: Drug delivery program delivered through public or private mail at reduced costs.

MAINTENANCE OF EFFORT (MOE): A requirement of the Medicare catastrophic coverage act that affects employers with plans that duplicate 50% or more of the new catastrophic benefits. Under MOE, they have to maintain their effort by providing eligible employees, retirees, or dependents with additional benefits or a refund equal in value to the duplicated benefits.

MAJOR DENTAL: Include crowns and bridges, inlays, on-lays and facings, periodontics, endodontics, orthodontics, surgical extraction of wisdom teeth, and dentures. Precious metal fillings and gold may also be included in major dental insurance. See HMO, MCO, and Health Insurance.

MAJOR DIAGNOSIS: The medical condition that consumes the most resources in a given health care encounter.

MAJOR HOSPITALIZATION INSURANCE: A type of medical-expense health insurance that provides benefits for most hospitalization expenses incurred, up to a high limit, subject to a large deductible. Such contracts may contain internal maximum limits and a percentage participation clause (sometimes called coinsurance clause). Distinguished from major medical in that it pays benefits only when the insured is hospitalized. See HMO, MCO, and Health Insurance.

MAJOR MEDICAL EXPENSE INSURANCE: Policies designed to help offset the heavy medical expenses resulting from catastrophic or prolonged illness or injury. They generally provide benefits payments for 75%–80% of most types of medical expenses above a deductible paid by the insured. See HMO, MCO, Health Insurance, and Surgical Expense Insurance.

MAJOR TEACHING HOSPITALS: Hospitals with an approved graduate medical education program and a ratio of interns and residents to beds of 0.25 or greater (varies). See Indirect Medical Education Adjustment.

MALDISTRIBUTION: The dearth or excess of health care providers or entities for a given population, health plan, or cohort.

MALINGERING: Feigning a disability to collect health insurance benefits, especially following a recovery from a covered disability.

MALPRACTICE: Improper professional actions or the failure to exercise proper professional skills by a professional advisor, such as a physician, physical therapist, or hospital. See Malpractice Insurance.

MALPRACTICE INSURANCE: Insurance against the risk of suffering financial damage due to professional misconduct or lack of ordinary skill. Malpractice requires that the patient prove some injury and that the injury was the result of negligence on the part of the professional. See Malpractice.

MALPRACTICE INSURANCE EXPENSE: A component of the Medicare relative value scale. See Malpractice Insurance.

MANAGED BEHAVIORAL HEALTH PROGRAM: A program of managed care specific to psychiatric or behavioral health care. This usually is a result of a carve-out by an insurance company or managed care organization (MCO). Reimbursement may be in the form of subcapitation, fee for service, or capitation. See Carve-Out.

MANAGED CARE: (1) An integrated system of health insurance, financing, and service delivery functions involving risk sharing for the delivery of health services and defined networks of providers. (2) Any system of health payment or delivery arrangements where the health plan attempts to control or coordinate use of health services by its enrolled members to contain health expenditures, improve quality, or both. Arrangements often involve a defined delivery system of providers with some form of contractual arrangement with the plan. See Health Maintenance Organization, Independent Practice Association, Preferred Provider Organization. (3) Approaches to health services delivery and benefit design that integrate management and coordination of services with financing to influence utilization, cost, quality, and outcomes. See HMO and MCO.

MANAGED CARE ORGANIZATION (MCO): A prepaid or cost-effective health care plan that has restrictions and is similar to an HMO. See HMO, IPA, PPO, and Health Insurance.

MANAGED CARE PAYMENT SUSPENSION: Includes nonpayment for health maintenance organizations (HMO), competitive medical plans, and other plans that provide health services on a prepayment basis, which is based either on cost or risk, depending on the type of contract they have with Medicare. See Medicare + Choice.

MANAGED CARE PLAN: A health plan with a defined system of selected providers that contract with the plan. Enrollees have a financial incentive to use participating providers that agree to furnish a broad range of services to them. Providers may be paid on a prenegotiated basis. See Health Maintenance Organization, Point-of-Service Plan, and Preferred Provider Organization.

MANAGED CARE PLAN WITH POINT OF SERVICE (POS) OPTION: A managed care plan that allows the use of outside providers, drugs, vendors, or facilities, for an additional charge. See Health Maintenance Organization, Point-of-Service Plan, and Preferred Provider Organization.

MANAGED COMPETITION: A health insurance system that bands together employers, labor groups, and others to create insurance purchasing groups; employers and other collective purchasers would make a specified contribution toward insurance purchase for the individuals in their group; the employer's set contribution acts as an incentive for insurers and providers to limit and control expenses and premiums.

MANAGED FEE-FOR-SERVICE: The cost of covered services paid by the insurer after services have been received. Various managed care tools such as pre-certification, second surgical opinion, and utilization review. See Discount.

MANAGED INDEMNITY PLAN: An insurance plan that combines the features of an indemnity plan with cost containment mechanisms. See Health Insurance, HMO, and MCO.

MANAGEMENT INFORMATION SYSTEMS: A health care information technology system that gathers, stores, analyzes, and manipulates information for medical and economic executive decisions. All hardware and software required for electronic support of a health insurance company. See EDI and HIPAA.

MANAGEMENT SERVICES ORGANIZATION (MSO): A management entity owned by a hospital, physician organization, or third party. The MSO contracts with payers and hospitals or physicians to provide services such as negotiating fee schedules, handling administrative functions, and billing and collections. See IPA.

MANAGING PHYSICIAN: See Gatekeeper, Hospitalist, and Intensivist.

MANDATED BENEFITS: State legislatures have passed statutes requiring any health plans being offered in the state to include certain treatments for coverage. These treatments may include chiropractic care, mental and nervous disorder coverage, routine mammograms, and organ transplants. See Exclusions and Coverage.

MANDATED EMPLOYER INSURANCE: Employers are required to provide health benefit coverage for their employees. See ERISA and Worker's Compensation Insurance.

MANDATED ENROLLMENT: A group of patients required to enter a certain managed medical care program.

MANDATED INSURANCE BENEFITS: The minimum health insurance coverage specified by government statute. See ERISA, Worker's Compensation Insurance, and Exclusions.

MANDATED PROVIDERS: Types of providers of medical care whose services must be included by state or federal law. See Doctors.

MANUAL: A field book containing rates, classifications, and underwriting rules for a particular insurance company. The public cost per unit of health, disability, or long-term care insurance.

MANUAL RATES: Rates developed based upon the health plan's average claims data and then adjusted for group specific demographic, industry factor, or benefit variations. See Rates and Manual Ratings.

MANUAL RATING: The calculation of the insurance premium rate from a manual classifying the types on a general basis, such as by industries, without reference to the particular conditions of an individual case. See Rates and Experience Rating.

MARGIN: Error adjustment when estimating advanced health insurance premium rates or reserve requirements.

MARGINAL COST: The additional cost incurred by increasing the scale of a program (usually differs from average cost by one unit).

MARGOLIN ACT: Worker's compensation insurance related act from California that suggests a series of penalties and fines for a delay in administering covered benefits.

MARKETABLE SECURITIES: Short-term claims that can be sold or bought in the capital markets (T-bills, CDs, short-term paper loans).

MARKET AREA: The targeted geographic area or areas of greatest market potential. The market area does not have to be the same as the post acute facility's catchment area. See Service Area.

MARKET ASSISTANCE PLAN (MAP): A plan promulgated by the Department of Insurance to assist buyers to obtain certain types of insurance when they are limited in availability.

MARKET BASKET INDEX: An index of the annual change in the prices of goods and services providers used to produce health services. There are separate market baskets for prospective payment system (PPS) hospital operating inputs and capital inputs and skilled-nursing facility, home health agency, and renal dialysis facility operating and capital inputs.

MARKETING DIRECTOR: Individual responsible for marketing a managed care plan, whose duties include oversight of marketing representatives, advertising, client relations, and enrollment forecasting.

MARKET RATE INTEREST: The current fair value trade rate for the same or similar securities. Usury rate. See Simple Interest and Compound Interest.

MARKET RISK: Health insurance company risks involving psychology of the managed care marketplace.

MARKET SEGMENTATION: Dividing a total market into individually smaller niche marketplaces.

MARKET VALUE (MV): The price of medical or health care services, bought or sold on the open market, with transparency, free flow of information, and no coercion.

MASSAGE THERAPY (MASSOTHERAPY, SOMATOTHERAPY): Any method that involves pressing or similarly manipulating a person's soft tissues to promote the person's well-being.

MASTER CONTRACT: A single health or other insurance policy of a company and its employees. See Master Policy.

MASTER FILE: The active working file of an insurance company that contains all the billing and current status information for each policy.

MASTER PATIENT/MEMBER INDEX: An index or file with a unique identifier for each patient or member that serves as a key to a member's health record.

MASTER POLICY: The contract of health insurance issued to the employer, association, or other named group under a group insurance plan that contains all the terms, conditions, and benefits of the agreement. Individual employees participating in the group plan receive individual certificates that state the benefits but usually not all the details of the plan contained in the master policy. See Master Contract, Insurance Policy, and Clause.

MASTER-SERVANT RULE: Assumption that an employer is liable for the negligent acts of employees.

MATERIAL FACT: In insurance, vital information required for an underwriting decision. A statement of something that is done or exists is of such importance that disclosure (or failure to disclose) would alter an underwriting decision or loss settlement.

MATERIAL MISREPRESENTATION: The falsification of a material fact that may affect the outcomes of insurance policy determinations.

MATERNITY BENEFIT: A medical expense health insurance benefit that covers all or a portion of the costs arising from pregnancy and childbirth. In individual health policies, maternity benefits are often excluded from coverage unless purchased with additional premium.

MATERNITY CARE: Services associated with pregnancy and delivery from the first obstetrical visit to the first postpartum visit. It includes the hospital stay for delivery.

MATURITY: The end of the life for a fixed income marketable security. The date on which a health care loan, bond, or debenture comes due; both principal and any accrued interest due must be paid.

MATURITY FACTOR: An adjustment factor used to modify health insurance claim invoices when less than a year of history is available.

MAXIMUM ALLOWABLE CHARGE: The amount set by an insurance company as the highest amount that can be charged for a particular medical service. The limit on billed or invoiced charges for Medicare patients by nonparticipating providers.

MAXIMUM ALLOWABLE COST (MAC) LIST: A list of prescriptions where the reimbursement will be based on the cost of the generic product.

MAXIMUM AVERAGE INDEXED MONTHLY EARNINGS: Regarding the calculation of Social Security benefits, an average earnings base determined by indexing credited earnings of a worker in terms of average earnings in a current year (per formula) and used to determine the amount of benefits when eligibility for benefits arises after 1978 (except that the pre-1979 method is used in 1979 through 1983 for retirement benefits only, if it produces higher benefits) if the worker has maximum taxable earnings in all computation years, that would give him or her maximum indexed earnings.

MAXIMUM AVERAGE MONTHLY WAGE: Regarding the calculation of Social Security benefits, an average earnings base used to determine the amount of benefits when eligibility for benefits arises before 1979 (and in 1979 through 1983 for retirement benefits only, if it produces higher benefits than the post-1978 method), if the worker has had maximum taxable earnings for a sufficient number of years.

MAXIMUM CLAIM LIABILITY: The highest amount of insurance claims for which a group is held liable.

MAXIMUM DEFINED DATA SET: Under HIPAA, this is all of the required data elements for a particular standard based on a specific implementation specification. An entity creating a transaction is free to include whatever data any receiver might want or need. The recipient is free to ignore any portion of the data that is not needed to conduct their part of the associated business transaction, unless the inessential data is needed for coordination of benefits.

MAXIMUM DISABILITY POLICY: A form of noncancelable disability income insurance that limits the insurance company's liability for any one claim, but not the aggregate amount of all claims.

MAXIMUM OUT OF POCKET: A predetermined limited amount of money an individual must pay out of pocket, before an insurance company or (self-insured employer) will pay 100% for an individual's health care expenses.

MAXIMUM PLAN BENEFIT COVERAGE: A predetermined and limited amount of money a managed care plan will pay per period certain.

MAXIMUM PROBABLE LOSS: The largest insurance loss expected in a risk under normal circumstances.

MAXIMUM WAGE BASE: The maximum annual income level on which Social Security taxes are paid and credited for benefit calculation purposes.

MBIA (MUNICIPAL BOND INSURANCE ASSOCIATION): An association of five insurance companies (The Aetna Casualty & Surety Co., Fireman's Fund Insurance Companies, The Travelers Indemnity Company, CIGNA Corporation, and The Continental Insurance Company) that offers insurance policies on qualified municipal issues under which the payment of principal and interest when due is guaranteed, in the event of issuer default. The two principal rating agencies assign their highest ratings to all hospital and municipal issues insured by MBIA.

McCARREN-FERGUSON ACT: A Federal statute that generally exempts insurance activities from federal antitrust enforcement where states regulate these activities.

MCO (MANAGED CARE ORGANIZATION): Refers to any type of organizational entity providing managed medical care, such as an HMO, PPO, etc.

MCO (MANAGED CARE ORGANIZATION) STANDARDS: These are standards that states set for plan structure, operations, and the internal quality improvement or assurance system that each MCO must have to participate in the Medicaid program.

MEAN (ARITHMETIC): The measure of central location commonly called the average. Calculated by adding together all the individual values in a group of measurements and dividing by the number of values in the group. See Median and Mode.

MEAN (GEOMETRIC): The mean or average of a set of data measured on a logarithmic scale. The expected loss.

MEAN RESERVE: The average of the initial insurance reserve and the terminal reserve, computed as of the middle of the policy year; one-half the sum of the initial and terminal reserves.

MEDIAN: The measure of central location that divides a set of data into two equal parts. See Mean and Mode.

MEDIATE: To settle differences between two parties.

MEDICAID: A Title 19 Federal program, run and partially funded by individual states to provide medical benefits to certain low-income people. The state, under broad federal guidelines, determines what benefits are covered, who is eligible, and how much providers will be paid. All states but Arizona have Medicaid programs.

MEDICAID ALLIED MANPOWER: This category includes some 60 occupations or specialties that can be divided into 2 large categories based on time required for occupational training. The first category includes those occupations that require at least a baccalaureate degree (e.g., clinical laboratory scientists and technologists, dietitians and nutritionists, health educators, medical record librarians, and occupational speech and rehabilitation therapists). The second group includes those occupations that require less than a baccalaureate degree (e.g., aides for each of the above categories as well as medical assistants and radiology technicians).

MEDICAID MCO: A managed care organization that provides comprehensive services to Medicaid beneficiaries, but not commercial or Medicare enrollees.

MEDICAID AND MEDICARE PATIENT AND PROGRAM PROTECTION ACT: Federal law, since 1987, that enacts criminal penalties against a person who knowingly offers, pays, solicits, or receives payment to encourage services or a medical item for which payment is made by these programs.

MEDICAID-ONLY MCO: A managed care organization that provides comprehensive services to Medicaid beneficiaries, but not commercial or Medicare enrollees.

MEDICAID QUALIFYING TRUST: Irrevocable living trust in which the grantor forfeits control of assets placed in the trust, but retains the right to its income, as the assets can be distributed to the beneficiary at the grantor's death.

MEDI-CAL: A federal, state-operated and administered program that provides medical benefits for certain low-income persons. This is California's version of the federal Medicaid program.

MEDICAL ADVISORY COMMITTEE: Managers who deal with care issues brought to it by a health insurance company medical director.

MEDICAL ASSISTANT: A doctor's helper in clinical or administrative matters who is usually not an allied health care professional.

MEDICAL ATTENDANCE: Treatment or care by a legally qualified physician.

MEDICAL CARE EVALUATION: A component of a quality assurance program that looks at the process of medical care. See Medical Examination.

MEDICAL CARE EVALUATION STUDIES (MCES): The name given to a generic form of health care review in which problems in the quality of the delivery and organization of health care services are addressed and monitored. A program based on MCES is recommended as a way of meeting the federal government's requirements for an internal quality assurance program for federally qualified HMOs.

MEDICAL CARE INSURANCE: See Medical Expense Insurance.

MEDICAL CARE PLANS: A form of group insurance.

MEDICAL CODE SETS: Codes that characterize a medical condition or treatment. These code sets are usually maintained by professional societies and public health organizations. See EDI and HIPAA.

MEDICAL COST RATIO (MCR): Compares the cost of providing service to the amount paid for the service. See Medical Loss Ratio.

MEDICAL DIVISION EMPLOYMENT: Physicians are employed by the hospital or hospital subsidiary and are incorporated as employees into the integrated delivery system.

MEDICAL EXAMINATION: The physical examination of a proposed insured, for health or life insurance, usually conducted by a licensed physician or other qualified medical personnel who acts in the capacity of the insurer's agent, the results of which become part of the application, and are attached to the policy contract. The so-called nonmedical in reality is a short-form medical report and is filled out by the agent. Various company rules, such as amount of insurance applied for or already in force, age of applicant, sex, past physical history, data revealed by inspection report, etc., determine whether the examination shall be medical or nonmedical.

MEDICAL EXAMINER: A doctor who examines applicants or claimants on behalf of, and as an agent for, an insurance company.

MEDICAL EXPENSE INSURANCE: One of two major categories of health insurance (the other being disability income insurance), these policies cover the out-of-pocket medical costs that result from accident and sickness—medical, dental, surgical, and hospital expenses. Includes coverage under the names Hospital-Surgical Expense Insurance and Medical Care Insurance. Types of coverage include basic and comprehensive. See Health Insurance, HMO, or MCO.

MEDICAL FOUNDATION: Usually a nonprofit health care delivery system composed of affiliated hospitals, doctors, and health care providers. Also known as a Foundation Model.

MEDICAL GROUP PRACTICE: The American Group Practice Association (AGPA), the American Medical Association (AMA), and the Medical Group Management Association (MGMA) define medical group practice as: "provision of health care services by a group of at least three licensed physicians engaged in a formally organized and legally recognized entity sharing equipment, facilities, common records, and personnel involved in both patient care and business management." See GPWW and IPA.

MEDICAL IMPAIRMENT BUREAU: Previous name for the Medical Information Bureau. See Medical Information Bureau (MIB).

MEDICAL INFORMATICS: Medical informatics is the systematic study, or science, of the identification, collection, storage, communication, retrieval, and analysis of data about medical care services to improve decisions made by physicians and managers of health care organizations. See Medical Management Information Systems.

MEDICAL INFORMATION BUREAU (MIB): A service organization that collects medical data on life and health insurance applicants and stores this information for exchange among member insurance companies. Its purpose is to guard against fraud and concealment by helping the companies uncover pertinent health facts about new applicants.

MEDICAL INSURANCE: Health insurance that provides payment for medical, surgical, or hospital expenses. See Health Insurance, MCO, and HMO.

MEDICAL LOSS RATIO: The relationship of medical insurance premiums paid out for claims. Also Medical Cost Ratio.

MEDICALLY NECESSARY: A term used to describe the supplies and services provided to diagnose and treat a medical condition in accordance with the standards of good medical care. The amount of revenues from health insurance premiums that is spent to pay for the medical services covered by the plan. Usually referred to by a ratio, such as 0.95, which means that 95% of premiums were spent on purchasing medical services. The goal is to keep this ratio below 1.00—preferably in the 0.75 range—because a managed care organization or insurance company's profit comes from premiums. See Emergent, Urgent, and Utilization Review.

MEDICALLY NEEDY: Patients eligible for Medicaid whose medical bills and total income is below certain limits.

MEDICALLY UNNECESARY CARE (MUC): A term used to describe that part of a stay in a health care facility, as determined by a case manager, as excessive to diagnose and treat a medical condition in accordance with the standards of good medical practice and the medical community. For example, the stay was too long, or was available in a less costly or more efficient setting.

MEDICALLY UNNECESSARY DAYS: Inpatient hospital stay deemed not needed or excessive.

MEDICAL MANAGEMENT: Techniques used in clinical or administrative medicine to reduce costs and enhance health care.

MEDICAL MANAGEMENT INFORMATION SYSTEM (MMIS): A data system that allows payers and purchasers to track health care expenditure and utilization patterns. See Management Information Systems and Medical Informatics.

MEDI-CAL NET PATIENT REVENUE: Medi-Cal gross patient revenue minus Medi-Cal deductions from revenue. For hospitals, it includes disproportionate share payments received from SB 855.

MEDICAL PAYMENT INSURANCE: A form of health coverage in automobile insurance that covers payment without liability for medical or similar expenses.

MEDICAL RECORDS INSTITUTE: An organization that promotes the development and use of electronic health care record. See EDI and HIPAA.

MEDICAL REPORT: An information document completed by a physician or other approved examiner and submitted to an insurance company to supply medical evidence of insurability, or lack of insurability. It also includes a report of such information provided the company in relation to a claim.

MEDICAL SAVINGS ACCOUNT (MSA): A health insurance option consisting of a high-deductible insurance policy and a tax-advantaged savings account. Individuals pay for their own health care up to the annual deductible by withdrawing from the savings account or paying out of pocket. The insurance policy would pay for most or all costs of covered services once the high deductible is met. See Health Savings Account (HSA) and Reinsurance.

MEDICAL SPENDING ACCOUNT: A type of flexible medical savings count. See Medical Saving Account (MSA), Flexible Spending Account (FSA), and Health Savings Account (HSA).

MEDICAL/SURGICAL: Also known as unspecified general acute care (GAC; i.e., beds not designated as perinatal, pediatric, ICU, CCU, acute respiratory, burn center, ICNN, or acute rehabilitation).

MEDICAL SURVEILLANCE: The monitoring of potentially exposed individuals to detect early symptoms of disease.

MEDICAL TECHNOLOGY: Includes drugs, devices, techniques, and procedures used in delivering medical care and the support systems for that care. See Medical Management Information Systems.

MEDICAL TREATMENT EFFECTIVENESS PROGRAM (MedTEP): A component of Agency for Health Care Policy and Research to study and improve the effectiveness and appropriateness of clinical practice. See AHCPR.

MEDICAL UNDERWRITING: A way for insurance companies to rate the risk of insuring certain individuals or group applicants. The degree of risk then establishes premiums or the denial of coverage. See Underwriter.

MEDICARE: A nationwide, federal health insurance program for people aged 65 and older. It also covers certain people under 65 who are disabled or have chronic kidney disease. Medicare Part A is the hospital insurance program; Part B covers physicians' services. Created by the 1965 Title 18 amendment to the Social Security Act.

MEDICARE ADVANTAGE PLAN: A plan with additional choices for Part A and B recipients, except those with end-stage renal disease. Used to be Medicare+Choice plans. Older terminology.

MEDICARE APPROVED AMOUNT: The Medicare payment amount for a covered service that may be less than the actual amount charged. See Approved Charge.

MEDICARE CARRIER: Private company contracted to pay Medicare Part A and B bills.

MEDICARE CATASTROPHIC COVERAGE: Federal Act of 1982, which was repealed in 1989, that increased benefits under Medicare Parts A and B.

MEDICARE+CHOICE: A program created by the Balanced Budget Act of 1997 to replace the existing system of Medicare risk and cost contracts. Beneficiaries will have the choice during an open season each year to enroll in a Medicare+Choice plan or to remain in traditional Medicare. Medicare+Choice plans may include coordinated care plans (HMOs, PPOs, or plans offered by provider-sponsored organizations); private fee-for-service plans; or plans with Medical Savings Accounts. See Medicare Advantage.

MEDICARE+CHOICE MEDICAL SERVICES ACCOUNT: A health insurance account created by contributions from the Centers for Medicare and Medicaid Services (CMS, formerly HCFA) to pay out-of-pocket medical expenses for Medicare beneficiaries. The accounts are used in conjunction with high-deductible, catastrophic health care policies.

MEDICARE+CHOICE PLAN: A health plan, such as a Medicare managed care plan or private fee-for-service plan, offered by a private company and approved by Medicare. Used as an alternative to the original Medicare plan. See Medicare Advantage.

MEDICARE CHOICES DEMONSTRATION: A demonstration project designed to offer flexibility in contracting requirements and payment methods for Medicare's managed care program. Participating plans include provider-sponsored organizations and preferred provider organizations. Plans are required to submit encounter data to HCFA (now CMS), and most will test new risk-adjustment methods.

MEDICARE COST CONTRACT: A contract between Medicare and a health plan under which the plan is paid on the basis of reasonable costs to provide some or all of Medicare-covered services for enrollees. See Medicare Cost Report.

MEDICARE COST REPORT (MCR): An annual report required of all institutions participating in the Medicare program. The MCR records each institution's total costs and charges associated with providing services to all patients, the portion of those costs and charges allocated to Medicare patients, and the Medicare payments received. See Medicare Cost Contract.

MEDICARE COVERAGE: Medicare Parts A and B.

MEDICARE CURRENT BENEFICIARY SURVEY (MCBS): A longitudinal survey administered by Health Care Financing Administration (CMS) that provides information on specific aspects of beneficiary access, utilization of services, expenditures, health insurance coverage, satisfaction with care, health status and physical functioning, and demographic information.

MEDICARE ECONOMIC INDEX (MEI): An index that tracks changes over time in physician practice costs. From 1975 through the present, increases in prevailing charge screens are limited to increases in the MEI.

MEDICARE GAP INSURANCE: See Medigap.

MEDICARE MANAGED CARE PLAN: Medicare + Choice or Medicare Advantage Plans.

MEDICARE PART A: Medicare hospital compensation program.

MEDICARE PART B: Medicare physician compensation program.

MEDICARE PART B PREMIUM REDUCTION: A managed care organization able to use its adjusted excess premiums to reduce Medicare Part B premiums for members. Available since FY 2003.

MEDICARE PART C: Medicare managed care compensation program.

MEDICARE PART D: Medicare drug compensation program.

MEDICARE PLUS: Program to offer private health plans to Medicare beneficiaries, as proposed under the conference agreement passed by the Congress in November 1995. See Medicare Part C, Medicare Advantage, and Medicare HMO.

MEDICARE PREMIUM COLLECTION CENTER (MPCC): A Medicare direct billing contractor.

MEDICARE PRIVATE FEE-FOR-SERVICE PLANS: Abridged type of Medical Advantage Plan, which determines reimbursement amounts, rather than the insurance plan. Extra benefits may or may not be possible at higher or lower premium costs.

MEDICARE PROVIDER ANALYSIS AND REVIEW (MedPAR) FILE: A Health Care Financing Adminstration (CMS) data file that contains charge data and clinical characteristics, such as diagnoses and procedures, for every hospital inpatient bill submitted to Medicare for payment.

MEDICARE RISK CONTRACT: A contract between Medicare and a health plan under which the plan receives monthly capitated payments to provide Medicare-covered services for enrollees and thereby assumes insurance risk for those enrollees. A plan is eligible for a risk contract if it is a federally qualified HMO or a competitive medical plan.

MEDICARE SAVINGS ACCOUNT: Medicare medical savings account (MSA) health insurance with a high deductible, along with a savings account to pay health care expenses and medical bills.

MEDICARE SAVINGS PROGRAM: A state-sponsored but federally administered Medicaid program that helps pay Medicare deductibles and insurance premiums.

MEDICARE SECONDARY PAYER: When another health insurance payer reimburses medical expenses prior to Medicare reimbursement.

MEDICARE SELECT: A type of Medicare supplement insurance that has lower premiums in return for a limited choice of beneficiaries: They will use only providers who have been selected by the insurer as preferred providers. Also covers emergency care outside the preferred provider network. See Medicare Advantage.

MEDICARE SUMMARY NOTICE: An explanation of benefits for medical services or durable medical equipment rendered by a Medicare participating provider or vendor.

MEDICARE SUPPLEMENT INSURANCE POLICY (Medigap): Health insurance policy that provides additional individual benefits under Medicare. See Medicare Wrap and Medigap.

MEDICARE UNDERWRITING: The federal health benefit program for elderly persons and disabled that covers over 35,000,000 beneficiaries, or over 14% of the United States, with an annual cost of over $120 billion. Medicare pays for 25% of all hospital care and 23% of all physician services. This high cost is the source of constant debate in Congress. This refers to the Medicare program, the largest single payer in United States.

MEDICARE WRAPAROUND INSURANCE: There are 10 standardized Medigap insurance plan policies (A–J) with specific packages of benefits. See Medicare Supplement Insurance Policy.

MEDIGAP INSURANCE: Privately purchased individual or group health insurance policies designed to supplement Medicare coverage. Benefits may include payment of Medicare deductibles, coinsurance, and balance bills, as well as payment for services not covered by Medicare. Medigap insurance must conform to 1 of 10 federally standardized benefit packages.

MEDIGAP PLAN: Plan purchased by Medicare enrollees to cover copayments, deductibles, and health care goods or services not paid for by Medicare.

MEDIGAP POLICY: A privately purchased insurance policy that supplements Medicare coverage and meets specified requirements set by Federal statute and the National Association of Insurance Commissioners.

MEMBER: A person eligible to receive, or receiving, benefits from an HMO or insurance policy. Includes both those who have enrolled or subscribed and their eligible dependents. See Policy Holder.

MEMBER MONTH: For each member, the recorded count of the months that the member is covered. See Per Member Per Month (PMPM) and Capitation.

MEMBERS PER YEAR: The number of members eligible for health plan coverage on a yearly basis.

MENTAL DISORDER: A person with a chronic psychiatric impairment and whose adaptive functioning is moderately impaired. Also used to describe the nursing care given to such person. See Behavioral Health.

MENTAL DISORDERED (MD): Mental disorders, such as schizophrenia, paranoia. A special treatment program (STP) for mentally disordered patients provided in licensed skilled-nursing facility (SNF) beds. In facilities with licensed SNF beds, two separate patient populations are served, each requiring distinctly different staff and services: (a) MD patients (generally younger than 65 years old, with specific mental needs) are served in facilities with licensed SNF beds and that also have approved STP for MD patients; and (b) general SN patients (mostly geriatric with various physical health needs) are served in facilities with licensed SNF beds but which have no STPs.

MENTAL HEALTH PARITY ACT: The idea in 1996 that mental health care is covered in the same way as physical health care.

MENTAL HEALTH CARE PROVIDER: Psychologist, psychiatrist, social worker, or other licensed provider of mental health care services.

MENTAL ILLNESS: Any condition that has an emotional origin or effect. Alcoholism or chemical or drug dependencies are not included. See Behavioral Health.

MERCHANDISING AIDS: Any of an assortment of charts, brochures, pamphlets, or other visuals that an agent may employ to assist him or her in health insurance or other selling activities.

MESSENGER MODEL: A method of setting fees for loose, non-risk-bearing managed care organizations, such as IPAs or PHOs. A designated agent must act as a messenger, shuttling individual physician information to the payer and vice versa. This method meets the criteria of antitrust laws that bar physicians from sharing any practice data or fee information. See IPA, PHO, HMO, MSA, or MCO.

META-ANALYSIS: A systematic, typically quantitative method for combining information from multiple studies.

METROPOLITAN STATISTICAL AREA: A geographic area that includes atleast one city with 50,000 or more inhabitants, or a Census Bureau-defined urbanized area of at least 50,000 inhabitants, and a total manpower shortage area population of at least 100,000 (75,000) in New England, for example.

MIDLEVEL PRACTITIONER: Nurse practitioners, certified nurse-midwives, and physicians' assistants that have been trained to provide medical services otherwise performed by a physician. Midlevel practitioners practice under the supervision of a doctor of medicine or osteopathy who takes responsibility for the care they provide. Physician extender is another term for these personnel.

MINIMAL CARE: Ambulatory care for self-sufficient patients at their end stage of recovery.

MINIMUM PREMIUM: A minimum premium is the smallest amount of premium the insurer requires to be paid in the first year of a health insurance contract.

MIRROR HMO: False health plan with an intermediary attempt to negotiate health care reimbursement down, with resale to another HMO. See Faux or Silent HMO.

MISCELLANEOUS EXPENSES: Ancillary expenses, usually hospital charges other than daily room and board. Examples would be x-rays, drugs, and lab fees. The total amount of such charges that will be reimbursed is limited in most basic hospitalization policies.

MISNOMER: A wrong name. See Mirror HMO.

MISQUOTE: An incorrect estimate of an insurance premium.

MISREPRESENTATION: A false statement as to past or present material fact made in an HMO, managed care organization, life, or health insurance application and intended to induce an insurance company to issue a policy it would not otherwise issue or to rate the policy more favorably than it otherwise would have. See Agent. See Broker. See Fraud and Abuse.

MISSION STATEMENT: The guiding statement of a health care organization that describes its identity and attributes, along with its reason for existence, goals, and objectives.

MISSTATEMENT OF AGE: Giving the wrong age for oneself in an application for health insurance or for a beneficiary who is to receive benefits on a basis involving a health contingency. See Representations and Fraud and Abuse.

MIXED MODEL HMO: A type of HMO that combines certain characteristics of two or more HMO models.

MODALITY: Method of treatment for physical disorders.

MODE: A measure of central location, the most frequently occurring value in a set of data points. See Mean and Median.

MODE OF PAYMENT: The frequency with which health insurance premiums are paid (e.g., annually, semiannually, monthly, etc.).

MONEY MARKET FUND: An investment vehicle whose primary objective is to make higher interest securities available to the average investor who wants immediate income and high investment safety. This is accomplished through the purchase of high-yield money market instruments, such as U.S. government securities, bank certificates of deposit, and commercial paper.

MONEY MARKET INSTRUMENTS: Obligations that are commonly traded in the money market. Money market instruments are generally short-term and highly liquid.

MONEY SUPPLY: The amount of money in circulation. The money supply measures used by the Federal Reserve System are: (a) M1—Currency in circulation + demand deposit + other check-type deposits: (b) M2—M1 + savings and small denomination time deposits + overnight repurchase agreements at commercial banks + overnight Eurodollars + money market mutual fund shares; (c) M3—M2 + large-denomination time deposits

(Jumbo CDs) + term repurchase agreements; (d) M4—M3 + other liquid assets (such as term Eurodollars, bankers acceptances, commercial paper, Treasury securities, and U.S. Savings Bonds).

MONTHLY ANNIVERSARY: The same day as the health insurance policy date for each succeeding month. If the policy date is the 29th, 30th, or 31st of a month, in any month that has no such day, the monthly anniversary is deemed to be the last day of that month.

MOODY'S INVESTORS SERVICE, INC.: An independent subsidiary of Dun & Bradstreet. The firm provides debt, solvency ratings, and economic information to investors regarding hospitals and other health care organizations.

MORALE HAZARD: A hazard arising from indifference to loss because of the existence of insurance. It is different than a moral hazard. See Risk and Peril.

MORAL HAZARD: The effect of personal reputation, character, associates, personal living habits, financial responsibility, and environment (as distinguished from physical health) on an individual's general insurability. It is different than a morale hazard. See Risk, Peril, and Risk Management.

MORAL RISK: Financial worth and moral condition as reviewed by a study of habits, environment, mode of living, and general reputation that an underwriter must take into consideration in determining whether an applicant for insurance is a standard insurable risk. This information is usually obtained from inspection reports. See Hazard and Peril.

MORBIDITY: A measure of disease incidence or prevalence in a given population, location, or other grouping of interest. See Mortality.

MORBIDITY RATE: The ratio of the incidence of sickness to the number of well persons in a given group of people over a given period of time. It may be the incidence of the number of new cases in the given time or the total number of cases of a given disease or disorder. See Mortality Rate.

MORBIDITY TABLE: A table showing the incidence of sickness at specified ages in the same fashion that a mortality table shows the incidence of death at specified ages.

MORBIDITY TABLES (RATES): A collection of data used to estimate the amount of loss as a result of disability resulting from accident or sickness. These figures are used to determine health insurance rates. Similar to the mortality table used in life insurance computation.

MORTALITY: A measure of deaths in a given population, location, or other grouping of interest. In insurance, the relative incidence of death as measured within a given age group.

MORTALITY, ESTIMATED: The mortality assumed in advance of actual experience for a given group over a given period, usually for an insured group for a coming year, as contrasted to that actually experienced and measured at the end of the assumed period.

MORTALITY EXPERIENCE: The rate at which participants in a pension or insurance plan have died or are assumed to die. The effect of deaths that occur during operations of an insurance plan. The mortality assumed in advance of actual experience for a given group over a given period, usually for an insured group for a coming year, as contrasted to that actually experienced and measured at the end of the assumed period.

MORTALITY, EXPERIENCED: The actual mortality experienced, usually in an insured group, as contrasted to that estimated or anticipated.

MORTALITY FACTOR: One of the basic factors needed to calculate basic premium rates. It uses mortality tables in attempting to determine the average number of deaths at each specific age that will occur each year.

MORTALITY, RATE OF: The ratio of the number of deaths in a given group in a year's time to the total number in the group exposed to the risk of death.

MORTALITY RATE, AGE ADJUSTED: The incidence of death standardized for a given age to be useful for comparisons between different populations or within the same population during varying periods of time.

MORTALITY RATE, AGE SPECIFIC: The ratio of deaths in a specified age group to the population of the same group during a specified period of time.

MORTALITY RATE, CAUSE SPECIFIC: The ratio of deaths from a specified cause in any given group for a given period of time.

MORTALITY RATE, CRUDE: The ratio of total deaths to total population during a given period of time, unadjusted by age, sex, or other factors.

MORTALITY RATE (INFANT): A ratio expressing the number of deaths among children aged younger than 1 year reported during a given time period divided by the number of births reported during the same time period. The infant mortality rate is usually expressed per 1,000 live births.

MORTALITY RATE (NEONATAL): A ratio expressing the number of deaths among children from birth up to but not including 28 days of age divided by the number of live births reported during the same time period. The neonatal mortality rate is usually expressed per 1,000 live births.

MORTALITY RATE (POSTNEONATAL): A ratio expressing the number of deaths among children from 28 days up to but not including 1 year of age.

MORTALITY RISK: The risk of death. The risk carried by a life insurance company and sometimes called the pure insurance risk. The degree of risk is the difference between the policy reserve (usually equal to the cash value of a permanent life policy) and the face amount of the policy. See Morbidity Risk.

MORTALITY SAVINGS: The savings occurring when actual mortality losses are less than the amount calculated from the mortality table used.

MORTALITY TABLE: A listing of the mortality experience of individuals by age and sex used to estimate how long a male or female of a given age is expected to live. The mortality table is the basis for calculating the risk factor, which in turn determines the gross premium rate.

MORTGAGE DISABILITY INSURANCE: A specific type of disability income insurance that pays benefits (often directly to the mortgage holder) during a total disability of the insured, or until the mortgage is paid up.

MOST FAVORED NATION CLAUSE: A provider clause stipulating that the latter will not pay the provider more than the lowest discounted price the provider gives to any other health plan.

MOTIVATING STORIES: Personal stories told by an agent in a sales interview to illustrate and emphasize the importance of adequate insurance coverage or of the uses of a particular plan.

MSO (Managed Services Organization): MSOs may contract with physicians (individually or in groups) to provide administrative and practice-management services. One of the following: (a) Medical Staff Organization—An organized group of physicians, usually from one hospital, into an entity able to contract with others for the provision of services; or (b) Management (or Medical) Services Organization—An entity formed by, for example, a hospital, a group of physicians, or an independent entity, to provide business-related services, such as marketing and data collection, to a group of providers like an Independent Physicians Association (IPA), Physician Hospital Organization (PHO), or Clinic Without Walls (CWW).

MULTIDISCIPLINARY: Treatment that involves care provided by a wide range of specialists.

MULTI EMPLOYER HEALTH PLAN: A group health insurance plan sponsored by more than two employers and their related employee benefits organization.

MULTIPLE EMPLOYER TRUST (MET): A legal trust established by a plan sponsor that brings together a number of small, unrelated employers for the purpose of providing group medical coverage on an insured or self-funded basis.

MULTIPLE EMPLOYER WELFARE ARRANGEMENT (MEWA): As defined in a 1983 Amendment to the Employee Retirement Income Security Act (ERISA) of 1974, an employee welfare benefit plan or any other arrangement providing any of the benefits of an employee welfare benefit plan to the employees of two or more employers. MEWAs that do not meet the ERISA definition of employee benefit plan and are not certified by the U.S. Department of Labor may be regulated by states. MEWAs that are fully insured and certified must only meet broad state insurance laws regulating reserves. See ERISA.

MULTIPLE OPTION PLAN: Health care plan that lets employees or members choose their own plan from a group of options, such as HMO, PPO, or major medical plan. See Cafeteria Plan or Flexible Benefits Plan.

MULTIPLE SURGICAL PROCEDURES: More than one surgical procedure performed at a given time.

MULTISPECIALTY GROUP: A group of doctors who represent various medical specialties and who work together in a group practice.

MULTIYEAR BUDGET: Extended series of income and outflow projects, for 2–7 years.

MUNICIPAL SECURITIES RULES MAKING BOARD or MSRB: An independent self-regulatory organization established by the Securities Acts Amendment of 1975, which is charged with primary rulemaking authority over dealers, dealer banks, and brokers in municipal securities. Its 15 members represent three categories: (a) securities firms; (b) bank dealers; and (c) the public; each category has equal representation on the Board.

MUTUAL ASSENT: The mutual offer and acceptance in an insurance policy that makes it a legally enforceable agreement.

MUTUAL COMPANY: A health or life insurance company that has no capital stock or stockholders. Rather, it is owned by its policy owners and managed by a board of directors chosen by the policy owners. Any earnings, in addition to those necessary for the operation of the company and contingency reserves, are returned to the policy owners in the form of policy dividends. See Stock Company.

MUTUALIZATION: The process of converting a stock insurance company to a mutual insurance company, accomplished by having the company buy in and retire its own shares.

N

NAIC: National Association of Insurance Commissioners is an organization of insurance regulators from all states and dependent areas.

NAIC LONG-TERM-CARE INSURANCE MODEL: Minimum standards for a long-term-care insurance policy as set forth by the National Association of Insurance Commissioners (NAIC): (a) guaranteed renewable contract; (b) no health care exclusions; (c) policy summary provision; (d) free-look period; and (e) custodial and skilled-nursing care benefits.

NAME-BRAND DRUG: A drug manufactured by a pharmaceutical company that has chosen to patent the drug's formula and register its brand name. See Generic Drug.

NAMED INSURED: In a life, long-term care, disability, or health insurance contract, the person or persons, organization, firm, or corporation specifically named as the insured(s) in the policy. See Member and Policy Holder.

NAMED PERIL POLICY: A health insurance policy, such as cancer, where named perils are listed.

NAPRAPATHY: System of bodywork founded in 1905 by chiropractic professor Oakley G. Smith, author of *Modernized Chiropractic* (1906). It encompasses nutritional, postural, and exercise counseling. Naprapathic theory holds: (a) that soft connective tissue in a state of contraction can cause neurovascular interference; (b) that this interference may cause circulatory congestion and nerve irritation; and (c) that reducing this interference (primarily by hand) paves the way for optimal homeostasis. The major form of Naprapathy in the United States is the Oakley Smith Naprapathic Method, taught by the Chicago National College of Naprapathy. See Alternative Health Care.

NASD: National Association of Securities Dealers.

NASDAQ: National Association of Securities Dealers Automated Quotations.

NATIONAL ACCOUNT: Large group health insurance accounts that have employees in more than one geographic area that are covered through a single national contract for health coverage.

NATIONAL ASSOCIATION OF HEALTH DATA ORGANIZATIONS: A group that promotes the development and improvement of state and national health information systems.

NATIONAL ASSOCIATION OF INSURANCE BROKERS, INCORPORATED (NAIB): Voluntary association of insurance brokers organized for the exchange of information and recommendations to state legislatures. See Big I.

NATIONAL ASSOCIATION OF INSURANCE COMMISSIONERS (NAIC): An association of state life, health, Property & Casualty, and other insurance commissioners attempting to solve insurance regulatory problems, create uniform legislation and regulations, and promote life insurance company solvency and responsibility. See Big I.

NATIONAL ASSOCIATION OF INSURANCE COMMISSIONERS MODEL CODE: A set of rules proposed by the NAIC in 1975 to establish minimum standards and guidelines to assure full and truthful disclosure to the public of all material and relevant information in the advertising and promotion of life insurance products.

NATIONAL ASSOCIATION OF SECURITIES DEALERS (NASD): A voluntary association of brokers or dealers in over-the-counter (OTC) securities organized on a nonprofit, non-stock-issuing basis. The general aim is to protect investors in the OTC market. It is the self-regulatory organization (SRO) for brokers or dealers in the OTC market.

NATIONAL ASSOCIATION OF SECURITIES DEALERS AUTOMATED QUOTATIONS (NASDAQ): An electronic data terminal device furnishing subscribers with instant identification of market makers and their current quotations, updated continuously.

NATIONAL ASSOCIATION OF STATE MEDICAID DIRECTORS (NASMD): An association of state Medicaid directors. NASMD is affiliated with the American Public Health Human Services Association (APHSA).

NATIONAL CENTER FOR HEALTH STATISTICS: A federal organization within the Centers for Disease Control and Prevention that collects, analyzes, and distributes health care statistics. The NCHS maintains the *International Classification of Diseases* (9th Rev. Clinical Modification) codes.

NATIONAL CLAIMS HISTORY (NCH) SYSTEM: A HCFA data reporting system that combines both Part A and Part B claims in a common file. The National Claims History system became fully operational in 1991.

NATIONAL COMMISSION ON STATE WORKER'S COMPENSATION LAWS: The national insurance group, first commissioned in 1971, to study state worker's compensation laws. See OSHA.

NATIONAL COMMITTEE FOR QUALITY ASSURANCE (NCQA): A nonprofit organization created to improve patient care quality and health plan performance in partnership with managed care plans, purchasers, consumers, and the public sector.

NATIONAL DRUG CODE (NDC): Classification system for drug identification, similar to the Uniform Product Code, used by a physician or medical group.

NATIONAL HEALTH EXPENDITURES: Total spending on health services, prescription, and over-the-counter drugs and products, nursing home care, insurance costs, public health spending, and health research and construction.

NATIONAL HEALTH INSURANCE: The government as the single payer of medical bills. Key features often include: federal financing from general tax revenues, beneficiary contributions or payroll taxes, government fee controls, and prospective budgets.

NATIONAL INSURANCE ASSOCIATION, INCORPORATED (NIA): An association of insurance companies formed for the exchange of information and ideas on common insurance related problems of African-Americans.

NATIONAL MEDIAN CHARGE: The national median charge is the exact middle amount of the amounts charged for the same medical service. This means that half of the hospitals and community mental health centers charged more than this amount and the other half charged less than this amount for the same service.

NATIONAL PRACTITIONER DATA BANK (NPDB): A computerized data bank maintained by the federal government that contains information on physicians against whom malpractice claims have been paid or certain disciplinary actions have been taken. Hospitals and other agencies pay a fee to access these records. Many regulatory agencies now require hospitals to utilize the NPDB prior to credentialing physicians at their facilities.

NATIONAL PROVIDER REGISTRY: The organization envisioned for assigning national provider IDs.

NATIONAL STANDARD FORMAT: Generically, this applies to any nationally standardized data format, but it is often used in a more limited way to designate the Professional EMC NSF, a 320-byte flat file record format used to submit professional claims.

NATIONAL STANDARD PER VISIT RATES: National rates for each home health disciplines based on historical claims data. Used in payment of low utilization payment adjustments and calculation of outliers.

NATIONAL UNIFORM BILLING COMMITTEE (NUBC): An organization, chaired and hosted by the American Hospital Association, that maintains the UB-92 hardcopy institutional billing form and the data element specifications for both the hardcopy form and the 192-byte UB-92 flat file electronic media claims format. The NUBC has a formal consultative role under HIPAA for all transactions affecting institutional health care services.

NATIONAL UNIFORM CLAIM COMMITTEE (NUCC): An organization chaired and hosted by the American Medical Association that maintains the HCFA-1500 claim form and a set of data element specifications for professional claims submission via the HCFA-1500 claim form, the Professional EMC NSF, and the X12 837. The NUCC also maintains the provider taxonomy codes and has a formal consultative role under HIPAA for all transactions affecting nondental noninstitutional professional health care services.

NATURAL DEATH: Death by means other than accident, murder, or suicide.

NATURAL GROUP: For purposes of group insurance coverage, a natural group is defined as one organized for some purpose other than obtaining less expensive group insurance and must have been in existence for a satisfactory period of time (usually 2 years) before its members are eligible for a group insurance program.

NATURAL PREMIUM: The premium that is sufficient to pay for a given amount of insurance from one premium date to the next. A policy issued on this basis is called a *yearly renewable term policy*, and the net natural premium rate for it is called a *yearly renewable term rate*. The premium advances each year with the age of the insured. The yearly renewable term plan is usually impracticable because, at the older ages, few persons can afford or are willing to pay the necessary premiums.

NATUROPATHY: System of care where only natural herbs and medicines are used.

NCPDP BATCH STANDARD: A National Council for Prescription Drug Programs (NCPDP) format for use by low-volume dispensers of pharmaceuticals, such as nursing homes.

NCPDP TELECOMMUNICATION STANDARD: A National Council for Prescription Drug Programs (NCPDP) standard designed for use by high-volume dispensers of pharmaceuticals, such as retail pharmacies.

NCQA: National Committee for Quality Assurance.

NEEDS ASSESSMENT: Systematic appraisal of the type, depth, and scope of a health problem.

NEGATIVE PLEDGE: A covenant bond that limits a medical provider, health care entity, or durable medical equipment provider from giving a real estate lien (claim) to another entity or creditor. See DME.

NEGLECT: Vendors or health care providers that do not render the goods or services needed to avoid harm or illness. The failure to exercise proper care.

NEGLIGENCE: Degree of care used by the ordinary and prudent person; may be caused by omission or commission.

NEONATAL INTENSIVE CARE UNIT (NICU): A hospital unit with special equipment for the care of premature and seriously ill newborn infants.

NEONATOLOGY: Medical care, treatment, study, and intervention for high-risk newborn babies.

NEPHROLOGY: The medical and surgical care of kidney and kidney-related ailments.

NET: The amount by which a health care company's total assets exceed its total liabilities, representing the value of the owner's interest, or equity in the company.

NET ACOUNTS RECEIVABLE: The amount projected to be received by a payer of health care services.

NET ASSETS: Assets minus liabilities.

NET ASSETS TO TOTAL ASSETS: net assets/total assets.

NET BENEFITS: The total discounted benefits minus the total discounted health insurance costs. See Benefits and Exclusions.

NET COST: A term ordinarily referring to the actual cost of health insurance to a policy owner in a mutual company after the policy dividends are deducted from the premiums deposited. Because there are no dividends on nonparticipating policies, the net cost of such policies is equal to the total premiums paid. See Expenses.

NET INTEREST COST (NIC): A common method of computing the interest expense to the issuer of issuing hospital revenue bonds, which usually serves as the basis of award in a competitive sale. NIC takes into account any premium and discount paid on the issue. NIC represents the dollar amount of coupon interest payable over the life of the serial issue, without taking into account the time value of money (as would be done in other calculation methods, such as the true interest cost method). Although the term net interest cost actually refers to the dollar amount of the issuer's interest cost, it is also used to refer to the overall rate of interest to be paid by the issuer over the life of the bonds.

NET LINE: Gross line on an individual risk, less all reinsurance ceded. Also, the maximum amount of loss on a particular risk to which an insurer or reinsurer will expose itself without reinsurance or retrocession.

NET LOSS: The amount of loss sustained by a health insurance company after all claims have been met

NET PATIENT SERVICES REVENUE: The revenue a health care entity or medical provider has the legal right to collect.

NET PREMIUM: (1) premium paid minus health insurance agent's commission; (2) the original premium minus any returned premium; (3) the net charge for insurance cost only minus expenses or contingencies; (4) a participating premium minus dividends paid or anticipated. See Premium. See Rates.

NET PREMIUM RATE: The amount of the health insurance premium before loading for expense.

NET PRESENT VALUE (NPV): The difference in amount between initial payment and related future cash inflows after cost of capital adjustments (interest rate). See Simple Interest and Compound Interest.

NET PROFITS: A health insurance term broadly used to describe only the profits remaining after including all earnings and other income or profit and after deducting all expenses and charges of every character, including interest, depreciation, and taxes.

NETWORK: An affiliation of providers through formal and informal contracts and agreements. Networks may contract externally to obtain administrative and financial services. A list of physicians, hospitals, and providers for a managed care organization. See IPA, MSA, PHO, and HMO.

NET WORKING CAPITAL: The difference between current asset and current liabilities for a health care entity.

NETWORK MODEL HMO: An HMO that contracts with several different medical groups, often at a capitated rate. Groups may use different methods to pay their physicians. A health plan that contracts with multiple physician groups to deliver health care to members. Usually limited to large single or multispecialty groups. Distinguished from group model plans that contract with a single medical group, independent practice associations that contract through an intermediary, and direct contract model plans that contract with individual physicians in the community. See Group-Model HMO, Health Maintenance Organization, and Independent Practice.

NEURO-LINGUISTIC PROGRAMMING (NLP, NEUROLINGUISTICS): Quasi-spiritual behavior-modification (or performance psychology) technique whose crux is modeling, or NLP modeling (i.e., imitating the behavior of high achievers). Richard Bandler and John Grinder initially formulated NLP in 1975, reputedly duplicating the magical results of several top communicators and therapists. (These included Milton H. Erickson, MD, the originator of Ericksonian Hypnosis.) Advanced Neuro Dynamics, Inc., in Honolulu, Hawaii, has promoted a style of NLP that "recognizes the importance of the human spirit and its connection with the mind and body." Pure NLP is the brand of NLP promoted by The Society of Neuro-Linguistic Programming.

NEUROLOGY: Medical and surgical care and treatment of nervous system disorders.

NEWBORN CARE: All physician services provided to a baby during the mother's hospitalization.

NEWBORNS' AND MOTHERS' HEALTH PROTECTION ACT (NMHPA): Law that mandates coverage for hospital stays for childbirth cannot generally be less than 48 hr for normal deliveries or 96 hr for cesarean section births.

NEWSPAPER POLICY: Limited health insurance policy sold by some newspaper companies to increase circulation.

NO FAULT INSURANCE: Health care insurance benefits coverage regardless of the at-fault party of an accident; originally automotive.

NOMINAL VALUE: A measurement of economic amount that is not corrected for change in price over time (inflation). Thus, not expressing a value in terms of constant prices. See Real Value.

NOMINATOR: In insurance, one who provides a referred lead, that is, gives the name (often with qualifying information) of a prospective buyer of health insurance or a prospective recruit.

NONADMITTED ASSETS: In insurance, assets by general accounting standards that do not qualify under state law for insurance reserve purposes, such as furniture, fixtures, bonds in default, certain securities, etc.

NONADMITTED COMPANY: A company not licensed to do business in a particular state. Also called an unauthorized company.

NONADMITTED REINSURANCE: Reinsurance for which no credit is given in the ceding company's annual report because the reinsurer is not licensed to do business in the ceding company's jurisdiction.

NONASSESSABLE CONTRACT OR POLICY: An insurance policy that limits the liability of policy owners to the amount of premiums paid. The policy owners cannot be assessed additional premiums or amounts.

NONASSIGNABLE CONTRACT OR POLICY: An insurance policy that the owner cannot legally assign to a third party.

NONCANCELABLE GUARANTEED RENEWABLE HEALTH INSURANCE: Health insurance policy not subject to change, alteration, termination, or premium increase.

NONCANCELABLE HEALTH INSURANCE POLICY: A health policy that the insured has the right to continue in force (by the payment of premiums as set forth in the contract) for a substantial period of time, during which period the insurance company has no unilateral right to make any change in any provision or cancel the policy. Both the premium and renewability are guaranteed.

NONCANCELABLE INCOME DISABILITY INSURANCE: Income interruption or termination disability insurance that remains in force at the option of the insurer.

NONCOMPOS MENTIS: Latin for "Not sound in mind."

NONCONFINING SICKNESS: An illness that prevents the insured from working, but does not confine the insured to his or her home, a hospital, or a sanitarium.

NONCONTRACTING PROVIDER: An eligible provider who has not entered into a contracting provider agreement with a HMO, managed care organization, or health insurance company. Payment for covered services is sent directly to the member and cannot be signed over to the provider. The member is responsible for amounts in excess of the maximum payment allowance. The noncontracting provider is responsible for collecting payment from the member. Payment can usually be sent directly to an out-of-state provider. See Doctor.

NONCONTRIBUTORY: Health insurance where the covered participant pays no part of the premium.

NONCURRENT ASSETS: Assets with a life of more than 1 year.

NONCURRENT LIABILITIES: Liabilities with a life of more than 1 year.

NONDISABLING INJURY: Injury that does not qualify the insured for total disability insurance benefits, as some ability to work is retained. See Illness and Disability.

NONDUPLICATION OF BENEFITS: A provision in some health insurance policies specifying that benefits will not be paid for amounts reimbursed by others. In group insurance, this is usually called coordination of benefits. See Coordination of Benefits.

NONFORMULARY DRUG: A drug or medication not listed and approved on a health insurance plan coverage schedule.

NONGROUP: A directly enrolled cohort without affiliation for medical or other insurance.

NONMALEFICENCE: Ethical principle of managed care to not harm their members.

NONMEDICAL HEALTH OR LIFE INSURANCE: Life, disability, or health insurance issued without a medical examination. The term applied to the medical portion of a life or disability insurance application that accepts a health questionnaire completed on the applicant over his or her signature and does not require a medical examination.

NONMEDICAL REPORT: A form completed by the applicant, giving certain information as to health required by an insurance company for issuance of insurance when a medical examination is not required.

NONOCCUPATIONAL DISABILITY: Disease or injury that is not job related. See Worker's Compensation Income Insurance.

NONOCCUPATIONAL HEALTH INSURANCE: Health insurance that covers off-the-job accidents and sickness, also referred to as unemployment compensation disability insurance. A health insurance policy that does not cover disability resulting from injury or sickness covered by workers' compensation insurance.

NONOPERATING EXPENSES: Health care entity expenses incurred though non-health care-related activities, like marketing, sales, and advertising.

NONOPERATING INCOME: Health care entity income received though non-health care-related activities, like marketing, sales, and advertising.

NONPARTICIPATING PHYSICIAN: A physician who does not sign a participation agreement and, therefore, is not obligated to accept assignment on all Medicare claims. See Assignment, Participating Physician, Participating Physician, and Supplier Program.

NONPHYSICIAN PRACTITIONER: A health care professional who is not a physician. Examples include advanced practice nurses and physician assistants.

NONPLAN PROVIDER: A health care provider without a contract with an insurer; similar to a nonparticipating provider.

NONPRICE RATIONING: Free health care services on a first-come-first served basis.

NONPROFIT INSURANCE COMPANY: Companies exempted from some taxes to provide health or medical expense insurance on service basis.

NONPRORATING POLICY: An insurance policy in which the benefits stipulated in the policy will be paid whether or not the insured changes his or her occupation.

NONRECOURSE FINANCING: Loans for which partners, both general and limited, have no personal liability. In health care facility real estate programs, only the value of such loans, if qualified, is part of the partners' basis in the partnership.

NONRESIDENT AGENT: Insurance agent licensed in a state in which he is not a resident.

NONSMOKER: The health characteristic of not using tobacco products, considered by an insurance company, when issuing, life, health, and long-term care insurance.

NONSYSTEMIC CONDITION: A local health condition, injury, or ailment not affecting the whole person.

NORTH CAROLINA HEALTH CARE INFORMATION-COMMUNICATIONS ALLIANCE: An organization in North Carolina that promotes the advancement and integration of information technology into the health care industry.

NOSOCOMIAL: Originating or beginning in a hospital, as with an infection.

NOTE: A written, short-term promise of an issuer to repay a specified principal amount on a date certain, together with interest at a stated rate, payable from a defined source of anticipated revenue. Notes usually mature in 1 year or less, although notes of longer maturities are also issued. The following types of notes are common in the municipal hospital-revenue bond market: (a) Bond Anticipation Notes (BANs): Notes issued by a governmental unit, usually for capital health care projects, which are paid from the proceeds of the issuance of long-term bonds; (b) Construction Loan Notes (CLNs): Notes issued to fund construction of hospital projects. CLNs are repaid by the permanent financing, which may be provided from bond proceeds or some prearranged commitment; (c) Revenue Anticipation Notes (RANs): Notes issued in anticipation of receiving hospital or other revenues at a future date; (d) Tax Anticipation Notes (TANs): Notes issued in anticipation of future tax receipts, such as receipts of ad valorem taxes that are due and payable at a set time of the year.

NOTES PAYABLE: A legal obligation to pay creditors or holders of a valid lien or claim. See Accounts Payable.

NOT-FOR-PROFIT: Ownership group that includes all church-related and other facilities that are organized and operated under a policy by which no trustee or other person shares in the profits or losses of the enterprise.

NOTICE OF ENROLLMENT RIGHTS: Should an employee decline enrollment in a group health plan at his or her first opportunity, an employer would provide to the employee a notice of enrollment rights. This notice advises the employee of what to expect should he or she wish to enroll at a later date.

NOTICE OF MEDICARE BENEFITS: A notice to show what action was taken on a claim. See Explanation of Medicare Benefits.

NOTICE OF MEDICARE PREMIUM PAYMENT DUE—HCFA 500: The billing notice sent to Medicare beneficiaries who must pay their Medicare premium directly. Notices are sent either monthly or quarterly.

NOTIFICATION REQUIREMENTS: Ensuring that a patient receives the appropriate level of care by reviewing admissions and procedures before or after they are provided. Examples of notification requirements include precertification, admission review, prior approval, and continued stay review.

NUBC EDI TAG: The NUBC EDI Technical Advisory Group, which coordinates issues affecting both the NUBC and the X12 standards. See EDI Section.

NUISANCE: A product or service that endangers life or health.

NURSE: Informal or formal term for a helper or giver of health care interventions, diagnosis, or treatment.

NURSE FEES: A provision in a medical expense reimbursement policy calling for reimbursement for the fees of nurses other than those employed by the hospital.

NURSE PRACTITIONER: Registered nurse qualified and specially trained to provide primary care, including primary health care in homes and in ambulatory care facilities, long-term care facilities, and other health care institutions. Nurse practitioners generally function under the supervision of a physician but not necessarily in his or her presence. They are usually salaried rather than reimbursed on a fee-for-service basis, although the supervising physician may receive fee-for-service reimbursement for their services. Are also considered midlevel practitioners. See RN and LPN.

NURSERY: A hospital perinatal unit for normal newborns that includes incubators for nondistressed, low-birth-weight babies.

NURSE TRIAGE: A screening process done by nurses to prioritize patient complaints and ailments.

NURSING EXPENSE PROVISION: In health insurance, provides per diem benefits to the insured if that individual requires nursing care. The nurse generally must be a private duty registered nurse (RN) and not a member of the insured's immediate family.

NURSING FACILITY: An institution that provides skilled-nursing care and rehabilitation services, to injured, functionally disabled, or sick persons. Formerly, distinctions were made between intermediate care facilities (ICFs) and skilled-nursing facilities (SNFs). The Omnibus Budget Reconciliation Act of 1987 eliminated this distinction effective October 1, 1990, by requiring all nursing facilities to meet SNF certification requirements.

NURSING HOME: A residence facility that provides room, board, and help in the activities of daily living.

NURSING HOME INSURANCE: A medical expense health insurance policy offered primarily to senior citizens to provide residential or convalescent nursing home care. The National Association of Insurance Commissioners bill, accepted by most states, requires that a nursing home policy that covers only convalescent care must have that limitation stated clearly on the face of the policy.

NURSING HOME PROVISION: Provides health insurance benefits of some specified amount if the insured is confined to a nursing home when no longer needing hospital care.

NURSING NOTES: Patient care records rendered by the nursing staff and entered into the patient medical record.

NURSING SERVICES: The cost centers that include care given to persons who are partially or totally unable to care for themselves, have health or mental problems, and require convalescent or restorative services. Included are the following nursing services: (a) skilled-nursing care; (b) intermediate care; (c) mentally disordered care; (d) developmentally disabled care; (e) subacute care; (f) hospice inpatient services; and (g) other routine services. Also included are consultation and evaluation services.

O

OBJECTIONS: Questions or concerns raised by prospects during the agent's presentation, sometimes validly, sometimes as a means of evasion.

OBJECTIONS IN THE INTERVIEW: Concerns or negative statements expressed to the agent by the insurance sales prospect regarding the agent's recommendations.

OBJECTIONS TO THE INTERVIEW: Objections raised by the prospect to granting an insurance agent an interview.

OBLIGATORY TREATY: In insurance, a reinsurance contract under which the business covered by the contract must be ceded by the ceding company in accordance with specific contract terms and must be accepted by the reinsurer.

OBSERVATION UNIT: A hospital department that cares for inpatients for less than 23 hr and 59 minutes.

OBSOLETE CARE: No longer generally accepted health care, usually in the eyes of the insurance or managed care company.

OBSTETRICAL/GYNECOLOGICAL (OB/GYN) CARE PROVIDER: A selected gynecological and maternity health care manager. He or she will evaluate a health condition and either treat or coordinate required gynecological or maternity services.

OBSTETRICS: This is the medical treatment that relates to pregnancy, childbirth, and maternity services. Obstetrics should not be confused with gynecology that covers reproductive conditions in women.

OCCUPANCY RATE: A measure of the usage of the licensed beds during the reporting period that is derived by dividing the patient days in the reporting period by the licensed bed days in the reporting period. A measure of health facility inpatient use, showing the percentage of beds (excluding beds in suspense) occupied during the reporting period. It is determined by dividing patient (census) days by licensed or available bed days (the number of beds multiplied by number of calendar days in reporting period). The percentage of facility beds occupied during the reporting period. It is determined by dividing patient days by the quantity: average number of licensed beds, excluding those beds in suspense, multiplied by number of calendar days in the reporting period, with that result multiplied by 100 to convert it to a percentage. [Patient days divided by (number of beds × number of days in reporting period) × 100].

OCCUPATIONAL ACCIDENT: An accident that arises from and occurs in the course of employment. See Disability and Disability Income Insurance.

OCCUPATIONAL CLASSIFICATION: Groupings of occupations by equivalent degrees of inherent hazard to which they are subject. A system of classifications used by different insurance companies for purposes of underwriting and rating health insurance policies in particular.

OCCUPATIONAL DISEASE: Impairment of health caused by continued exposure to conditions inherent in a person's occupation or a disease caused by or resulting from the nature of an employment See Hazard, Peril, and Illness.

OCCUPATIONAL HAZARD: A danger inherent in the insured's line of work. See Peril and Illness.

OCCUPATIONAL HEALTH: Activities undertaken to protect and promote the health and safety of employees in the workplace, including minimizing exposure to hazardous substances, evaluating work practices, and environments to reduce injury, and reducing or eliminating other health threats. See OSHA.

OCCUPATIONAL INJURY (OR SICKNESS): An injury or sickness arising out of, or in the course of, one's employment.

OCCUPATIONAL MANUAL: A book listing occupational classifications for various types of work.

OCCUPATIONAL POLICY: A plan that insures a person against both off-the-job and on-the-job accidents or sicknesses.

OCCUPATIONAL RISK: A condition in an occupation that increases the possibility of accident, sickness, or death.

OCCUPATIONAL SAFETY & HEALTH ACT (OSHA): Act passed by U.S. Congress that became effective in April 1971. It is found in the Code of Federal Regulations, Title 29, Chapter XVII, Part 1910. Its purpose is to reduce occupational hazards through direct intervention, while promoting a safety and health culture through compliance assistance, cooperative programs, and strong leadership; and maximize OSHA's effectiveness and efficiency by strengthening its capabilities and infrastructure.

OCCUPATIONAL SAFETY & HEALTH ACT (OSHA) BLOOD-BORNE STANDARD: Standard to reduce occupational exposure to blood-borne diseases, like AIDS, Hepatitis B, Syphilis, etc. See OSHA.

OCCUPATIONAL THERAPIST: A practitioner of occupational therapy.

OCCUPATIONAL THERAPY: Health care physical therapy to assist in the gain back of lost usual activities of daily living, former job, or occupation.

OCCURRENCE: An accident or sickness that results in an insured loss.

ODDS: The probable number of incidents of a given occurrence in a statistical universe or representative sample, expressed as a ratio to the probable number of nonoccurrences.

OFFER: An applicant's signing and submitting a written application for insurance, accompanied by the first premium.

OFFER AND ACCEPTANCE: (1) An offer occurs by signing an application, having a physical examination, and prepaying the first premium. Policy issuance and delivery as applied for, constitute acceptance by the company. (2) Offer made by the company and premium payment constitutes acceptance by the applicant.

OFFEREE: One to whom a health insurance policy offer is made.

OFFERING MEMORANDUM: Written document that describes the terms and conditions of a health care organizations private placement.

OFFEROR: One who makes a health insurance policy offer.

OFFICE OF HEALTH MAINTENANCE ORGANIZATIONS (OHMO): The office within the Department of Health and Human Services that is responsible for overseeing federal government activity regarding HMOs.

OFFICE OF INSPECTOR GENERAL (OIG): The office responsible for auditing, evaluating, and criminal and civil investigating for Department of Health and Human Services (DHHS), as well as imposing sanctions, when necessary, against health care providers. Unconstrained federal unit within the DHHS that performs health care audits, investigates medical fraud and abuse cases, collects data and performs special monitoring functions. See FBI, Fraud and Department of Justice.

OFFICE OF THE INSPECTOR GENERAL: See OIG.

OFFICE OF PERSONNEL MANAGEMENT (OPM): The federal agency that administers the agency that a managed care plan contracts to provide coverage for federal employees.

OFFICE OF PREPAID HEALTH CARE OPERATIONS AND OVERSIGHT (OPHCOO): The latest name for the federal agency that oversees federal qualification and compliance for HMOs.

OFFICE VISIT: Visiting a provider or physician in an office setting for services.

OHTA: Office of Health Technology Assessment.

OLD-AGE BENEFIT FOR SPOUSE OF WORKER: Under U.S. Social Security, a monthly benefit paid to the wife or husband of an individual who is receiving old-age benefits, provided the spouse has been married to that individual for at least 1 year (or if they are the natural or adoptive parents of a mutual child).

OLD-AGE SURVIVOR'S AND DISABILITY INSURANCE: The actual name for Social Security, a United States federal system of social insurance benefits for aged workers and their eligible family members, eligible surviving family members of deceased workers, and disabled workers and their eligible family members, set up by the 1935 Social Security law, with compulsory participation for all eligible persons, and with benefits and contribution rates determined by schedule or formulas provided by Congress.

OLD-AGE AND SURVIVORS INSURANCE: The retirement and death benefits under U.S. Social Security.

OLDER AGE POLICY: In health insurance, medical care policy issued to persons aged 65 years or older to supplement government-sponsored programs, such as Medicare.

OMBUDSPERSON OR OMBUDSMAN: A person within a managed care organization or a person outside of the health care system (such as an appointee of the state) who is designated to receive and investigate complaints from beneficiaries about quality of care, inability to access care, discrimination, and other problems that beneficiaries may experience with their managed care organization. This individual often functions as the beneficiary's advocate in pursuing grievances or complaints about denials of care or inappropriate care.

OMD: Oriental medical doctor. DOM stands for doctor of oriental medicine.

OMISSIONS: Failure to act.

OMNIA PRO AEGROTO: Latin phrase that means "all for the patient."

ONUS (ONUS PROPONDI): Latin phrase that means "the burden of proof."

OON: Out of Network.

OPEN ACCESS: Open access arrangements allow members to see participating providers, usually specialists, without referral from the health plan's gatekeeper. These types of arrangements are most often found in an independent physician association-model HMOs.

OPEN CERTIFICATE: An insurance policy under which the rates and policy provisions may be changed. Fraternal benefit societies are required by law to issue this type of certificate.

OPEN COVER: In insurance, a reinsurance facility under which risks of a specified category may be declared and insured.

OPEN DEBIT: A life and health insurance debit (territory) currently without an agent.

OPEN-ENDED HMO: Enrollees are allowed to receive services outside the HMO provider network without referral authorization, but are usually required to pay an additional copay or deductible.

OPEN-END QUESTION: In an insurance sales interview, a question that elicits an opinion from the prospect or that requires more than a simple yes or no response.

OPEN ENROLLMENT: The annual period during which people in a dual choice health benefits program can choose among the two (or more) plans, being offered. Also, may be the period during which a federally qualified HMO must make its plan available without restrictions to individuals who are not part of a group.

OPEN ENROLLMENT PERIOD: After the initial open enrollment period, the time where eligible persons may change health or benefit plans usually without evidence of insurability or waiting periods. This period of time usually occurs annually.

OPEN FORMULARY: A list of drugs that a health plan prefers, but does not mandate physicians to prescribe.

OPENING INVENTORY: The cost of durable medical equipment and other medical supplies on hand at the beginning of the year.

OPEN-PANEL HMO: A type of HMO in which any doctor or provider who meets the HMO's specific standards can be contract with the HMO to provide services to the members.

OPEN PHO: A physician-hospital organization available to all eligible hospital medical staff members.

OPERATING ACTIVITIES: The main business activities of a health care organization.

OPERATING BED: A bed or cot ready and available for patient use.

OPERATING BUDGET: The operational inflow and outflow projections of a health care entity.

OPERATING CASH FLOW: The cash flows received from the main business activities of a health care organization.

OPERATING EXPENSES: The expenses incurred from the main business activities of a health care organization.

OPERATING INCOME: The income earned from the main business activities of a health care organization.

OPERATING LEASE: A short-term loan for daily operations.

OPERATING MARGIN: Income (loss) from health care operations plus mortgage interest expenses plus other interest expenses divided by net patient service revenue. This ratio indicates the percentage of net patient service revenue that remains as income after operating expenses, except interest expense, have been deducted.

OPERATING REVENUES: The revenues generated by a health care entity through its operational activities and provision of medical services.

OPERATIONS: In insurance, the normal activities of an insurance company or agency in the course of conducting its business.

OPERATIVE NOTES: Surgical notes of an operating procedure(s) created by the surgeon.

OPHTHALMOLOGIST: A trained and licensed medical or osteopathic doctor who specializes in treating conditions and diseases of the eye. A medical eye doctor. See MD/DO.

OPHTHALMOLOGY: Care and treatment of eye disorders by an MD/DO.

OPL: Other Party Liability.

OPPORTUNITY HEALTH CARE COSTS: The value of health care opportunities foregone because of an intervention project.

OPTICIAN: Nonphysician specialist who fits, adjusts, and dispenses glasses and other optical devices based on the written prescription of a licensed physician or optometrist.

OPTIMAL HEALTH: Optimal health is a balance of physical, emotional, social, spiritual, and intellectual health.

OPTIONAL BENEFIT: An additional benefit offered by an insurance company that may be included in a policy at the applicant's request, usually for an additional premium. Waiver of premium and accidental death benefit riders are examples of optional benefits.

OPTIONAL RENEWAL: Health insurance contract giving the holder a right to continue or terminate coverage at any premium due date.

OPTOMETRIST: Nonphysician specialist in the examination, diagnosis, treatment, and management of diseases and disorders of the visual system, the eye, and associated structures, as well as the diagnosis of related systemic conditions. See OD.

OR: Operating Room.

ORAL SURGEON: Provider licensed to perform diagnosis and treatment of oral conditions requiring surgical intervention. See DDS or DMD.

ORGANIZATIONAL DETERMINATION: A health insurance or managed care plan's decision to pay or appeal medical services payment decisions after an appeal is filed.

ORGANIZED CARE: An advanced form of integrated health care delivery through a continuum of care.

ORGANIZED CARE SYSTEM: Often used to discuss a more evolved form of integrated delivery systems (IDSs) and Community Care Networks (CCNs). This relatively new term describes the result of mergers and alliances between and among physicians, health systems, and managed care organizations. These systems often have the same performance imperatives as IDSs and CCNs: (a) improve health status; (b) integrate delivery; (c) demonstrate value; (d) improve efficiency of care delivery and prevention; and (e) meet patient and community needs.

ORGAN PROCUREMENT: Refers to hospital, physician, laboratory, administrative, and other miscellaneous costs related to the harvesting, preparation, preservation, and transportation of an organ for transplant. Organ procurement does not include fees for the purchase of an organ.

ORIGINAL ISSUE DISCOUNT: An amount by which the par value of a hospital or other security exceeds its public offering price at the time it was originally offered to an investor. The original issue discount is amortized over the life of the security and, on a municipal security, is generally treated as tax-exempt interest. When the investor sells the security before maturity, any profit realized on such sale is figured (for tax purposes) on the adjusted cost basis, which is calculated for each year the security is outstanding by adding the accretion value to the original offering price. The amount of the accretion value (and the existence and total amount of original issue discount) is determined in accordance with the provisions of the Internal Revenue Code and the rules and regulations of the Internal Revenue Service.

ORIGINAL MEDICARE PLAN: The federal 1965 Medicare Health Insurance plan for seniors with unlimited freedom of choice; traditional Medicare. See Medicare Parts A and B.

ORTHOMOLECULAR MEDICINE (ORTHOMOLECULAR NUTRITIONAL MEDICINE, ORTHOMOLECULAR THERAPY): Approach to therapy whose centerpiece is megavitamin therapy. Orthomolecular medicine encompasses hair analysis, orthomolecular nutrition (a variation of megavitamin therapy), and orthomolecular psychiatry. Linus Carl Pauling, PhD (1901–1994), coined the word *orthomolecular*. The prefix *ortho* means straight, and the implicit meaning of *orthomolecular* is "to straighten (correct) concentrations of specific molecules." The primary principle of orthomolecular medicine is that nutrition is the foremost consideration in diagnosis and treatment. Its purported focus is normalizing the balance of vitamins, minerals, amino acids, and similar substances in the body.

ORTHOPEDICS: The branch of medicine that involves the care and treatment of muscle and skeleton diseases.

OSHA (OCCUPATIONAL SAFETY & HEALTH ACT): Act passed by U.S. Congress that became effective in April 1971. It is found in the Code of Federal Regulations, Title 29, Chapter XVII, Part 1910. Its purpose is to reduce occupational hazards through direct intervention, while promoting a safety and health culture through compliance assistance, cooperative programs, and strong leadership; and maximize OSHA's effectiveness and efficiency by strengthening its capabilities and infrastructure.

OTHER CARRIER LIABILITY: The decision with dual benefits covered of which health plan will be the primary insurer.

OTHER INCOME BENEFITS (BENEFIT INTEGRATION): While disabled, an insured may be eligible for benefits from other sources. Benefits payable under the long-term disability plan may be offset (reduced) by other sources of disability income such as Social Security, workers compensation, or disability benefits received from other employer-sponsored plans.

OTHER INSURANCE CLAUSE: Statement of what is to be done if any other insurance policy embraces the covered claim.

OTHER MANAGED CARE ARRANGEMENT: Other Managed Care Arrangement is used if the plan is not considered a primary care case management, prepaid health plan, comprehensive managed care organization (MCO), Medicaid-only MCO, or health insuring (insurance) organization.

OTHER PROVIDERS: Health providers other than facilities and practitioners, such as hospice agencies, ambulance services, and retail pharmacies.

OTHER TEACHING HOSPITALS: Hospitals with an approved graduate medical education program and a ratio of interns and residents to beds of less than 0.25.

OTHER URBAN AREA: A metropolitan statistical area with a population of less than 1 million, or a New England County Metropolitan Area with fewer than 970,000 people.

OTHER WEIRD ARRANGEMENT (OWA): A general acronym that applies to any new or bizarre managed care plan that has thought up a new twist. See Hybrid.

OTOLARYNGOLOGIST: A physician who specializes in the medical and surgical care and treatment of the head and neck, including the ears, nose, and throat, but excluding the eyes.

OTOLARYNGOLOGY: The medical and surgical care and treatment of the head and neck, including the ears, nose, and throat, but excluding the eyes.

OUT OF AREA: A reference to services that are outside a certain geographic area generally referred to as the service area.

OUT-OF-AREA BENEFITS: The coverage allowed to HMO members for emergency situations outside of the prescribed geographic area of the HMO. The coverage generally is restricted to emergency services.

OUT-OF-AREA COVERAGE: Coverage of benefits in an area that would normally be outside the health plan's coverage service area.

OUT-OF-AREA SERVICES: When covered persons receive services outside of the normal coverage area. These services are usually only covered in cases of emergency or when prior approval is given, unless otherwise stated in the contract.

OUTCOME: A clinical outcome is the result of medical or surgical intervention or nonintervention.

OUTCOME AND ASSESSMENT INFORMATION SET: A group of data elements that represent core items of a comprehensive assessment for an adult home care patient and form the basis for measuring patient outcomes for purposes of outcome-based quality improvement (OBQI). This assessment is performed on every patient receiving services of home health agencies that are approved to participate in the Medicare or Medicaid programs.

OUTCOME DATA: Data that measure the health status of people enrolled in managed care resulting from specific medical and health interventions.

OUTCOME EVALUATION: Outcome evaluation is used to obtain descriptive data on a project and to document short-term results. Task-focused results are those that describe the output of the activity (e.g., the number of public inquiries received as a result of a public service announcement). Short-term results describe the immediate effects of the project on the target audience (e.g., percentage of the target audience showing increased awareness of the subject). Information that can result from an outcome evaluation includes: (a) knowledge and attitude changes; (b) expressed intentions of the target audience; (c) short-term or intermediate behavior shifts; and (d) policies initiated or other institutional changes made.

OUTCOME INDICATOR: An indicator that assesses what happens or does not happen to a patient following a process; agreed upon desired patient characteristics to be achieved; undesired patient conditions to be avoided.

OUTCOME MANAGEMENT: A clinical result of medical or surgical intervention or nonintervention. It is thought that through a database of outcomes experience, caregivers will know better which treatment modalities result in consistently better outcomes for patients. Outcome management may lead to the development of clinical protocols.

OUTCOME MEASUREMENT: This process measures the results of specific medical treatments in an effort to discern a pattern and develop reliable practice patterns for providers to follow that keep care quality high, while delivering cost-effective medicine.

OUTCOMES: The clinical, administrative, and economic results achieved through health care intervention and treatment.

OUTCOMES AND EFFECTIVENESS RESEARCH: Medical or health services research that attempts to identify the clinical outcomes (including mortality, morbidity, and functional status) of the delivery of health care.

OUTCOMES MANAGEMENT: Providers and payers alike wish to find a method of managing care in a way that would produce the best outcomes. Managed care organizations are increasingly interested in learning to manage the outcome of care rather than just managing the cost of care. It is thought that through a database of outcomes experience, caregivers will know better which treatment modalities result in consistently better outcomes for patients. Outcomes management may lead to the development of clinical protocols.

OUTCOMES MEASUREMENT SYSTEM: A method used to track clinical treatment and responses to that treatment. The methods for measuring outcomes are quite varied among providers. Much disagreement exists regarding the best practice or tools to utilize to measure outcomes. In fact, much disagreement exists in the medical field about the definition of outcome itself. See Outcomes.

OUTCOMES RESEARCH: Research on measures of changes in patient outcomes (i.e., patient health status and satisfaction resulting from specific medical and health interventions). Attributing changes in outcomes to medical care requires distinguishing the effects of care from the effects of the many other factors that influence patients' health and satisfaction. With the elimination of the physician's fiduciary responsibility to the patient, outcomes data is gaining increasing importance for patient advocacy and consumer protection. Payers to identify potential partners on the basis of good outcomes use outcomes research.

OUTCOMES STANDARDS: Long-term objectives that define optimal, measurable future levels of health status, maximum acceptable levels of disease, injury, or dysfunction, or prevalence of risk factors.

OUTLAY: The issuance of checks, disbursement of cash, or electronic transfer of funds made to liquidate an expense regardless of the fiscal year the service was provided or the expense was incurred. When used in the discussion of the Medicaid program, outlays refer to amounts advanced to the states for Medicaid.

OUTLIER: Cases with extremely long lengths of stay (day outliers) or extraordinarily high costs (cost outliers) compared with others classified in the same diagnosis-related group. Hospitals receive additional prospective payment plan payment for these cases.

OUTLIER THRESHOLDS: The day and cost cutoff points that separate inlier patients from outlier patients.

OUT-OF-NETWORK BENEFITS: With most HMOs, a patient cannot have any services reimbursed if provided by a hospital or doctor who is not in the network. With preferred provider organizations and other managed care organizations, there may exist a provision for reimbursement of out-of-network providers. Usually involves a higher copayment or a lower reimbursement. See Point of Service Plans, Benefits, and Exclusions.

OUT-OF-NETWORK ITEMS AND SERVICES: Health care coverage for a person who elects to receive care from a nonparticipating provider when covered under the contract. In these cases, the deductible or copayment may be higher.

OUT-OF-NETWORK PROVIDER: A health care provider with whom a managed care organization does not have a contract to provide health care services. Because the beneficiary must pay either all of the costs of care from an out-of-network provider or their cost-sharing requirements are greatly increased, depending on the particular plan a beneficiary is in, out-of-network providers are generally not financially accessible to Medicaid beneficiaries. See Doctor.

OUTPATIENT: A person who receives care at a clinic or hospital without being admitted to that facility as an overnight or resident patient.

OUTPATIENT CARE: Care given a person who is not bedridden.

OUTPATIENT DIAGNOSTIC RIDER: Insurance contract clause for outpatient diagnostic tests.

OUTPATIENT PROSPECTIVE PAYMENT SYSTEM (OPPS): A payment method that establishes rates, prices, or budgets before services are rendered and costs are incurred for outpatients. Providers retain or absorb at least a portion of the difference between established revenues and actual costs. See PPS.

OUTPATIENT REVIEW: Quality program to assess outpatient care and treatment.

OUTPATIENT SURGERY: Surgery on a nonhospital admission basis.

OUTPATIENT VISITS: Included are emergency room visits, outpatient clinic visits, referred ancillary service visits, home health care contacts, and day care days, where the outpatient is treated and released the same day. Also included are outpatient ambulatory surgery visits, renal dialysis visits, observation care visits, psychiatric visits, chemical dependency visits, hospice outpatient visits, and adult day health care visits.

OUT-OF-PLAN PROVIDER: Physician who has not entered into a contract with an HMO or other health insurance carrier. See Doctor.

OUT-OF-POCKET COSTS: Total costs paid directly by consumers for insurance copayment and deductibles, prescription or over-the-counter drugs, and other services.

OUT-OF-POCKET EXPENSE: Cost borne directly by a patient without the benefit of insurance or additional out-of-pocket expenses, such as deductibles or copayments. See Co-payment and Deductible.

OUT-OF-POCKET LIMIT: A cap placed on out-of-pocket costs, after which benefits increase to provide full coverage for the rest of the year.

OUT-OF-POCKET MAXIMUM: The maximum amount of expenses, as set by a health care plan that a person is obligated to pay directly during each calendar year.

OUTSTANDING BUSINESS: Life and health insurance issued but not yet placed in force.

OVER-AGE INSURANCE: Health insurance issued beyond an age normally issued, such as 65 years.

OVER-THE-COUNTER DRUGS (OTC): A drug that can be purchased without a prescription. See Generic and Trade Drugs.

OVER-THE-COUNTER SECURITY: As thousands of companies have insufficient shares outstanding, stockholders, or earnings to warrant application for listing on the New York Stock Exchange, securities of these companies are traded in the over-the-counter market between firms who act either as agents for their customers or as principals (for themselves).

OVER-THE-COUNTER SELLING: A nonagency system of marketing whereby the insured obtains insurance by going directly to the insurance company. Savings bank life insurance departments and certain direct writers engage in over-the-counter selling.

OVER INSURANCE: More insurance in force than required.

OVERLAPPING DEBT: The hospital issuer's proportionate share of the debt of other local governmental units that either overlaps it (the issuer is located either wholly or partly within the geographic limits of the other units) or underlies it (the other units are located within the geographic limits of the issuer). The debt is generally apportioned based upon relative assessed values.

OVERRIDE: Insurance claims payments when after adjudication that is not automated in nature.

OVERRIDING COMMISSION: Commission paid to a general agent, special agent, agent, or manager in addition to the commission paid the agent or broker who secures the application or renewal of the insurance contract.

OWNER: The person designated as the owner of an insurance policy, with all rights contained in the policy. The owner is so designated on the policy application and may or may not be the insured. Also referred to as the policy owner or policyholder.

OWNERSHIP OF EXPIRATIONS: A company agreement, ordinarily found in the life and health fields, stating that certain details of a policy (such as expiration) will not be revealed to any other agent or broker except the originating agent, thus permitting the original agent to contact the client for renewal or extension of a policy.

P

PACKAGE: A combination of several different types of health insurance coverage.

PACKAGE PRICING: Combines the fees for the professional and institutional services associated with a procedure into a single payment. Package pricing, also known as service bundling or global pricing, sets the price of the bundled procedures and therefore implicitly controls the volume of services provided as part of the global service.

PAID AMOUNT: The portion of a submitted charge that is actually paid by both third-party payers and the insured, including copayments and balance bills. For Medicare this amount may be less than the allowed charge if the submitted charge is less, or it may be more because of balance billing.

PAID AS BILLED: Medical invoice paid as submitted without change or adjudication.

PAID BUSINESS: Insurance for which the application has been signed, the medical examination completed, and the settlement for the premium tendered.

PAID CLAIMS: Amounts paid to providers based on the health plan.

PAID CLAIMS LOSS RATIO: Paid claims divided by total premiums.

PANDEMIC: An epidemic occurring over a very wide area (several countries or continents) and usually affecting a large proportion of the population.

PAPER PROFIT: An unrealized profit on a security still held. Paper profits are realized only when a security is sold at prices above the cost of acquisition.

PARAMEDICAL: A nonphysician health care provider.

PARAMEDICAL EXAM: An examination by a nonphysician health care provider.

PARAMEDICAL TREATMENT: Treatment by a nonphysician medical provider.

PARENT ORGANIZATION: A health care entity that owns another health care company.

PAR MAIL ORDER DRUG PROVIDER: A prescription medication vendor who has a contract or service agreement with a health plan to provide medications to the plan's members via mail order.

PAROL EVIDENCE RULE: A legal concept that states when an agreement has been executed in writing, any prior oral agreements must have been included in the written agreement to be considered by a court of law.

PAR PHARMACY: A pharmacy that has a contract or service agreement with an insurer to provide medications to the plan's members directly.

PAR PRESCRIBER: A participating provider who is licensed to prescribe drugs to patients.

PART A MEDICARE: Medical Hospital Insurance (HI) under Part A of Title XVIII of the Social Security Act, which covers beneficiaries for inpatient hospital, home health, hospice, and limited skilled nursing facility services. Beneficiaries are responsible for deductibles and copayments. Part A services are financed by the Medicare HI Trust Fund, which consists of Medicare tax payments.

PART B MEDICARE: Medicare Supplementary Medical Insurance (SMI) under Part B of Title XVII of the Social Security Act, which covers Medicare beneficiaries for physician services, medical supplies, and other outpatient treatment. Beneficiaries are responsible for monthly premiums, copayments, deductibles, and balance billing. Part B services are financed by a combination of enrollee premiums and general tax revenues.

PART C MEDICARE: Medicare managed care compensation program. See MEDICARE + Choice.

PART D MEDICARE: Medicare Drug Program.

PARTIAL CAPITATION: An insurance arrangement where the payment made to a health plan is a combination of a capitated premium and payment based on actual use of services; the proportions specified for these components determine the insurance risk faced by the plan. See Capitation.

PARTIAL DISABILITY: In health insurance, an illness or injury that prevents an insured from performing a significant part, but not all, of his or her occupational duties. Disability income policies often provide partial disability benefits.

PARTIAL HOSPITALIZATION PROGRAM (PHP): Acute level of psychiatric treatment normally provided for 4 or more hours per day. Normally includes group therapies and activities with homogeneous patient populations. Is used as a referral step-down from inpatient care or as an alternative to inpatient care. Unlike intensive outpatient or simple outpatient services, PHP provides an attending psychiatrist, onsite nursing and social work. Reimbursed by payers at a rate that is roughly one half of inpatient psychiatric hospitalization day rate. Patients do not spend the night in the partial hospital.

PARTIAL HOSPITALIZATION SERVICES: Additional services provided to mental health or substance abuse patients that provides outpatient treatment as an alternative or follow-up to inpatient treatment.

PARTIAL RISK CONTRACT: A contract between a purchaser and a health plan, in which only part of the financial risk is transferred from the purchaser to the plan.

PARTICIPANT: A person covered by an insurance policy.

PARTICIPATING PHYSICIAN: A physician who signs a participation agreement to accept assignment on all Medicare claims for 1 year. A primary care physician in practice in the payer's managed care service area that has entered into a contract. Participating other entities may include: hospitals, pharmacists, outpatient treatment and diagnostic centers, and other allied health care providers.

PARTICIPATING PHYSICIAN AND SUPPLIER PROGRAM (PAR): A program that provides financial and administrative incentives for physicians and suppliers to agree in advance to accept assignment on all Medicare claims for a 1-year period.

PARTICIPATING PROVIDER: Any provider licensed in the state of provision and contracted with an insurer.

PARTICIPATION: The number of employees enrolled compared with the total number eligible for coverage. Many times, a minimum participation percentage is required.

PAR VALUE: The face or stated value of a fixed income security.

PATHOLOGIST: A medical doctor or doctor of osteopathy who practices pathology.

PATHOLOGY: The laboratory study of disease, human tissue, and corpses.

PATIENT: The person or health insurance member receiving health care benefits, medical care, outpatient services, long-term care, drug therapy, disability benefits, or durable medical equipment; regardless of the ability to pay.

PATIENT ACUITY: Intensity of a patient care rated from I (minimal) to intensive care IV.

PATIENT ADVOCATE: See Advocate.

PATIENT BILL OF RIGHTS: A report prepared by the President's Advisory Commission on Consumer Protection and Quality in the Health Care Industry in an effort to ensure the security of patient information, promote health care quality, and improve the availability of health care treatment and services. The report lists a number of rights, subdivided into eight general areas that all health care consumers should be guaranteed and describes responsibilities that consumers need to accept for the sake of their own health.

PATIENT LIABILITY: The dollar amount that an insured is legally obligated to pay for services rendered by a provider.

PATIENT LIFTS: Patient moving equipment.

PATIENT MIX: The number and types of patients in a health care environment.

PATIENT ORIGIN: The geographic origin of the patient as determined by the patient's zip code.

PATIENT ORIGIN STUDY: A study, generally undertaken by an individual health program or health plan agency, to determine the geographic distribution of the residences of the patients served by one or more health programs. Such studies help define catchment and medical trade areas and are useful in locating and planning the development of new services.

PATTERN ANALYSIS: The clinical and statistical analysis of data sets.

PAYER: An entity that assumes the risk of paying for medical treatments. This can be an uninsured patient, a self-insured employer, a health plan, or an HMO.

PAYER-ID: Centers for Medicare and Medicaid's term for their pre-HIPAA National Payer ID initiative.

PAYMENT RATE: The total payment that a hospital or community mental health center gets when they give outpatient services to Medicare patients. The total amount paid for each unit of service rendered by a health care provider, including both the amount covered by the insurer and the consumer's cost sharing: sometimes referred to as payment level. Also used to refer to capitation payments to health plans. For Medicare payments to physicians, this is the same as the allowed charge.

PAYMENT REVIEW PROGRAMS: A program used to discover medical fraud and health care abuse by provider and practitioners.

PAYMENT SAFEGUARDS: Activities to prevent and recover inappropriate Medicare benefit payments including Medicare secondary payer, medical review or utilization review, provider audits, and fraud and abuse detection.

PAYOR: See Payer.

PAY OR PLAY: Philosophy for employers to provide health care insurance for employees or pay the government to provide it.

PAY AND PURSUE: Coordination of insurance benefits administered after claims payment.

PCCM: A Primary Care Case Management program is a Freedom of Choice Waiver program, under the authority of §1915(b) of the Social Security Act. States contract directly with primary care providers who agree to be responsible for the provision or coordination of medical services to Medicaid recipients under their care. Currently, most PCCM programs pay the primary care physician a monthly case management fee in addition to receiving fee-for-services payment.

PCP (Primary Care Provider): A Doctor who serves as a group member's personal doctor and first contact in a managed care system. PCPs include family and general practitioners, internists, pediatricians, and OB/GYNs.

PCP CAPITATION: A reimbursement system for health care providers of primary care services that receive a prepayment every month. The payment amount is based on age, sex, and plan of every member assigned to that physician for that month. Specialty capitation plans also exist but are little used.

PEDIATRICIAN: A medical doctor or doctor of osteopathy who specializes in the care and treatment of children.

PEDIATRIC ONCOLOGY: Diagnosis and treatment of cancer disorder in children.

PEDIATRICS: The medical care and treatment of children by a medical doctor or doctor of osteopathy.

PEER REVIEW: (1) An organization contracting with HCFA (Health Care Financing Administration/Centers for Medicare and Medicaid Services) that reviews the medical necessity and the quality of care provided to Medicare beneficiaries; formerly called Utilization and Quality Control Peer Review Organization. (2) An organization that contracts with HCFA to investigate the quality of health care furnished to Medicare beneficiaries and to educate beneficiaries and providers. Peer Review Organizations also conduct limited review of medical records and claims to evaluate the appropriateness of care provided. See Utilization Review.

PEER REVIEW ORGANIZATION (PRO): An organization established by the Tax Equity and Fiscal Responsibility Act of 1982 (TEFRA) to review quality of care and appropriateness of admissions, readmissions, and discharges for Medicare and Medicaid.

PENALTY: Charging out of health care network patients a premium for using nonparticipating medical providers.

PENDED: A situation in which it is not known whether an authorization has or will be issued for delivery of a health care service, and the case has been set aside for review.

PENETRATION: The percentage of business that an HMO is able to capture in a particular subscriber group or in the market area as a whole.

PER ACCIDENT LIMIT: Maximum benefits a company will pay for a liability insurance claim resulting from a particular accident.

PER CAPITA HEALTH CARE SPENDING: Annual spending on health care per person.

PER CAUSE DEDUCTIBLE: Requirement that a deductible be made for each separate illness or accident before benefits are paid.

PERCENTAGE PARTICIPATION: A provision in a health insurance contract that states that the insurer will share losses in an agreed proportion with the insured. An example would be an 80–20 participation where the insurer pays 80% and the insured pays the 20% of losses covered under the contract. Often erroneously referred to as coinsurance.

PERCENTAGE PARTICIPATION DEDUCTIBLE: Stop-loss amount over which a health insurance plan pays all of the costs in a percentage participation plan.

PER DIEM: Total medical reimbursement per day, rather than by actual charges and services.

PER DIEM PAYMENTS: Fixed daily payments which do not vary with the level of services used by the patient. This method generally is used to pay institutional providers, such as hospitals and nursing facilities. See Per Diem Rates.

PER DIEM RATES: Fixed daily rates that do not vary with the level of services used by the patient. This method generally is used to pay institutional providers, such as hospitals and nursing facilities. See Per Diem Payments.

PERFORMANCE BUDGET: Projected performance goals, along with line item projections of inflows and outflows that measure a health care entities performance.

PERFORMANCE MEASURE: A gauge used to assess the performance of a process or function of any organization. Quantitative or qualitative measures of the care and services delivered to enrollees (process) or the end result of that care and services (outcomes). Performance measures can be used to assess other aspects of an individual or organization's performance, such as access and availability of care, utilization of care, health plan stability, beneficiary characteristics, and other structural and operational aspect of health care services.

PERFORMANCE MEASURES: A specific measure of how well a health plan does in providing health services to its enrolled population. Can be used as a measure of quality. Examples include percentage of diabetics receiving annual referrals for eye care, mammography rate, or percentage of enrollees indicating satisfaction with care.

PERFORMANCE STANDARDS: Standards an individual provider is expected to meet, especially with respect to quality of care. The standards may define volume of care delivered per time period. Thus, performance standards for obstetrician or gynecologist may specify some or all of the following office hours and office visits per week or month: on-call days, deliveries per year, gynecological operations per year, etc.

PERIL: The possible cause of an insurance loss. See Loss and Hazard.

PERINATAL UNIT: A maternity and newborn service for the provision of care during pregnancy, labor, delivery, postpartum, and neonatal periods with appropriate staff, space, equipment, and supplies. Commonly called maternity or obstetrical beds.

PERIODIC INTERIM PAYMENT: The prepayment of health care benefits to a provider based on historical averages.

PERIODS OF CARE (HOSPICE): A set period of time for hospice care after a doctor's statement of eligibility.

PERMANENT DISABILITY: A long-range disability that will last for an indefinite. See Disability and Disability Income Insurance.

PERMANENTLY RESTRICED NET ASSET: Assets donated with ties or restrictions.

PERMANENT PARTIAL DISABILITY: An injury or sickness causing a partial disability from which there is no recovery.

PERMANENT PARTIAL DISABILITY BENEFITS: Benefits paid for a disability that impairs earnings capacity, but that does not involve total inability to work.

PERMANENT TOTAL DISABILITY: Total disability from which a person is not expected to recover. When used as a definition of disability qualifying for insurance benefits (usually in life insurance waiver-of-premium provision), the disability is stipulated as permanent if it persists for a specified number of months, usually six. Definitions found in disability income policies will vary.

PERMANENT TOTAL DISABILITY BENEFITS: Payments to an individual who is totally unable to work or who qualified under a specific policy. Such compensation may be limited to a maximum time or a maximum amount, but if unlimited may continue for life.

PER MEMBER PER MONTH (PMPM): Generally used by HMOs and their medical providers as an indicator of revenue, expenses, or utilization of services per member per 1-month period (i.e., "we receive a capitation payment of $20 per member per month").

PER MEMBER PER YEAR (PMPY): Generally used by HMOs and their medical providers as an indicator of revenue, expenses, or utilization of services per member per year (i.e., "Our patients come in to see the doctor on an average of 3.4 times per member per year").

PERPETUITY: An indefinite period of time.

PERSISTENCY RATE: The percentage or number of health insurance or managed care policies remaining in force or that have not been canceled for nonpayment of premium during their term.

PERSONAL CARE: Nonskilled, personal care, such as help with activities of daily living like bathing, dressing, eating, getting in and out of bed or chair, moving around, and using the bathroom. It may also include care that most people do themselves, like using eye drops. The Medicare home health benefit does pay for personal care services.

PERSONAL HEALTH CARE EXPENDITURES: These are outlays for goods and services relating directly to patient care. The part of total national or state health expenditures spent on direct health care delivery, including hospital care, physician services, dental services, home health, nursing home care, and prescription drugs.

PERSONAL INJURY: Bodily harm.

PER THOUSAND MEMBERS PER YEAR (PTMPY): A common way of reporting utilization. The most common example of hospital utilization, expressed as days PTMPY.

PHANTOM PROVIDERS: Medical practitioners for whom the patient receives no direct bill, as from a pathologist or anesthesiologist.

PHARMACEUTICAL CARDS: Identification cards issued by a pharmacy benefit management plan to plan members that assist pharmacy benefits managers in processing and tracking pharmaceutical claims. Also known as drug cards or drug prescription cards.

PHARMACY: A licensed agency that distributes medicinal drugs.

PHARMACY BENEFITS MANAGER: The administrator of a drug benefit plan for an insurance company.

PHARMACY AND THERAPEUTICS COMMITTEE: Health care panel that selects the drugs used in a managed care plan.

PHP: Prepaid Health Plan is an entity that either contracts on a prepaid, capitated risk basis to provide services that are not risk-comprehensive services, or contracts on a nonrisk basis. Additionally, some entities that meet the definition of HMOs are treated as PHPs through special statutory exemptions.

PHYSICAL CONDITION: The current status of one's health.

PHYSICAL EXAMINATION: A medical examination given by a doctor for the underwriting of an insurance policy.

PHYSICAL EXAMINATION AND AUTOPSY PROVISION: An insurance provision that states that the insurance company has the right to require a physical examination of the insured or an autopsy on a deceased insured (if not prohibited by state law). The purpose of this provision is to allow the insurance company to protect itself from fraudulent claims or to determine if the cause of a loss was an accident or sickness or if drugs or alcohol contributed to a loss.

PHYSICAL HAZARD: That type of hazard that arises from the physical characteristics of an individual (e.g., impediments of hearing or sight). It may exist because of a current condition, past medical history, or physical condition present at birth. See Peril.

PHYSICAL IMPAIRMENT: A physical defect that makes an applicant a below average risk. See Disability.

PHYSICALLY IMPAIRED RISK: A person having a physical impairment or disease that may affect his or her acceptability as a risk.

PHYSICAL MEDICINE SERVICES: The medical care provided by a facility and rendered by, or under the direction of, a practitioner to a covered person pursuant to the health plan. Physical medicine services shall include, but not be limited to, rehabilitation services and worker injury services.

PHYSICAL THERAPIST: A trained medical person who provides rehabilitative services and therapy to help restore bodily functions, such as walking, speech, the use of limbs, etc.

PHYSICAL THERAPY: Illness, injury, or disease treatment by mechanical means, such as exercise, light, heat, or paraffin baths.

PHYSICIAN: See Doctor.

PHYSICIAN ASSISTANT (PA): A medical provider with more than 2 years of advanced training that acts as a physician surrogate, but without an unlimited license to practice medicine, and only under the supervision of a doctor. Also known as Physician Extender. See MD, DPM, DDS, DO, etc.

PHYSICIAN ATTESTATION: The requirement that the attending physician certify, in writing, the accuracy and completion of the clinical information used for diagnosis-related groups assignment.

PHYSICIAN CONTINGENCY RESERVE (PCR): Portion of a claim deducted and held by a health plan before payment is made to a capitated physician. The revenue withheld from a provider's payment to serve as an incentive for providing less expensive service. A typical withhold is approximately 20% of the claim. This amount can be paid back to the provider following analysis of his or her practice and service utilization patterns. See Withhold.

PHYSICIAN EXPENSE POLICY: A medical expense health plan that reimburses the policy owner for the cost of a physician's services (other than surgical). Commonly referred to as a basic medical policy.

PHYSICIAN HOSPITAL ORGANIZATION (PHO): Alignment of medical providers, doctors, and health care facilities that negotiate with insurance companies, managed care organizations, HMOs, and other insurance entities.

PHYSICIAN HOSPITAL ORGANIZATION (CORPORATION) (PHO-C): Typically, is owned jointly by a hospital and a physician group. The PHO, in turn, contracts with hospitals and physicians for the delivery of services to payers under contract to the PHO. It can also provide management services and perform other services typically associated with a medical services organization.

PHYSICIAN INCENTIVE PLAN: Any doctor or allied health care provider or entity compensation plan based on cost-efficient and quality care delivery.

PHYSICIAN INCOME: Net doctor income after expenses and before taxes.

PHYSICIAN ORGANIZATION (PO): (1) A structure in which a hospital and physicians—both in individual and group practices—negotiate as an entity directly with insurers. (2) An organization that contracts with payers on behalf of one or more hospitals and affiliated physicians. The PO may also undertake utilization review, credentialing, and quality assurance activities. Physicians retain ownership of their own practices, maintain significant business outside the PO, and typically continue in their traditional style of practice.

PHYSICIAN PAYMENT REVIEW COMMISSION (PPRC): Created by Congress in 1986, to monitor and recommend changes in the current Medicare reimbursement procedures.

PHYSICIAN PRACTICE MANAGEMENT CORPORATION: A private or public company that acquires or partners with medical providers, facilities, or entities for profit.

PHYSICIAN PROFESSIONAL COMPONENT EXPENSES: Fees paid to hospital-based physicians and residents for services provided for direct patient care.

PHYSICIAN PROFILING: The process of compiling data on physician treatment, surgery, or prescribing patterns and comparing physicians' actual patterns to expected patterns within select categories. Also known as economic profiling.

PHYSICIAN'S DESK REFERENCE: An annual manufacturer's manual listing prescription drugs and related pharmaceuticals.

PHYSICIAN SERVICES: One portion of national health care expenditures. Includes physicians' overhead administrative expenses, and income.

PHYSICIAN'S EXPENSE POLICY: A medical expense health plan that reimburses the policy owner for the cost of a physician's services (other than surgical). Commonly referred to as a basic medical policy.

PHYSICIAN AND SURGEON'S PROFESSIONAL LIABILITY INSURANCE: Malpractice insurance.

PHYSICIAN'S WORK: A measure of the physician's time, physical effort and skill, mental effort and judgment, and stress from iatrogenic risk associated with providing a medical service; as a component of the Medicare relative value scale.

PIA: Primary Insurance Amount. See Social Security.

PLACED BUSINESS: Health insurance policies whose applications have been examined and the policies issued and delivered to the policy owners, who have paid the first premiums.

PLACEMENT FOR ADOPTION: The assumption that one waiting for the adoption of a child has a legal obligation to the financial support of that child.

PLAN ADMINISTRATION: A term often used to describe the management unit with responsibility to run and control a managed care plan—includes accounting, billing, personnel, marketing, legal, purchasing, possibly underwriting, management information, facility maintenance, and servicing of accounts. This group normally contracts for medical services and hospital care.

PLAN AGE: The time period a health plan has been in operation.

PLAN OF CARE: A doctor's anticipated written medical or surgical treatment plan. See Care Map.

PLAN DOCUMENT: The document that contains all of the provisions, conditions, and terms of operation of a pension or health or welfare plan. This document may be written in technical terms as distinguished from a summary plan description (SPD) that under Employee Retirement Income Security Act of 1974 must be written in a manner calculated to be understood by the average plan participant.

PLAN FUNDING: Method that an employer or other payer or purchaser uses to pay medical benefit costs and administrative expenses.

PLAY OR PAY: Employers would be required to provide health insurance to their employees or to pay a special government program tax.

PM: Per member.

PMPM: Per member per month.

PMPY: Per member per year.

PODIATRIST: A medical and surgical specialty doctor for conditions of the foot, ankle, and lower leg. See DPM and Doctor.

PODIATRY: The medical and surgical care and treatment of foot, ankle, and leg-related diseases and injuries by a podiatrist.

POINT-OF-SALE: The health insurance agent making a presentation to a prospect. Also refers to sales aids, such as visuals, charts, and proposals used by an agent in an interview.

POINT OF SERVICE: An HMO plan which allows the member to pay little or nothing if they stay within the established HMO delivery system, but permits members to choose and receive services from an outside doctor, any time, if they are willing to pay higher copayments, deductibles, and possibly monthly premiums. Also called an open-ended plan.

POINT-OF-SERVICE PLAN (POS): Also known as an open-ended HMO. (1) A managed-care plan that combines features of both prepaid and fee-for-service insurance. Health plan enrollees decide whether to use network or nonnetwork providers at the time care is needed and usually are charged sizable copayments for selecting the latter. See Health Plan, Health Maintenance Organization, and Preferred Provider Organization. (2) A health plan in which enrollees select providers either within or outside of a preferred network, with copayment or deductibles higher for out-of-network providers. (3) A health plan with a network of providers whose services are available to enrollees at a lower cost than the services of nonnetwork providers. POS enrollees must receive authorization from a primary care physician to use network services. POS plans typically do not pay for out-of-network referrals for primary care services. Often may encourage, but do not require, members to choose a primary care physician. As in traditional HMOs, the primary care physician acts as a gatekeeper when making referrals; plan members may, however, opt to visit nonnetwork providers at their discretion. Subscribers choosing not to use the primary care physician must pay higher deductibles and copays than those using network physicians.

POLICY: The basic written contract between the health insurer and the policy owner. The policy together with the application and all endorsements and attached papers, constitutes the entire contract of insurance.

POLICY ANNIVERSARY: In insurance, the anniversary of the date of issue of a policy, as shown in the policy schedule.

POLICY DEVELOPMENT: The process whereby public health agencies evaluate and determine health needs and the best ways to address them.

POLICY HOLDER: The person who holds possession of an insurance policy.

POLICY PERIOD: In insurance, the length of time during which the policy contract provides protection. Also called policy term.

POLICY PLANS: All the various insurance plans offered by an insurance company, as described in the rate book or manual published by the company.

POLICY REGISTER: A record maintained by an insurance company for noting the issuance of, and accounting for, all of its policies.

POLICY RESERVE: An unearned health insurance premium reserve.

POLICY SIGNIFICANCE: The significance of an evaluation's findings for policy and program development, as opposed to their statistical significance.

POLICY SPACE: The set of health insurance policy alternatives that are within the bounds of acceptability to policy makers at a given point in time.

POLICY SUMMARY: In insurance, an outline summary of a policy's provisions and financial make-up, provided by the agent to the insured (or prospective insured) to explain the policy. Some states require the agent to provide each applicant with a policy summary.

POOL: A method where each member of an insured group share risk.

POPULATION CARVE-OUTS: Provides health care to a designated population, targeted or defined by a specific health condition.

POPULATION AT NEED: Units of potential targets that currently manifest a particular condition.

POPULATION AT RISK: Segment of population with significant probability of having or developing a particular condition.

PORTABILITY: (1) An individual changing jobs would be guaranteed coverage with the new employer, without a waiting period or having to meet additional deductible requirements. (2) The requirement that insurers waive any preexisting condition exclusion for someone who was previously covered through other insurance as recently as 30 to 90 days earlier.

POSTPARTUM: The period of time following childbirth.

POTENTIALLY AVOIDABLE HOSPITALIZATIONS (PAHs): Admissions to a hospital that could have been avoided if adequate and timely health care had been available.

POWER OF APPOINTMENT: Authority granted to one person (called the donee) to appoint a person or persons who are to receive an estate or an income from a fund, after the testator's death, or the donee's death, or after the termination of an existing right or interest.

POWER OF ATTORNEY: Authority given one person (or entity) or act for and obligate another according to the instrument creating the power.

PP&E ASSETS PER BED: Property, plant, & equipment.

PPMC (PHYSICIAN PRACTICE MANAGEMENT CORPORATION): A firm that purchases physicians' practices in exchange for a percentage of the gross receivables. The PPMC leases the office back to the doctor or employs the doctor on a salaried basis. The PPMC then contracts with the areas managed care organizations.

PPO (PREFERRED PROVIDER ORGANIZATION): A select, approved panel of physicians, hospitals, and other providers who agree to accept a discounted fee schedule for patients and to follow utilization review and preauthorization protocols for certain treatments.

PPS INPATIENT MARGIN: A measure that compares PPS operating and capital payments with Medicare-allowable inpatient operating and capital costs. It is calculated by subtracting total Medicare-allowable inpatient operating and capital costs from total PPS operating and capital payments and dividing by total PPS operating and capital payments.

PPS OPERATING MARGIN: A measure that compares PPS operating payments with Medicare-allowable inpatient operating costs. This measure excludes Medicare costs and payments for capital, direct medical education, organ acquisition, and other categories not included among Medicare-allowable inpatient operating costs. It is calculated by subtracting total Medicare-allowable inpatient operating costs from total PPS operating payments and dividing by total PPS operating payments.

PPS YEAR: A designation referring to hospital cost reporting periods that begin during a given federal fiscal year, reflecting the number of years since the initial implementation of PPS. For example, PPS1 refers to hospital fiscal years beginning during federal fiscal year 2007, which was the first year of PPS. For a hospital with a fiscal year beginning July 1, PPS 1 covers the period from July 1, 2007, through June 30, 2008.

PRACTICAL NURSE: Also known as a vocational nurse, provides nursing care and treatment of patients under the supervision of a licensed physician or registered nurse. Licensure as a licensed practical nurse (LPN) or in California and Texas as a licensed vocational nurse (LVN) is required.

PRACTICE EXPENSE: The cost of nonphysician resources incurred by the physician to provide services. Examples are salaries and fringe benefits received by the physician's employees, and the expenses associated with the purchase and use of medical equipment and supplies in the physician's office. A component of the Medicare Resource Based Relative Value Scale (RBRVS).

PRACTICE EXPENSE RELATIVE VALUE: A value that reflects the average amount of practice expenses incurred in performing a particular service. All values are expressed relative to the practice expenses for a reference service whose value equals 1 practice expense unit. See Relative Value Scale.

PRACTICE GUIDELINES: An explicit statement of what is known and believed about the benefits, risks, and costs of particular courses of medical action intended to assist decisions by practitioners, patients, and others about appropriate health care for specific clinical conditions.

PRACTICE PARAMETERS: Strategies for patient management, developed to assist physicians in clinical decision-making. Parameters improve quality and assure appropriate utilization of health services.

PRACTITIONER: Any health care professional recognized by an insurer as licensed or accredited to provide covered services. Examples include certified nurse anesthetists, chiropractors, and doctor of medicine, doctor of osteopathy, oral surgeons, physical therapists, and podiatrists. See MD, DO, DPM, DDS, DMD, and OD.

PREADMISSION CERTIFICATION (PAC): The review of a patient's need for inpatient hospital care prior to admission. Under health plans that require PAC, this certification is a prerequisite for payment.

PREADMISSION REVIEW: The practice of reviewing claims for inpatient admission prior to the patient entering the hospital to assure that the admission is medically necessary.

PREADMISSION TESTING (PAT): Laboratory and other prescreening tests and examinations often required prior to being admitted to a medical facility as an inpatient.

PREAPPROACH: An insurance contact made by an agent to prospects, or potential prospects, by letter or other communication, to approach the prospects on the most favorable basis possible.

PREAUTHORIZATION: A method of monitoring and controlling utilization by evaluating the need for medical service prior to it being performed.

PRECERTIFICATION: The process of notification and approval of elective inpatient admission and identified outpatient services before the service is rendered.

PREDETERMINATION: An administrative procedure whereby a health provider submits a treatment plan to a third party before treatment is initiated. The third party usually reviews the treatment plan, monitoring one or more of the following: patient's eligibility, covered service, amounts payable, application of appropriate deductibles, and copayment factors and maximums. Under some programs, for instance, predetermination by the third party is required when covered charges are expected to exceed a certain amount. Similar processes: preauthorization, precertification, and preestimate of cost, pretreatment estimate, and prior authorization.

PREDICTABILITY: Expected insurance claims or losses.

PREDISABILITY EARNINGS: Amount of an employee's wages or salary that was in effect and covered by the plan on the day before the disability began. See Disability and Disability Income Insurance.

PREEXISTING CONDITION: In health insurance, an injury, sickness, or physical condition that existed before the policy effective date. Most individual policies will not cover a preexisting condition; most group policies will. Or: (a) A physical condition of an insured person that existed prior to the issuance of his policy or his enrollment in a plan and that may result in the limitation in the contract on coverage or benefits. (b) A physical condition including an injury or disease that was contracted or occurred prior to enrollment in the HMO. Federally qualified HMOs cannot limit coverage for preexisting conditions.

PREEXISTING CONDITION EXCLUSION: A practice of some health insurers to deny coverage to individuals for a certain period (e.g., 6 months) for health conditions that already exist when coverage is initiated. See Portability, Exclusions, and Benefits.

PREEXISTING CONDITION LIMITATIONS: A provision in insurance policies that excludes health conditions existing prior to coverage sign up. These limitations exclude specified conditions entirely or for a specified period. When an individual changes jobs and enrolls in a new insurance plan, these limitations can cause a critical gap in health benefits.

PREFERRED PROVIDER: A health plan with a network of doctors, medical providers, providers, health care facilities, and vendors, whose services are available to member enrollees and patients at lower cost than the services of nonnetwork providers. See PPO.

PREFERRED PROVIDER ORGANIZATIONS (PPO): (1) Are somewhat similar to independent physician associations and HMOs in that the PPO is a corporation that receives health insurance premiums from enrolled members and contracts with independent doctors or group practices to provide care. However, it differs in that doctors are not prepaid, but they offer a discount from normal fee-for-service charges. (2) A health plan with a network of providers whose services are available to enrollees at lower cost than the services of nonnetwork providers. PPO enrollees may self-refer to any network provider at any time. (3) A health plan in which enrollees receive services from a defined network of providers who agree to provide specific services for a set of fee. See IPA, PHO, and Preferred Provider.

PREFERRED RISK: A person whose physical condition, occupation, mode of living, and other characteristics indicate an above average life expectancy. See Risk and Peril.

PREFERRED RISK POLICIES: Life and health insurance, policies warranting a lower premium charge on the basis of rigid selection. Certain classes may be selected, such as business or professional people (e.g., where the mortality or morbidity experience is expected to be better than average).

PREFERRED STOCK: Owners of this kind of stock are entitled to a fixed dividend to be paid regularly before dividends can be paid on common stock. They also exercise claims to assets, in the event of liquidation, senior to common stockholders but junior to bondholders. Preferred stockholders normally do not have a voice in management.

PREGNANCY: The development of offspring in the uterus. Insurance coverage of this condition could include prenatal and postnatal care, childbirth, and complications of pregnancy.

PREINDUCTION TRAINING: Also called precontract training or precontract orientation. Training given to a prospective life or health insurance agent prior to becoming a full-time agency associate. Included is the study of licensing courses and other material geared to knowledge and skills development, plus activities designed to prepare for the career or eliminate the candidates.

PRELIMINARY OFFICIAL STATEMENT or RED HERRING: A preliminary version of the official statement which is used by an issuer or underwriters to describe the proposed issue of hospital or health care securities prior to the determination of the interest rate(s) and offering price(s). The preliminary official statement may be used by issuers to gauge underwriters' interest in an issue and is often relied upon by potential purchasers in making their investment decisions. Normally, offers for the sale of or acceptance of securities are not made on the basis of the preliminary official statement, and a statement to that effect appears on the face of the document generally in red print, which gives the document its nickname, red herring. The preliminary official statement is technically a *draft*. All further trades are in the floating secondary market.

PREMISES MEDICAL PAYMENTS INSURANCE: Supplemental coverage in business or personal insurance policies to cover the cost of medical or surgical expenses, as well as loss of income.

PREMIUM: The amount of money an insurance company charges for insurance coverage. (1) An amount paid periodically to purchase health insurance benefits. (2) The amount paid or payable in advance, often in monthly installments, for an insurance policy. A fee charged to plan subscribers and enrolled dependents that are covered under the contract for the insurance coverage provided. The insured and employer usually share the fee. A predetermined monthly membership fee that a subscriber or employer pays for the HMO coverage. (3) The sum of money that a contract holder pays or agrees to pay the health insurance company for the contract.

PREMIUM DEFICIENCY RESERVE: Supplementary reserve funds required of some life, disability, long-term care, and health insurance companies.

PREMIUM FINANCING: A policy holder contracts with a lender to pay the insurance premium on his or her behalf. The policy holder agrees to repay the lender for the cost of the premium, plus interest and fees. See Premium.

PREMIUM NOTICE: A formal note that an insurance premium is due. See Premium.

PREMIUM REVENUES: The amount earned from capitated medical service contracts.

PREMIUM SURCHARGE: Standard Part B Medicare premium of up to 10% additional for each year of the initial enrollment period, that Medicare was available but not covered. Medicare Part D has a similar surcharge.

PREMIUM TAXES: State income taxes on an insurer's premium income.

PREPAID ASSET: A benefit like rent or a health care insurance premium that is paid for in advance.

PREPAID GROUP PRACTICE: Prepaid Group Practice Plans involve multispecialty associations of physicians and other health professionals, who contract to provide a wide range of preventive, diagnostic, and treatment services on a continuing basis for enrolled participants.

PREPAID GROUP PRACTICE HEALTH PLAN: Prepaid health insurance plan in which physicians and other health professionals contract to provide a wide range of preventive, diagnostic, and treatment services to a group of enrolled participants.

PREPAID GROUP PRACTICE PLAN: A plan that specifies health services are rendered by participating physicians to an enrolled group of persons, with a fixed periodic payment made in advance by (or on behalf of) each person or family. If a health insurance carrier is involved, a contract to pay in advance for the full range of health services to which the insured is entitled under the terms of the health insurance contract. A health maintenance organization (HMO) is an example of a prepaid group practice plan.

PREPAID HEALTH PLAN: A contract between a health insurance entity and patients that agrees to provide covered medical benefits for a prepaid fixed sum. See Capitation and Prospective Payment System.

PREPAID HOSPITAL SERVICE PLAN: The common name for a health maintenance organization (HMO), a plan that provides comprehensive health care to its members, who pay a flat annual fee for services. See HMO.

PREPAID PREMIUM: An insurance premium paid prior to the due date.

PREPAID PRESCRIPTION PLAN: Drug reimbursement plan that is paid in advance.

PREPAYMENT: A method providing in advance for the cost of predetermined benefits for a population group, through regular periodic payments in the form of premiums, dues, or contributions including those contributions that are made to a health and welfare fund by employers on behalf of their employees.

PREPAYMENT PLANS: A term referring to health insurance plans that provide medical or hospital benefits in service rather than dollars, such as the plans offered by various HMOs.

PREPAYMENT OF PREMIUMS: In insurance, payment by the insured of future premiums, through paying the present (discounted) value of the future premiums or having interest paid on the deposit.

PRESCRIPTION: A written authorization for a prescription medication given by a participating physician prescriber.

PRESCRIPTION DEDUCTIBLE: An economic risk amount specified in a health care plan for a prescription drug program. See Generic Drug, Trade Drug, and Formulary.

PRESCRIPTION DRUG: Any medication that is approved by the Food and Drug Administration and, by law, requires a prescription. See Generic Drug, Trade Drug, and Formulary.

PRESCRIPTION DRUG CARD PLAN: Covered individuals are issued prescription drug cards that allow them to charge their drug purchases at participating pharmacies.

PRESCRIPTION ORDER OR REFILL: The dispensing of a prescription medication by a participating pharmacy as ordered by the prescriber.

PRESENT VALUE (PV): The amount of money that if invested at a specified rate of interest, will, at a given future time, accumulate to a specified sum that is calculated by: $PV = FV \times PVF$. See Present Value Factor (PVF) and Future Value (FV).

PRESENTEEISM: The employee practice of always being present at the workplace, often working longer hours even when there is nothing to do, or when ill.

PRESENT VALUE FACTOR (PVF): The discounting of future cash flow, such as account receivables by the formula: $[1/(1 + i)^n]$.

PRESTENCILED CLAIM: A preprinted health care claims form.

PREVALENCE: The number of cases of disease, infected persons, or persons with some other attribute, present at a particular time and in relation to the size of the population from which drawn. It can be a measurement of morbidity at a moment in time (e.g., the number of cases of hemophilia in the country as of the first of the year).

PREVAILING CHARGE: One of the screens that determined a physician's payment for a service under the Medicare usual, customary, and reasonable (UCR) payment system. In Medicare, it was the 75th percentile of customary charges, with annual updates limited by the Medicare Economic Index.

PREVALENCE RATE: The proportion of persons in a population who have a particular disease or attribute at a specified point in time or over a specified period of time.

PREVENTION: Actions taken to reduce susceptibility or exposure to health problems (primary prevention), detect and treat disease in early stages (secondary prevention), or alleviate the effects of disease and injury (tertiary prevention). The set of activities designed to increase health and decrease morbidity and mortality in a population, cohort, or other insurance-related risk group.

PREVENTION MEASURES: Actions taken to reduce susceptibility or exposure to health problems, to detect and treat disease in early stages, or to alleviate the effects of disease and injury.

PREVENTIVE CARE: Health care that emphasizes prevention, early detection, and early treatment, such as colorectal cancer screening, yearly mammograms, and flu shots, thereby reducing the costs of health care in the long run.

PREVENTIVE CARE SERVICES: Health care that emphasizes health maintenance and the prevention of disease through measures, such as routine physical exams and immunizations.

PREVENTIVE HEALTH CARE: Health care that seeks to prevent or foster early detection of disease and morbidity and focuses on keeping patients well in addition to health them while they are sick.

PREVENTIVE HEALTH SERVICES: Services intended to prevent the occurrence of a disease or its consequences. See HMO, MCO, and PPO.

PRICE CEILINGS: Legal maximum charges for health services resulting in a shortage. See Price Floors.

PRICE FLOORS: Legal minimum charges for health services resulting in a glut. See Price Ceilings.

PRICER: Software modules in Medicare claims processing systems, specific to certain benefits, used in pricing claims, most often under prospective payment systems.

PRICER OR REPRICER: A person, an organization, or a software package that reviews procedures, diagnoses, fee schedules, and other data and determines the eligible amount for a given health care service or supply. Additional criteria can then be applied to determine the actual allowance, or payment, amount.

PRIMACY: Health insurance coverage that takes precedence when one or more insurance or other policies cover the same loss.

PRIMARY CARE: A basic level of health care provided by the physician from whom an individual has an ongoing relationship and who knows the patient's medical history. Primary care services emphasize a patient's general health needs, such as preventive services, treatment of minor illnesses and injuries, or identification of problems that require referral to specialists. Traditionally, primary care physicians are family physicians, internists, gynecologists, and pediatricians. (a) Basic or general health care usually rendered by general practitioners, family practitioners, internists, obstetricians and pediatricians—often referred to as primary care practitioners. (b) Professional and related services administered by an internist, family practitioner, obstetrician-gynecologist, or pediatrician in an ambulatory setting, with referral to secondary care specialists, as necessary. See Doctor, Hospitalist, and Intensivist.

PRIMARY CARE CASE MANAGEMENT (PCCM): A Medicaid managed care program in which an eligible individual may use services only with authorization from his or her assigned primary care provider. That provider is responsible for locating, coordinating, and monitoring all primary and other medical services for enrollees.

PRIMARY CARE NETWORK (PCN): A group of primary care physicians who share the risk of providing care to members of a given health plan.

PRIMARY CARE PHYSICIAN (PCP): A physician whose primary practice focus is internal medicine, family or general practice, obstetrician or gynecologist, and pediatrics. They generally provide treatment of routine illness and injuries and focus on preventive health care.

PRIMARY CARE PROVIDER (PCP): A primary care provider, such as a family practitioner, general internist, pediatrician, and sometimes an obstetrician or gynecologist. Generally, a PCP supervises, coordinates, and provides medical care to members of a plan. The PCP may initiate all referrals for specialty care.

PRIMARY COVER: In health insurance, coverage from the first dollar, perhaps after a deductible, as distinguished from an excess cover.

PRIMARY COVERAGE: A health plan without coordination of benefits consideration.

PRIMARY DISSEMINATION: Dissemination of the detailed findings of an evaluation to sponsors and technical audiences.

PRIMARY INSURANCE AMOUNT (PIA): Under U.S. Social Security, the worker's full retirement benefit at age 65 or disability benefit. Benefits at other than retirement ages or for others in the worker's family are expressed as percentages of the PIA.

PRIMARY PAYER: The insurer who pays the first medical claim. Medicare or other private health insurance.

PRIMARY PHYSICIAN CAPITATION: The amount paid to each physician monthly for services based on the age, sex, and number of the Members selecting that physician.

PRIMARY PLAN/SECONDARY PLAN: The primary plan includes benefits that are considered before any other health care plan for services rendered. The secondary health care plan assumes responsibility of payment for charges not covered by the primary plan as defined under their contract.

PRIMARY MANAGEMENT (PM): A Freedom of Choice Waiver program, under the authority of §915(b) of the Social Security Act. States contract directly with primary care providers who agree to be responsible for the provision or coordination of medical services to Medicaid recipients under their care. Currently, most PM programs pay the primary care physician a monthly case management fee in addition to receiving fee-for-services payment.

PRIMARY SOURCE VERIFICATION: A process through which an HMO or managed care organization validates credentialing information from the organization that originally conferred or issued the credentialing element to the medical practitioner.

PRINCIPAL: The applicant for or subject of insurance. An individual or company charged with the performance of certain obligations. The money due under an insurance policy. The party to a transaction, but not a broker or agent. The person who designates another as his or her agent. A sum lent or employed as a fund or investment, as distinguished from its income or profits. The capital sum as distinguished from interest or profits. The original amount (as of a loan) of the total due and payable at a certain date. The capital sum of a mortgage loan.

PRINCIPAL DIAGNOSIS: That condition established after study to be chiefly responsible for occasioning the admission of the patient to the hospital for care. This definition may not apply to patients receiving long-term care (skilled nursing or intermediate care) or physical rehabilitation care, because of issues concerning reimbursement. The medical condition that is ultimately determined to have caused a patient's admission to the hospital. The principal diagnosis is used to assign every patient to a diagnosis-related group.

PRINCIPAL DIAGNOSTIC GROUP: The major group of diseases, disorders, and conditions as listed in, and roughly corresponding to, the chapters of the *International Classification of Diseases*, 9th Rev., Clinical Modification (ICD-9-CM).

PRIOR APPROVAL: A notification requirement for certain elective medical procedures, such as cosmetic surgery. Receiving written prior approval will ensure receipt of full benefits.

PRIOR APPROVAL RATING: The prereview and scrutiny of certain life, health, and other insurance forms use before use.

PRIOR AUTHORIZATION: The review and approval of health care or specific services by an insurer prior to coverage. Prior authorization is needed before health services are received under most health plan contracts.

PRIOR CARRIER DEDUCTIBLE CREDIT: A benefit that allows covered persons or their dependents credit for deductibles already accumulated for the calendar year under their employer's previous health insurance program. The amount of deductible met under the covered person's prior insurance for the same calendar year can be applied toward their new deductible requirement.

PRIOR CONFINEMENT REQUIREMENT: Mandate that the insured must have been in a hospital or health care facility prior to receiving long-term care insurance benefits.

PRIOR DEDUCTIBLE CREDIT: A provision that allows a member or family to apply any deductible credit.

PRIOR INSURANCE: An insurance policy in force before a present policy.

PRIOR SERVICE: Continuous health plan membership card indicating the date of inception to current date of coverage.

PRIVATE CONTRACT: A contract between you and your doctor(s) who have elected out of the Medicare Program. See Concierge Medicine. The provider may not bill Medicare for 2 years, and there are no limits on the insured's charges that must be paid in full.

PRIVATE DUTY NURSING: Nursing services provided in the home by an approved registered nurse (RN) or a licensed practical nurse (LPN) that last for extended periods of time.

PRIVATE EXPENDITURES: These are outlays for services provided or paid for by nongovernmental sources—consumers, insurance companies, private industry, and philanthropic and other nonpatient care sources.

PRIVATE INSURANCE: See Social Insurance.

PRIVATE INUREMENT: The payment for medical goods, services and equipment, at above market rates, at the expenses of tax-exempt healthcare entities (501 [c] 3 charitable or community healthcare facilities and hospitals).

PRIVATE NONCOMMERICAL HEALTH INSURANCE: See Health Insurance, HMO, and PPO.

PRIVATE PAY: Patients who are financially responsible for their own care and are not covered by a third-party payer program.

PROBABILITY: The likelihood or relative frequency of an event.

PROBABLE LIFE CURVE: Primarily with respect to health and life insurance, a statistical curve used to plot future probable mortality based on past experience.

PROBABLE LIFETIME: Based on actuarial statistics, the average expected longevity of any given individual at a particular age.

PROBATIONARY PERIOD: The specified number of days after a health insurance policy is issued during which time coverage is not provided for certain sicknesses. This period protects the insurance company against preexisting conditions. Also called incubation period.

PROBATIONARY PROVISION: A provision in health insurance policies to exclude benefits for sickness beginning within a specified number of days, such as 15 or 30, following the policy date. Its purpose is to reduce the number of claims for sickness that may have had their inception prior to the policy date and to prevent antiselection on the part of persons who know they are in ill health.

PROCEDURALIST: A medical provider that performs interventions and treatments, such as dentist, podiatrists, surgeon, etc. Noncognitive medical provider or doctor.

PROCEDURE: A medical intervention to fix a health problem or to learn more about it. For example, surgery, tests, and putting in an intravenous line are procedures.

PROCEDURE CODE: *International Classification of Diseases*, 9th Rev., code system.

PROCESS EVALUATION: Process evaluation examines the procedures and tasks involved in implementing a program. This type of evaluation also can look at the administrative and organizational aspects of the program.

PRODUCE: An insurance agent (salesman) who sells many policies.

PRODUCT: The medical care, goods, treatments, drugs, or services administered to a health care plan member or patient.

PRODUCTION: The sales volume of a health insurance company, an agency, or a producer, measured in face amount of protection or in premium dollars.

PRODUCTION CLUB: An organization within a particular insurance company and bearing a company-oriented name, composed of agents who meet or exceed specified production standards set by the club or the company. Club conferences or conventions constitute the primary activity resulting from qualification.

PRODUCTIVE HOURS: The sum of hours worked by all employees in a specific classification in a given cost center during the reporting period. Hours worked do not include vacation or sick leave and other paid time off.

PRODUCTIVITY: The ratio of outputs (goods and services produced) to inputs (resources used in production). Increased productivity implies that the hospital or health care organization is either producing more output with the same resources or the same output with fewer resources.

PRODUCT MARGIN: Total contribution margin minus avoidable fixed costs. See Contribution Margin and Fixed Cost.

PROFESSIONAL COMPONENT: The portion of health care delivery charges provided by a medical provider and allocated as a cost of physician services.

PROFESSIONAL FEES: Monies paid to contracted medical providers, while nursing compensation is usually a line-item labor item. See Surgical Fee Schedule.

PROFESSIONAL LIABILITY INSURANCE: The insurance physicians purchase to help protect themselves from the financial risks associated with medical liability claims. See Malpractice.

PROFESSIONAL REVIEW ORGANIZATION: An organization that reviews the services provided to patients in terms of medical necessity professional standards and appropriateness of setting. See Peer Review.

PROFESSIONAL STANDARDS REVIEW (PSRO): A physician-sponsored organization charged with reviewing the services provided patients who are covered by Medicare, Medicaid, and maternal and child health programs. The purpose of the review is to determine if the services rendered are medically necessary; provided in accordance with professional criteria, norms, and standards; and provided in the appropriate setting.

PROFESSIONAL STANDARDS REVIEW ORGANIZATION (PSRO): Organization responsible for determining whether care and services provided were medically necessary and meet professional standards regarding eligibility for reimbursement under the Medicare and Medicaid programs. A group, founded in 1972, that monitors federal health insurance programs. See Peer Review.

PROFILE: Aggregated data in formats that display patterns of health care services over a defined period of time.

PROFILE ANALYSIS OR PROFILING: Review and analysis of profiles to identify and assess patterns of health care services. Expressing a pattern of practice as a rate or some measure of utilization or outcome (as functional status, morbidity, or mortality) aggregated over time for a defined population of patients. This is used to compare with other practice patterns. May be used for physician practices, health plans, or geographic areas.

PROFITABILITY RATIOS: A financial success measurement of a health care organization.

PROFIT CENTER: Health care organizational units responsible for earning revenues and controlling their own costs. These health care entities include traditional, capitation, and administrative subunit profit centers.

PROFORMA FINANCIAL STATEMENTS: Estimates or projections of the four consolidated financial statements: (a) Balance Sheet; (b) Cash Flow Statement; (c) Net Income Statement; and (d) Statement of Operations.

PROGRAM ALL INCLUSIVE FOR THE ELDERLY (PACE): A medical, social, and long-term care program for fragile senior citizens, sponsored by various state Medicaid programs to keep them functioning in the community for as long as possible.

PROGRAM MANAGEMENT: A Centers for Medicare and Medicaid Services (CMS) operational account. Program management supplies the agency with the resources to administer Medicare, the federal portion of Medicaid, and other agency responsibilities. The components of program management are Medicare contractors, survey and certification, research, and administrative costs.

PROGRAM MANAGEMENT AND MEDICAL INFORMATION SYSTEM (PMMIS): An automated system of records that contains records primarily of current Medicare-eligible end-stage renal disease (ESRD) patients, but also maintains historical information on people no longer classified as ESRD patients because of death, successful transplantation, or recovery of renal function. The PMMIS contains medical information on patients and the services that they received during the course of their therapy. In addition, it contains information on ESRD facilities and facility payment.

PROGRESSIVE IMPAIRMENT: Gradual deterioration of the body as a result of a disease like cancer or AIDS.

PROGRESSIVE RATES: A method employed by some HMOs in which they implement new rates monthly, quarterly, or semiannually.

PROHIBITED RISK: Any class that an insurance company will not cover, for any reason.

PROJECTED COSTS: Claims or retention costs projected for a given patient population for a specific time period.

PROJECTION: An estimate of future numbers based upon the extension of present relationships, but which may also incorporate expected changes in such relationships. In insurance, an estimate of future conditions, such as mortality, morbidity, sales, lapse rate, etc.

PROMISE TO PAY: As specified in a policy, the insurance company's stated agreement to make payment of all stipulated sums to designated beneficiaries in the event of certain, specified occurrences.

PROMOTION: Health education and the fostering of healthy living conditions and lifestyles.

PROOF OF LOSS: A mandatory health insurance policy provision stating that the insured must provide a signed and completed claim form to the insurance company within 90 days of the date of loss.

PROPERTY, PLANT, AND EQUIPMENT (PP&E) ASSETS PER BED: Net property, plant, and equipment, plus construction in progress, divided by available beds. This ratio indicates the property, plant, and equipment associated with each available bed.

PROPOSAL: A sales presentation or illustration of facts and figures pertaining to a plan of health insurance, as shown to a prospect by an agent.

PROPRIETARY EQUIPMENT: Capital investment assets of a health care facility.

PROPRIETARY HOSPITAL: A hospital or other facility that provides medical services for a profit.

PRO RATA: According to a calculated share or portion; in proportion.

PRO RATA CANCELLATION: The termination of a health insurance contract or bond, with the premium charge being adjusted in proportion to the exact time the protection has been in force. When the policy is terminated midterm by the insurance company, the earned premium is calculated only for the period coverage was provided. For example: an annual policy with premium of $1,000 is cancelled after 40 days of coverage at the company's election. The earned premium would be calculated as follows: 39/365 days × $1,000 = .10 × $1,000 = $106.

PRO RATA PREMIUM: A fractional premium.

PRO RATA RATE: A short-term health insurance premium rate proportionate to the rate for a longer term.

PRO RATA UNEARNED PREMIUM RESERVE: In health insurance, a reserve calculated to represent the unearned portion of the liability to policy owners to be discharged in the future with future protection, by return to the policy owner in event of cancellation or by reinsuring the business with another insurer.

PRORATE: Adjustment of health policy benefits for any reason of change in occupation or significant or existence of other coverage.

PRORATING: The proportionate reduction in the amount of health insurance benefits payable as provided in the contract; for example, because the insured has changed to a more hazardous occupation since the issuance of medical policy, or because benefits payable by all the insured's disability insurance exceed his or her current or average earnings over the preceding 2 years, or because he or she is actually older than stated in a life insurance application, etc.

PRORATION: The modification of health insurance policy benefits because of a change in the insured person's occupation or the existence of other insurance.

PROSPECT: A potential insurance purchaser; an individual or business meeting the following qualifications: (a) has a need for insurance; (b) can afford the coverage; (c) qualifies as an insurable risk; and (d) can be approached by the agent under favorable circumstances. A potential purchaser about who too little is known to determine if these four qualifications are met is called a suspect.

PROSPECT FILE: A health insurance agent's card of computerized listing of present clients, prospects, and suspects, usually arranged according to alphabet and by date to contact.

PROSPECTING: The process of identifying and contacting people and businesses to discuss their health insurance needs.

PROSPECTING RATING PLAN: The formula in a reinsurance contract for determining reinsurance premium for a specified period on the basis, in whole or in part, of the loss experience of a prior period.

PROSPECTIVE FUTURE SERVICE BENEFIT: In a pension plan, that portion of a participant's retirement benefit relating to his or her period of credited service to be rendered after a specified current date.

PROSPECTIVE PAYMENT: A method of paying health care providers in which rates are established in advance. Providers are paid these rates regardless of the costs they actually incur.

PROSPECTIVE PAYMENT SYSTEM (PPS): The private and federal medical systems that reimburse health care providers based on diagnostic-related groups (DRGs). (1) The Medicare system used to pay hospitals for inpatient hospital services; based on the DRG classification system. (2) Medicare's acute care hospital payment method for inpatient care. Prospective per-case payment rates are set at a level intended to cover operating costs in an efficient hospital for treating a typical inpatient in a given DRG. Payments for each hospital are adjusted for differences in area wages, teaching activity, care to the poor, and other factors. Hospitals may also receive additional payments to cover extra costs associated with atypical patients (outliers) in each DRG. Capital costs, originally excluded from PPS, have been phased into the system. Today, capital payments are usually on a fully prospective, per-case basis. See Managed Care, HMO, and Capitation.

PROSPECTIVE RATING: A method used to arrive at the reinsurance rate and premium for a specified period, based in whole or in part on the loss experience of a prior period.

PROSPECTIVE REIMBURSEMENT: Any method of paying hospitals or other health programs in which amounts or rates of payment are established in advance regardless of the costs they actually incur. See Capitation.

PROSPECTIVE RESERVE: A life or health insurance reserve computed as the present value of assumed future claims minus the present value of net premiums, both values computed on the basis of assumed rates of interest.

PROSPECTIVE REVIEW: A method of reviewing possible hospitalization, prior to admission, to determine necessity of confinement, outpatient alternatives, and estimated reasonable length of stay. See Retrospective Review and Utilization Review.

PROSTHETIC APPLIANCE: A device used as artificial substitutes to replace a missing natural part of the body; also a device to improve the performance of a natural function. Prosthetic appliances do not include eyeglasses, hearing aids, orthopedic shoes, arch supports, orthotic devices, trusses, or examinations for their prescription or fitting.

PROTECTED HEALTH INFORMATION (PHI): Individually identifiable health care and private medical information, according to HIPAA. Personal health care information transmitted or maintained in any form or medium, which is held by a covered entity or its business associate. Identifies the individual or offers a reasonable basis for identification. Is created or received by a covered entity or an employer Relates to a past, present, or future physical or mental condition, provision of health care, or payment for health care. See HIPAA.

PROTECTION: Elimination or reduction of exposure to injuries and occupational or environmental hazards. Synonymous term for health, disability, or managed care insurance or plan coverage.

PROVIDER: Any licensed physician or institution that provides health care services. See Doctor.

PROVIDER AGREEMENT: Physician contract with a health insurance company, producing rules and billing regulations.

PROVIDER DIRECTORY: A listing of all physicians, ancillary services, and facilities that participate in a plan.

PROVIDER DISCOUNTS: The amount of money contracting health care providers deduct from their charge because of contracts between themselves and a health plan. See Discount.

PROVIDER EFFECTIVE DATE: The date that a provider is admitted into an insurance plan network.

PROVIDER EXCESS: Specific or aggregate stop-loss coverage extended to a provider instead of a payer or employer.

PROVIDER ID NUMBER: Computer numeric identifier given to a health care entity or provider for tracking and payment purposes.

PROVIDER MANUAL: A book that details plan coverage, utilization rules, and billing instructions for plan network providers.

PROVIDER NETWORKS: A preselected list of medical providers who may be chosen by patients in a particular health care or insurance plan.

PROVIDER NUMBERS: Unique identifying numbers assigned to each network provider by the plan. These numbers are used for referrals, claims, and all other communication with the health plan.

PROVIDER RELATIONS DEPARTMENT: Division of a managed care organization that educates providers and resolves their concerns.

PROVIDERS: Institutions and individuals that are licensed to provide health care services (e.g., hospitals, physicians, pharmacists, etc.). See Doctors and Medical Provider.

PROVIDER SAVINGS: An amount of money saved because of contracts between a health plan and participating providers.

PROVIDER SURVEY DATA: Data collected through a survey or focus group of providers who participate in the Medicaid program and have provided services to enrolled Medicaid beneficiaries. The state or a contractor of the state may conduct the survey.

PROVIDER TAXONOMY CODES: An administrative code set for identifying the provider type and area of specialization for all health care providers. A given provider can have several provider taxonomy codes. This code set is used in the X12 278 referral certification and authorization and the X12 837 claim transactions and is maintained by the National Uniform Claim Committee.

PROVISIONS FOR BAD DEBT: An operational estimate of ARs that will not likely be paid. See Bad Dept Expenses and Write Offs.

PRUDENT LAYPERSON STANDARD: The criteria that a prudent layperson would use to decide if a health problem requires emergency room care. Situations that meet these criteria cannot result in claims denial for the member.

PRUDENT MAN RULE: Anyone acting for another—in a fiduciary or trust capacity—to make judgments and act as would a prudent person. Most states have adopted this rule, named after a court case decided in 1830, which provides that a person acting in a fiduciary capacity (e.g., a hospital trustee, executor, custodian, etc.) is required to conduct himself faithfully and exercise sound judgment when investing monies under his care.

PSN (Provider Sponsored Network): These range from loose alliances between physicians to legal entities formed between hospitals and physicians for the purposes of managed care contracting.

PSO (Provider Sponsored Organization): A term used in Medicare reform legislation to define a provider-sponsored health plan that would be licensed to provide coverage of the Medicare benefits package. See IPA, PHO, MSO, and GPWWs.

PSYCHIATRIC FACILITY (PARTIAL HOSPITALIZATION): A facility for the diagnosis and treatment of mental illness on a 24-hr basis, by or under the supervision of a physician. See Behavioral Health.

PSYCHIATRIC HEALTH FACILITY (PHF): A facility that provides 24-hr inpatient care for mentally disordered, incompetent. Such care usually includes, but not be limited to, the following basic services: psychiatry; clinical psychology; psychiatric nursing; social work; rehabilitation; drug administration; and appropriate food services for those persons whose physical health needs can be met in an affiliated hospital or in outpatient settings.

PSYCHIATRIC RESIDENTIAL TREATMENT CENTER: A facility or distinct part of a facility for psychiatric care that provides a total 24-hr therapeutically planned and professionally staffed group living and learning environment.

PSYCHIATRY: The diagnosis and treatment of mental, emotional, and drug-related disorders by a medical doctor or doctor of osteopathy.

PSYCHOKINESIS (PK, cryptokinesis, telekinesis, telergy): Alleged production or control of motion, or influencing of an event, mentally, without the use of bodily mechanisms. The word "telekinesis" implies involvement of the occult.

PSYCHOLOGIST: A doctor who diagnoses and treats mental and emotional disorders but is not a medical doctor or doctor of osteopathy.

PSYCHOTHERAPY (psychotherapeutics, therapy): Treatment of mental and emotional disorders or "adjustment" problems mainly with psychological techniques. Its major categories are individual psychotherapy and group psychotherapy. Psychotherapy ranges from specialist therapy to informal conversations, and from science-oriented techniques (e.g., rational-emotive therapy [RET]) to quackery, applied pop psychology, religious counseling, and methods akin to mesmerism. Psychotherapists include clinical psychologists, clinical social workers, "counselors," psychiatric nurses, and psychiatrists.

PUBLIC HEALTH: Activities that society does collectively to assure the conditions in which people can be healthy. This includes organized community efforts to prevent, identify, preempt, and counter threats to the public's health.

PUBLIC HEALTH DEPARTMENT OR DISTRICT: Local (county or multi-county) health agency, operated by local government, with oversight and direction from a local board of health, which provides public health services throughout a defined geographic area.

PUBLIC OFFERING: The first or initial time a company sells securities to raise money in the open markets.

PUBLIC USE MEDICAL FILE: Nonidentifiable medical data that is within the public domain.

PULMONARY MEDICINE: The study and diagnosis and treatment of lung and lung-related breathing disorders.

PULMONOLOGIST: A medical doctor or doctor of osteopathy that diagnoses and treats lung and lung-related breathing disorders.

PURCHASER: This entity not only pays the premium but also controls the premium dollar before paying it to the provider. Included in the category of purchasers or payers are patients, businesses, and managed care organizations. Although patients and businesses function as ultimate purchasers, managed care organizations and insurance companies serve a processing or payer function.

PURE PREMIUM: Premium to cover pure cost only, without marketing, salary, advertising, commissions, or sales-loading expenses.

PURE RISK: A loss or no-loss situation, without the chance of gain. See Hazard and Peril.

PURGE: Removing health care data from electronic files.

PY: Per Year.

Q

QARI: The Quality Assurance Reform Initiative was unveiled in 1993 to assist states in the development of continuous quality improvement systems, external quality assurance programs, internal quality assurance programs, and focused clinical studies.

QI: Broadly, the alleged vital force that underlies functioning of body, mind, and spirit. According to Qigong theory, Qi encompasses air and internal Qi, or true Qi, which includes essential Qi (vital energy).

QUALIFICATION LAWS: Rules governing the license of insurance agents and brokers as stipulated from state to state and detailing such matters as license fee and methods of revoking and suspending an agent's license. See Qualified Prospect.

QUALIFIED MEDICAL CHILD SUPPORT ORDER (QMCSO): A medical child support order that requires parents to provide health coverage for their children.

QUALIFIED MEDICAL EXPENSE (QME): Defined by IRS Code 213(d) as an expense used to alleviate or prevent a mental defect, illnesses, or physical defects.

QUALIFIED MEDICARE BENEFICIARY (QMB): A person whose income level is such that the state pays the Medicare Part B Premiums, deductibles and copayments.

QUALIFIED PROSPECT: One who meets the qualifications of an insurance sales prospect, as opposed to a suspect, who may or may not be qualified.

QUALIFYING EVENT: An occurrence (such as death, termination of employment, divorce, etc.) that triggers an insured's protection under COBRA, which requires continuation of benefits under a group insurance plan for former employees and their families who would otherwise lose health care coverage.

QUALIFYING INDIVIDUALS: A Medicaid-sponsored program for those who need assistance paying Part B Medicare health insurance premiums.

QUALIFYING PREVIOUS COVERAGE: Benefits or coverage that has been in effect for at least 1 year, provides benefits similar to or exceeding those of the standard plan and is provided under: (a) any group health insurance (excluding self-insured plans); (b) an individual health benefit plan, including coverage issued by an HMO, a fraternal benefit society, a nonprofit medical and surgical plan, or a nonprofit hospital service plan; or (c) an organized delivery system. Medicare, Medicare Supplement, or Short-Term Major Medical is usually not a qualifying previous coverage.

QUALITY: Can be defined as a measure of the degree to which delivered health services meet established professional standards and judgments of value to the consumer. Quality may also be seen as the degree to which actions taken or not taken maximize the probability of beneficial health outcomes and minimize risk and other untoward outcomes, given the existing state of medical science and art. Quality is frequently described as having three dimensions: (a) quality of input resources; (b) quality of the process of services delivery (the use of appropriate procedures for a given condition); and (c) quality of outcome of service use (actual improvement in condition or reduction of harmful effects). Quality programs are commonly called QA, TQM, QI, CQI, and other acronyms, all referring to the process of monitoring quality in systematic ways. See Quality Assurance.

QUALITY-ADJUSTED LIFE YEAR (QALY): A common measure of health status or treatment outcome used in cost-utility analysis; it combines morbidity and mortality data.

QUALITY ASSURANCE (QA): Activities and programs intended to assure the quality of care in a defined medical setting. Such programs include peer or utilization review components to identify and remedy deficiencies in quality. The program must have a mechanism for assessing its effectiveness and may measure care against preestablished standards.

QUALITY ASSURANCE REFORM INITIATIVE (QARI): A process developed by the Health Care Financing Administration to develop a health care quality improvement system for Medicaid-managed care plans.

QUALITY BUSINESS: In life, long-term care, disability, and health insurance, a term used to describe the staying power of an agent's business. It is characterized by good persistency, satisfactory mortality, and low acquisition and maintenance costs.

QUALITY OF CARE: The degree or grade of excellence with respect to medical services received by patients and administered by providers. Criteria typically include technical competence, need, appropriateness, etc. See Quality of Life.

QUALITY COMPASS: Rating product developed by the National Committee for Quality Assurance and based on the Health Plan and Employer Information Data set initiative to rate health plans to a specific set of performance measures.

QUALITY IMPROVEMENT (QI): Also called performance improvement (PI). This is the more commonly used term in health care, replacing QA. QI implies that concurrent systems are used to continuously improve quality, rather than reacting when certain baseline statistical thresholds are crossed. Quality improvement programs usually use tools such as cross-functional teams, task forces, statistical studies, flow charts, process charts, Pareto charts, etc. See Quality Assurance.

QUALITY IMPROVEMENT ORGANIZATION (QIA): Usually a group of doctors or other health care experts, paid by the federal government to monitor medical quality in hospitals, clinics, offices, emergency rooms, operating rooms, ambulatory surgical centers, and other emerging health care organizations. See Pareto charts, etc. See Quality Assurance.

QUALITY OF LIFE: An assessment to evaluate the impact of a disease or a medical service on the social, physiological, mental, intellectual, and general well-being of individuals. See Quality of Care.

QUALITY OF LIFE ENDPOINTS: The characteristics measured in quality of life research (e.g., pain, ability to function, and sense of well-being). See Quality of Life.

QUALITY MANAGEMENT: A formal set of activities to assure the quality of services provided. Quality management includes quality assessment and corrective actions taken to remedy any deficiencies identified through the assessment process. See Quality Improvement and Quality Assurance.

QUARANTINE BENEFIT: A benefit paid for loss of time resulting from the quarantining of an insured by health authorities.

QUARANTINE INDEMNITY: An insurance benefit paid for loss of time while the insured is quarantined because of exposure to a contagious disease.

QUARTER OF COVERAGE: With regard to eligibility for Social Security benefits, a unit of coverage is credited to an individual worker for each portion of a calendar year's covered wages or self-employment income that equals or exceeds the amount per quarter specified by law for the year. Not more than one may be credited to a calendar quarter and not more than four in a calendar year. Exception: No quarter that (a) began after his or her death; (b) lay within a period of disability (other than the first or last quarter of such period); or (c) has not yet begun can ever be a quarter of coverage.

QUASI CONTRACT: An obligation similar in nature to an insurance contract, arising not from an agreement of the parties but from some relation between them or from a voluntary act of one of them. Also, a situation imposed by law to prevent unjust enrichment or injustice and not dependent on agreement of the parties to the contract.

QUASI-INSURANCE INSTITUTIONS: A term referring to social insurance plans under government authority and direct supervision that have some but not all of the characteristics of insurance. Examples are Social Security's old-age and survivors benefits, unemployment insurance, Medicare, Medicaid, etc.

QUASI-JUDICIAL BODIES: Some federal agencies, such as the Federal Trade Commission that have powers similar to a judicial body, thus permitting them to enforce their regulations and rules.

QUASI-PUBLIC CORPORATION: An incorporated organization privately operated but in which some general interest of the public is evident. The line of demarcation is not clear when a private company comes into this classification. Charitable and religious companies are quasi-public.

QUATERNARY CARE: Highly sophisticated medical care provided by specialty physicians, in specialty settings, like organ transplants and serious poly trauma treatment.

QUICK ASSETS: Cash or those assets that can quickly be converted into cash.

QUICK ASSET RATIO: The ratio of cash, accounts receivable, and marketable securities to current liabilities. Also called acid test.

QUICK RATIO: A measure of health care entity financial liquidity: (cash + marketable securities + accounts receivable/current liabilities). See Ratio Analysis.

QUID PRO QUO: Latin for this for that, or one thing for another, such as the consideration in an insurance contract, which requires the exchange of something of value by both parties for there to be a valid contract.

QUI FACIT PER ALIUM, FACIT PER SE: He who acts through another acts himself (i.e., the acts of the agent are the acts of the principal).

QUINQUENNIAL MILITARY SERVICE DETERMINATION AND ADJUSTMENTS: Prior to the Social Security Amendments of 1983, determinations were made every 5 years about the costs arising from the granting of deemed wage credits for military service prior to 1957; and annual reimbursements were made from the general fund of the Treasury Department to the health insurance (HI) trust fund for these costs. The Social Security Amendments of 1983 provided for (1) a lump-sum transfer in 1983 for (a) the costs arising from the pre-1957 wage credits and (b) amounts equivalent to the HI taxes that would have been paid on the deemed wage credits for military service for 1966 through 1983, inclusive, if such credits had been counted as covered earnings; (2) quinquennial adjustments to the pre-1957 portion of the 1983 lump-sum transfer; (3) general fund transfers equivalent to HI taxes on military deemed wage credits for 1984 and later, to be credited to the fund on July 1 of each year; and (4) adjustments as deemed necessary to any previously transferred amounts representing HI taxes on military deemed wage credits.

QUI TAM: Latin phrase for "in the name of the King." A legal mechanism in the Federal False Claims Act (FCA) that allows a person to sue those committing health care fraud, on behalf of the government.

QUOTE: An estimate of the cost of insurance, based on information supplied to the insurance company by the applicant.

R

RACE-SPECIFIC MORTALITY RATE: A mortality rate limited to a specified racial group. Both numerator and denominator are limited to the specified health group.

RADIOLOGIST: A physician who specializes in radiology.

RADIOLOGY: The Medical diagnosis and treatment of disease using radioactive isotopes.

RADIX: Chart derived from mortality tables, used in the health and life insurance industry.

RAILROAD RETIREMENT: System that provides retirement and other benefits, including eligibility for Medicare, for railroad workers.

RAILROAD TRAVEL POLICY: Form of Accident Insurance policy sold in railroad stations by ticket agents or by vending machines.

RATE BAND: The allowable variation in insurance premiums as defined in state regulations. Acceptable variation may be expressed as a ratio from highest to lowest (e.g., 2:1) or as a percent from the community rate (e.g., +/−15%).

RATED: A rated health insurance policy is one issued on a substandard risk with higher than standard premiums.

RATED POLICY: A higher than standard premium charged, for some specific cause or reason, in a health life, disability, or other insurance policy.

RATE MANUAL: A list of charges by an insurance company for nonstandard premiums.

RATE REVIEW: A review of a health care entity, hospital, or doctor's office practice to evaluate economic, fiscal, and other financial data or that of a health insurance company regarding premium rate setting policies.

RATE SPREAD: The difference between the highest and lowest rates that a health plan charges small groups. The National Association of Insurance Commissioners Small Group Model Act limits a plan's allowable rate spread to 2 to 1.

RATING: The premium classification given to a person who applies for health insurance. The term is usually used when an applicant is designated as a substandard risk. A higher premium reflects an increased health, illness, or accident risk.

RATING IN AGE: An insurance applicant of substandard risk.

RATING BUREAU: An organization that classifies and promulgates insurance rates and, in some cases, compiles data and measures hazards of individual risks in terms of rates in given geographical areas.

RATING CLASS: The rate class into which a health insurance risk, especially an impaired risk, has been placed.

RATING EXPERIENCE: The determination or adjustment of the premium rate for an individual group, partially or wholly on the basis of that group's own previous experience.

RATING, MERIT: The determination of an insurance rate for an individual risk based on its variation in hazard from the average or standard for its class.

RATIO ANALYSIS: A method of analyzing a business entities' financial condition calculated from line items in the financial statements. There are four major categories: (a) liquidity; (b) profitability; (c) capitalization; and (d) activity.

RBRVS: Resource-Based Relative Value Sale.

REAL VALUE: A measurement of economic amount corrected for change in price over time (inflation). Thus, expressing a value in terms of constant prices. See Nominal Value.

REASONABLE CHARGES: Under Medicare or a major medical policy, the customary charges for similar services made by physicians. The range of prevailing charges for physicians engaged in specialty practices may be different from one locale to another.

REASONABLE AND CUSTOMARY CHARGE: The charges or fees that are common within a geographic area. These fees are reasonable if they are within the average charge for service parameters for that area, and if the charges for participating providers are what have been contracted with the health plan.

REBATE: A controversial insurance practice where a portion of an agent's commission, or anything of value, is given to the prospective insured as an inducement to buy. Rebates are illegal in most states. See Twisting and Churning.

REBATING: Granting any form of inducement, favor, or advantage to the purchaser of an insurance policy that is not available to all under the standard policy terms. Rebating in some states is a penal offense for which both the agent and the person accepting the rebate can be punished by fine or imprisonment, and in virtually all states the agent is subject to revocation of license. See Rebate.

REBILL: To bill again for noncovered or nonpaid services.

RECAPTURE: With respect to reinsurance, the action of a ceding company in taking back an insurance policy previously ceded to a reinsurer.

RECEIPT: A written acknowledgment of a payment.

RECIDIVISM: The frequency of the same patient returning to the hospital for the same presenting problems.

RECIPIENT: An individual covered by the Medicaid program; however, now referred to as a beneficiary.

RECIPROCITY: Agreement among two or more HMOs whereby a member of one HMO who is temporarily out of his or her HMO's service area may receive treatment from another HMO for illness or injury, normally of an acute nature, that cannot be postponed until the member returns to the home service area.

RECISION OF COVERAGE: Cancellation of insurance or health care coverage because information received on the medical questionnaire was untrue, inaccurate, or incomplete.

RECONCILIATION: A method of applying premiums, dues, or bills to health insurance policies.

RECONCILIATION CODE: Computer code used to settle a health claim within a reasonable payment range.

RECONSTRUCTIVE SURGERY: Any surgery used in the restoration of any part of the body to obtain its original function.

RECOUPMENT: The recovery by Medicare of any Medicare debt by reducing present or future Medicare payments and applying the amount withheld to the indebtedness.

RECURRENT DISABILITY: Recurrent disability insurance provision designed to protect an employee who tries to return to work but becomes disabled again from the same or a related cause. If this happens within a certain period of time, the employee will be considered disabled from the original disability and will not be subject to a new elimination period. This encourages an employee to return to work without fear of losing benefits. See Long-Term Care and Disability Insurance.

RECURRENT DISABILITY PROVISION: A provision that specifies a period of time during which the recurrence of a disability from the same accident or sickness is considered to be a continuation of the prior disability, thereby eliminating the need for a second deductible period.

RECURRENT HOSPITALIZATION PROVISION: A health insurance provision that specifies a period of time (usually 6 months) during which the recurrence of a disability from an accident or sickness is considered a continuation of the prior disability, thereby eliminating a new deductible charge.

RED HERRING: Preliminary prospectus of an underwriter for securities offerings. Normally, offers for the sale of or acceptance of securities are not made on the basis of the preliminary official statement, and a statement to that effect appears on the face of the document generally in red print, which gives the document its nickname, red herring. See Public Offering.

RED LINE: The practice of denying insurance coverage to high-risk groups or individuals.

REDUCED MORAL HAZARD: A condition or provision that discourages an insured from trying to make a profit through his or her insurance. The suicide clause and the duplication of benefits clause are examples.

REDUCTIONS: Decrease in benefits of a health insurance policy as a result of a certain condition. See Discounts and Exclusions.

RE-ENROLLMENT: The number of subscribers currently enrolled plus those who elect to join the HMO less those subscribers who leave the HMO.

REFERRAL AUTHORIZATION: A verbal or written approval of a request for a member to receive medical services or supplies outside of the participating medical group. See Gatekeeper and Managed Care.

REFERRAL CENTER (TRIAGE CENTER, CALL CENTER, 24-HR CERTIFI-CATION): This is a mechanism established by health plans to direct patients to approved hospitals and doctors. Often the Referral Center serves a UR function and certified or precertifies the care. These centers are also used by hospitals to refer patients to certain doctors, reduce use of the emergency room, or to provide follow-up patient contact. Managed care organizations use these centers as their central hub of communications with patients and providers at the time of service.

REFERRAL PHYSICIAN: A physician who has a patient referred to him by another source for examination or surgery or to have specific procedures performed on the patient, usually because the referring source is not prepared or qualified to provide the needed service. See Doctor and Gatekeeper.

REFERRAL POOL: An amount set aside to pay for noncapitated services provided by a primary care provider, services provided by a referral specialist, or emergency services.

REFERRAL SERVICES: Medical services arranged for by the physician and provided outside the physician's office other than hospital services.

REFERRED OR REFERRAL: A participating provider's written request to have a covered person receive benefit coverage for services rendered by a nonparticipating provider as well as the insurer's written approval for such request.

REFERRED LEAD: A prospect obtained when a client, prospect, or friend personally refers the insurance agent to someone else, often with an introductory phone call, letter, or brief note on the back of the agent's card. See Qualified Prospect.

REFERRING PHYSICIAN: A physician who sends a patient to another source for examination or surgery or to have specific procedures performed on the patient, usually because the referring physician is not prepared. See Gatekeeper and Internist.

REFINEMENT: The correction of relative values in Medicare's relative value scale that was initially set incorrectly.

REFLEXIVE CONTROLS: Outcome measures taken on participating targets before interventions and used as control observations.

REGENSTRIEF INSTITUTE: A research foundation for improving health care by optimizing the capture, analysis, content, and delivery of health care information. Regenstrief maintains the logical observation and identifier names and codes coding system that is being considered for use as part of the HIPAA claim attachments standard.

REGIONAL HOME HEALTH INTERMEDIARY (RHHI): A private company that contracts with Medicare to pay home health bills and check on the quality of home health care.

REGIONAL OFFICE: The Centers for Medicare and Medicaid Services (CMS) have many (ROs) that work closely together with Medicare contractors in their assigned geographical areas on a day-to-day basis. Several of these ROSs monitor network contractor performance, negotiate contractor budgets, distribute administrative monies to contractors, work with contractors when corrective actions are needed, and provide a variety of other liaison services to the contractors in their respective regions.

REGISTERED NURSES (RNs): Registered nurses are responsible for carrying out physician's instructions. They supervise practical nurses and other auxiliary personnel who perform routine care and treatment of patients. Registered nurses provide nursing care to patients or perform specialized duties in a variety of settings from hospital and clinics to schools and public health departments. A license to practice nursing is required in all states. For licensure as an RN, an applicant must have graduated from a school of nursing approved by the state board for nursing and have passed a state board examination. See LPN.

REGULAR MEDICAL BENEFIT: The stipulated health insurance benefit for physician's services that usually is on a per diem basis.

REGULAR MEDICAL EXPENSE INSURANCE: Provides benefits for payment of doctor fees for nonsurgical care, commonly in a hospital, but also at home or at a physician's office. Frequently contained in hospital and surgical expense policies. See Health Insurance.

REHABILITATION: A restorative process through which an individual with end-stage renal disease develops and maintains self-sufficient functioning consistent with his or her capability. The return to a recognized, acceptable, and attainable physical, mental, motional, social, and economic usefulness for employment.

REHABILITATION BENEFITS: Insurance benefits paid for physical and mental rehabilitation.

REHABILITATION CLAUSE: Any clause in a health insurance or disability income policy describing benefits intended to assist a disabled policy owner in vocational rehabilitation.

REHABILITATION SERVICES: The medical care related to rehabilitation rendered by a practitioner to a covered person pursuant to the health plan.

REIMBURSE: To pay back.

REIMBURSEMENT: The payment of an amount of money for the loss of an insurance claim. In insurance, payment to the insured for a covered expense or loss incurred by or on behalf of the insured. See Usual, Customary, and Reasonable and Capitation.

REIMBURSEMENT BENEFITS: Provisions under which the actual expense incurred by the insured (usually for medical, nursing, and hospital treatment) are paid.

REINSTATEMENT: Policy owners' rights, by the terms of most life insurance policies, to reinstate lapsed policies within a reasonable time after lapse, provided they present satisfactory evidence of insurability, pay back premiums, and interest. The right is usually denied if a policy has been surrendered for its cash value.

REINSURANCE: (1) A contract by which an insurer procures a third party to insure it against loss or liability by reason of such original insurance. (2) The practice of an HMO or insurance company of purchasing insurance from another company to protect itself against part or all the losses incurred in the process of honoring the claims of a policyholder. Also referred to as *stop loss* or *risk control* insurance. (3) Insurance purchased by another health or managed care plan to mitigate the risks pertaining to stop-loss, aggregate stop-loss, out of area, solvency protection, and other risks and perils. See Insurance.

REINSURANCE ASSUMED: The portion of risk that the reinsurer accepts from the original reinsurer; the premium for an assumption of reinsurance.

REINSURANCE, AUTOMATIC: An agreement between the ceding company and the reinsurer whereby the latter agrees to automatically cover all amounts above the original company's retention limit, up to an agreed maximum.

REINSURANCE BROKER: An individual or organization that places reinsurance through a reinsurance underwriter. See Insurance Broker and Agent.

REINSURANCE CEDED: The portion of risk that the original insurer transfers to the reinsurer. Also know as the premium for a cession of reinsurance.

REINSURANCE, COINSURANCE PLAN: An arrangement whereby the original insuring company cedes to a reinsurer the amount of the original contract that exceeds its retention limits and continues that amount of reinsurance in force throughout the life of the contract.

REINSURANCE CREDIT: Credit taken on its annual statement by a ceding insurance company for reinsurance premiums ceded and losses recoverable.

REINSURANCE, SURPLUS SHARE: A type of reinsurance in which the writing company cedes all of the coverage in a given policy above a certain retention limit.

REINSURER: A special type of insurer that assumes all or a part of the insurance or reinsurance written by another insurer. See Insurance.

REJECTION: Refusal to underwrite a risk; or the denial of a claim by an insurer.

REJECT STATUS: The encounter data did not pass the front-end edit process. Medicare plus choice organizations need to correct the data and resubmit.

RELATIONSHIP CODE: The relationship of sex and gender between an insurance policyholder and a member.

RELATIVE VALUE SCALE (RVS): Is the compiled table of relative value units (RVUs), which is a value given to each procedure or unit of service. As payment systems, RVS is used to determine a formula that multiplies the RVU by a dollar amount, called a converter. See California RVS.

RELATIVE VALUE UNIT (RVU): The unit of measure for a relative value scale. RVUs must be multiplied by a dollar conversion factor to become payment amounts.

RELEASE: Give up or abandon an enforceable right.

REMITTANCE ADVICE: A health service report for specific insurance members.

RENAL TRANSPLANT CENTER: A hospital unit that is approved to furnish transplantation and other medical and surgical specialty services directly for the care of end-stage renal disease transplant patients, including inpatient dialysis furnished directly or under arrangements.

RENEWAL: Continuance health care insurance of coverage.

RENEWAL COMMISSIONS: Payment to an insurance agent for continued health care, disability, life, long-term care, or other insurance of coverage.

REOPENING: Action taken, after all appeal rights are exhausted, to reexamine or question the correctness of a determination, a decision, or cost report otherwise final.

REPLACEMENT INSURANCE: Insurance that substitutes coverage under one policy for coverage under another policy.

REPORT CARD: A medical quality improvement assay or written report.

REPORT OF ELIGIBILITY: A schedule of health insurance or managed care plan categories for members or eligible dependents.

REPORTING PERIOD: The period of time for which a report encompasses. For financial data, this period normally consists of 12 consecutive calendar months (or thirteen 4-week periods) that begin on the first day of a month and end on the last day of a month. Other reporting periods may consider with a calendar quarter, a semiannual period, or any consecutive calendar period of time.

REPRESENTATIONS: Statements made by an applicant on a health insurance application that the applicant attests are substantially true to the best of his or her knowledge and belief, but which are not warranted as exact in every detail, as compared to warranties. See Clause, Policy, and Contract.

REPRESENTATIVE: See insurance agent or broker.

REQUESTOR: An entity that formally requests access to the Centers for Medicare and Medicaid Services (CMS) data.

RERELEASE: When a requestor formally requests permission to re-release Centers for Medicare and Medicaid (CMS) data that has been formatted into statistical or aggregated information by the recipient. CMS is responsible for reviewing the files or reports to ensure that they contain no data elements or combination of data elements that could allow for the deduction of the identity of the Medicare beneficiary or a physician and that the level of cell size aggregation meets the stated requirement.

RES CARE/B & C HOME: Refers to a Residential Care Facility, sometimes called a Board and Care Home. The provision of room and board, personal services, supervision, and assistance in transportation, guidance, and training to sustain the activities of daily living is Res Care. Medication and nursing are not included.

RESCUE PROCEDURES: The procedures of removing blood from a body and then returning that blood to the same body, as well as removing blood from one body and infusing it into another body.

RESERVES: Monies earmarked by health plans to cover anticipated claims and operating expenses. A fiscal method of withholding a certain percentage of premiums to provide a fund for committed but undelivered health care and such uncertainties as: (a) longer hospital utilization levels than expected; (b) overutilization of referrals; and (c) accidental catastrophes, etc. Providing a fund for committed but undelivered health services or other financial liabilities. A percentage of the premiums support this fund. Businesses other than health plans also manage reserves. For example, hospitals document reserves as that portion of the account receivables they hope to collect but have some doubt about collectability. Rather than book these amounts as income, hospitals will reserve these amounts until paid.

RESIDENT AGENT: An agent domiciled in the state in which he or she sells insurance. See Agent. See Broker.

RESIDENTIAL CARE: The provision of room and board, personal services, supervision, and assistance in transportation, guidance, and training to sustain the person in the activities of daily living. Medication and nursing are not included. See Res Care/B & C Home.

RESIDENTIAL TREATMENT CENTER: A health care facility providing residential care.

RESIDUAL BENEFIT: Relates to the part of anything remaining or its residue. In health insurance, a generally variable, long-term partial disability benefit tied to the insured's actual income loss. The percentage amount of loss is often measured on a monthly basis.

RESIDUAL DISABILITY: Inability to perform one or more important business duties for the time period usually required for such duties. A physical or mental disability that limits an insured's earning ability even though he or she may be able to work full time.

RESIDUAL DISABILITY INCOME INSURANCE: Pro rata income replacement coverage for an individual with a residual disability (Lost income/Prior income × Benefit for Total Disability).

RESIDUAL SUBSCRIBER: A separate medical bill or invoice used when a health plan or insurance policy holder or member has a dependent with a different plan.

RES IPSA LOQUITOR: Latin phrase for "The facts speak for themselves." An accident could not have occurred without negligence (e.g., surgical sponge left in the abdomen following an operation).

RESOURCE-BASED RELATIVE VALUE SCALE (RBRVS): (1) A schedule of values assigned to health care services that give weight to procedures based on resources needed by the provider to effectively deliver the service or perform that procedure. Unlike other relative value scales, the RBRVS ignores historical charges and includes factors such as time, effort, technical skill, practice cost, and training cost. Established as part of the Omnibus Reconciliation Act of 1989, Medicare payment rules for physician services were altered by establishing an RBRVS fee schedule. This payment methodology has three components: (a) a relative value for each procedure; (b) a geographic adjustment factor; and (c) a dollar conversion factor. (2) A Medicare weighting system to assign units of value to each *Current Procedural Terminology* code (procedure) performed by physicians and other providers. See UCR and Capitation.

RESPITE CARE: Temporary or intermittent nursing home care, assisted living, or other type of long-term-care program, to allow caregivers a rest. Or a hospital admission where the main reason for the admission is to provide temporary relief for a person who normally cares for a patient at home. See Long-Term Care Insurance and Activities of Daily Living.

RESPONDEAT SUPERIOR: A general rule in law that a principal or employer is liable for an agent or representative's acts performed on behalf of the principal's business.

REST CURE: Time spent in a nursing home, sanitarium, hospice, or rest home for custodial care.

RESTORATION OF BENEFITS: A provision in many Major Medical Plans that restores a person's lifetime maximum benefit amount in small increments after a claim has been paid. Usually, only a small amount ($1,000–$3,000) may be restored annually.

RESTRAINTS: Any manual or mechanical device to restrict individual movement or patient motion.

RESTRICTED DONATIONS: A conditional donation.

RESTRICTED FORMULARY: A limited set of drugs or medicinal benefits available for health plan, managed care, or insurance members.

RESTRICTIONS: In life or health insurance, limitations or exclusions in a policy.

RETAINED EARNINGS: Profits that a business entity keeps to further its mission statement, goals, and objections.

RETAINER: An ongoing fee paid to a professional person to engage his or her services.

RETENTION: The portion of the health or life insurance premium that is used by an insurance company for administrative costs.

RETENTION DEDUCTIBLE: An insurance clause that stipulates in the absence of underlying coverage, a deductible will apply.

RETROSPECTIVE PREMIUM: An insurance premium establishing method in which current costs are adjusted to reflect the prior year's loss or health claim experience. See Retrospective Rate.

RETROSPECTIVE RATE: An insurance rating method in which current rates are adjusted to reflect the prior year's aggregate or individual rating experience. See Retrospective Premium.

RETROSPECTIVE RATE DERIVATION (RETRO): A rating system whereby the employer becomes responsible for a portion of the group's health care costs. If health care costs are less than the portion the employer agrees to assume, the insurance company may be required to refund a portion of the premium.

RETROSPECTIVE REIMBURSEMENT: The payment to a health care provider or entity prior to the deliverance of medical services.

RETROSPECTIVE REVIEW: A method of reviewing patient care, after hospital discharge, to determine quality, necessity, and appropriateness of care. See Utilization Review, Retrospective Review Process, and Quality Assurance.

RETROSPECTIVE REVIEW PROCESS: A review that is conducted after services are provided to a patient. The review focuses on determining the appropriateness, necessity, quality, and reasonableness of health care services provided. Becoming seen as least desirable method; supplanted by concurrent reviews. See Utilization Review.

RETURN ON ASSETS (ROA): Net income expressed as an average of total assets.

RETURN COMMISSION: That percentage of a commission paid to an agent by an insurance company that must be returned in the event a policy is canceled.

RETURN ON EQUITY: Net income expressed as a percentage of total equity.

RETURN ON INVESTMENT (ROI): The percentage of loss or gain from an investment.

RETURN ON NET ASSETS: Excess revenues over expenses/net assets.

RETURN ON NET WORTH (RONW): Excess of corporate insurance company end of year net worth.

RETURN FOR NO CLAIM: A provision in some health policies stating that if no claims have been paid during the term of the policy (or after the policy has been in force for a specified time), the insurance company will refund a portion of the premium.

RETURN PREMIUM: The amount due the policy owner if an insurance policy is canceled, reduced in amount, or reduced in rate. See Premium and Rate Setting.

RETURN ON TOTAL ASSETS: Excess revenues over expenses/total assets.

RETURN TO WORK PROVISION: Encourages employees to return to work as soon as they become physically able, an additional incentive is usually provided for a certain period of time, and is called a return to work provision.

REVENUE ATTAINMENT: Achieving the amount of revenues budgeted.

REVENUE BUDGET: An operating and nonoperating revenue forecast.

REVENUE CODE: Payment codes for services or items in FL 42 of the UB-92 found in Medicare or National Uniform Billing Committee (NUBC) manuals (42X, 43X, etc).

REVENUE ENHANCEMENT: Augmenting traditional revenue sources of the enterprise with new sources, products, or health care services.

REVENUE SHARE: The proportion of a practice's total revenue devoted to a particular type of expense. For example, the practice expense revenue share is that proportion of revenue used to pay for practice expense.

REVENUE VOLUME VARIANCE: (Actual volume − budget volume) × actual volume.

REVERSE CAPITATION: A payment method that capitates medical specialists but pays primary care physicians at some fee-for-service rate.

REVERSE MEMBERSHIP: Health insurance policy member with a new ID number and not previously the subscriber.

REVIEW OF CLAIMS: Using information on a claim or other information requested to support the services billed to make a determination.

REVOCATION: Cancellation of the power or authority previously conferred.

REVOLVING CREDIT LINE: A continuous line of credit up to a prenegotiated limit.

REWRITTEN: A revised health policy or a new policy issued on an insured that has previously let his or her coverage lapse.

RHEUMATOLOGIST: A physician who specializes in rheumatology.

RHEUMATOLOGY: The study of human arthritic, rheumatic, and related collagen vascular conditions.

RHU: registered health underwriter. See Insurance Agent, Agent, Certified Medical Planner®, CMP®, Certified Financial Planner®, and CFP®.

RIDER: A description of covered health services that is attached to a health plan's insurance contract. See Clause and Policy.

RIGHT TO RENEW: A written guarantee in an insurance policy that enables the policy owner to continue coverage for another policy term.

RIGHTS OF INDIVIDUALS: (a) Receive notice of information practices; (b) to view and copy own records; (c) request corrections; (d) obtain accounting of disclosures; (e) request restrictions and confidential communications; and (f) file complaints.

RIMS: risk and insurance management society.

RISK: The uncertainty of financial loss. Refers to finances used for providing patient care. For example, an HMO that offers prepaid care for a given premium is at risk because it must provide care within the premium funds available. See Peril.

RISK-ADJUSTED CAPITATION: A method of payment to either an organization or individual provider that takes the form of a fixed amount per person per period and that is varied to reflect the health characteristics of individuals or groups of individuals. See Capitation and Prospective Payment System.

RISK ADJUSTER: A measure used to adjust payments made to a health plan on behalf of a group of enrollees to compensate for spending, which is expected to be lower or higher than average, based on the health status or demographic characteristics of the enrollees. See Risk.

RISK ADJUSTMENT: Risk adjustment uses the results of risk assessment to fairly compensate plans that, by design or accident, end up with a larger-than-average share of high-cost enrollees. Increases or reductions in the amount of payment made to a health plan on behalf of a group of enrollees to compensate for health care expenditures that are expected to be higher or lower than average.

RISK ASSESSMENT: (1) The means by which plans and policy makers estimate the anticipated claims costs of enrollees. (2) Identifying and measuring the presence of direct causes and risk factors that, based on scientific evidence or theory, are thought to directly influence the level of a specific health problem. See Risk and Risk Management.

RISK-BASED CAPITAL: Insurance company capital requirement based on its risk of operations.

RISK-BASED CAPITAL RATIO: The capital of an insurance company, minus its liabilities, required to support its risk-based operations and investments.

RISK-BASED HEALTH MAINTENANCE ORGANIZATION/COMPETITIVE MEDICAL PLAN: A type of managed care organization. After any applicable deductible or copayment, all of an enrollee or member's medical care costs are paid for in return for a monthly premium. However, because of the lock-in provision, all of the enrollee or member's services (except for out-of-area emergency services) must be arranged for by the risk-HMO. Should the Medicare enrollee or member choose to obtain service not arranged for by the plan, he or she will be liable for the costs. Neither the HMO nor the Medicare program will pay for services from providers that are not part of the HMO's health care system or network. See Managed Care.

RISK BEARER: Intentional or unintentional self-insurer. See Risk.

RISK-BEARING ENTITY: An organization that assumes financial responsibility for the provision of a defined set of benefits by accepting prepayment for some or all of the cost of care. A risk-bearing entity may be an insurer, a health plan, or self-funded employer; or a physician hospital organization or other form of provider-sponsored network. Health plans (except under employer self-insured programs) usually are risk-bearing. Providers and provider organizations if capitated, bear risk. There are 2 types of risk: (a) health insurance risk and (b) health business risk; each are calculated and considered separately. See Underwriter.

RISK CLASSIFICATION: Analysis of the uncertainty of financial loss. See Risk.

RISK COMMUNICATION: The production and dissemination of information regarding health risks and methods of avoiding them. See Risk Factor.

RISK CONTRACT: An arrangement between a managed health care plan and HCFA (now CMS) under §1876 of the Social Security Act. Under this contract, enrolled Medicare beneficiaries generally must use the plans' provider network. Capitation payments to plans are set at 95% of the adjusted average per capita cost. See Policy and Contract.

RISK CORRIDOR: A financial arrangement between a payer of health care services, such as a state Medicaid agency, and a provider, such as a managed care organization that spreads the risk for providing health care services. Risk corridors protect the provider from excessive care costs for individual beneficiaries by instituting stop-loss protections and they protect the payer by limiting the profits that the provider may earn. See Deductible.

RISK EXPERIENCE LOSS RATIO: The frequency and distribution of a health or other insurance company's health care claims or losses. See Risk Factor.

RISK FACTOR: Behavior or condition that, based on scientific evidence or theory, is thought to directly influence susceptibility to a specific health problem. See Peril.

RISK IDENTIFICATION: Determining and seeking hazards or perils. See Risk Management.

RISK LOAD: An underwriting factor that is multiplied into the rate to offset some adverse parameter of the group.

RISK MANAGEMENT: Measuring, identifying, and controlling potential adverse outcomes.

RISK MEASURE: Measure of the expected per capita costs of efficiently provided health care services to a defined group for a specified future period. See Rating.

RISK PHILOSOPHY: Personal or corporate view of risk management, insurance losses, perils, and hazards. See Self Insurance. See Risk Retention.

RISK POOLS: Legislatively created programs that unite those who cannot get insurance in the private market. Funding for the pool is subsidized through assessments on insurers or through government revenues. Maximum rates are tied to the rest of the market. See Adverse Selection.

RISK RETENTION: Personal or corporate policy of retaining and not eliminating, reducing, or transferring the possibility of hazard, illness, harm, or peril. See Self- Insurance.

RISK RETENTION ACT OF 1986: An amendment to the Product Liability Act of 1981, allowing for more efficient procedures for establishing risk retention groups See Self-Insurance.

RISK SELECTION: (1) The process by which health plans seek to enroll healthy, low-cost subscribers. (2) Enrollment choices made by health plans or enrollees on the basis of perceived risk relative to the premium to be paid. (3) Any situation in which health plans differ in the health risk associated with their enrollees because of enrollment choices made by the plans or enrollees (i.e., where one health plan's expected costs differ from another's because of underlying differences in their enrolled populations). See Risk Adjustment and Risk Pool.

RISK SHARING: A method by which medical insurance premiums are shared by plan sponsors and participants. In contrast to traditional indemnity plans in which insurance premiums belonged solely to insurance company that assumed all risk of using these premiums. Key to this approach is that the premiums are the only payment providers receive; provides powerful incentive to be parsimonious with care.

RISK, SPECULATIVE: A questionable gambling sort of risk involving uncertainty with respect to a given event that may produce a loss, but that may, on the other hand, produce a gain. See Peril.

ROLLING BUDGET: A continually updated budget process.

ROUTINE: Medical and surgical procedures or diagnostic interventions performed on a regular basis.

ROUTINE HOME CARE DAYS: Noncontinuous home hospice care.

ROUTINE NEWBORN CARE: The initial inpatient hospital physical examination of a newborn infant by a doctor other than the delivering physician or attendant anesthesiologist.

ROUTINE SERVICES (LTC): Various types of nursing care services (skilled nursing, intermediate care, mentally disordered care, developmentally disabled care, subacute care, hospice inpatient care, and other routine services) that are provided by health facilities and generally included in the daily service charge. Such services include room, dietary services, and minor medical supplies but exclude ancillary services for which a separate charge is made.

ROUTINE USE: The purposes identifiable medical data can be collected and the authority to release identifiable data.

RUN OFF: Insurance company liability for future health claims or losses to be paid by its reserve funds.

RURAL HEALTH CLINIC (RHC): A public or private hospital, clinic, or physician practice designated by the federal government as in compliance with the Rural Health Clinics Act (Public Law 95-210). The practice must be located in a medically underserved area or a health professions shortage area and use a physician assistant or nurse practitioners to deliver services. A rural health clinic must be licensed by the state and provide preventive services. These providers are usually qualified for special compensations, reimbursements, and exemptions.

RURAL HEALTH CLINICS ACT: Establishes a reimbursement mechanism to support the provision of primary care services in rural areas. Public Law 95-210 was enacted in 1977 and authorizes the expanded use of physician assistants, nurse practitioners, and certified nurse practitioners; extends Medicare and Medicaid reimbursement to designated clinics; and raises Medicaid reimbursement levels to those set by Medicare.

S

SAFE HARBOR: Acceptable payment practice that does not violate Stark, fraud and abuse laws, or office of inspector general health insurance payment regulations. See Fraud and Abuse.

SAFETY: A method of preventing illness, accidents or injury.

SAFETY ZONE: Substantial risk sharing arrangements between medical providers that must exist for competing doctors to share fee-related patient information without fear of antitrust violations.

SALARIED PROFESSIONALS: Highly trained individuals who work as employees of corporations, hospitals, or other medical facilities, government agencies, scientific and educational institutions, or other organizations.

SALARY ALLOTMENT INSURANCE: A life or health insurance plan arrangement for employees with an employer whereby regular forms of insurance are sold individually to employees on a payroll allotment basis, with premiums deducted from the wages of insured employees by the employer, who remits all premiums, generally in one monthly check, to the insurance company. Also called payroll deduction insurance, salary savings insurance, or payroll allotment plan.

SALES MANAGER: The home office or field management person responsible for managing those persons and activities that generate insurance sales. See Agent.

SALES QUOTA: A set goal or requirement, expressed in terms of dollars or units of insurance sales, for a specified period of use in supervision of selling efforts.

SAME DAY PROCEDURES: Procedures that once required a stay in hospital for several days completed on the same day of admission to keep the costs of hospitalization down. See Ambulatory Surgery Center.

SAME DAY SURGERY: Surgery performed on those patients admitted and discharged within 23 hr and 59 minutes.

SAME-DAY SURGERY CENTER: Surgical facilities and services for patients not needing overnight hospitalization. See Ambulatory Surgery Center.

SANCTION: Reprimand of a provider by a health plan.

SANITIZING: Purging health care information of its individually identifiable characteristics.

SCHEDULE: In health insurance, a list of specified amounts payable, usually for surgical operations, dismemberment, fractures, etc.

SCHEDULE OF BENEFITS (SOB): The section of a group plan outlining coverage, benefits, eligibility, and other features of the insurance plan.

SCHEDULED PREMIUM: The recommended or ideal premium in variable and universal life policies.

SCHEDULE OF INSURANCE: The list of individual terms, conditions, and provisions covered under one policy. Also, an inventory listing an insured's policies (e.g., in estate planning or total needs selling).

SCHEDULE POLICY: An insurance policy that covers, under separate insuring agreements in one policy, several hazards that are frequently handled under separate policies.

SCHOOL HEALTH AND RELATED SERVICES (SHRS): Medicaid option for children, including services such as audiology, speech therapy, psychological assessment, and counseling services.

SCORED SAVINGS: Amount of savings expected from enacting new legislation. Estimated by the Congressional Budget Office by calculating the difference in spending projected under current law and under the proposed legislation.

SCREEN: Insurance system for checking insureds, claims, and medical providers.

SCREENING: Physical examination and health history taken by an insurer before applicants are given the policy for they applied.

SECONDARY CARE: Services provided by medical specialists who generally do not have first contact with patients (e.g., cardiologist, urologists, dermatologists). In the United States, however, there has been a trend toward self-referral by patients for these services, rather than referral by primary care providers. This is quite different from the practice in England, where all patients must first seek care from primary care providers and are then referred to secondary or tertiary providers, as needed.

SECONDARY CARRIER: The health insurance plan that provides benefits after the primary payer has fulfilled its obligations.

SECONDARY COVERAGE: Health plan that pays costs not covered by primary coverage under coordination of benefits rules. Any insurance that supplements Medicare coverage. The three main sources for secondary insurance are employers, privately purchased Medigap plans, and Medicaid.

SECONDARY DISSEMINATION: Dissemination of summarized, often simplified, findings to audiences composed of stakeholders.

SECONDARY INSURANCE: Any insurance that supplements Medicare coverage. The three main sources for secondary insurance are employers, privately purchased Medigap plans, and Medicaid. See Insurance and Reinsurance.

SECONDARY MARKET: The public or private buying or selling of previously issued securities. See Public Offering.

SECONDARY PAYER: A health insurance plan that pays second-in-line for health care services. Private insurance, Medicare or Medicaid.

SECOND INJURY FUND: Fund used for a partially disabled employee who sustains a second or subsequent injury.

SECOND OPINION POLICY: A policy that allows a covered person to consult with two participating providers prior to scheduling a service. See Second Surgical Opinion.

SECOND SURGICAL OPINION: An opinion provided by a second physician, when one physician recommends surgery to an individual. Second surgical opinions are now covered under standard benefits in many health insurance plans. See Second Opinion.

SECTION 125 PLAN: A term used to refer to flexible benefit plans. The reference derives from the section of the Internal Revenue Service code that defines such plans and stipulates that employee contributions for life, health, disability, or long-term care insurance plans may be made with pretax dollars. See Flexible Spending Account (FSA).

SECTION 1115: Waiver that states could obtain from the federal government, which allowed them to set up managed care demonstration projects.

SECTION 1115 MEDICAID WAIVER: The Social Security Act grants the Secretary of Health and Human Services broad authority to waive certain laws relating to Medicaid for the purpose of conducting pilot, experimental, or demonstration projects that are likely to promote the objectives of the program. Section 1115 demonstration waivers allow states to change provisions of their Medicaid programs, including: eligibility requirements, the scope of services available, and the freedom to choose a provider, a provider's choice to participate in a plan, the method of reimbursing providers, and the statewide application of the program. Health plans and capitated providers can seek waivers through their state intermediaries.

SECTION 1902 (A) (1): Section of the Social Security Act that provides state Medicaid programs in all political subdivisions of the state.

SECTION 1902 (A) (10): Section of the Social Security Act that provides state Medicaid programs to those patients comparable in duration, scope, and amount.

SECTION 1902 (A) (23): Section of the Social Security Act that provides state Medicaid programs freedom to choose qualified medical providers to deliver covered services.

SECTION 1902 (R) (2): Section of the Social Security Act that allows state Medicaid programs to use more liberal income determination eligibility methods than those used for Supplemental Social Security Income (SSI) eligibility.

SECTION 1915(B) MEDICAID WAIVER: Section 1915(b) waivers allow states to require Medicaid recipients to enroll in HMOs or other managed care plans in an effort to control costs. The waivers allow states to: implement a primary care case-management system; require Medicaid recipients to choose from a number of competing health plans; provide additional benefits in exchange for savings resulting from recipients' use of cost-effective providers; and limit the providers from which beneficiaries can receive nonemergency treatment. The waivers are granted for 2 years, with 2-year renewals. Often referred to as a *freedom-of-choice waiver*.

SECTION 1915(C) MEDICAID WAIVER: Section of the Social Security Act that allows the states to waive various Medicaid requirements to establish alternative community-based health services for qualified individuals in qualified intermediate care facilities.

SECTION 1915(C)(7)(B) MEDICAID WAIVER: Section of the Social Security Act that allows the states to waive various Medicaid requirements to establish alternative community-based health services for developmentally disabled individuals in nursing facilities but still requiring specialized medical services.

SECTION 1929: Section of the Social Security Act that allows states to provide a wide range of community and home care services to functionally disabled individuals as an optional state medical services benefit.

SEER—MEDICARE DATABASE: Consists of a linkage of the clinical data collected by the Surveillance Epidemiology and End Results (SEER) registries with claims for health services collected by Medicare for its beneficiaries.

SEER PROGRAM: The Surveillance Epidemiology and End Results (SEER) Program of the National Cancer Institute is the most authoritative source of information on cancer incidence and survival in the United States.

SEGMENT: Under HIPAA, this is a group of related data elements in a transaction.

SEGMENTATION: Classes of different individuals, with different health insurance benefits, for a limited number of members.

SELECTIVE CONTRACTING: Section 1915 (B) option of the Social Security Act that allows the state development of a competitive contracting system for health care services.

SELF-FUNDED OR SELF-INSURED PLAN: A group health care plan funding arrangement in which the organization or employer sponsoring the plan takes complete financial responsibility for making all claims payments and pays all related medical expenses. See HSA and MSA.

SELF-FUNDING: The practice of an employer or organization assuming responsibility for health care losses of its employees. This usually includes setting up a fund against which claim payments are drawn and processing is often handled through an administrative services contract with an independent organization.

SELF-INFLICTED INJURY: An injury to the body of the insured inflicted by the insured that is generally excluded by health plans. See Illness, Accident, and Double Indemnity.

SELF-INSURANCE: An individual or organization that assumes the financial risk of paying for health care, disability, or other risks and perils. See Risk, HSA, MSA, and Re-Insurance.

SELF-INSURED: An individual or organization that assumes the financial risk of paying for health care, disability or other risks, hazards, and perils. Involves advanced financial arrangements to mitigate pure risk. See Insurance, Peril, Risk, HSA, MSA, and Re-Insurance.

SELF-INSURED HEALTH PLAN: Employer-provided health insurance in which the employer, rather than an insurer, is at risk for its employees' medical expenses. See HSA and MSA.

SELF-PAY: The individual responsible for insurance claims without a health insurance policy contract; also known as private pay.

SELF-RATING: In group insurance, a form of rating in which a large risk's premium is determined entirely by its own losses in a given period, plus an allowance for the insured's expenses.

SELF-REFERRAL: Specialty medical referral without insurance authorization.

SELF-REINSURANCE: The creation of a fund by an insurer to absorb losses beyond the insurer's normal retention.

SELLING INTERVIEW: A meeting between an insurance salesperson and a prospective buyer that has the objective of closing the sale.

SEMI-PRIVATE ROOM: A room in a hospital, nursing facility, or alternative facility that contains two or more beds.

SENIOR DIMENSIONS (SD): Older federal legislation that went into effect on February 1, 1985, allowing HMOs to enroll Medicare-eligible beneficiaries on an individual basis. Medicare pays participating plans, in advance, at a rate of 95% of Medicare's current average cost of providing medical services to its beneficiaries in a specific geographic area. In exchange, the HMO assumes total risk for the cost of care for medical-eligible members.

SENIOR PLAN: Refers to a benefit package offered by an HMO or other insurer to beneficiary's eligible for Medicare parts A and B.

SENSITIVITY: Extent to which the criteria used to identify the target population results in the inclusion of persons, groups, or objects at risk.

SENTINEL EVENT: An adverse health event that could have been avoided through appropriate care. An example would be hospitalization for uncontrolled hypertension that might have been avoided.

SENTINEL SURVEILLANCE: A surveillance system in which a prearranged sample of reporting sources agrees to report all cases of one or more specific conditions.

SERVICE: Medical care and items, such as medical diagnosis and treatment; drugs and biologicals; supplies, appliances, and equipment; medical social services; and use of hospital, rural primary care hospital, or skilled-nursing facilities.

SERVICE AREA: The geographic area served by a private Medicare fee-for-service insurer or health care provider.

SERVICE CARVE-OUTS: A service carve-out provides a set of specific services outside a mainstream plan; these services might be administered separately and reimbursed on either a capitated or a fee-for-service basis. See Carve-Outs and Exclusions.

SERVICE CATEGORY DEFINITION: The type of medical or health services defined in the service category.

SERVICE CENTERS: Health care service or department that meets the quality and quantity requirements of the organization.

SERVICE INSURER: Agreement to pay health care vendors under contract arrangements, such as Blue Cross or Blue Shield.

SERVICE LIMITATIONS: Dollar amounts or time limits applied to certain services.

SERVICE MIX: Range of health care services offered by a medical provider or health care organization.

SERVICE OFFERINGS: Standard medical practice offerings of a physician, as opposed to others like house calls, specialty visit participation, and office ambience that are variable.

SERVICE QUALITY: Enhancing the value of a product through service that meets or exceeds customer expectations. See Quality Management and Quality Improvement.

SETTLEMENT: Payment of an insurance claim. It implies that both the policy owner and the insurance company are satisfied with the amount and the method of payment.

SEVERITY ADJUSTMENT: See case mix adjustment.

SEX-SPECIFIC MORTALITY RATE: A mortality rate among either males or females.

SHADOW CONTROLS: Health care experts and participant judgments used to estimate net impact.

SHADOW PRICES: Imputed or estimated health insurance costs not valued accurately in the marketplace. Shadow prices also are used when market prices are inappropriate because of regulation or externalities.

SHARED RISK POOL FOR REFERRAL SERVICES: In capitation, the pool established for the purpose of sharing the risk of costs for referral services among all participating physicians. See Risk.

SHARED SAVINGS: A provision of most prepaid health care plans in which at least part of the providers' income is directly linked to the financial performance of the plan.

SHELL LABORATORY: A storefront medical laboratory that outsources tests to another laboratory and is usually owned by the referring or participating physicians. See Fraud and Abuse.

SHERMAN ANTITRUST ACT: Established as national policy, the concept of a competitive marketing system by prohibiting companies from attempting to (a) monopolize any part of trade or commerce or (b) engage in contracts, combinations, or conspiracies in restraint of trade. The Act applies to all companies engaged in interstate commerce and to all companies engaged in foreign commerce.

SHOCK LOSS: An insurance claim or loss that is so large as to materially affect the underwriting averages, such as that might occur through an epidemic or major natural disaster.

SHOE BOX: The phenomenon where insured members place health care deductible invoices in a shoebox for safekeeping and then lose or fail to submit them for payment.

SHOE BOX EFFECT: When an indemnity-type benefits plan has a deductible, there may be beneficiaries who save up their receipts to file for reimbursement at a later time.

SHORT-PERIOD INSURANCE: Insurance issued for terms of less than 1 year.

SHORT RATE: The rate charged for insurance taken for a period of less than 1 year.

SHORT-STAY HOSPITALS: Those hospitals in which the average length of stay is less than 30 days. The American Hospital Association and National Master Facility Inventory (a National Center for Health Statistics dataset) define short-term hospitals as hospitals in which more than half the patients are admitted to units with an average length of stay of less than 30 days.

SHORT-TERM DISABILITY: Disability usually lasting less than 2 years. See Disability, Activities of Daily Living, Long-Term Insurance, and Disability Income Insurance.

SHORT-TERM DISABILITY INCOME POLICY: A disability income policy with benefits payable for a limited period of time, and often with a waiting period as short as 30 days before benefits become payable.

SHORT-TERM FINANCING: Financing repaid within 12 months.

SHORT-TERM POLICY: An insurance contract in effect for less than 1 year.

SICKNESS: Any physical illness, disorder, or disease including pregnancy, but not mental illness. See Injury and Illness.

SICKNESS INSURANCE: A form of health insurance against loss by illness or disease. It does not include accidental bodily injury. See Insurance, Illness, and Injury.

SIDE EFFECT: A problem caused by drugs or medical treatment.

SILENT PPOs: Called voluntary PPOs, wrap-around PPOs, or blind PPOs. They act like brokers by selling patients' discounts to parties that do not guarantee them volume. For example, a PPO contracted with a patient sells the patient's discounts to an insurer, who applies the discounts to the patient's bills. See mirror or faux HMO.

SIMPLE INTEREST: Interest earned on the principal sum only, with no interest computed on interest or interest past due, as in compound interest.

SINGLE COVERAGE: Coverage for the plan member only.

SINGLE DISMEMBERMENT: The loss of one hand, one foot, or sight in one eye.

SINGLE DRUG PRICER (SDP): The SDP is a drug-pricing file containing the allowable price for each drug-covered incident to a physician's service, drugs furnished by independent dialysis facilities that are separately billable from the composite rate, and clotting factors to inpatients. The SDP is in effect, a fee-schedule similar to other Centers for Medicare and Medicaid Services fee schedules.

SINGLE PAYER: In an attempt to provide universal coverage to all residents of a state or country, the state (or country) becomes the single payer for all health care bills.

SINGLE PAYER SYSTEM: A single, government fund pays for everyone's health care using tax revenue.

SINGLE-SPECIALTY GROUP PRACTICE: Physicians in the same specialty pool their expenses, income, and offices.

SINGLE STATE AGENCY (SSA): The SSA designation requiring a single state agency to administer its Medicaid health insurance plan.

SITE-OF-SERVICE DIFFERENTIAL: The monetary difference paid as a different medical provider renders the same service in a different medical practice. One example would be an examination in an emergency room versus in a family doctor's office.

SITE VISIT: The physical quality monitoring of a health care facility as mandated by the Centers for Medicare and Medicaid Services (older HCFA) and various other HMO, managed care organization, or similar agencies, every 1–2 years.

SIXTH OMNIBUS RECONCILIATION ACT OF 1985 (OBRA/SOBRA): Portions of this Act created quality review organizations (QROs) and empowered QROs and peer review organizations (PROs) to monitor quality of care for Medicare recipients enrolled in HMOs, provided for civil monetary penalties for plans that failed to provide proper care, and restricted the types of physician incentives that a managed care plan may use when providing care for Medicare recipients.

SKILLED CARE: Trained rehabilitation or nursing care services.

SKILLED-NURSING FACILITY (SNF): (1) Provide registered nursing services around the clock. (2) An institution that has a transfer agreement with one or more hospitals, provides primarily inpatient skilled nursing care and rehabilitative services, and meets other specific certification requirements. See Long-Term Care Insurance, Activities of Daily Living, and Hospice.

SKIMMING: The practice in health programs paid on a prepayment or capitation basis, and in health insurance, of seeking to enroll only the healthiest people as a way of controlling program costs. See Fraud and Abuse.

SLIDING SCALE COMMISSION: An insurance commission adjustment on earned premiums under a formula whereby the actual commission (paid by a reinsurer to a ceding insurer) varies inversely with the loss ratio, subject to a maximum and minimum. See Rebate, Twisting, and Churning.

SLIDING SCALE DEDUCTIBLE: A deductible that is not set at a fixed amount, but rather varies according to income.

SLIDING SCALE MODEL: A discounted fee schedule based on the patients' ability to pay.

SMALL EMPLOYER: Any entity that is active in business and that employs at least 2, but not more than 50, eligible employees (those who work full-time).

SMALL-GROUP MARKET (SGM): The insurance market for products sold to groups that are smaller than a specified size, typically employer groups. The size of groups included usually depends on state insurance laws and thus varies from state to state, with 50 employees the most common size (3–99).

SMALL-GROUP POOLING: A term used by many carriers to refer to all or segments of small group businesses when combined into a pool or pools. See Risk Pool and Rate.

SMALL MARKET INSURANCE (SMI): Niche, but large potential, insurance market purchasing space for small to medium-sized businesses that are not public companies and are usually privately held.

SMALL MARKET INSURANCE (SMI) REFORM: Recent changes in the marketing of insurance to small businesses in order to increase the availability and affordability of coverage.

SOCIAL/HEALTH MAINTENANCE ORGANIZATION (SHMO): A prepaid, Congress-mandated plan that provides consolidated health care and support services (such as long-term care benefits) to its members. See Medicare and Medicaid.

SOCIAL INDICATOR: Periodic measurements designed to track the course of a social problem over time.

SOCIAL INSURANCE: Compulsory plan under which participants are entitled to certain benefits as a matter of right. The plan is administered by a state or federal government agency aimed at providing a minimum standard of living for lower and middle wage groups. Social Security, unemployment compensation, etc., are social insurance programs. See Medicare and Medicaid.

SOCIAL INSURANCE PROGRAMS: Encompasses all the insurance benefit (pecuniary or service) programs provided for the public, or large segments of it, by federal, state, or local governments, including: old-age, survivor's, and disability insurance; Medicare and Medicaid; unemployment compensation; workers' compensation; compulsory temporary disability insurance; railroad retirement; railroad unemployment and temporary disability insurance; assistance to the blind and to dependent children, etc. See Medicare and Medicaid.

SOCIAL SECURITY: Programs provided under the U.S. Social Security Act, originally passed in 1935 and now including Medicare; Medicaid; old-age, survivors, and disability insurance; and a variety of grants-in-aid. Government programs that provide economic security to the public. For example, social insurance, public assistance, family allowances, grants-in-aid, maternity benefits, etc.

SOCIAL SECURITY ACT: Federal legislation providing social insurance on a national scale.

SOCIAL SECURITY BENEFIT, PRIMARY: Retirement income for life, payable to a worker without dependents under the old-age, survivor's, and disability insurance section of the Federal Social Security Act.

SOCIAL SECURITY BENEFITS: Benefits provided for eligible workers and their families under Social Security programs; can be placed in three general categories: survivor benefits, retirement benefits, and disability benefits.

SOCIAL SECURITY FREEZE: The fixation of Social Security benefits at a certain dollar amount or fixed percentage.

SOCIAL SECURITY, INTEGRATION UNDER SECTION 401: Regulations in accordance with §401 of the Internal Revenue Code regarding the manner in which benefits under a private employee retirement plan and benefits under Social Security must be related so that the private plan does not discriminate in favor of higher paid employees.

SOCIAL SECURITY OFFSET: The avoidance of supplicate Social Security benefits, according to some prescribed formal or calculations.

SOCIAL WORKER: One who provides social services to a community cohort.

SOLE COMMUNITY HOSPITAL (SCH): A hospital which (a) is more than 50 miles from any similar hospital; (b) is 25 to 50 miles from a similar hospital and isolated from it at least 1 month per year by snow or is the exclusive provider of services to at least 75% of its service area populations; (c) is 15 to 25 miles from any similar hospital and is isolated from it at least 1 month per year; or (d) has been designated as an SCH under previous rules. The Medicare diagnosis-related group (DRG) program makes special optional payment provisions for SCHs, most of which are rural, including providing that their rates are set permanently so that 75% of their payment is hospital-specific and only 25% is based on regional DRG rates.

SOLE PROPRIETORSHIP INSURANCE: Life and health insurance purchased for the purpose of handling the business continuity problems arising in a sole proprietorship.

SOLE PROVIDER HEALTH INSURANCE: Insurance or managed care coverage for the owner of a small business, or his or her employees. See HMO and Managed Care.

SOLICITOR: A licensed employee of a health insurance agent, company, or broker that acts for the agent or broker in some circumstances.

SOLO PRACTICE: A physician who practices alone or with others but does not pool income or expenses. See Gatekeeper and Internist.

SOLVENCY: Individual or corporate fiscal health.

SOUND HEALTH CLAUSE: A clause sometimes included in a policy that states that the policy will not take effect on delivery unless the applicant is alive and in good health.

SOUND NATURAL TEETH: Teeth that are (a) free of active or chronic clinical decay; (b) have at least 50% bony support; and (c) are functional in the arch.

SPECIAL AGENT: A health, life disability, long-term care, or other insurance agent representing his or her company in an exclusive territory. See Agent and Broker.

SPECIAL CLASS: The status of an insurance applicant who cannot qualify for a standard policy, but may secure one with a rider waiving the payment for a loss involving certain existing health impairments. He or she may be required to pay a higher premium or the policy may be issued with lesser benefits than those requested.

SPECIAL ELECTION PERIOD: A set time limit to change health plans or return to the original Medicare plan. The special election period is different from the special enrollment period (SEP).

SPECIAL ENROLLMENT PERIOD (SEP): A set time to sign up for Medicare Part B if not elected during the initial enrollment period, because of group health plan coverage through an employer or union.

SPECIAL FEATURES: Health insurance policy benefits paid with respect to losses other than those covered by principal sum and loss of time. Hospital and surgical benefits are among these.

SPECIAL HAZARD: In insurance, a risk of more than average size, duration, or danger.

SPECIAL INDEMNITIES: Health insurance policy provisions that extend the coverage of the policy or more clearly define the risks covered.

SPECIALIST: Any health professional who has specific training and certification in a particular area of medical care. See Internal Medicine.

SPECIAL PUBLIC-DEBT OBLIGATION: Securities of the U.S. Government issued exclusively to the old-age, survivor's, and disability insurance; disability insurance; hospital or health insurance; supplementary medical insurance (SMI) trust funds; and other federal trust funds. Section 1841(a) of the Social Security Act provides that the public-debt obligations issued for purchase by the SMI trust fund shall have maturities fixed with due regard for the needs of the funds. The usual practice in the past has been to spread the holdings of special issues, as of every June 30, so that the amounts maturing in each of the next 15 years are approximately equal. Special public-debt obligations are redeemable at par at any time.

SPECIALTY CASE RATE: The fee paid to a medical specialist or specialty facility to cover all global services or treatments.

SPECIALTY CONTRACTOR: A Medicare contractor that performs a limited Medicare function, such as coordination of benefits, statistical analysis, etc.

SPECIALTY HMOs: Specialty HMOs provide their members one or more limited health care benefits or services (e.g., pharmacy, vision, dental, mental health or rehabilitation services) and are based on any of the HMO model types.

SPECIALTY PLAN: Medicare advantage that provides more focused care for some patients, such as diabetics.

SPECIALTY PPOS: Specialty PPOs are designed similarly to regular health coverage PPOs, but provide one or more limited benefits (e.g., pharmacy, vision, dental, mental health, rehabilitation, or workers' compensation).

SPECIFIC INSTRUMENT: A set of quality of life questions that examine a narrow and clearly defined area of quality of life.

SPECIFICITY: Extent to which the criteria used to identify the target population results in the exclusion of persons, groups, or objects not at risk.

SPECIFIC LOW INCOME MEDICARE BENEFICIARIES (SLMB): The Medicare Program that pays for Part B premiums for those with PART A, limited resources and low monthly incomes.

SPECIFIC MARKET: As a market for insurance, a group of people or businesses with common needs, usually of the same occupation. Teachers, grocers, and surgeons, for example, constitute specific markets. This is compared with general markets, such as merchants, medical professionals, etc.

SPECIFIC PERILS: A health insurance or other policy that provides stated benefits, usually of large amounts, toward the expense of the treatment of a stated peril or hazard named in the policy. See Specific Disease Insurance.

SPECIFIED DISEASE INSURANCE: A health insurance, HMO, or managed care organization policy that provides stated benefits, usually of large amounts, toward the expense of the treatment of the disease or diseases named in the policy. See Specific Perils.

SPECULATIVE: See Risk, Hazard, and Perils.

SPEECH LANGUAGE THERAPY: Medical instructions and therapy to strengthen and regain speech skills.

SPELL OF ILLNESS: A period of consecutive days, beginning with the first day on which a beneficiary is furnished inpatient hospital or extended care services, and ending with the close of the first period of 60 consecutive days thereafter in which the beneficiary is in neither a hospital nor a skilled-nursing facility.

SPEND DOWN: A term used in Medicaid for persons whose income and assets are above the threshold for the state's designated medically needy criteria, but are below this threshold when medical expenses are factored in. The amount of expenditures for health care services, relative to income, that qualifies an individual for Medicaid in states that cover categorically eligible, medically indigent individuals. Eligibility is determined on a case-by-case basis.

SPIDER GRAPHS/CHARTS: A technique or tool developed by Ernst and Young, to combine analyses of a market's level of managed care evolution with an internal readiness review. It involves three steps: Market Assessment, Internal Analysis, and Gap Analysis. Components of the graph include: Network formation, Managed care penetration, Utilization levels, Reimbursement, Excess inpatient capacity, Geographic distribution, Commercial premium, Physician integration, Managed care characteristics, Employer and purchaser base, Outcomes management, Strategic alignment, Organization and Governance, Access to markets, Delivery systems, Medical management, Finance, Performance management, and Information technology.

SPILLOVER CASH FLOW: Direct or indirect cash flow change that occurs elsewhere in a health care organization when another project is executed.

SPONSORED DEPENDENT: One who requires more than half of his or her support as defined by the Internal Revenue Code.

SPOUSE: A husband or wife as the result of a marriage legally recognized in the United States.

STACKING: The use of multiple insurance policy claims for financial gain.

STAFF-MIX: Amount and type of medical staff in various categories and departments.

STAFF MODEL HMO: (1) Physicians are employed and salaried by consumer owners and services are provided exclusively to HMO plan enrollees.

(2) An HMO in which physicians practice solely as employees of the HMO and usually are paid a salary. See Group-Model HMO, Health Maintenance Organization, and PPO.

STANDARD AMOUNT: An amount used as the basis for payment under a prospective payment system. It is intended to represent the national average operating cost of inpatient treatment for a typical Medicare patient in a reasonably efficient hospital in a large urban or other area. Standardized amounts are based on Medicare costs reported by hospitals for cost reporting periods ending in 1982, adjusted for geographic location and certain hospital characteristics, such as teaching activity. The adjusted amounts are updated to the year of payment by an annual update factor.

STANDARD BENEFITS PACKAGE: (1) A core set of health benefits that everyone in the country should have—either through their employer, a government program, or a risk pool. (2) A defined set of health insurance benefits that all insurers are required to offer. See Benefit Package.

STANDARD OF CARE: A clinical protocol that is agreed upon by the involved professional community; it then represents the standard of care. See Malpractice.

STANDARD CLASS RATE (SCR): Base revenue requirement per member, for a health plan, multiplied by demographic information to determine monthly premium rates.

STANDARD DEATH RATE: That ratio between the total number of deaths in a year and the total number living, after proportional adjustment has been made in the numbers living and dying in each age group to fit some standard distribution of lives by age, thus permitting comparison of overall mortality rates of different groups free from the distortions that arise from different distributions by age.

STANDARD POLICY: A health care policy issued with standard provisions and at standard rates; not rated or with special restrictions. See Standard Risk.

STANDARD PREMIUM: A basic premium charge for health, life, disability, managed medical care, or other insurance policy, without exclusions, riders, or additional benefits or risks. See Risks, Insurance, and Standardized Amount.

STANDARD PRESCRIBER IDENTIFICATION NUMBER (SPIN): A National Council of Prescription Drug Program unique identifier for medicinal prescribers.

STANDARD PROVISIONS: The usual health insurance policy items, terms, and conditions required by the Uniform Provisions Law, a National Association of Insurance Commissioners model bill enacted by virtually all jurisdictions.

STANDARD RISK: A person who meets an insurer's underwriting criteria for standard health insurance policies. A person entitled to insurance protection without extra rating or special restrictions; a risk meeting the same conditions as the tabular risks on which rates are based. See Risk and Peril.

STANDARDS: Accepted measures of comparison having quantitative or qualitative value.

STANDARDS TRANSACTION: Under HIPAA, this is a transaction that complies with the applicable HIPAA standard.

STANDARD WORKER'S COMPENSATION INSURANCE: See Worker's Compensation.

STARK BILL: Federal law that prevents physicians from Medicare patients to entities which they or their immediate family have a vested financial interest, and bars doctors from referring Medicare patients for 11 types of health care services.

STATE BUY-IN: The term given to the process by which a state may provide supplementary medical insurance coverage for its needy, eligible persons through an agreement with the federal government under which the state pays the premiums for them.

STATE DISABILITY PLAN: State-funded insurance programs to treat job-related injuries or cover claims for job related injury expenses.

STATE FUND: Account established by a state agency to funded insurance programs like worker's compensation or disability insurance to cover claims for job related injury expenses.

STATE HIGH RISK POOL: State-funded nonprofit-making program for the medically uninsured. Premiums are typically 125%–150% standard carrier health insurance rates.

STATE INSURANCE ASSISTANCE PROGRAMS: State-sponsored federally funded program for free health insurance advice to patients with Medicare.

STATE INSURANCE DEPARTMENT: State agency to offer advice on Medigap plans and other health insurance issues.

STATE-MANDATED BENEFIT LAWS: State laws that require insurers to cover specified health services or for services from certain health care providers. The Employee Retirement Income Security Act of 1974 exempts self-funded insurers from mandated benefits.

STATE MEDICAL ASSISTANCE OFFICE: State-sponsored advisory program providing information on health claims, insurance bills, and prescription drug coverage.

STATEMENT OF CASH FOWS: Uses and sources of cash in an organization over time.

STATEMENT OF OPERATIONS: Summary of revenues and expenses during an accounting period affecting unrestricted net assets.

STATE MUTUAL: Policy holder insurance company that operates in one or more states.

STATE SUPERVISION AND REGULATION: Initiated by the McCarran Ferguson Act of 1945 (Public Law 15), and declared that insurance regulation is to be done by individual state associations. However, the National Association of Insurance Commissions is a federal body with similar interests through its tax policies and regulations. See NAIC and State Taxation of Insurance.

STATE SURVEY: The Centers for Medicare and Medicaid Services (CMS) have entered into agreements with agencies of state governments, typically the agency that licenses health facilities within the state health departments, to conduct surveys of Medicare participating providers and suppliers for purposes of determining compliance with Medicare requirements for participation in the Medicare program.

STATE SURVEY AGENCY: State department that inspects Medicare facilities and providers.

STATE TAXATION OF INSURANCE: Authority of the individual states to tax insurance companies in the range of 2–4 of premiums.

STATE UNIFORM BILLING COMMITTEE: A state-specific affiliate of the National Uniform Billing Committee.

STATIC BUDGET: Single activity level estimation budget.

STATISTICS BUDGET: Method of medical service identification by payer type.

STATUS CHANGE: A lifestyle event that may cause a person to modify their health benefits coverage category. Examples include, but are not limited to, the birth of a child, divorce, or marriage. See Qualifying Event.

STATUS LOCATION: An indicator on a health claim record describing the queue where the claim is currently situated and the action that needs to be performed on the claim.

STATUTORY REGULATIONS: State rules by mandating principles of financial statement preparation for insurance companies.

STATUTORY RESERVES: State-mandated solvency reserves enabling insurance companies to pay current and future claims.

STATUTORY RESTRICTIONS: State law insurance company rules of fairness, reasonable, and transparency regarding rate-making decisions and premium-setting policies.

STEERAGE DISCOUNTS: A health care payer's agreement to send patients to preselected medical providers, in return for discounted fees.

STEP CARE: A graduated treatment protocol indicating to HMO providers the order in which they will administer different therapies for a given condition.

STEP-DOWN METHOD: Cost (indirect) allocation strategy redirected expenses to which payment is attached.

STEP-FIXED COSTS: Fixed costs that increase in total at certain points as the level of activity increases.

STEP-UP BENEFITS: Benefit offerings if a health a plan package includes one of the following benefit structures in a particular service category: (a) more than one optional supplemental benefit; (b) both a mandatory and optional benefit; or (c) both an additional and optional benefit.

STOCK COMPANY: In insurance, a company that is owned and controlled by a group of stockholders whose investment in the company provides the capital necessary for the issuance of guaranteed, fixed premium, and nonparticipating policies. The stockholders share in the profits and losses of the company. Some stock companies also issue participating policies.

STOCKHOLDER: An individual who owns some part or share of an incorporated stock company. The stock shares represent proof of ownership. The stockholders select a board of directors and share in the company's profits and losses.

STOCKHOLDERS' EQUITY: In a stock insurance company selling participating life insurance, the sum of the net worth accounts allocated to the nonparticipating stockholders' branch.

STOP LOSS: The practice of an HMO or insurance company of protecting itself or its contracted medical groups against part or all losses above a specified dollar amount incurred in the process of caring for its policyholders. Usually involves the HMO or insurance company purchasing insurance from another company to protect itself. Also referred to as reinsurance.

STOP-LOSS INSURANCE: Insuring with a third party against a risk that a managed care organization cannot financially and totally manage. For example, a comprehensive prepaid health plan can self-insure hospitalization costs with one or more insurance carriers.

STOP-LOSS LIMIT: A way medical providers limit economic risks in cases where costs are greater than reimbursement amounts.

STOP-LOSS REINSURANCE: Insurance that protects a ceding company against an excessive amount of aggregate claim losses during a certain period of time or over a percentage of earned premium income.

STRAIGHT DEDUCTIBLE CLAUSE: Insurance policy clause that specifies either the dollar amount or percentage of loss that the insurance does not cover.

STRATEGIC BIAS: Bias in response to a questionnaire, caused by a belief that a particular answer is in the respondent's best interest.

STRATEGIC DECISIONS: A health care organization's capital investment choices that are used to increase its market position in a certain locale.

STRATEGIC FINANCIAL PLANNING: Strategy and budgeting methodology to reach strategic targets and financial goals.

STRATEGIC NATIONAL IMPLEMENTATION PROCESS: A national workgroup for electronic data interchange effort for helping the health care industry identify and resolve HIPAA implementation issues. See WEDI.

STRATEGIC PLANNING: The way in which a health care entities' mission is positioned for the future.

STRATIFICATION OF LOSSES: Risk management technique whereby health or other insurance claims and losses are categorized into subsets for further analysis. See Risk Management.

STRONG HOLISM: A health care aspect of super naturalistic pantheism, or Spinozism, which holds that nature is divine. According to strong holism, the universe is uninterrupted in substance and the unbroken whole, and all things have instantaneous interconnections.

SUBACUTE CARE: Usually a comprehensive inpatient program for those who have experienced a serious illness, injury, or disease, but who do not require intensive hospital services. The range of services considered subacute can include infusion therapy, respiratory care, cardiac services, wound care, rehabilitation services, postoperative recovery programs for knee and hip replacements, and cancer, stroke, and AIDS care. See Primary, Secondary, Tertiary, and Quaternary Care.

SUBCAPITATION: An arrangement that exists when an organization being paid under a capitated system contracts with other providers on a capitated basis, sharing a portion of the original capitated premium. Can be done under carve-out, with the providers being paid on a per member per month basis. See Capitation and Prospective Payment Systems.

SUBJECT PREMIUM: A base or standard insurance premium. See Rate and Rate Setting.

SUBMITTED CHARGE: The charge submitted by a provider to the patient or a payer. See Paid Amounts.

SUBORDINATED DEBT: Junior debt.

SUBROGATION: The recovery of the cost of services and benefits provided to the insured of one managed care organization that other parties are liable.

SUBROGATION WAIVER: Relinquishing the rights of subrogation.

SUBSCRIBER: An individuals meeting the health plans' eligibility requirement that enrolls in the health plan and accepts the financial responsibility for any premiums, copayments, or deductibles. See Insured.

SUBSCRIPTION POLICY: An insurance policy to which two or more insurance companies may subscribe, indicating on the policy the share of the risk to be borne by each company.

SUBSIDIARY: A health care organization owned or managed by another entity.

SUBSTANDARD HEALTH INSURANCE: Insurance coverage for those patients with a serious medical condition, illness, past medical history, or otherwise unhealthy background, whose physical or mental conditions are such that they are rated below standard in the premium setting process. See Risk Management, Peril, Hazard, and Substandard Risk.

SUBSTANDARD RISK: A person whose health risk is greater than average for his or her age. Substandard rating factors include various medical conditions, such as diabetes, hypertension, and heart ailments; high-risk occupations, such as airline pilots, race car drivers, miners, and high-altitude construction workers; high-risk avocations or hobbies, such as scuba diving or sky diving; detrimental habits or addictions, such as smoking or a history of drug use or alcohol abuse; and possible moral turpitude as evidenced by excessive gambling, criminal convictions, and bankruptcy. Substandard risks, if covered at all, are usually charged additional premium. See Peril.

SUBSTANTIAL FINANCIAL RISK: Medicare term for physician incentive plans, with a risk threshold of about 25%.

SUICIDE PROVISION: Most life insurance policies provide that if the insured commits suicide within a specified period, usually 1 or 2 years after date of issue, the company's liability will be limited to a return of premiums paid.

SUI JURIS: An individual who may enter into a legal and binding contract, uncontrolled by another person.

SUITABILITY: Refers to the agent's legal responsibility under the Securities and Exchange Commission requirements to determine, within reason, the suitability of a variable life product for a given prospect or client.

SUMMARY OF CLAIMS PROCESSED (SOCP): A summary sent to the member showing how much the health insurer paid, what the member's financial responsibility may be, and any provider write-offs.

SUMMARY PLAN DESCRIPTION: This is a recap or summary of the health benefits provided under the plan. It is used most often with employees covered by self-funded plans.

SUNK COST: Cost previously incurred and unchangeable.

SUPERANNUATED: Antiquated; incapacitated or disqualified for active work by advanced age; retired.

SUPERANNUATION: To become antiquated; to become incapacitated or disqualified for active work because of old age or infirmity.

SUPERBILL: A form that specifically lists all of the services provided by the physician. It cannot be used in place of the standard AMA form. See Claim.

SUPPLEMENTAL ACCIDENT: First dollar health insurance coverage for an accident.

SUPPLEMENTAL BENEFITS: Benefits contracted for by an employer group that are outside of, or in addition to, the basic health plan.

SUPPLEMENTAL HOSPITAL PLAN: A health care policy to cover out-of-pocket expenses from other health care plans.

SUPPLEMENTAL INSURANCE: Any private health insurance plan held by a Medicare beneficiary, including Medigap policies and post-retirement health benefits.

SUPPLEMENTAL MAJOR MEDICAL INSURANCE: See Supplemental Medical Insurance (SMI).

SUPPLEMENTAL MEDICAL INSURANCE (SMI): The part of the Medicare program that covers the costs of physicians' services, outpatient laboratory and x-ray tests, durable medical equipment, outpatient hospital care, and certain other services. This voluntary program requires payment of a monthly premium, which covers 25% of pro-ram costs. Beneficiaries are responsible for a deductible and coinsurance payments for most covered services. Also called Part B coverage or benefits.

SUPPLEMENTAL SECURITY INCOME (SSI): A federal income support pro-ram for low-income disabled, aged, and blind persons. Eligibility for the monthly cash payments is based on the individual's current status without regard to previous work or contributions.

SUPPLIER: A provider of health care services, other than a practitioner, that is permitted to bill under Medicare Part B. Suppliers include independent laboratories, durable medical equipment providers, ambulance services, orthotist, prosthetist, and portable x-ray providers.

SUPPLIES BUDGET: Predicting fixed and variable supplies.

SUPPORTING SERVICE PROVIDER: A health care professional who provides supporting or ancillary services under the direction of a primary care or referral provider.

SURCHARGE: An extra charge applied by the insurer.

SURGICAL EXPENSE INSURANCE: A basic health insurance policy that provides benefits to pay for surgical costs including fees for the surgeon, the anesthesiologist, and the operating room.

SURGICAL INDEMNITIES: Fixed indemnities for certain surgical operations specified in the policy or in provisions attached to the policy.

SURGICAL INSURANCE BENEFITS: A form of health insurance against loss due to surgical expenses. See Hospital Insurance and Health Insurance.

SURGICAL SCHEDULE: A list or table of cash or payments in a health or managed care insurance policy.

SURPLUS: The amount by which assets exceed liabilities. Also, with respect to reinsurance, the portion of a ceding company's gross amount of insurance on a risk remaining after deducting the retention established by the ceding company.

SURPLUS ACCOUNT: The difference between a company's assets and liabilities. Net surplus includes contingency reserves and unassigned funds, whereas gross surplus also includes surplus assigned for distribution as dividends.

SURPLUS BUSINESS: In life and health insurance, business placed by agents who are not full time, regular representatives of the insurance company to which they are directing the business.

SURPLUS LINES TAX: A tax imposed by state law when coverage is placed with an insurer not licensed or admitted to transact business in the state where the risk is located. Unlike premium tax for admitted insurers, the surplus lines tax is not included in the premium and must be collected from the policyholder and remitted to the state.

SURRENDER: To terminate or cancel a life health insurance policy before the maturity date.

SURVEILLANCE: To closely watch or monitor health care, services, or treatment.

SURVEY: Systematic collection of information from a defined population, usually by means of interviews or questionnaires administered to a sample of units in the population.

SURVIVAL CURVE: A curve that starts at 100% of the study population and shows the percentage of the population still surviving at successive times for as long as information is available. May be applied not only to survival as such, but also to the persistence of freedom from a disease or health complication or some other endpoint.

SURVIVOR BENEFIT: A lump sum payment that will provide benefits to the insured's eligible survivors in the event the insured dies while receiving disability payments. This is an optional benefit in most policies.

SURVIVOR MONTHLY INCOME FOR DEPENDENT CHILD: Under Social Security, a monthly benefit paid to each eligible child of a fully or currently insured deceased individual until the child reaches the age of 18 years (age 22 if a full-time student in a public or accredited school or college) or beyond if the child is disabled, unless the child marries.

SURVIVOR MONTHLY INCOME FOR WIDOW OR WIDOWER: Under Social Security, a monthly benefit paid to an eligible widow or widower (aged 60 or older) of a deceased covered individual.

SURVIVOR MONTHLY INCOME FOR WIDOW OR WIDOWER WITH CHILD (CHILDREN) IN HIS OR HER CARE: Under Social Security, a monthly benefit paid to an eligible widow or widower of a deceased fully insured or currently insured individual, who has in his or her care a child (or children) of the deceased aged younger than 16 years (or disabled) and eligible for a child's benefit. Such benefits are in addition to those payable to the child. (They do not continue to the widow or widower beyond the child's age of 16, by virtue of the child's receiving a benefit beyond 18–21 years of age, as a student.)

SURVIVOR SPOUSE: Spouse of a deceased health plan member eligible for insurance coverage.

SUSPECT PROCEDURE: Medical intervention of doubtful value or one done mainly for compensation and tagged for utilization review.

SUSPENSE: Occurs when a licensee requests that their license, or some licensed beds, be temporarily taken out of service, or when the Department of Health Services does so on its own.

SUSTAINABLE GROWTH RATE (SGR): The target rate of expenditure growth set by the SGR system. The SGR is similar to the performance standard under the volume performance standard system, except that the target depends on growth of gross domestic product instead of historical trends.

SUSTAINABLE GROWTH RATE SYSTEM: A revision to the volume performance standard system, proposed by the Congress and the Administration. This system would provide an alternative mechanism for adjusting fee updates for the Medicare Fee Schedule. The mechanism would use a single conversion factor, base target rates of growth on growth of gross domestic product, and change the method for calculating the conversion factor update to eliminate the 2-year delay.

SWAP MATERNITY: A provision granting immediate maternity coverage in a group health insurance plan but terminating coverage on pregnancies in progress upon termination of the plan. The term swap means providing the coverage at the beginning of the policy where it is not usually provided, but not providing it after the end of the policy where it usually is provided.

SWEDISH MASSAGE: The most common form of bodywork in Western countries. Its originator, Peter Hendrik (Per Henrick) Ling (17761839), of Sweden, was a fencing master, physiologist, and poet. His method was called the "Ling system" or the "Swedish movement treatment." Dr. S. W. Mitchell introduced Swedish massage in the United States. It is based on scientific anatomy and often vigorous. The aim of Swedish massage is to improve circulation of blood and lymph.

SWING-BED HOSPITAL: A hospital participating in the Medicare swing-bed program. This program allows rural hospitals with fewer than 100 beds to provide skilled postacute care services in acute-care beds.

SWITCH MATERNITY: A provision for group health maternity coverage on female employees only when their husbands are included in the plan as dependents.

SWOT ANALYSIS: Strengths, Weakness, Opportunities, and Threats. A management methodology of competitive behavior.

SYNCHRONICITY (SYNCHRONISTIC PRINCIPLE): "Causal connecting principle," the supposed equivalent of a cause. Carl Jung posited synchronicity, which he equated with the Tao to describe meaningful but apparently accidental concurrences or sequences of events.

T

10-DAY FREE LOOK PROVISION: A life and health insurance policy provision (often required by law) giving the policy owner 10 days to review a new policy. If the policy owner is not satisfied with the policy, it can be returned to the insurance company for a 100% refund of premium paid. Coverage is then canceled from the date of issue and the insurance company is not liable for any claims. Some state laws require a 20-day free look provision.

24-HOUR COVERAGE: Health insurance coverage that removes the sometime artificial boundary between occupational and nonoccupationally related health care claims.

TABULAR PLANS: A retrospective rating system method that lists basic, minimum, and maximum premium rates for health, life, managed care, disability, or other insurance policies.

TAFT-HARTLEY HEALTH PLANS: One way private sector unionized employees can get health and other benefits. Taft-Hartley Plans can be formed by a single employer, but this is unusual. Multiemployer funds are almost always set up under §302(c)(5) of the Taft-Hartley Act, more formally known as the Labor Management Relations Act of 1947, which covers private sector employees. Taft-Hartley plans have five basic characteristics: (a) one or more employers contribute to the plan; (b) the plan is collectively bargained with each participating employer; (c) the plan assets are managed by a joint board of trustees, labor, and management; (d) assets are placed in a trust fund; and (e) mobile employees can change employers provided it is with a participating employer.

TANF: Temporary Assistance for Needy Families. A Federally sponsored public assistance program that replaced Aid to Families With Dependent Children (AFDC) in 1996.

TANGIBLE ASSETS: Assets with physical presence, volume, and space.

TAO: The experience of everything or the universal Way.

TARGET: The unit (individual, family, community) to which a program intervention is directed.

TARGET POPULATION: Cohort based on age, gender, clinical focus, and target geographic areas.

TAXABLE INCOME: Gross income minus certain deductions and exemptions, from which the income tax due is determined.

TAXABLE YEAR: A period of time for which a report is to be made by a person or business, of income received, allowable deductions, etc., for income tax purposes. This is generally a calendar year for individuals, but may be another acceptable 12-month period (fiscal year) for businesses. A taxpayer on the cash basis is required to include items in gross income in the taxable year received; a taxpayer on the accrual basis is required to include items in gross income in the taxable year they accrue.

TAX EQUITY AND FISCAL RESPONSIBILITY ACT OF 1982 (TEFRA): Legislation that established target rate of increased limits on reimbursements for inpatient operating costs per Medicare discharge. A facility's target amount is derived from costs in a base year updated to the current year by the annual allowable rate of increase. Medicare payments for operating costs generally may not exceed the facility's target amount. These provisions may still apply to hospitals and units excluded from prospective payment systems.

TCM: traditional Chinese medicine.

TEACHING SUPPORT (NET): Teaching allowances minus clinical teaching support funds.

TECHNICAL COMPONENT: The portion of a *Current Procedural Terminology* code that includes equipment, supplies, or facilities.

TECHNOLOGY ASSESSMENT: In health policy, a synthesis of information on the safety, effectiveness, and cost of a service or technology to predict how providing it would affect patients and the health care system.

TELEMEDICINE: The use of telecommunications (i.e., wire, radio, optical, electromagnetic channels transmitting voice data, Wi-Fi, Wi-Max, broadband T lines, and/or video) to facilitate medical diagnosis, patient care, or medical learning. Many rural areas are finding uses for telemedicine in providing oncology, home health, emergency room, radiology, and psychiatry among others. Medicaid and Medicare provide some limited reimbursement for certain services provided to patients via telecommunication. See EDI, HIPAA.

TELEMETRY BED: Hospital bed with instruments for patient monitoring from a remote location.

TELEMETRY UNIT: Hospital department with multiple telemetry beds.

TEMPORARY: An insurance agent licensed for a brief period of time; usually 90 days.

TEMPORARY PARTIAL DISABILITY: A disability that causes some loss of activity and income-earning ability and from which full recovery is expected. Used mainly in workers' compensation insurance.

TEMPORARY RECEIPT: A form given by a life or health insurance agent to the policy owner paying a premium when the premium receipt book or the official premium receipt is not available or when the premium cannot be officially receipted because the grace period has expired.

TEMPORARY STAFFING AGENCY SERVICES: Nursing and other staffing obtained through a nurse registry or other temporary help agency.

TEMPORARY TOTAL DISABILITY: A disability that causes complete loss of income-earning ability and from which full recovery is expected. Used mainly in workers' compensation insurance.

TERM: Health or life insurance policy that makes no provisions for renewal or termination, other than by expiration. A specified period of time.

TERMINAL ILLNESS BENEFIT: Clause in a life, health, or disability insurance policy suggesting an early benefit if diagnosed with a terminal illness within a given time period.

TERMINAL VALUE (TV): Value at the end of fixed or variable maturity, the sale of an asset, or the salvage price of a piece of equipment.

TERTIARY CARE: Medical care requiring a setting outside of the routine, community standard; care to be provided within a regional medical center having comprehensive training, specialists, and research training. See Primary, Secondary, and Quaternary Care.

TERTIARY CENTER: A large medical care institution, usually a teaching hospital that provides highly specialized care.

ThD: Doctor of theology.

THEORY OF PROBABILITY: An area of mathematics from which comes the law of large numbers (also called law of simple probability and Poisson's law), that is the mathematical principal on which insurance is based. See Law of Large Numbers.

THERAPEUTIC ALTERNATIVES: Drug products that provide the same pharmacological or chemical effect in equivalent doses.

THERAPEUTIC SUBSTITUTION: Dispensing by a pharmacist of a therapeutically equivalent drug product without contacting the prescribing physician for his permission to change the order. Generally, a Pharmacy and Therapeutics (P&T) Committee will formally approve specific types of substituting, and only those that can be made independently by a pharmacist health plan will often outsource certain responsibilities to third-party administrators (TPAs). TPAs are prominent players in the managed care industry. Therapeutic substitution always requires physician committee approval.

THIASOI: Ancient Greek benevolent societies considered a step in the evolution of life and health insurance.

THIRD-PARTY ADMINISTRATOR (TPA): Organizations with expertise and capability to administer all or a portion of the claims process.

THIRD-PARTY PAYER: A public or private organization that pays for or underwrites coverage for health care expenses.

THIRD-PARTY PAYMENT: (a) Payment by a financial agent such as an HMO, insurance company, or government rather than direct payment by the patient for medical care services. (b) The payment for health care when the beneficiary is not making payment, in whole or in part, in his own behalf.

THRESHOLD STANDARDS: Rate or level of illness or injury in a community or population that, if exceeded, should signal alarms for renewed or redoubled action.

TICKLER: A file designed to jog one's memory and call attention to something at a certain time. In life health or other kinds of insurance, the policy-expiration and premium-due tickets are examples of this device.

TIER: A specific list or level of drugs used in a health insurance plan.

TIME OF PAYMENT OF CLAIMS PROVISION: A mandatory, health insurance provision specifying how long an insurance company has to pay claims.

TIME-SERIES ANALYSIS (EVALUATION): Reflexive designs that rely on relatively long series of repeated outcome measurements taken before and after an intervention.

TITLE XVIII: Another term for Medicare.

TITLE XIX: Another term for Medicaid.

TOKEN PAYMENT: A form of copayment, usually a nominal payment, made by the patient for a service or supply item.

TORT: A wrongful act (or failure to act) by one person that gives another person the right to sue for damages.

TORT REFORM: Changes in the legal rules governing medical malpractice lawsuits.

TOTAL ASSET TURNOVER: Total revenues/total assets.

TOTAL BUDGET: Otherwise known as a global budget, a cap on overall health spending.

TOTAL DISABILITY: Inability to perform work all physical and cognitive work functions and Depends on the specific wording of an insurance policy. See Disability, Disability Income Insurance, and Partial Disability.

TOTAL MARGIN: A measure that compares total hospital revenue and expenses for inpatient, outpatient, and nonpatient care activities. Calculated by subtracting total expenses from total revenue and dividing by total revenue.

TOTAL QUALITY MEDICAL MANAGEMENT (TQMM): Method of defining and measuring medical quality through an integrated reporting system of patient satisfaction, input, feedback, physician opinions, process improvements, and outcomes measurement; used to continually assess care.

TOTAL REVENUE: Medical service price, times medical service, or product quantity.

TPA (THIRD PARTY ADMINISTRATOR): An administrative organization, other than the employee benefit plan or health care provider, that collects premiums, pays claims, or provides administrative services.

TRADITIONAL: A prepaid fee-for-service health plan that gives members maximum choice, allowing them to seek medical care from any health care provider without reduction of benefits.

TRANSACTING INSURANCE: The solicitation, inducements, and negotiations leading to a contract of insurance.

TRANSACTION: Medical goods or services transferred or rendered for compensation.

TRANSACTIONAL ANALYSIS (TA): System of psychotherapy created by psychiatrist Eric Berne, MD (d. 1970), and the subject of two bestsellers: *Games People Play: The Psychology of Human Relationships* (1964), and *I'm OK ... You're OK* (1967). Fundamental to TA is the hypothesis that ego-states attitudes during transactions and corresponding sets of behavior patterns fall into three categories: (a) parental (perceptive or didactic, admonitory); (b) adult (evaluative); and (c) childlike (emotional and creative).

TRANSFER: Movement of a patient between hospitals or between units in a given hospital. Medicare, a full diagnosis-related group rate is paid only for transferred patients that are defined as discharged.

TRANSFER PAYMENT: A payment (transfer of money) from one group to another without use of any physical resource.

TRANSFER OF RISK: Shifting all or part of a risk to another party, such as an insurance company, for a premium fee. See Insurance, Risk, and Peril.

TRANSIENT PATIENTS: Patients who receive treatments on an episodic basis and are not part of a facilities regular caseload.

TRANSITIONAL CARE: Patient care for those no longer in acute need.

TRANSPLANT: The surgical procedure that involves removing a functional organ from either a deceased or living donor and implanting it in a patient needing a functional organ to replace their nonfunctional organ.

TRANSPLANT BENEFIT: Total disability insurance benefit whereby a monthly payment is made to an organ donor.

TRAUMA: A physical injury caused by personal violence or brute mechanical force.

TRAUMATIC INJURY: In general, damage of a physical nature caused by accidental means and not resulting from disease or illness. See Illness and Injury.

TRAVEL-ACCIDENT INSURANCE: A form of health insurance limiting coverage to accidents occurring while the insured is traveling.

TRAVEL-ACCIDENT POLICIES: Health insurance policies that limit the payment of benefits.

TREATING PHYSICIAN: The licensed practitioner that actually provides care to the patient while hospitalized (i.e. a specialist or hospital-based physicians). (The Primary Care provider is not always the admitting or treating physician, but will make "social rounds" on their patients, thus freeing them up to do more in office work.) See Gatekeeper, Doctor, and Internist.

TREATMENT: Patient care intended to correct or relieve the underlying problem and its symptoms.

TREATMENT EPISODE: The period of treatment between admission and discharge from a modality (e.g., inpatient, residential, partial hospitalization, and outpatient). Many health care statistics and profiles use this unit as a base for comparisons.

TREATMENT FACILITY: Any facility, either residential or nonresidential, that is authorized to provide treatment for mental illness or substance abuse. See Hospital.

TREND ANALYSIS: A method of horizontal analysis in which potential line item changes are compared with a previous year.

TREND FACTOR: The rate at which medical costs are changing because of such factors as prices charged by medical care providers, changes in the frequency and pattern of utilizing various medical services, cost-shifting, and use of expensive medical technology.

TRIAGE: The act of categorizing patients according to acuity and by determining which need services first. Most commonly occurs in emergency rooms, but can occur in any health care setting. It is the classification of ill or injured persons by severity of condition. Designed to maximize and create the most efficient use of scarce resources of medical personnel and facilities. Managed care organizations, health plans, and provider systems are setting up programs or clinics called *triage centers*. These centers serve as an extension of the utilization review process, as diversions from emergency room care or as case management resources. These triage centers also serve to steer patients away from more costly care (for example, a child with a cold is steered away from an emergency room). Triage can be handled on the telephone and be called a preauthorization center, crisis center, call center, or information line.

TRICARE (formerly CHAMPUS): Insurance program for Veterans and civilian dependents of members of the military. Triple option managed care program from the Department of Defense, including these options: (a) HMO; (b) PPO; and (c) Standard insurance. See CHAMPUS.

TRICARE FOR LIFE (TFL): Expanded Medicare eligibility for uniformed services retirees, their eligible survivors, family, and some former spouses. See TRICARE and CHAMPUS.

TRIPLE-OPTION PLAN: Insurance plans offering three options from which an individual may choose, usually: traditional indemnity, HMO, and PPO. See Cafeteria Plan, CHAMPUS, and TriCare.

TRUE GROUP PLAN: Health, life, managed care, disability, or other insurance policy arrangement where all employees of a company are eligible for plan acceptance regardless of history, mental, or physical findings.

TRUE NEGATIVES: Eligibles who have not received any services through the managed care plan, as evidenced by the absence of a medical record and any encounter data. True negatives signify potential access problems and should be investigated by the managed care plan.

TRUSTEE: Agent or individual acting on behalf of a health care entity.

TRUST FUND: Separate accounts in the U.S. Treasury, mandated by Congress, whose assets may be used only for a specified purpose. For the supplemental medical insurance trust fund, monies not withdrawn for current benefit payments and administrative expenses are invested in interest-bearing federal securities, as required by law; the interest earned is also deposited in the trust fund. See Medicare.

TRUST FUND RATIO: A short-range measure of the adequacy of the trust fund level; defined as the assets at the beginning of the year expressed as a percentage of the expenditures during the year.

TTY: Teletypewriter communications device (older term and device).

TURNAROUND TIME: The number of days from the receipt of a claim to the payment of that claim.

TWISTING: Inducing the termination of a health or life insurance policy to purchase a new one and generate sales commissions for the agent.

TWO-PERSON COVERAGE: Insurance coverage for a plan member, plus the member's spouse or dependent child.

TWO-PERSON MEMBERSHIP: Managed care or health insurance members for the insured and one dependent person.

TYPE OF CONTRACT: A health insurance membership classification.

TYPE OF CONTROL: A combination of ownership category and legal organization: (a) Legal Organization—Corporation, division of a corporation, partnership, proprietorship, or other; (b) Ownership—Not for profit (church related or other not for profit), investor owned, or governmental.

U

UB-92 UNIFORM BILL 1992: Bill form used to submit health insurance claims for payment by third parties. Similar to HCFA 1500, but reserved for the inpatient component of health services. Also known as HCFA (CMS) Form 1450.

UBERRIMAE FIDEI CONTRACT: Latin phrase for utmost good faith, which assumes that all parties in good faith enter into insurance contracts.

UCR: A method of profiling prevailing fees in an area and reimbursing providers based on that profile. See Usual, Customary, and Reasonable and Surgical Fee Schedule.

UCR REDUCTION SAVINGS: The dollar amount or economic differential saved between the actual medical charges submitted for patient care and the allowed charges according to some proscribed payment schedule.

ULTIMATE MORTALITY TABLE: A mortality table based on life insurance experience after the first few (usually five) policy years from date of issue have been excluded. The purpose is to show the rate of mortality by attained age after the effects of selection (by medical examination, etc.) have worn off.

ULTIMATE NET LOSS: That total sum that the insured or any company as insurer or both, becomes legally obligated to pay, such as legal, medical, and investigation costs.

ULTRA VIRES: Latin phrase meaning beyond power of authority. A company offering insurance products and services without a charter or is a good example of this concept.

UMPIRE: An arbitrator. See Umpire Clause.

UMPIRE CLAUSE: In some insurance policies, a provision that, in the event the insured and the insurance company cannot agree on a claim settlement, each party is to select an arbitrator, and the two arbitrators then select an umpire. The insured and the insurance company agree to abide by the decision of the majority vote of the arbitrators and umpire.

UNACCRUED: Most often, this describes medical insurance income resulting from payments received but not yet due. See Accrual Basis of Accounting.

UNALLOCATED BENEFIT: A reimbursement provision in health insurance policies, usually for miscellaneous hospital and medical expenses, that does not specify how much will be paid for each type of treatment, examination, or the like, but only sets a maximum that will be paid for all such treatments.

UNALLOCATED CASH REPRESENT: Health insurance premiums that are received but not credited within a given time period.

UNALLOCATED CLAIM EXPENSE: Expenses of loss adjustment that a health insurance company incurs but cannot charge specifically to any single claim, such as claim department salaries and office overhead. See Expense.

UNAUTHORIZED INSURANCE: Insurance written by a company not licensed to do business in the state or country in which it sold the policy. See Insurance and Mutual Company.

UNAUTHORIZED INSURER: An insurance company not licensed to do business in a particular state.

UNBUNDLED: Itemizing or fragmenting each component of a medical or health care service or procedure separately. This can often result in higher overall costs. See Unbundling and Bundled.

UNBUNDLING: Billing of each component of a medical service or procedure separately. This can often result in higher overall costs. See Unbundled.

UNCOMPENSATED CARE: Care rendered by hospitals or other providers without payment from the patient or a government-sponsored or private insurance program. It includes both charity care, which is provided without the expectation of payment, and bad debts, for which the provider has made an unsuccessful effort to collect payment due from the patient.

UNCOVERED EXPENSE: A cost incurred by the patient that his or her insurance policy or HMO contract does not cover and was unknown previously.

UNDERGRADUATE MEDICAL EDUCATION: The medical training provided to students in medical school.

UNDERINSURANCED: A state or condition in which inadequate insurance is carried to satisfy an individual's or business's insurance needs in the event of the insured's death or illness.

UNDERLYING INSURANCE: The amount of insurance or reinsurance on a risk that attaches before the next higher excess layer of insurance or reinsurance attaches.

UNDERWRITER: Technically, the person who writes his or her name under a health insurance agreement, accepting all or part of the risk. Often refers to the home office employee (Home Office Underwriter) who reviews the facts about the risk, accepts or declines the risk, and assigns the rate—the home office underwriter. Also, used in reference to the agent offering the health insurance (Field Underwriter), because the agent does exercise underwriting discretion in selecting the risks (prospects) he or she contacts. See Insurance.

UNDERWRITING: (1) Insurance function bearing the risk of adverse price fluctuations during a particular period. (2) Analysis of a group that is done to determine rates or to determine whether the group should be offered coverage at all. A related definition refers to health screening of each individual applicant for insurance and refusing to provide coverage for preexisting conditions. See Underwriter.

UNDERWRITING DEPARTMENT: That department or division of an insurance company that handles underwriting.

UNDERWRITING PROFIT (OR LOSS): The profit (or loss) received from insurance or reinsurance premiums, as contrasted to that realized from investments. Also, the excess of premiums over claims paid and expenses (profit), or the excesses of claims paid and expenses over premiums (loss).

UNEARNED INCOME: An individual's income derived from investments, as opposed to salary or wages.

UNEARNED PREMIUM: That portion of written premium applicable to the unexpired or unused part of the period for which the premium has been charged. Thus, in the case of an annual premium, at the end of the first month of the premium period, eleven-twelfths of the premium is unearned.

UNEARNED REINSURANCE PREMIUM: That part of the reinsurance premium applicable to the unexpired portion of policies that are reinsured.

UNEMPLOYMENT COMPENSATION: Benefit payments paid to unemployed workers who meet the qualification requirements of the law, the requirements being that the worker not be unemployed voluntarily; that the worker have worked in employment covered by the law; that the worker be willing and able to take employment if offered; and that an initial waiting period of unemployment has elapsed before compensation is paid.

UNFAVORABLE VARIANCE: Occur when actual health care insurance premiums are lower than expected budgets premiums. The opposite of Favorable Variance.

UNIFIED HEALTH CARE SYSTEM: A plan that includes health insurance, workers compensation, and health-related auto insurance under one policy or program.

UNIFIED INSURANCE: Health insurance coverage that is provided through a single insurance policy.

UNIFORM BILLING CODE OF 1982: See UB-82.

UNIFORM BILLING CODE OF 1992: See UB-92.

UNIFORM CLAIM FORM: All insurers and self-insurers would be required to use a single claim form and standardized format for electronic claims.

UNIFORM CLAIM TASK FORCE: An organization that developed the initial HCFA-1500 Professional Claim Form. The National Uniform Claim Committee later assumed the maintenance responsibilities.

UNIFORM INDIVIDUAL ACCIDENT AND SICKNESS POLICY AND PROVISIONS ACT: Mandatory and optional state health insurance benefits. See Appendix.

UNIFORM POLICY PROVISIONS: See Uniform Set of Health Services.

UNIFORM PROVISIONS: Operating conditions of a health insurance policy mandated by law.

UNIFORM SET OF HEALTH SERVICES: A broad range of health services including: (a) a comprehensive and affordable uniform benefits package of personal health services delivered by competing certified health plans; (b) a variety of services provided through the public health system; and (c) health system support, such as clinical research and health personnel education.

UNILATERAL CONTRACT: A contract in which only one party pledges anything. Health insurance is a unilateral contract because only the insurance company can be sued for breach of contract. See Adhesion Contract.

UNINSURABLE RISK: A risk that fails to meet an insurance company's standards and is thus deemed uninsurable. See Insurable Risk, Risk, and Risk Management.

UNINSURED POPULATION: An estimated 44 million Americans. See Medicaid and State Health Insurance.

UNIQUE PROVIDER IDENTIFICATION NUMBER: A medical provider's identification number (issued by CMS) that is used on Medicare claims. See UPIN.

UNIT/DAY: A meter, volume, or benchmark of health care (office visits, hospital days).

UNITED NATIONS RULES FOR ELECTRONIC DATA INTERCHANGE FOR ADMINISTRATION, COMMERCE, AND TRANSPORT: An international electronic data interchange format. Interactive X12 transactions use the EDIFACT message syntax.

UNIT INPUT INTENSITY ALLOWANCE: The amount added to, or subtracted from, the hospital input price index to yield the prospective payment system update factor.

UNIT OF MEDICAL SERVICE: A unit of measure for health care services. System of payments based on the number of units delivered.

UNIVERSAL ACCESS: The right and ability to receive a comprehensive, uniform, and affordable set of confidential, appropriate, and effective healthcare services.

UNIVERSAL CARE: Socialized health care, such as the UK, Canada, France, and most countries in the world. Few countries have the private insurance programs as the primary form of health care, as in the United States. See Universal Coverage.

UNIVERSAL COVERAGE: A type of government-sponsored health plan that would provide health care coverage to all citizens. This is an aspect of Clinton's original health plan in the mid-1990s and is an attribute of national health insurance plans similar to those offered in other countries, such as the UK or Canada.

UNIVERSAL PRECAUTIONS: Recommendations issued by the Centers for Disease Control and Prevention (CDCP) to minimize the risk of transmission of blood-borne pathogens, particularly HIV and HBV, by health care and public safety workers. Barrier precautions are to be used to prevent exposure to blood and certain body fluids of all patients.

UNLICENSED INSURER: An unauthorized insurer and nonadmitted company.

UNREPORTED CLAIMS: Medical claims that have not yet been reported to the insurance company. Also, the reserve set up to meet those claims. See IBNR.

UNRESTRICED NET ASSETS: All assets of a health, life, disability, or managed care insurance company not encumbered by covenants (i.e., legal restrictions). See Assets.

UNRESTRICED NET REVENUES: All revenues of a health, life, disability, or managed care insurance company not encumbered by covenants (i.e., legal restrictions). See Revenues.

UPCODING: The practice of a provider billing for a procedure that pays better than the service actually performed. See Fraud and Abuse.

UPDATE: A process by which contact, contract, insurance, clinical, and medical plan information is updated in a health insurance management system using Mobile Digital Communications Networks (MDCN), and electronically downloaded to the client (patient).

UPDATE FACTOR: The year-to-year increase in base payment amounts for prospective payment systems (PPS) and excluded hospitals and dialysis facilities. The update factors generally are legislated by the Congress after considering annual recommendations provided by the Prospective Payment Assessment Commission (ProPAC) and the Secretary of Health and Human Services. ProPAC's update factors are intended to reflect changes in the prices of inputs used to provide patient care services, as well as changes in productivity, technological advances, quality of care, and long-term cost-effectiveness of services. ProPAC recommends separate update factors for PPS hospital operating payments, PPS hospital capital payments, the Tax Equity and Fiscal Responsibility Acts of 1982–83 target amounts for PPS-excluded hospitals and distinct-part units, and composite rate payments to dialysis facilities. See ProPAC.

UPIN: A medical provider's identification number (issued by CMS) that is used on Medicare claims. See Unique Provider Identification Number.

URAC: Utilization Review Accreditation Committee. See Quality Management and Quality Assurance.

URGENT CARE: The treatment of unexpected sickness or injuries that are not life-threatening but require immediate attention. See Emergency Care.

URGENT CARE CENTER: Short-term care facility for all non-life-threatening illnesses or injuries. See Emergency Center.

URGENTLY NEEDED CARE: Health care for a sudden illness or injury that needs medical care right away, but is not life threatening.

URGENT NEEDS: Urgent public health problems and unmet needs in various communities. The Health Services Act of 1993 allocated $20 million to enable the public health system to respond to these urgent health needs.

URGENT SERVICES: Benefits covered in an evidence of coverage that is required to prevent serious deterioration of an insured's health that results from an unforeseen illness or injury.

URGI-CENTER: A licensed medical center that provides urgent care. See ASC.

UROLOGIST: A physician who specializes in urology.

UROLOGY: The medical and surgical diagnosis and treatment of the kidneys, genitourinary system, and related structures.

US PER CAPITA COST (USPCC): The national average cost per Medicare beneficiary, calculated annually by the Office of the Actuary.

USUAL, CUSTOMARY, AND REASONABLE (UCR): Health insurance plans that pay a physician's full charge if it is reasonable and does not exceed his or her usual charges and the amount customarily charged for the service by other physicians in the area.

USURIOUS RATE OF INTEREST: Interest charged in excess of the maximum rate of interest that the law allows. Not to be confused with the legal rate of interest, which is the rate applied by law when there is no agreement by the parties as to the rate of interest.

USURY: Excess rate of interest over the legal rate charged to a borrower for use of money. Each state has its own definition of the exact rate and conditions that result in usury.

UTAH HEALTH INFORMATION NETWORK: A public–private coalition in the State of Utah for reducing health care administrative costs through the standardization and electronic exchange of health care data.

UTILITY: Preference for, or desirability of, a specific level of health status.

UTILITY FUNCTION: A mathematical function in health insurance statistics that associates a number with each of a set of feasible alternatives.

UTILITY MEASUREMENT: Quality of life measured as a single number (usually from 0 to 1) along a continuum from worst (death) to best (full health). See Quality of Life.

UTILIZATION: Use of services. Utilization is commonly examined in terms of patterns or rates of use of a single service or type of service, such as hospital care, physician visits, or prescription drugs. Measurement of utilization of all medical services in combination is usually done in terms of dollar expenditures. Use is expressed in rates per unit of population at risk for a given period, such as the number of admissions to the hospital per 1,000 persons aged older than 65 per year or the number of visits to a physician per person per year for an annual physical. See Prospective Utilization Review.

UTILIZATION REVIEW: Evaluation of the necessity, appropriateness, and efficiency of the use of medical services and facilities. Helps insure proper use of health care resources by providing for the regular review of such area as admission of patients, length of stay, services performed, and referrals. See Retrospective Utilization Review.

V

VALIDATION: The process by which the integrity and correctness of health data are established. Validation processes can occur immediately after a data item is collected or after a complete set of data is collected.

VALUATION, ASSET: The process of determining the value of a company's investments or other assets.

VALUATION PERIOD: A period of years that is considered as a unit for purposes of calculating the status of a medical trust fund.

VALUE: The worth of anything, often expressed in terms of money, but not necessarily so. The present worth of all the rights to future benefits arising from ownership of the thing valued.

VALUE-ADDED NETWORK: A vendor of electronic data interchange communications and translation services. See EDI.

VALUED BASIS OF PAYMENT: An arrangement whereby the insurance company agrees to pay to, or on behalf of, the insured upon occurrence of a defined loss a specified amount of money, regardless of the extent of such loss.

VALUE HEALTH CARE PURCHASING: The bulk purchases of medical supplies, equipment, or services to harvest economy of scale cost savings.

VARIABLE COSTS: Medical services costs that remain the same per unit, but change with variations in activity over the relevant range. See Fixed Cost and Mixed Cost.

VARIABLE LABOR BUDGET: Labor expense projection that changes over time with overtime and work outages.

VARIANCES: The differences obtained from subtracting actual results from expected or budgeted results.

VEHICLE: An inanimate intermediary in the indirect transmission of an agent that carries the agent from a reservoir to a susceptible host.

VENDOR: A facility or medical practitioner who provides service to insured patients for a fee.

VERTICAL ANALYSIS: A method of financial statement analysis that compares line item percentages. See Horizontal Analysis.

VERTICAL INTEGRATION NETWORK (VIN): Alliance of medical providers rendering a spectrum or continuum of health care services for the needs of a specific population cohort.

VETERANS ADMINISTRATION HEALTH CARE SYSTEM: A federally funded health care system for veterans with service-related medical problems. See CHAMPUS and TriCare.

VIATICAL SETTLEMENT: A transaction in which a life insurance policy-holder who is terminally ill sells his or her rights to the policy in exchange for immediate payment of a portion of the death benefits.

VIATICATION: The discounted sale by terminally ill patients of their cash value accumulation life insurance policy for value to enjoy living benefits.

VIRTUAL CORPORATION: Health care entity that can conserve cash, labor, liabilities, financial risk, and other assets by outsourcing most services.

VIRTUAL INTEGRATION: A pattern of strategic alliances designed to win the cost advantages of affiliation without the overhead disadvantages of ownership.

VIRULENCE: The proportion of persons with clinical disease, who after becoming infected, become severely ill or die. See Vector and Vehicle.

VISION CARE COVERAGE: A health care plan usually offered only on a group basis that covers routine eye examinations and that may cover all or part of the cost of eyeglasses and lenses.

VISION SURVEY AND ANALYSIS: Examination given by an eye doctor that may include a case history, refraction, coordination measurements and tests, prescription of lenses as needed, and verification of lenses, if prescribed.

VIS MAJOR: Act of God accident in which no one is responsible.

VITAL FORCE: (i.e., bioenergy, cosmic energy, cosmic energy force, cosmic force, cosmic life energy, cosmic life force, élan vital, energy of being, force of life, force vitale, inner vital energy, internal energy, life energy, life force, life force energy, life power, life source energy, nerve energy, nerve force, personal energy, spirit, subtle energy, universal energy, universal life energy, universal life energy power, universal life force, universal life force energy, universal life principle, vital cosmic force, vital element, vital energy, vital energy force, vitality, vital life force, vital life force energy, vitalistic principle, vitality energy, vital life spirit, vital magnetism, vital principle, vital spirit): Alleged nonmaterial force that sustains life, whose aspects include the following:

- Animal magnetism (mesmerism)
- Archetypal energy (dream work)
- Astral light (Theosophy)
- Aura (energy field work, Kirlian diagnosis)
- Bioelectrical energy (magical aromatherapy)
- Biological energy (neural therapy)
- Biomagnetic energy (Physio-Spiritual Etheric Body healing)
- Biomagnetism (de la Warr system)
- Bioplasmic energy (Bioplasmic healing)
- Body energy (Magno-Therapy, Zero Balancing)
- Chi (Chinese medicine)
- Core energy (inner self-healing process)
- Divine Energy (7 Keys Meditation Program)

- Divine-healing energy (Emotional Energetic Healing)
- Divine power (religious healing)
- Dynamism (homeopathy)
- Earth energy (Iron Shirt Chi Kung)
- Eeck (Eckankar)
- Energy body (core energetics, Pranic Healing)
- Essence (Diamond Approach)
- Etheric body (curative eurhythmy)
- Etheronic force (Edgar Cayce tradition)
- God Force (Rainbow Diet)
- Healing dolphin energy (Lifeline)
- Healing light energy (Chi Nei Tsang)
- Innate healing energy (homeovitics)
- Innate intelligence (chiropractic)
- Jariki (Zazen)
- Ki (shiatsu)
- Kundalini (kundalini yoga)
- Libidinal energy (Jungian psychology)
- Life-fields, L-Fields (radionics)
- Liquid light of sex
- Living energy (Living Energy Training)
- Magical energies (magical diet)
- Magnetic energy (magnet therapy)
- Manna (kahuna healing)
- MariEL (MariEL)
- Moon energy (Celtic magic)
- Orgone (Reichian Therapy)
- Pneuma (bioenergetics)
- Prana (Ayurveda)
- Psychic energy (psychic healing)
- Reiki (Reiki)
- Ruach, ruah (Judaism)
- Seichim (Seichim)
- Seiki (seiki-jutsu)
- Sexual energy (Gnosis, Tantra)
- Shakti (spiritual midwifery)
- Shin-ki (Shinkiko)
- Shintsu-Riki® (Kobayashi Technique)
- Soul (Christianity)
- Tai do (the way)
- Tachyon energy (electromagnetic healing)
- Transformation energy (Cellular Theta Breath)
- Universal creative healing energy (Planetary Herbology)

- Universal Fifth Dimensional Energy (Alchemia)
- Vis medicatrix nature (naturopathy)

See Alternative Health Care.

VITAL STATISTICS: Systematically tabulated information about births, marriages, divorces, and deaths, based on registration of these vital health insurance events.

VOLUME AND INTENSITY OF SERVICES: The quantity of health care services per enrollee, taking into account both the number and the complexity of the services provided.

VOLUME OFFSET: See Behavioral Offset.

VOLUME PERFORMANCE STANDARDS (VPS): A mechanism to adjust updates to fee-for-service payment rates based on how actual aggregate.

VOLUME PERFORMANCE STANDARD (VPS) SYSTEM: The VPS system provides a mechanism to adjust fee updates for the Medicare Fee Schedule based on how annual increases in actual expenditures compare with previously determined performance standard rates of increase.

VOLUNTARY EMPLOYEE BENEFICIARY ASSOCIATION (VEBA): A trust established under IRS Code 501(c)(9) that can be used to prefund health care.

W

WAITING PERIOD: The length of time an individual must wait to become eligible for benefits for a specific condition after overall coverage has begun. In general, the duration of time before a person is eligible for participation, coverage, or benefits under a group insurance or retirement plan or for benefits under a health policy or disability provision. For example, the time between the beginning of an insured's disability and the commencement of the period for which benefits are payable; also called elimination period in individual health policies. See Elimination Period.

WAIVE: A legal term meaning to surrender a right or privilege.

WAIVER: Approval that the Health Care Financing Administration (HCFA, the former federal agency that administered the Medicaid program, now CMS) may grant to state Medicaid programs to exempt them from specific aspects of Title XIX, the federal Medicaid law. Most federal waivers involve loss of freedom of choice regarding which providers beneficiaries may use, exemption from requirements that all Medicaid programs be operated throughout an entire state, or exemption from requirements that any benefit must be available to all classes of beneficiaries (which enables states to experiment with programs only available to special populations). See CMS and Estoppel.

WAIVER OF PREMIUM PROVISION: A provision available in many life insurance policies and in disability income health policies that exempts the insured from the payment of premiums after he or she has been disabled for a specified period of time (usually 6 months in life policies and 90 days or 6 months in health policies).

WAIVER OF PREMIUM WITH DISABILITY INCOME RIDER: A life insurance rider that pays a monthly income and waives the policy owner's obligation to pay further premiums in the event that he or she becomes totally and permanently disabled.

WARRANTIES (REPRESENTATIONS): Almost every state provides that all statements made by a health and life insurance policy applicant, whether in the application or to the medical examiner, are considered, in the absence of fraud, to be representations and not warranties. The distinction is crucial because a warranty must be literally true. Even a small breach of warranty, even if by error, could be sufficient to render the policy void, whether the matter warranted is material or not and whether or not it had contributed to the loss.

WARRANTY, IMPLIED: A warranty that is assumed to be a part of a contract even though not expressly included.

WEIGHTED AVERAGE APPROACH: Charge-setting method based on the number and types of medical interventions and the financial requirements of the health care enterprise.

WEIGHT AND HEIGHT TABLE: A statistical table providing such information as average weight and height for men and women by age. Such tables may be prepared by the Actuarial Society of America and the Association of Life Insurance Medical Directors or by individual insurance companies.

WELL-BABY DAYS: Nonacute, newborn nursery days; refers to condition of baby, not location.

WELLNESS: Preventive medicine associated with lifestyle and preventive care that can reduce health care utilization and costs. See Illness, Sickness, and Injury.

WILLINGNESS TO PAY: The maximum amount of money that an individual is prepared to give up to ensure that a proposed health care measure is undertaken.

WITHHOLD: The portion of the monthly capitation payment to physicians withheld by the HMO until the end of the year or other time period to create an incentive for efficient care. The withhold is at risk (i.e., if the physician exceeds utilization norms, he does not receive it). It serves as a financial incentive for lower utilization.

WITHHOLD POOL: The amount withheld from a primary care provider's capitation payment or a specialist's payment amount to cover excess expenditures of his or a group's referral or other pool. See Withhold.

WORK CLAUSE: Under social security, a provision that all or part of a recipient's benefits will be lost if he or she earns over a certain amount of money in a given year. However, there are no restrictions on earnings after age 70.

WORKERS' COMPENSATION BENEFITS: Life and health insurance coverage for employees while they are on the job. The employer pays premiums. Each state sets the benefit schedule and requirements. Coverage includes medical expenses, disability income, dismemberment, and death benefits. By providing workers' compensation benefits, the employer's liability for injuries and sickness on the job is usually eliminated.

WORKERS' COMPENSATION CATASTROPHE COVERS: Excess of loss reinsurance purchased by primary insurance companies to cover their unlimited medical and compensation liability under the workers' compensation laws.

WORKERS' COMPENSATION INDEMNITY BENEFITS: Benefits that replace an employee's wages while the employee is unable to work because of a work-related injury or illness.

WORKERS' COMPENSATION INSURANCE: Private or state-sponsored insurance program that provides income, health care, medical and surgical, mental health, drug, rehabilitation, and death and survivor benefits given to a worker injured on the job while a covered member.

WORKERS' COMPENSATION INSURANCE BENFITS: Income, medical, surgical and mental, drug, rehabilitation, death and survivor benefits given to a worker injured on the job while a covered member.

WORKERS' INJURY SERVICES: The medical care related to worker injury rendered by a practitioner to a covered person pursuant to the health plan.

WORKGROUP FOR ELECTRONIC DATA INTERCHANGE: A health care industry group that has a formal consultative role under the HIPAA legislation.

WORKING CAPITAL CYCLE: The activities of a health care entity that include: (a) securing cash; (b) turning cash into medical and other resources; (c) using resources for providing health care services; and (d) billing patients again to repeat the cycle.

WORKING CAPITAL, NET: Current assets minus current liabilities.

WRAPAROUND PLAN: Refers to insurance or health plan coverage for copays and deductibles that are not covered under a member's base plan.

WRITE: To insure, underwrite, or sell a life or health insurance product.

WRITTEN: Health or other insurance in which the policy has been taken and issued.

WRITTEN BUSINESS: Insurance business for which applications have been signed by the applicant, but for which policies are not yet in force; classified as paid business.

WRITTEN PREMIUM: That entire amount of premium on policy contracts that has been issued by an insurance company.

Z

Z TABLE: A mortality table showing ultimate experience on insured lives and computed from the experienced mortality on life policies issued by major companies from 1925 to 1934. The Z Table was a step in the development of the Commissioners Standard Ordinary Table of Mortality.

ZERO-BASED BUDGETING: A budget method that requires accountability for the line item existence and funding needs of existing and new health services programs.

ZERO PREMIUM: Medicare managed care plans in which there is no extra premium payment for a member above the monthly Medicare Part B payment for all beneficiaries.

ZONE SYSTEM: A system developed by the National Association of Insurance Commissioners for the triennial examination of insurers, under which teams of examiners are formed from the staffs of several states in each of several geographical zones. The results of their examinations are then accepted by all states in which the insurance company is licensed, without the necessity of each such state having to conduct its own examination.

Acronyms and Abbreviations

A

AA: anesthesia assistant

AAA: Ambulance Association of America

AAA: American Academy of Actuaries

AAA: American Academy of Allergists

AAA: American Arbitration Association

AAA: Area Agency on Aging

AAAAS: American Association of Accreditation of Ambulatory Surgery

AAAASF: American Association for the Accreditation of Ambulatory Surgical Facilities, Inc.

AAAHC: Accreditation Association for Ambulatory Health Care

AAAHF: Accreditation Association for Ambulatory Healthcare Facilities

AAAS: American Association for the Advancement of Science

AABB: American Association of Blood Banks

AABD: Aid to Aged, Blind, and Disabled

AACCN: American Association of Critical Care Nurses

AACN: American Association of Colleges of Nursing

AACP: American Association of Colleges of Pharmacy

AACPDM: American Academy for Cerebral Palsy and Developmental Medicine

AACR: American Association for Cancer Research

AACT: abbreviated account query

AAE: American Association of Endodontists

AAETS: American Academy of Experts in Traumatic Stress

AAFP: American Academy of Family Physicians

AAH: American Association for Homecare

AAHA: American Association of Homes for the Aging

AAHAM: American Association of Healthcare Administrative Management

AAHC: American Accreditation Healthcare Commission (Formerly URAC)

AAHCP: American Academy of Home Care Physicians

AAHE: Association for the Advancement of Health Education.

AAHKS: American Association of Hip and Knee Surgeons

AAHP: American Association of Health Plans

AAHPC: American Academy of Hospice and Palliative Care

AA/HR: affirmative action/human relations

AAHRP: Association for the Accreditation of Human Research Protection Programs

AAHS: American Association for Hand Surgery

AAHSA: American Association for Homes and Services for the Aging

AAI: accredited advisor in insurance

AAI: Alliance of American Insurers

AAIS: American Association of Insurance Services

AAL: actuarial accrued liability

AALU: Association of Advanced Life Underwriting

AAMA: American Association of Medical Assistants

AAMC: The American Association of Medical Colleges

AAMR: American Association on Mental Retardation

AAN: American Academy of Neurology

AAN: American Academy of Nursing

AANA: American Association of Nurse Anesthetists

AANN: American Academy of Neuroscience Nurses

AANOS: The American Academy of Neurological and Orthopedic Surgeons

AANS: American Academy of Neurological Surgeons

AAO: American Academy of Ophthalmology

AAOFAS: American Association of Orthopedic Foot and Ankle Surgeons

AAOHN: American Association of Occupational Health Nurses

AAOM: American Academy of Oral Medicine

AAOO: American Academy of Ophthalmology and Otolaryngology

AAOP: American Academy of Oral Pathology

AAOPP: American Association of Osteopathic Postgraduate Physicians

AAOS: American Academy of Orthopedic Surgeons

AAP: American Academy of Pediatrics

AAP: American Academy of Psychotherapists

AAP: Association for the Advancement of Psychoanalysis

AAP: Association of Academic Physiatrists

AAP: American Accreditation Program

AAP: American Association of Pathologists

AAP: Association of American Physicians

AAPA: American Academy of Physician Assistants

AAPA: American Association of Pathologist Assistants

AAPB: American Association of Pathologists and Bacteriologists

AAPCC: adjusted annual per capita cost

AAPCC: adjusted average per capita cost

AAPCC: American Association of Poison Control Centers

AAPHD: American Association of Public Health Dentists

AAPHP: American Association of Public Health Physicians

AAPI: American Accreditation Program, Inc.

AAPL: American Academy of Psychiatry and the Law

AAPM: American Association of Physicists in Medicine

AAPMR: American Academy of Physical Medicine and Rehabilitation

AAPOS: American Association for Pediatric Ophthalmology and Strabismus

AAPP: American Academy on Physician and Patient

AAPPO: American Association of Preferred Provider Organizations

AAPS: American Association of Pharmaceutical Scientists

AAPS: American Association of Plastic Surgeons

AAPSM: American Academy of Podiatric Sports Medicine

AAPT: American Association of Pharmacy Technicians

AAR: annual average rate

AARC: American Association for Respiratory Care

AARDA: American Autoimmune Related Diseases Association

AARF: additional adjusted reduction factor

AARP: American Association of Retired People

AART: American Association for Respiratory Therapy

AAS: American Analgesia Society

AASD: American Academy of Stress Disorders

AASH: American Association for the Study of Headache

AASP: American Association of Senior Physicians

AAST: American Association for the Surgery of Trauma

AATS: American Association for Thoracic Surgery

AAU: Association of American Universities

AAWD: American Association of Women Dentists

AAWM: American Academy of Wound Management

AAWP: American Association of Women Podiatrists

AB: bachelor of arts (latartium baccalaureus)

ABA: American Board of Anesthesiologists

ABAT: American Board of Applied Toxicology

ABC: activity-based costing

ABC: American Blood Commission

ABD: aged, blind, and disabled

ABHES: Accrediting Bureau of Health Education Schools

ABM: activity-based management

ABMS: American Board of Medical Specialties

ABMT: autologous bone marrow transplant

ABN: advance beneficiary notice

ABNS: American Board of Nursing Specialties

ABO: adjusted blind onset

ABPANC: American Board of Peri-Anesthesia Nursing Certification, Inc.

ABQUARP: American Board of Quality Assurance and Utilization Review Physicians

ABS: American Back Society

ABSS: applied behavioral sciences specialist

ABTA: American Brain Tumor Association

ABV: accredited in business of possible valuation

AC: appeals council

AC: augmentative communication

AC: alternative care

ACA: American Chiropractic Association

ACA: American College of Apothecaries

ACAAI: American College of Asthma, Allergy, and Immunology

ACC: ambulatory care center

ACC: American College of Cardiology

ACCME: Accreditation Council for Continuing Medical Education

ACCP: Alliance for Cervical Cancer Prevention

ACCP: American College of Chest Physicians

ACCP: American College of Clinical Pharmacy

ACD: alternative care determination

ACE: Aetna claim exchange

ACE: adjusted current earnings

ACE: affiliated covered entity

ACE: average current earnings

ACEP: American College of Emergency Physicians

ACER: Annual Contact Evaluation Report

ACF: administration for children and families

ACF: adult care facility

ACF: alternative care facility

ACF: ambulatory care facility

ACG: American College of Gastroenterology

ACG: adjusted clinic groups

ACG: ambulatory care group

ACH: automated clearing-house

ACHCA: American College of Health Care Administrators

ACHE: American Congress of Healthcare Executives

ACI: audit controls integrity

ACI: average cost of illness

ACID: automated continuing investigation of disability

ACIL: American Council of Independent Laboratories

ACLA: American Clinical Laboratory Association

ACLD: Association for Children with Learning Disabilities.

ACLI: American Council of Life Insurance

ACLM: American College of Legal Medicine

ACLPS: Academy of Clinical Laboratory Physicians and Scientists

ACLPS: Academy of Clinical Laboratory Physicians and Scientists

ACLS: advanced cardiac life support

ACLU: American College of Life Underwriters

ACMA: American Occupational Medical Association.

ACMD: associate chief medical director

ACME: Advisory Council on Medical Education

ACME: automated classification of medical entities

ACME: Alliance for Continuing Medical Education

ACMI: American College of Medical Informatics

ACNHA: American College of Nursing Home Administrators

ACNM: American College of Nuclear Medicine Nutrition

ACNM: American College of Nurse Midwives

ACNP: acute care nurse practitioner

ACNP: American College of Nuclear Physicians

ACOE: Accreditation Council on Optometric Education

ACOEM: American College of Occupational and Environmental Medicine

ACOEP: American College of Osteopathic Emergency Physicians

ACOG: American College of Obstetricians and Gynecologists

ACOHA: American College of Osteopathic Hospital Administrators

ACO-HNS: American Council of Otolaryngology—Head and Neck Surgery

ACOI: American College of Osteopathic Internists

ACOM: American College of Occupational Medicine

ACOMS: American College of Oral and Maxillofacial Surgeons

ACOOG: American College of Osteopathic Obstetricians and Gynecologists

ACOP: American College of Osteopathic Pediatricians

ACOP: approved code of practice

ACORDE: A Consortium on Restorative Dentistry Education

ACOS: American College of Osteopathic Surgeons

ACOS: associate chief of staff

ACOS/AC: associate chief of staff for ambulatory care

ACP: accelerated claims process

ACP: American College of Pathologists

ACP: American College of Pharmacists

ACP: American College of Physicians

ACP: American College of Prosthodontists

ACP: American College of Psychiatrists

ACPA: American Cleft Palate Association

ACPE: American College of Physician Executives

ACPE: American Council on Pharmaceutical Education

ACPM: American College of Preventive Medicine

ACPOC: Association of Children's Prosthetic-Orthotic Clinics

ACPS: advanced claims processing system

ACR: adjusted community rating

ACR: ambulance call report

ACR: American College of Radiology

ACR: American College of Rheumatology

ACRF: ambulatory care research facility

ACRM: American Congress on Rehabilitation Medicine

ACRP: adjusted community rate proposal

ACRPI: Association of Clinical Research for the Pharmaceutical Industry

ACS: Ambulatory Care Services

ACS: American Cancer Society

ACS: American Chemical Society

ACS: American College of Surgeons

ACSIUG: ambulatory care special-interest user group

ACSM: American College of Sports Medicine

ACSOG: American College of Surgeons Oncology Group

ACSW: Academy of Certified Social Workers

ACT: anxiety control training

ACT: asthma care training

ACTA: American Cardiology Technologists Association

ACV: alternative care value

ACYF: Administration on Children Youth and Families (Department of Health and Human Services)

AD: admission and discharge

AD: admitting diagnosis

ADA: American Diabetes Association

ADA: American Dental Association

ADA: American Dietetic Association

ADA: Americans With Disabilities Act

ADADS: alcohol and drug abuse data system

ADAMHA: Alcohol, Drug Abuse and Mental Health Administration

ADAP: alcohol and drug abuse patient

ADASP: Association of Directors of Anatomic and Surgical Pathology

ADB: accidental death benefit

ADC: adult day care

ADC: Alzheimer's Disease Center

ADC: average daily census

ADD: accidental death and dismemberment

ADD: Administration on Developmental Disabilities

ADE: adverse drug event

ADEA: Age Discrimination in Employment Act of 1967

ADEA: American Dental Education Association

ADEAR: Alzheimer's Disease Education and Referral Center

ADFS: alternative delivery and financing system

ADG: ambulatory diagnostic group

ADHA: American Dental Hygienists Association

ADL: activities of daily living

ADM: alcohol, drug abuse, and mental health

ADM: alcohol, drug, or mental disorder

ADMC: advance determination of Medicare coverage

ADMD: alcohol, drug, and mental disorders

ADP: automatic data processing

ADPL: average daily patient load

ADPL-BAS: average daily patient load-bassinet

ADPL-IP: average daily patient load-inpatient

ADPL-T: average daily patient load-total

ADR: adverse drug reaction

ADR: alternative dispute resolution

ADRG: adjacent diagnostic-related group

ADS: alternative delivery system

ADSC: average daily service charge

ADT: admission, discharge, and transfer

AECHO: Aetna Electronic Claim Home Office

AEP: appropriateness evaluation protocol

AET: Annual Earnings Test

AEVCS: automated eligibility verification claims submission

AFAR: American Federation for Aging Research

AFC: adult foster care

AFDC: aid to families with dependent children

AFDS: alternative finance delivery system

AFEHCT: Association for Electronic Health Care Transactions

AFPE: American Foundation for Pharmaceutical Education

AFS: alternative financing system

AG: affiliated group

AGNIS: a gnomic nursing information system

AGPA: American Group Practice Association

AGPAM: American Guild of Patient Account Managers

AGS: American Geriatric Society

AH: Accident and Health Insurance

AHA: American Heart Association

AHA: American Hospital Association

AHAF: American Health Association Foundation

AHC: alternative health care

AHC: automated clearing house

AHCA: Agency for Health Care Administration

AHCA: American Health Care Association

AHCPR: Agency for Health Care Policy and Research

AHEC: Area Health Education Center

AHF: American Health Foundation

AHF: American Hepatic Foundation.

AHF: American Hospital Formulary

AHF: Associated Health Foundation

AHIA: Association of Health Insurance Agents

AHIMA: American Health Information Management Association

AHIP: Assisted Health Insurance Plan

AHIS: Automated Hospital Information System

AHMA: American Holistic Medicine Association

AHMC: Association of Hospital Management Committees

AHN: army head nurse

AHN: assistant head nurse

AHP: accountable health plan

AHP: assistant house physician

AHPA: American Health Planning Association

AHRP: Alliance for Human Research Protections

AHRQ: Agency for Healthcare Research and Quality

AHS: Academy of Health Sciences

AHS: American Hearing Society

AHS: American Hospital Society

AHS: area health service

AHS: assistant house surgeon

AHSA: American Health Security Act

AHSN: Assembly of Hospital Schools of Nursing

AHSR: Association for Health Services Research

AI: accident and indemnity

AI: accident insurance

AI: aged individual

AIA: American Insurance Association

AICPA: American Institute of Certified Public Accountants

AIM: advanced informatics in medicine

AIME: average indexed monthly earnings

AIMR: Association for Investment and Research

AIMS: Abnormal Involuntary Movement Scale

AIMTSH: Association for Information Management and Technology Staff in Health

AIPM: Association of Immunization Program Managers

AIR: American Institute of Research

AJAO: American Juvenile Arthritis Organization

AL/ALF: assisted living/assisted living facilities

ALC: assisted living center

ALFA: Assisted Living Federation of America

ALIMD: Association of Life Insurance Medical Directors

ALJ: administrative law judge

ALOH: average length of hospitalization

ALOS: average length of service

AM: alternative medicine

AMA: against medical advice

AMA: American Management Association

AMA: American Medical Association

AMAP: American Medical Accreditation Program

AMAP: Approved Medication Administration Personnel

AMBHA: American Managed Behavior Healthcare Association

AMC: academic medical center

AMCP: Academy of Managed Care Pharmacy

AMCPA: American Managed Care Pharmacy Association

AMCR: Association for Managed Care Review

AMCRA: American Managed Care and Review Association

AMDCP: American Medical Directors Certification Program

AMDF: American Macular Degeneration Foundation

AMDPA: Arkansas Medical Dental and Pharmaceutical Association

AME: agreed medical examiner

AME: average monthly earnings

AMEE: Association for Medical Education in Europe

AMFAR: American Foundation for AIDS Research

AMGA: American Medical Group Association

AMI: Advancement of Medical Instrumentation

AMIA: American Medical Informatics Association

AMP: automated medical payment

AMP: average manufacturer's price

AMPRA: American Medical Peer Review Association

AMPS: automated Medicaid payment system

AMRA: American Medical Records Association

AMSR: assigned medical security responsibility

AMW: average monthly wage

AN: account number

ANA: American Nurses Association

ANA-PAC: American Nurses Association-Political Action Committee

ANCC: American Nurses Credentialing Center

ANDA: abbreviated new drug approval

ANF: American Nurses Foundation

ANPR: advanced notice of proposed rule-making

ANS: American National Standards

ANSI: American National Standards Institute

AO: administrative official

AO: at occupation

AOA: Administration on Aging

AOA: American Optometric Association

AOA: American Osteopathic Association

AOB: alcohol on breath

AOB: assignment of benefits

AOC: administrator on call

AOCP: American Osteopathic College of Pathologists

AOD: administrator on duty

AOD: alleged onset date

AOD: alleged onset of disability

AODA: alcohol and other drugs of abuse

AOFAS: American Orthopedic Foot and Ankle Society

AONE: American Organization of Nurse Executives

AOPA: American Orthotic and Prosthetic Association

AOR: assignment of rights

AORN: Association of Perioperative Registered Nurses

AOS: Academic Orthopedic Society

AOT: assisted outpatient treatment

AOTA: American Occupational Therapy Association

AOTP: automated one time payment

AP: accounts payable

AP: additional premium

AP: administrative proceedings

AP: Appeals Department

AP: Attending Physician

APA: Academy of Physician Assistants

APA: American Paralysis Association

APA: American Pharmaceutical Association

APA: American Psychiatric Association

APA: American Psychological Association

APC: ambulatory payment classification

APC: amended payroll certification

APCC: adjusted per capita cost

APDRG: all patient diagnosis-related groups

APEXPH: assessment protocol for excellence in public health

APF: American Pathology Foundation

APG: ambulatory payment groups

APHA: American Public Health Association

APHAP: acute partial hospitalization program

APHP: acute partial hospitalization program

API: applications program interface

API: Association for Pathology Informatics

APIC: Association for Practitioners in Infection Control

APMA: American Pharmaceutical Project Managers Associates

APMA: American Podiatric Medical Association

APMA: American Podiatric Medical Association

APP: application

APPP: American Preferred Provider Plan

APR: adjusted payment rate

APR: average percentage rate

APR-DRG: all patient refined diagnosis-related group

APS: American Pain Society
APS: Attending Physician Statement
APSF: Anesthesia Patient Safety Foundation
APT: admission per thousand
APTA: American Physical Therapy Association
APTD: aid to the permanently and totally disabled
AQA: Alternate Quality Assessment Survey
AQD: alleged quarter of disability
AR: accounts receivable
AR: acknowledged receipt
ARC: AIDS-related complex
ARC: Association for Retarded Citizens
ARCF: American Respiratory Care Foundation
ARDA: assistant regional director for administration
ARDEN: Arden Syntax Medical Logic Modules
AREA: Academic Research Enhancement Award
ARF: adjustment of reduction factor
ARIA: American Risk and Insurance Association
ARNP: advance registered nurse practitioner
ARP: American Registry of Pathology
ARPA: Advanced Research Projects Agency
ARU: automated response unit
AS: admission scheduling
ASA: accredited senior appraiser
ASA: American Society of Anesthesiologists
ASA: Association of the Society of Actuaries

ASAHP: American Society of Allied Health Professionals
ASAP: American Society for Automation in Pharmacy
ASB: American Society of Biomechanics
ASBME: Associated Students of Biomedical Engineering
ASC: Accredited Standards Committee
ASC: Administrative Services Contract
ASC: ambulatory surgical center
ASC: American Standards Committee
ASCA: Administrative Simplification Compliance Act
ASCHP: American Society of Clinical Hospital Pharmacists
ASCII: American Standard Code for Information Interchange
ASCLC: American Society for Clinical Laboratory Science
ASCLU: American Society of Chartered Life Underwriters
ASCO: American Society of Clinical Oncology
ASCP: American Society of Clinical Pathologists
ASCP: American Society of Consultant Pharmacist
ASCS: admission scheduling and control system
ASF: ambulatory surgical facility
ASFC: agency-sponsored family care
ASHA: American School Health Association
ASHA: American Speech-Language-Hearing Association
ASHMM: American Society for Hospital Materials Managers

ASHNR: American Society of Head and Neck Radiology

ASHP: American Society of Health-System Pharmacists

ASHRM: American Society for Healthcare Risk Management

ASI: accident and sickness insurance

ASIA: American Spinal Injury Association

ASIM: American Society of Insurance Management

ASIM: American Society of Internal Medicine

ASL: American sign language

ASME: Association for the Study of Medical Education

ASMI: American Sports Medicine Institute

ASO: administrative services only

ASO: administrative services organization

ASP: active server page

ASP: application services provider

ASPH: Association of School of Public Health

ASPL: American Society for Pharmacy Law

ASPMN: American Society of Pain Management Nurses

ASR: age/sex rate

ASS: administrative simplification section

ASS: administrative simplification standards

ASTHO: Association of State and Territorial Health Officials

ASTM: American Society for Testing Materials

ATLS: advanced trauma life support

ATRA: American Tort Reform Association

ATSDR: Agency for Toxic Substances and Disease Registry

AUA: American Urology Association

AUMP: agreed upon medical procedure

AUP: agreed upon procedure

AUR: ambulatory utilization review

AV: actual value

AVC: Association of Vitamin Chemists

AVG: ambulatory visit group

AWHONN: Association of Women's Health, Obstetric and Neonatal Nurses

AWI: average wage index

AWOL: absent without leave

AWP: any willing provider

AWP: average wholesale price

AYD: alleged year of disability

B

BAA: business agency announcement

BAA: business associate agreement

BA: benefit authorizer

BA: budget authority

BA: business associate

BAC: Beneficiary Advisory Committee

BAC: business associate contract

BAR: billing, accounts receivable

BARS: Behaviorally Anchored Rating Scale

BBA: Balanced Budget Act of 1997

BBRA: Balanced Budget Refinement Act of 1999

BC: blind child

BCBSA: Blue Cross-Blue Shield Association

BCF: benefit continuity factor
BCI: blind countable income
BCM: billing and collection master
BCP: benefit continuous provision
BDN: benefits delivery network
BDOC: bed days of care
BEA: break-even analysis
BEA: Bureau of Economic Affairs
BEA: Bureau of Economic Analysis
BEC: benefit entitlement code
BEC: Benefits Executive Council
BEER: Benefits Estimate Earnings Record
BENCAT: beneficiary category
BEP: break-even point
BEPIPD: break-even point in patient dollars
BEPIPU: break-even point in patient units
BERD: behavior event requiring documentation
BH: boarding home
BHCAG: buyers health care action group
BHR: Bureau of Human Resources
BHU: basic health unit
BI: bodily injury
BIC: beneficiary identification code
BID: twice a day
BIF: beneficiary in force
BIP: Benefit Integrity Department
BIPA: Benefits Improvement and Protection Act
BIR: benefit initial recomputation
BLS: Bureau of Labor Statistics
BLS: basic life support
BM: budget month
BME: biomedical engineer
BMET: biomedical engineer technician

BNI: Beneficiary Notices Initiative
BOAN: beneficiary's own account number
BOD: beneficial occupancy date
BOH: board of health
BOI: blind individual
BOML: bill of medical lading
BOPUD: benefit overpayment/ underpayment data
BOSS: burial operations support system
BOSSN: beneficiary's own Social Security number
BPB: borderline personality disorder
BPHC: Bureau of Primary Health Care
BPO: Bureau of Program Operations
BQA: Bureau of Quality Assurance
BQCA: Bureau of Quality Compliance Assurance
BRA: beneficiary residing abroad
BRAT: behavioral research and therapy
BRFS: Behavioral Risk Factor Survey
BRFSS: behavioral risk factor surveillance system
BRI: benefit rate increase
BRIN: biomedical research infrastructure network
BS: balance sheet
BS: blind services
BSN: bachelor's of science in nursing
BSR: bill summary record
BTC: beneficiary telephone code
BTCG: brain tumor cooperative group
BTD: beneficiary telephone number data
BTM: benefit termination month

BTP: benefit termination period
BUR: billing update record
BVA: Blind Veterans Association
BVA: board of veterans' appeals
BWE: blind worker's expense
BY: base year

C

CA: certified acupuncturist
CA: certified aromatherapist
CA: claims authorizer
CA: current assets
CAAHEP: Commission on Accreditation for Allied Health Education Programs
CAC: carrier advisory committee
CAC: certified alcoholism counselor
CACN: clinical ambulatory care network
CAD: change of address
CAE: claims administrative expense
CAF: civil assets forfeiture
CAH: care at home
CAH: critical access hospital
CAHPS: consumer assessments of health plans study
CAIRS: child and adult integrated reporting system
CalPERS: California Public Employees Retirement System
CALSO: claims automated lump sum operations
CAN: American College of Neuropsychiatrists
CAN: American College of Nutrition
CAN: Certified Nursing Administration
CAN: claimant account number
CAP: capitated ambulatory plan

CAP: capitation
CAP: client assessment profile
CAP: client assistance
CAP: clinical assessment profit
CAP: College of American Pathologists
CAPA: certified ambulatory peri-anesthesia nurse
CAPS: claims adjusted processing system
CARF: Commission on Accreditation of Rehabilitation Facilities
CARN: certified addiction registered nurse
CASA: clinic assessment software application
CASAC: certified alcoholism and substance abuse counselor
CASB: Cost Accounting Standards Board
CASCON: case control
CAT: catastrophic claims
CAWR: combined annual wage reporting
CBA: certified business appraiser
CBA: cost benefit analysis
CBC: Center for Beneficiary Choice
CBER: Center of Biological Evaluation and Research
CBO: community-based organization
CBO: Congressional Budget Office
CBO: cost budget office
CBOC: community-based outpatient clinic
CBPPMI: Cain Brothers Physician Practice Management Index
CC: complications
CC: controllable cost
CCA: certified cost accountant

CCA: claims adjustment and analysis

CCC: Certificate of Clinical Competency

CCC: Code of Corporate Conduct

CCDC: certified chemical dependency counselor

CCF: Claim Correction Form

CCG: check claim group

CCH: certified clinical hypnotherapist

CCI: Correct Coding Initiative

CCM: certified case manager

CCMU: critical care medical unit

CCN: chronic care network

CCN: community care network

CCN: correspondence control number

CCO: chief compliance officer

CCO: complete care organization

CCP: Coordinated Care Program

CCR: continuing care record

CCR: cost to charge ratio

CCRC: continuing care retirement communities

CCRN: certified critical care registered nurse

CCS: complications and/or comorbidities

CCTC: clinical computer training center

CD: chemical dependency

CDA: certified dental assistant

CDB: childhood disability benefits

CDC: Centers for Disease Control and Prevention

CDC: chemical dependency counselor

CDC: Claims Distribution Center

CDCI: Chronic Disease Care Index

CDE I: certified disability evaluator I

CDE: certified diabetic educators

CDI: continuing disability investigation

CDM: certified disease manager

CDMRP: Congressionally Directed Medical Research Program

CDN: Claims Disability Notice

CDR: continuing disability review

CDRH: chemical dependency recovery hospital

CDS: chemical dependency specialist

CDSC: contingent deferred sales charge

CDT: Commissioners Disability Table

CDT: current dental terminology

CDU: critical decision units

CE: consultation and examination

CE: consultative examination

CE: continuing education

CE: covered entity

CEA: cost-effectiveness analysis

CEBS: certified employee benefits specialist

CEC: Covert Earnings Card

CEMPM: Center for Education in Medical Practice Management

CEN: certified emergency nurse

CEO: chief executive officer

CER: capital expenditure review

CERT: Centers for Education and Research on Therapeutics

CERT: computer emergency response team

CF: conversion factor

CFA: cash flow analysis

CFA: chartered financial analyst

CFAA: Computer Fraud and Abuse Act

CFC: certified financial consultant

CFFA: certified forensic financial analyst

CFM: cash flow management

CF/MR: Intermediate Care Facility for the Mentally Retarded

CFO: certified financial officer

CFO: chief financial officer

CFOI: Bureau of Labor Statistics Census of Fatal Occupational Injuries

CFP©: certified financial planner©

CFR: Code of Federal Regulations

CFS: Cash Flow Statement

CFS: Consolidated Financial Statements

CGL: commercial general liability

CHA: Catholic Health Association

CHAMPUS: Civilian Health and Medical Program of the Uniformed Services

CHAMPVA: Civilian Health and Medical Program of the Veteran's Administration

CHAP: Community Health Accreditation Program

CHC: certified health consultant

CHC: community health center

CHCC: comprehensive health care clinic

CHCS: composite health care system

CHDM: conceptual health data model

CHE: certified health care executive

ChFC: chartered financial consultant

CHHA: certified home health agency

CHI: consumer health information

CHIM: College of Healthcare Informatics Management

CHIME: College of Healthcare Informatics Management Executives

CHIN: Community Health Information Network

CHIP: Children's Health Insurance Programs

CHIPAS: community health purchasing alliance

CHMIS: community health management information systems

CHMSA: critical health manpower shortage area

CHN: cooperative health care networks

CHP: comprehensive health planning

CHPA: community health purchasing alliances

CHPDAC: California Health Policy and Data Advisory Commission

CHPS: Center for Health Policy Studies

CHRIS: computerized human resource information system

CHRP: College of Health-Related Professions

CHTP: certified healing touch practitioner

CI: coding institute

CIB: child insurance benefits

CIC: certified insurance counselor

CIC: clinical incident response capability

CICE: certified independent chiropractic examiner

CIDC: Bureau of Chronically Ill and Disabled Children

CIET, 1961: Commissioners Industrial Extended Term Mortality Table, 1961

CII: Childhood Immunization Initiative

CIL: center for independent living

CIM: certified IRB manager
CIM: Coverage Issues Manual
CIO: chief information officer
CIP: case in progress
CIS: clinical information system
CISO: chief information security officer
CISS: community integrated services system
CIT: center for intensive treatment
CITI: Collaborative IRB Training Initiative
CIU: Claims Investigative Unit
CLA: conversional living arrangement
CLASS: claims acquisition and submission system
CLCCP: Comprehensive Limiting Charge Compliance Program
CLIA: Clinical Laboratory Improvement Amendment
CLIN: contract line item number
CLRA: Children's Leukemia Research Association
CLT: capitation liability theory
CLU: chartered life underwriter
CM: case mix
CM: computation month
CM: contribution margin
CMA: certified management accountant
CMA: current month accrual
CMAR: current money amount of reduction
CMBA: currently monthly benefit amount
CMC: certified management consultant (international)
CMCM: comprehensive Medicaid case management
CMD: certified medical director

CME: Council on Medical Education
CME: continuing medical education
CMHC: community mental health center
CMHC: certified mental health counselor
CMI: case-mix index
CMM: Center for Medicare Management
CMM: comprehensive major medical
CMN: Certificate of Medical Necessity
CMO: case management organization
CMOP: Consolidated Mail Outpatient Pharmacy
CMP: civil monetary penalty
CMP: Claims Modernization Project
CMP: competitive medical plan
CMP©: certified medical planner©
CMR: clinical medical records
CMR: contribution margin ratio
CMREF: Cardiovascular Medical Research and Education Fund
CMS: Centers for Medicare and Medicaid Services
CMS: cryptographic message syntax
CMT: certified massage therapist
CMT: certified medical transcriptionist
CMUR: concurrent medical utilization review
CMV: controlled medical vocabulary
CMV: current market value
CNAICNT: certified nurse aide or certified nurse technician
CNH: community nursing home
CNHI: Committee for National Health Insurance

CNM: certified nurse midwife

CNOR: certified nurse in the operating room

CNS: clinical nurse specialist

COA: Certificate of Authority

COB: coordination of benefits

COBRA: Consolidated Omnibus Budget Reconciliation Act

COC: Certificate of Coverage

COE: center of excellence

COG: children's oncology group

COI: Certificate of Insurance

COI: conflict of interest

COI: cost of illness

COL: cost of living

COLA: cost of living adjustment

COM: College of Medicine

COM: current operating month

COMSP: cost of medical service provided

CON: certificate of need

CON: College of Nursing

CONRA: Centers of Biological Research and Education

COO: chief operating officer

COP: College of Pharmacy

COP: conditions of participation

COPC: community-oriented primary care

COPE: Council on Optometric Practitioner Education

COPH: College of Public Health

COPH: community-oriented public health

COPPA: Children's Online Privacy Protection Act

COPPR: children's online privacy protection rule

CORBAMed: common object request broker architecture for medicine

CORF: comprehensive outpatient rehabilitation facility

COSS: common object service specifications

COT: chain of trust

COTA: certified occupational therapy assistant

COTH: Council of Teaching Hospitals

COTS: commercial-off-the-shelf

CP: cerebral palsy

CP: clinical psychologist

CPA: certified public accountant

CPAC: Competitive Pricing Advisory Committee

CPAN: certified post-anesthesia nurse

CPD: Certified Processing Department

CPE: certified physician executive

CPEHS: Consumer Protection and Environmental Health Service

CPEP: carrier performance and evaluation program

CPEP: comprehensive psychiatric emergency program

CPG: Clinical Practice Guidelines

CPHA: Commission on Professional and Hospital Activities

CPHQ: certified physician in healthcare quality

CPHQ: certified professional in healthcare quality

CPI: consumer price index

CPIA: current primary insurance amount

CPM: clinical path method

CPN: certified pediatric nurse

CPO: claims processing organization

CPOE: computerized physician order entry

CPR: computer-based patient record

CPR: critical payment record

CPR: customary, prevailing, and reasonable

CPRI: Computer-based Patient Record Institute

CPRI: Consolidation of Computer-based Patient Record Institute

CPRS: computerized patient record system

CPS: Child Protective Services

CPS: critical payment system

CPSS: Committee on Payment and Settlement Systems

CPT: *Current Procedural Terminology*

CPT-4: *Current Procedural Terminology*, 4th ed.

CQAS: carrier quality assurance system

CQI: continuous quality improvement

CR: capitation rate

CR: carrier replacement

CR: change request

CR: chemical restraints

CR: claims representative

CR: continuing review

CRAHCA: Center for Research in Ambulatory Healthcare Administration

CRC: community rating by class

CRCA: Clinical Research Curriculum Award

CRD: chronic renal disease

CRF: Continuing Review Form

CRISP: computer retrieval of information on scientific projects

CRL: certificate revocation list

CRNA: certified registered nurse anesthetist

CRPC: chartered retirement planning counselor

CRR: Continuing Review Report

CRRN: certified rehabilitation registered nurse

CRRN-A: certified rehabilitation registered nurse–advanced

CRTT: certified respiratory therapist technician

CRVS: California Relative Value Studies

CS: customer satisfaction

CSHCN: children with special health care needs

CSI, 1961: Commissioners Standard Industrial Mortality Table, 1961

CSI: claims status inquiry

CSI: Customer Satisfaction Index

CSO: clinical services organization

CSO: Commissioners Standard Ordinary Mortality Table

CSR: Center for Scientific Review

CSR: cost summary review

CST: certified surgical technologist

CSW: clinical social worker

CTA: Chain of Trust Agreement

CTSU: Cancer Trial Support Unit

CUA: cost utility analysis

CUC: Conference of Urban Counties

CUR: current unreduced rate

CUREX: current unreduced expenses

CUWI: current unvalidated wage items

CV: cost variance

CVA: certified valuation analysts

CVPA: cost volume profit analysis

CWCO: current worker's compensation offset

CWF: common working file

CWT: compensated work therapy

CY: computation year
CY: current (calendar) year

D

DA: date of admission
DA: direct assistance
DA: disability assistance
DAA: drug addition/alcohol
DABPS: diplomate American Board of Podiatric Surgery
DAC: disabled adult child
DACUS: death, alert, control, and update system
DAW: dispense as written
DB: death benefit
DB: direct broker
DBL: disability benefit law
DBO: death benefit only
DBR: daily board and room hospital benefit
DBRHB: daily board and room hospital benefit
DC: diagnostic code
DC: differential cost
DC: direct cost
DC: disabled child
DC: doctor of chiropractic
DC: dual choice
DCA: deferred compensation administrator
DCA: duplicate confirmation administrator
DCC: Data Content Committee
DCC: debt cancellation contract
DCF: date claim filed
DCG: diagnostic cost group
DCH: Department of Community Health

DCHV: Domiciliary Care for Homeless Veterans
DCI: detailed claim information
DCI: duplicate coverage inquiry
DCN: document control number
DCO: direct contracting organization
DCOM: distributed component object model
DD: data dictionary
DD: developmental disability or developmental delay
DDC: Developmental Disabilities Council
DDE: direct data entry
DDPC: Developmental Disabilities Planning Council
DDR: discharged during referral
DDS: dependent data suffix
DDS: disability determination system
DDS: doctor of dental surgery
DE: disability examiner
DE: dual entitlement
DEA: Department of Elderly Affairs
DEA: Drug Enforcement Agency
DeCC: Dental Content Committee
DED: Disability Evaluation Division
DEERS: Defense Enrollment Eligibility Reporting System
DEFRA: Deficit Reduction Act
DEMS: dual entitlement maintenance system
DEQ: disability earnings query
DEQY: detailed earnings query
DES: data encryption standard
DESI: drug efficiency study and implementation
DFQC: deemed federal quarters of coverage

DGEMS: Documentation Guidelines for Evaluation Management Services

DHAC: Department of Health and Aged Care

DHANP: diplomate of Homeopathic Academy of Naturopathic Physicians

DHHS: Department Health and Human Services

DHO: disability hearing officer

DHS: Department of Health and Human Services

DHS: designated health services

DI: disability insurance

DI: disabled individual

DI: double indemnity

DIB: disability insurance benefit(s)

DIBCESS: disability cessation

DIC: dependency and indemnity compensation

DIC: disability indicator code

DIF: DMERC Information Form

Dipl Ac: diplomate of acupuncture

Dipl CH: diplomate in Chinese herbology

DIRCON: direct contact

DISML: Disability Insurance State Manual

DISPRO: disproportionate share

DITC: Disability Insurance Training Council

DIWC: disabled individual, worker, or child

DKA: did not keep appointment

DLI: date last insured

DLN: document locator number

DLP: date of last payment

DM: direct measurement

DM: divisor months

DMACS: DMERC Medicare automated claims system

DMAIC: define, measure, analyze, improve, and control

DMC: disabled minor child

DMCA: Digital Millennium Copyright Act

DMD: data management division

DMD: doctor of dental medicine

DME: durable medical equipment

DMEPOS: durable medical equipment, prosthetics/orthotics, and supplies

DMERC: durable medical equipment regional carriers

DMIS: Defense Medical Information System

DMW: deemed military wages

DN: discrepancy notice

DN: distinguished name

DNH: deceased number holder

DNR: do not renew

DNR: do not resuscitate

DO: doctor of osteopathy

DOA: date of admission

DOA: dead on arrival

DOB: date of birth

DOC: died of other causes

DOD: date of death

DoD: Department of Defense

DOE: date of entitlement

DOE: date of examination

DOE: Department of Education

DOE: direct order entry

DOH: Department of Health (See HHS)

DOI: Department of Insurance

DOJ: Department of Justice

DOL: Department of Labor

DON: Director of Nursing

DOR: date of receipt
DOS: date of service
DOS: date of surgery
DOSRL: date of suspension or termination
DOT: date of transfer
DOV: date of voucher
DPA: data protection authority
DPC: Discharge Planning Committee
DPH: Department of Public Health
DPH: doctor of public health
DPM: doctor of podiatric medicine
DPN: designated provider network
DPP: deferred payment plan
DPR: drug price review
DPT: days per thousand
DQA: director of quality assurance
DRA: Deficit Reduction Act
DRC: delayed retirement credits
DRC: diagnostic related category
DRG: diagnosis-related group
DRL: Directory of Licensure Requirements
DRP: Disclosure Reporting Page
DrPH: doctor of public health
DRS: data retrieval system
DRS: Designated Record Set
DRS: Disability Review Section
DS: directional services
DS: disabled spouse
DS: disproportionate share
DS: Downs' syndrome
DSA: digital signature algorithm
DSC: doctor of surgical chiropody
DSc: doctor of science
DSCSHN: Division of Services for Children With Special Health Needs
DSH: disproportionate share hospital

DSM: *Diagnostic and Statistical Manual of Mental Disorders*
DSM: disease state management
DSMB: Department of Safety and Monitoring Board
DSM-III: *Diagnostic & Statistics Manual of Mental Disorders* (3rd ed.)
DSM-IV: *Diagnostic & Statistics Manual of Mental Disorders* (4th ed.)
DSMO: Designated Standard Maintenance Organization
DSP: demisit-sine-prole, or died without issue
DSS: decision support system
DSS: Department of Social Services
DSS: digital signature standard
DSTU: draft standards for trial use
DTC: direct to consumer
DTF: dental treatment facility
DTR: dental treatment room
DTx: day treatment
DUA: date use agreement
DUE: drug use evaluation
DUMERC: durable medical equipment regional carriers
DUR: drug use/utilization reviews
DUR: drug utilization review
DVE: diagnostic vocational evaluation
DVR: data validation reviews
DWB: disabled widow(er) benefits
DWI: driving while intoxicated
DX: diagnosis

E

EA: evaluate and advise
EAC: estimated acquisition cost

EACH: essential access community hospital

EAP: emergency advanced payment

EAP: Employee Assistance Program

EBM: evidenced-based medicine

EBRI: Employee Benefit Research Institute

EC: electronic commerce

EC: Emergency Center

EC: environmental control

ECAP: electronic certification automated processing

ECF: extended care facility

ECHO: electronic computer health oriented

ECI: employment cost index

ECP: eligible contract participants

ECR: efficient consumer response

ED: Education Department

ED: Emergency Department

ED: emotionally disturbed

EdD: doctor of education

EDD: enhanced due diligence

EDGAR: Electronic Data Gathering, Analysis and Retrieval

EDI: electronic data interchange

EDIFACT: Electronic Data Interchange for Administrations, Commerce and Trade

EDIINT: electronic data interchange-internet integration

EDP: electronic data processing

EDS: electronic data systems

EEOC: Equal Employment Opportunity Commission

EER: eligibility enrollment screen

EFA: Epilepsy Foundation of America

EFT: electronic funds transfer

EGHP: employer group health plan

EHNAC: Electronic Healthcare Network Accreditation Commission

EHO: emerging healthcare organization

EHR: electronic health record

EI: economic index

EIN: employer identification number

EIS: executive information system

EKG: electrocardiogram

E/M: evaluation and management

EMC: electronic media claims

EMR: electronic medical record

EMR: experience modification rating

EMS: emergency management services

EMS: emergency medical service

EMTALA: Emergency Medical Treatment and Active Labor Act

ENA: Emergency Nurses Association

ENDOP: end of month control and summary operations

ENT: ear, nose, and throat

EO: errors and omissions

EOB: Explanation of Benefits

EOC: episode of care

EOC: evidence of coverage

EOC: Explanation of Coverage

EOD: established onset date

EOD: established onset of disability

EOI: evidence of insurability

EOM: end of month

EOMB: Explanation of Medical Benefits

EOQC: economic order quantity cost

EOR: explanation of review

EOS: economy of scale

EOY: end of year

EP: earned premium

EP: essential person

EPA: Environmental Protection Agency

EPE: extended period of eligibility

EPEA: expense per equivalent admission

EPF: electronic patient folder

EPHI: electronic protected health information

EPIC: Electronic Privacy Information Center

EPMPM: encounters per member per month

EPMPY: encounters per member per year

EPO: exclusive provider organization

EPSCoR: Experimental Program to Stimulate Competitive Research

EPSDT: early and periodic screening, diagnosis, and treatment

EQRO: external quality review organization

ER: earnings record

ER: emergency room

ERA: electronic remittance advice

ERA: Electronic Research Administration

ERA: expense reimbursement allowance

ERISA: Employee Retirement Income Security Act of 1974

ERL: electronic receipt listing

ERM: electronic record management

ERN: electronic remittance notice

ERNIF: earnings records not in file

ERP: Education Recognition Program

ERP: extended reporting policy

ERPSDT: early periodic screening diagnostic testing

ERTA: Economic Recovery Tax Act of 1981

ES: emergency services

ESDE: environmental safety data exchange

ESIGN: Electronic Signature in Global and National Commerce Act

ESOP: employee stock ownership plan

ESOT: employee stock ownership trust

ESQ: entitlement status query

ESRD: end-stage renal dialysis

ESRD: end-stage renal disease

ESS: enhanced security services

ESWL: extracorporeal shock wave lithotripsy

ETG: episodic treatment group

EtOH: alcohol on breath

EUROMED-ETS: Trusted Third Party Services for Healthcare in Europe

EUS: Earning Utilization Statement

EVOIL: economic value of individual life

EXD: exact duplicate

EXP: expedited appeals

EY: elapsed years

EY: eligibility years

F

FA: fiscal agent

FA: fraud and abuse

FAA: Federal Arbitration Act

FAAAI: Fellow of the American Academy of Allergy and Immunology

FAAFP: Fellow of the American Academy of Family Physicians

FAAN: Fellow of American Academy of Nurses

FAAN: Fellow of the American Academy of Neurology

FAAO: Fellow of the American Academy of Ophthalmology

FAAO: Fellow of the American Academy of Osteopathy

FAAOS: Fellow of the American Academy of Orthopedic Surgeons

FAAP: Fellow of the American Academy of Pediatrics

FAC: facility access controls

FAC: facility administration costs

FAC: freestanding ambulatory care

FACCP: Fellow of the American College of Chest Physicians

FACD: Fellow of the American College of Dentists

FACE: Fellow of the American College of Endocrinology

FACES-II: Family Adaptability and Cohesion Evaluation Scales, Version II

FACFAS: Fellow of the American College of Foot and Ankle Surgeons

FACN: Fellow of the American College of Neuropsychiatrists

FACOEP: Fellow of the American College of Osteopathic Emergency Physicians

FACOFP: Fellow of the American College of Osteopathic Family Physicians

FACOG: Fellow of the American College of Obstetricians and Gynecologists

FACOI: Fellow of the American College of Osteopathic Internists

FACOOG: Fellow of the American College of Osteopathic Obstetricians and Gynecologists

FACOP: Fellow of the American College of Osteopathic Pediatricians

FACOS: Fellow of the American College of Osteopathic Surgeons

FACP: Fellow of the American College of Physicians

FACP: final administrative cost proposal

FACPE: Fellow American College of Physician Executives

FACR: Fellow of the American College of Radiologists

FACS: Fellow of the American College of Surgeons

FACT: facility and activity center tracking

FACT: full account query

FAHS: Federation of American Health System

FAIR: fair access to insurance requirements

FALU: Fellow, Academy of Life Underwriters

FAOAO: Fellow of the American Osteopathic Academy of Orthopedics

FAOAS: Fellow of the American Osteopathic Academy of Sclerotherapy

FAOCA: Fellow of the American Osteopathic College of Anesthesiologists

FAOCAI: Fellow of the American Osteopathic College of Allergy and Immunology

FAOCD: Fellow of the American Osteopathic College of Dermatology

FAOCP: Fellow of the American Osteopathic College of Pathologists

FAOCPM: Fellow of the American Osteopathic College of Preventive Medicine

FAOCPR: Fellow of the American Osteopathic College of Proctology

FAOCR: Fellow of the American Osteopathic College of Radiology

FAOCRH: Fellow of the American Osteopathic College of Rheumatology

FAOCRM: Fellow of the American Osteopathic College of Rehabilitation Medicine

FAOSSM: Fellow of the American Orthopedic Society for Sports Medicine

FASA: Federated Ambulatory Surgery Association

FASB: Financial Accounting Standards Board

FB: fringe benefits

FBM: first benefit month

FBR: Federal Benefits Rates— Title XVI

FC: fixed cost

FCA: False Claims Act

FCCCD: Fair Credit and Charge Card Disclosure Act

FCER: Full Claims Earnings Record

FCH: family care home

FCII: Fellow of the Chartered Insurance Institute

FCMC: family-centered maternity care

FCN: financial control number

FCOVD: Fellow of the College of Optometrists in Vision Development

FCPA: Foreign Corrupt Practices Act

FCRA: Fair Credit Reporting Act

FDA: Food and Drug Administration

FDCPA: Fair Debt Collection Practices Act

FDO: formula-driven overpayment

FECA: Federal Employee's Compensation Act

FEHBP: Federal Employees Health Benefit Program

FEIN: federal employee identification number

FEMA: Federal Emergency Management Agency

FEP: Federal Employee Program

FERPA: Family Educational Rights and Privacy Act

FFP: federal financial participation

FFS: fee-for-service

FH: fair hearing

FHFMA: Fellow Healthcare Financial Management Association

FI: fiscal intermediary

FIA: Fellow of the Institute of Actuaries

FIB: Father's Insurance Benefits— Title II

FIC: fraternal insurance counselor

FICA: Federal Insurance Contributions Act

FICC: Fellow of the International College of Chiropractors

FIG: fiscal intermediary group

FIPS: federal information processing standard

FLA: federal living arrangements

FLMI: Fellow of the Life Management Institute

FLSA: Fair Labor Standards Act

FMAP: federal medical assistance percentage

FMAX: family maximum

FMC: Foundation for Medical Care

FMI: functional medical and integration management

FMLA: Family Medical Leave Act

FMO: financial management office

FMR: focused medical review

FMRC: Family Medicine Research Center

FNAAOM: Fellow of the National Academy of Acupuncture and Oriental Medicine

FOAB: federal old age benefits

FOCOO: Fellow American Osteopathic College of Ophthalmology and Otolaryngology

FOIA: Freedom of Information Act

FORE: Foundation for Osteoporosis Research and Education.

FP: family planning

FPA: Financial Planning Association

FPA: free of particular average

FPD: Federation of Physicians and Dentists

FPS: federal information processing standard

FQAM: Financial Quality Assurance Manager

FQC: federal quarters of coverage

FQHC: federally qualified health center

FQHMO: federally qualified health maintenance organization

FR: Federal Register

FRC: Federal Records Center

FSA: Fellow of the Society of Actuaries

FSA: flexible spending account

FSMB: Federation of State Medical Boards

FSR: Financial Status Report

FSS: frequent and substantially serviced

FTA: full-time attendance

FTAM: file transfer, access, and management

FTC: Federal Trade Commission

FTE: full-time equivalent

FTP: file transfer protocol

FTS: full-time student

FU: follow up

FUTA: Federal Unemployment Tax Act

FWA: federal wide assurance

FY: fiscal year

G

GA: general agent

GA: general assistance

GAAP: generally accepted accounting principles

GAAS: generally accepted auditing standards

GAB: General Adjustment Bureau

GAI: guaranteed annual income

GALEN: generalized architecture for languages, encyclopedias, and nomenclature

GAMA: General Agents and Managers Association

GAMC: General Agents and Managers Conference

GAO: General Accounting Office

GCG: good clinical guidelines

GCP: good clinical practices

GCRC: general research clinical group

GDP: gross domestic product

GDSA: governor-designated shortage area

GEC: geriatrics extended care

GEHA: Government Employees Hospital Association

GEHR: good electronic health record

GEP: guaranteed enrollment period

GEQC: government employment quarters of coverage

GERP: Geographic Expense Reimbursement Plan

GHAA: Group Health Association of America

GHP: group health plan

GLBA: Gramm-Lech-Bliley Act

GME: graduate medical education

GNP: gross national product

GOC: gynecologic oncology group

GOE: general office expense

GP: general practitioner

GPA: general public assistance

GPCI: Geographic Practice Cost Index

GPO: Group Purchasing Organization

GPR: gross profit margin

GPWW: group practice without walls

GSA: The Gerontological Society of America

GTEPS: General Telephone Electric Processing System

GUI: graphical user interface

GWVIS: Gulf War Veterans Information System

GWW: group without walls

H

HA: health affairs

HA: hearing assisted

HALLEX: Hearings, Appeals, and Litigation Law

HAP: Hospital Accreditation Program

HAR: hospital-associated representative

HAS: hospital administration services

HAT: hospital arrival time

HB: hospital based

HBA: Hill Burton Act

HBCS: Hospital Billing and Collection Service

HBO: Hospital Benefits Organization

HBP: hospital-based physician

HC: health care

HC: home care

HCAD: health care administrators

HCBWP: Home and Community-Based Waiver Program

HCC: hard copy claim

HCC: hierarchical coexisting condition

HCC: hierarchical condition category

HCCA: health care commuting area

HCCMC: Health Care Code Maintenance Committee

HCD: health care delivery

HCE: health care establishment

HCF: health care finder

HCFA: Health Care Financing Administration

HCFA 1500: Universal Billing Form

HCG: health care group

HCH: Health Care for the Homeless

HCHV: Health Care for Homeless Veterans

HCIA: health care investment analysts

HCIN: health care information network

HCIRC: Health Care Information Resource Center

HCIS: health care information systems

HCO: health care organization

HCPCS: HCFA Common Procedure Coding System

HCPP: health care prepayment plan

HCPR: health care provider records

HCQIA: Health Care Quality Improvement Act

HCQII: Health Care Quality Improvement Initiative

HCQIP: Health Care Quality Improvement Program

HCR: health care reform

HCRIS: Hospital Cost Report Information System

HCTA: health care trust account

HCTP: Health Consumer Training Program

HCUP: Healthcare Cost and Utilization Project

HDC: HCFA Data Center

HDE: humanitarian device exemption

HDI: Health Data Institute

HDS: health delivery system

HE: hearing examiner

HEA: home emergency assistance

HEAL: health education assistance loan

HEC: Health Eligibility Center

HEDIC: Health Electronic Data Interchange Corporation

HEDIS: Health Plan and Employer Data and Information Set

HEDITP: healthcare electronic data interchange trading partner

HEF: Health Education Foundation

HEP: high error profile

HERC: Health Economic Research Center

HEZ: health economic zone

HFMA: Healthcare Financial Management Association

HFPA: health facilities planning area

HFS: American Hospital Formulary Service

HFSG: healthcare finance study group

HH: hold harmless

HHA: home health agency

HHA: home healthcare agency

HHC: home health care

HHC: home health coverage

HHHA: homemaker home health aid

HHIC: Hawaii (Home) Health Information Corporation

HHL: home health line

HHO: Home Health Organization

HHOS: Medicare Health Outcomes Survey

HHPP: home health prospective payment

HHRG: home health resource group

HHS: Department of Health and Human Services (also DHHS)

HHSBG: Preventative Health and Human Services Block Grant

HHSSA: Home Health Services and Staffing Association

HI: health insurance

HI: hospital insurance

HIA: Health Insurance Part A

HIAA: Health Insurance Association of America

HIAM: Health Insurance Alpha Microfilm

HIB: Health Insurance Part B

HIB: hospital insurance benefits

HIBCC: Health Industry Business Communications Council

HIBRR: health insurance benefits rights and responsibilities

HIC: health information center

HIC: health insurance claim

HICA: health insurance claim account

HICDA: Hospital International Classification of Diseases

HICN: health insurance claim number

HICOIN: Health Insurance Central Office Inquiries Network

HICR: health insurance correction request

HIDA: Health Industry Distributors Association

HIDAD: health insurance daily actions dispersion

HIDUC: health insurance daily update control

HIDUP: health insurance daily update program

HIE: health insurance enrollment

HIEDIC: Health Industry EDI Corporation

HIFA: health insurance flexibility and accountability

HIGLAS: healthcare integrated ledger accounting system

HII: Health Insurance Institute

HIIM: Health Insurance Inquiries Manual

HIM: health information management

HIMA: Health Industry Manufacturers Association

HIMBEX: health insurance master billing exception

HIMEX: health insurance miscellaneous exception control

HIMF: Health Insurance Master File

HIMICS: Health Insurance Management Information Control System

HIMR: Health Insurance Master Record

HIMSS: Health Information and Management Systems Society

HIN: health industry number

HIN: health insurance network

HINN: hospital-issued notice of noncoverage

HIO: health insuring (insurance) organization

HIP: health insurance pamphlet

HIPAA: Health Insurance Portability and Accountability Act

HIPC: Health Insurance Purchasing Cooperative

HIPDB: Healthcare Integrity and Protection Data Bank

HIPPS: health insurance prospective payment system

HIQA: health insurance quality award

HIQR: health insurance online query response

HIRAM: health insurance reinstating alphabetic master

HIRD: health insurance reduction data

HIRO: health insurance regional office

HIRTF: health insurance reform task force

HIS: health information systems

HIS: health insurance system

HIS: Health Interview Survey

HISB: Health Informatics Standards Board

HISCC: Healthcare Informatics Standards Coordinating Committee

HISCR: health insurance screening and cross-referencing

HISDG: Health Information Systems Development Guide

HISKEW: health insurance skeleton eligibility write-off

HISM: Handbook of Information Security Management

HISMI: health insurance/ supplemental medical insurance

HISP: health infrastructure support program

HISPP: health informatics system planning panel

HISS: health insurance segmented sort system

HITF: Health Insurance Trust Fund

HIUM: health insurance utilization master

HIURPS: health insurance utilization records processing system

HIV: human immunodeficiency virus

HL7: health level 7

HLLP: hybrid lower layer protocol

HLQ: high level qualifier

HMDI: Hospital Medical and Dental Indemnity Corporation

HMO: health maintenance organization

HMOAA: Health Maintenance Organization Assistance Act

HMPSA: health manpower shortage area

HMQ: health insurance/master beneficiary record status query

HMSA: health manpower shortage area

HO: hearing officer

HOH: head of household

HON: Health on the Net Foundation

HOPD: Hospital Outpatient Department

HOPPS: hospital outpatient prospective payment system

HOR: home outcomes research

HOST: healthcare open systems and trials

HP: historical payment

HP: history and physical

HPA: health policy agenda

HPAC: Health Policy Advisory Center

HPB: historic payment basis

HPC: Health Policy Council

HPG: homogeneous patient groups

HPMS: health plan management system

HPPC: Health Plan Purchasing Corporation

HPPC: Health Plan Purchasing Cooperative

HPR: hospital peer review

HPSA: health professions shortage areas

HPSA: health provision shortage area

HR: hospital record

HRA: health risk assessment

HRAC: Human Research Advisory Committee

HRET: Hospital Research and Educational Trust

HREX: Human Radiation Experiments Information Management System

HRF: health-related facility

HRG: health research group

HRGA: high rate geographical area

HRP: holding the record open

HRPP: human research protection program

HRQL: health-related quality of life

HRSA: Health Resources and Services Administration

HSA: health savings account

HSA: health services agreement

HSA: health systems agency

HSOR: health services operations & readiness

HSP: health service plan

HSP: hospital specific portion

HSQB: health standards and quality bureau

HSR: hospital specific rate

HST: human subject training

HTML: hyper text markup language

HUB: historically underutilized business

HUD: Housing and Urban Development

HUD: humanitarian use device

HURA: health underserved rural area

HYBC: hypothetical base year calculations

I

IAAHU: International Association of Accident Health Underwriters

IADR: International Association for Dental Research

IAFP: International Association for Financial Planning

IAHU: International Association of Health Underwriters

IAM: information access management

IAP: interim assistance program

IAR: interim assistance reimbursement

IASP: International Association for the Study of Pain

IASS: Insurance Accounting and Statistical Society

IBC: Institutional Biosafety Committee

IBFS: interim billing and follow-up system

IBIA: International Biometric Association

IBNR: incurred but not reported

IBNRL: incurred but not reported losses

IC: indirect cost

ICA: International Claim Association

ICC: integrated case consultation

ICC: Interagency Coordinating Council

ICD: institute centers and division

ICD-9-CM: *International Classification of Diseases* (9th Rev. Clinical Modification)

ICD-10: *International Classification of Diseases* (10th Ed.)

ICECI: International Classification of External Causes of Injury

ICED: Index of Co-Existent Disease

ICF: intermediate care facility

ICF: International Cancer Foundation

ICFIMR: intermediate care facility including mental retardation

ICF/MR: intermediate care facility for the mentally retarded

ICF-MR: intermediate care facility-mental retardation

ICHP: Institute for Child Health Policy

ICIDH: International Classification of Impairments, Disability, and Handicaps

ICIDH-2: International Classification of Functioning, Disability, and Health

ICMA: Individual Case Management Association

ICN: internal control number

ICO: initial claims operation

ICPC-2: international classification of primary care

ICR: intelligent character recognition

ICRETT: International Cancer Technology Transfer Fellowships

ICRS: Initial Claims Review System

ICSI: Institute for Clinical Systems Integration

ICU: Intensive Care Unit

ID: identification

ID: initial determination

IDC: indirect costs

IDE: investigational device exemption

IDEA: Individuals With Disabilities Education Act

IDMA: Insurance Data Management Association

IDN: integrated network

IDS: integrated delivery system

IDTF: independent diagnostic testing facility

IEP: individual education program or plan

IEP: initial enrollment period

IETF: Internet engineering task force

IFCC: Institute for Family-Centered Care

IFS: Intensive Family Services

IFSP: individual family service plan

IGI: intergovernmental initiative

IGP: individual group practice

IHC: Internet Healthcare Coalition

IHCEBI: Interactive Health Care Eligibility Benefits Inquiry

IHCEBR: Interactive Health Care Eligibility Benefits Response

IHDS: integrated health delivery system

IHE: Integrating the Healthcare Enterprise

IHO: Integrated Healthcare Organization

IHP: individual habilitation plan or program

IHP: individual health plan

IHS: Indian Health Services

IHS: integrated healthcare system

IIA: Institute of Internal Auditors

IIA: Insurance Institute of America, Inc.

IIAA: Independent Insurance Agents Association

IIC: inflation index charge-customary

IIHI: individually identifiable health information

III: Insurance Information Institute

IIS: International Insurance Seminars, Inc.

IL: independent living

ILC: independent living center

iMBA: Institute of Medical Business Advisors, Inc.

IME: independent medical evaluation

IME: indirect medical education

IME: indirect medical evaluation (examination)

IMG: international medical graduates

IMO: integrated multiple option

IMPACC: intermediate payment critical case

IMS: integrated medical system

IMSDN: Integrated Medical Services Digital Network

IMSV: independent medical software vendors

INANE: International Academy of Nursing Editors

IND: investigational new drug

INH: in-office hours

INN: investigational nonproprietary names

INSECP: Internet security protocol

IOL: intra ocular lens

IOM: Institute of Medicine

IOS: intensity of service

IOV: initial office visit

IP: independent psychologist

IP: in-patient

IP: Internet protocol

IPA: independent physician association

IPA: individual practice association

IPFA: Incentive Program for Fraud and Abuse

IPL: independent physiological laboratory

IPN: Integrated Provider Network:

IPO: Individual Practice Organization

IPO: insured product option

IPO: Integrated Provider Organization

IPP: individual practice program

IPS: interim payment system

IQ: intelligence quotient

IR: income resources

IR: information and referral

IR: inherent reasonableness

IR: interest rate

IRAG: Integrated Healthcare Advisory Group

IRB: Institutional Review Board

IRC: Internal Revenue Code

IRD: independent research and development

IRF: inpatient rehabilitation facilities

IRIS: Insurance Regulatory Information System

IRS: Internal Revenue Service

IRVEN: Inpatient Rehabilitation Validation and Entry System

IRWE: impairment-related work expense

IS: information systems

ISHTAE: Implementing Secure Healthcare Telematic Applications in Europe

ISIS: Information Society Initiative for Standardization

ISM: in kind support and maintenance

ISMHO: International Society for Mental Health Online

ISN: Integrated Service Network

ISO: information security officer

ISO: Insurance Services Office

ISO: Internal Standards Organization

ISSIC: intensity of service, severity of illness criteria

IT: information technology

ITSEC: Information Technology Security Evaluation Criteria

IVR: interactive voice response

IXRDA: Independent X-Ray Dealers Association

J

JCAHO: Joint Commission on the Accreditation of Healthcare Organizations

JCWAA: Jobs Creation and Worker Assistance Act
JHITA: Joint Healthcare Information Technology Alliance
JIT: just in time
JTPA: Jobs Training Partnership Act
JV: journal voucher

K

KBS: knowledge-based system
KYC: know your customers

L

L2TP: layer 2 tunneling protocol
LA: living arrangement
LAc: licensed acupuncturist
LAP: last action processed
LBB: Legislative Budget Board
LCD: local coverage determination
LCDC: licensed chemical dependency counselor
LCED: level of care eligibility determination
LCER: Limiting Charge Exception Report
LCL: lowest charge
LCP: licensed clinical psychologist
LCSW: licensed clinical social worker
LD: learning disabilities or learning disabled
LDA: Learning Disabilities Association
LDO: legally defined overpayment
LEA: local education agency
LEP: limited English proficiency
LEP: low error profile
LFS: Laboratory Fee Schedule

LGHP: large group health plan
LHD: local health department
LISH: living in same household
LLB: bachelor of laws
LLP: limited liability partnership
LLP: limited license practitioner
LM: licensed midwife
LMER: last met earnings requirement
LMFT: licensed marriage and family therapist
LMHC: licensed mental health counselor
LMP: licensed massage practitioner
LMRP: Local Medical Review Policy
LMT: licensed massage therapist
LOA: leave of absence
LOB: line of business
LOI: Letter of Intent
LOINC: logical observation and identifier names and codes
LOS: length of stay
LOTR: licensed occupational therapist
LP: licensed psychologist
LPC: licensed professional counselor
LPHR: Act Local Public Health Reorganization
LPN: licensed practical nurse
LPT: legislative policy team
LRA: linear regression analysis
LRE: least restrictive environment
LRRA: Liability Risk Retention Act
LSC: life safety code
LSDP: lump sum death payment
LSW: licensed social worker
LTAC: long-term acute care
LTC: long-term care
LTCF: long-term care facility
LTCH: long-term care hospital

LTCU: Long-Term Care Unit
LTD: long-term disability
LTHHCP: Long-Term Home Health Care Program
LUPA: low utilization payment adjustment
LVN: licensed vocational nurse

M

MA: master of arts
MA: medical advisor
MA: medical assistance
MA: medical assistant
MAAA: member, American Academy of Actuaries
MAAC: maximum allowable actual charge
MABC: medical activity-based costing
MAC: major ambulatory category
MAC: master addiction counsel
MAC: maximum allowable charge
MAC: maximum allowable cost
MAC: Message Authentication Code
MAC: monitored anesthesia care
MACL: maximum allowable cost list
MADC: mean average daily census
MAF: medical assisted facility
MASS: medical analysis support system
MB: Medical Bureau
MBA: master's in business administration
MBA: Medical Business Advisors, Inc.
MBC: monthly benefit credited
MBHP: Managed Behavioral Health Program
MBP: monthly benefit payment
MBR: Master Beneficiary Record

MBRS: minority biomedical research support
M + C: Medicare plus Choice
MC: marginal change
MC: marginal cost
MC: medical consultant
MC: mixed cost
MCAT: Medical College Admissions Test
MCBA: masters certified business appraiser
MCBS: Medicare Current Beneficiary Survey
MCCA: Medicare Catastrophic Coverage Act
MCCF: Medical Care Collections Fund
MCE: medical care evaluation
MCH: maternal and child health
MCM: Medicare Carriers Manual
MCO: Managed Care Organization
MCP: Managed Care Program
MCPG: medical college physician's group
MCPI: Medical Consumer Price Index
MCR: medical cost ratio
MCR: modified community rating
MCS: medical consultant staff
MD(H): licensed homeopathic physician
MD: medical doctor
MDC: major diagnostic category
MDCP: Medically Dependent Children's Program
MDD: maximum daily dose
MDDRG: MD (Physician) diagnostic-related group
MDG: major diagnostic group
MDG: message design guidelines group

MDH: Medicare dependent hospital

MDN: message disposition notification

MDO: monthly debit ordinary

MDS: Minimum Data Set

MDSB: Medical Devices Standards Board

ME: maximum efficiency

ME: medical examiner

ME: medical expert

ME: mortality expense

Med: master of education

MEDISGRIPS: medical illness severity group system

MEDIX: medical data interchange

MedPAC: Medicare Payment Advisory Commission

Med-PAR: Medicare Provider Analysis and Review File

MEDPARD: Medicare Participating Suppliers Directory

MEDsupp: Medicare supplement insurance

MED-SURG: medical-surgical

MEDTEP: Medical Treatment Effectiveness Program

MEI: Medicare Economic Index

MEP: medical error profile

MEPS: Medical Expenditure Panel Survey

MER: Medical Evidence Record

MERFA: Medicare Education and Regulatory Fairness Act

MET: multiple employer trust

MEVA: medical economic value added

MEWA: multiple employer welfare arrangements

MF: medical foundation

MFAIC: Medicare Fraud and Abuse Information Coordinator

MFC: monetary and financial code

MFS: Medicare fee schedule

MFT: marriage and family therapist

MGCRB: Medicare Geographic Classification Review Board

MGMA: Medical Group Management Association

MHA: master's in healthcare administration

MHB: maximum hospital benefit

MH/CD: mental health/chemical dependency

MHDC: Massachusetts Health Data Consortium

MHDI: Minnesota Health Data Institute

MHR: mental health research

MHRH: mental health and retardation hospital

MH/SA: mental health/substance abuse

MHSS: military health service system

MHT: mental health therapist

MIA: medically indigent adult

MIA: Medicare inpatient adjudication

MIB: Medical Information Bureau

MIB: medical information bus

MIB: mother's insurance benefits

MICRA: Medical Injury Compensation Reform Act

MICU: Medical Intensive Care Unit

MID: medical assistance identification number

MIE: medical improvement expected

MILDEP: military department

MIME: Multipurpose Internet Mail Extension

MIRC: Medical Information Resource Center

MIRT: Myeloma Institute for Research and Therapy

MIS: management information system

MIS: medical information system

MISM: master of information systems management

ML: management latitude

MLF: maximum foreseeable loss

MLLP: minimal lower layer protocol

MLP: mid level practitioner

MLR: medical loss ratio

MLS: maximum loss expectancy

MM: member month

MMCO: Medicaid Managed Care Organization

MMDN: Managed Medical Data Networks

MMIS: Medical Management Information Systems

MMRF: Multiple Myeloma Research Foundation

MMWR: Morbidity and Mortality Weekly Report

MN: master of nursing

MOA: Medicare outpatient adjudication

MOEL: month of election

MOF: month of filing

MOSS: MIME Object Security Services

MOU: Memorandum of Understanding

MP: minimum premium

MP: multiperil premium

MPACT: Minimum Data Set for Post Acute Care Tool

MPCA: Medical Practice Cost Analysis

MPCA: Medical Project Cost Analysis

MPE: Medicaid presumptive eligibility

MPFS: Medicare Physician Fee Schedule

MPFSDB: Medicare Physician Fee Schedule Database

MPH: master of public health

MPI: Master Patient Index

MPI: Medicare provider identifier

MPIES: Medicare Physician Identification and Eligibility System

MPL: maximum probable loss

MPR: medical practice risk

MPV: minimum price variance

MR: management review

MR: marginal revenue

MR: medical records

MR: medical reexamination

MR: medical review

MRA: medical records administrator

MRD: Medical Records Department

MRE: medical research endowment

MRI: Medical Records Institute

MRN: Medicare Remittance Notice

MRP: maximum reimbursement point

MS: margin of safety

MS: master of science

MSA: medical savings account

MSD: master of science in dentistry

MSDS: Material Safety Data Sheet

MSFS: master's of science degree in financial services

MSGP: multi-specialty group practice

MSHJ: medical staff hospital joint venture

MS-HUG: Microsoft Health Users Group

MSN: master of science in nursing

MSN: Medicare Summary Notice

MSO: Management Services Organization

MSO: Medical Services Organization

MSP: Medicare secondary payer

MSPH: master of science in public health

MSS: masters in social service

MSS: Medical Social Services

MSS: Medical Source Statement

MSSR: minimum sole survivor rate

MSSW: master of science in social work

MSW: master of social work

MSW: medical social worker

MT: medical technician

MTDC: modified total direct costs

MTF: military treatment facility

MTS: Medicare Transaction System

MU: Marginal Utility

MUA: Medically Underserved Area

MUD: Medially Unnecessary Days

MUR: Medical Utilization Review

MVA: Medical Value Added

MVPC: Minority Veterans Program Coordinators

MVPS: Medicare Volume Performance Standard

MWS: Medical Warning System

N

NA: nursing assistant

NAACCR: North American Association of Central Cancer Registries

NAAOP: National Association for the Advancement of Orthotics & Prosthetics

NAAR: National Alliance for Autism Research

NABCO: National Alliance of Breast Cancer Organizations

NABP: National Association of Boards of Pharmacy

NAC: non-assigned claim

NACCHO: National Association of City and County Health Officials

NADONA: National Association of Directors of Nursing Administration

NAEHCA: National Association of Employers on Health Care Action

NAGNA: National Association for Geriatric Nurse Aides

NAHAM: National Association of Healthcare Access Management

NAHC: National Association for Home Care

NAHC: National Association of Healthcare Consultants

NAHDO: National Association of Health Data Organizations

NAHMOR: National Association of HMO Regulators

NAIA: National Association of Insurance Agents

NAIB: National Association of Insurance Brokers, Incorporated

NAIC: National Association of Insurance Commissioners

NAII: National Association of Independent Insurers

NAIP: National Association of Inpatient Physicians

NAIW: National Association of Insurance Women

NAM: National Association of Manufacturers

NAMES: National Association of Medical Equipment Suppliers

NAMOR: National Association of HMO Regulators

NANDA: North American Nursing Diagnosis Association

NAPFA: National Association of Personal Financial Advisors

NAPH: National Association of Public Hospitals

NAPHS: National Association of Psychiatric Health Systems

NAPHS: National Association of Public Psychiatric Hospitals

NAPM: National Association of Pharmaceutical Manufacturers

NARA: National Archives and Records Administration

NARD: National Association of Retail Druggists

NARSAD: National Alliance for Research on Schizophrenia and Depression

NAS: National Academy of Sciences

NAS: Non-Availability Statement

NASD: National Association of Securities Dealers

NASMD: National Association of State Medicaid Directors

NASW: National Association of Social Workers

NBCCEDP: National Breast and Cervical Cancer Early Detection

NCAHC: National Council on Alternative Healthcare

NCAN: national certified addiction counselor

NCBI: National Center for Biotechnology Information

NCC: national certified counselor

NCCA: National Commission for the Certification of Acupuncturists

NCCAM: National Center for Complimentary and Alternative Medicine

NCCF: National Childhood Cancer Foundation

NCCI: National Correct Coding Initiative Edits

NCCLS: National Committee for Clinical Laboratory Standards

NCCN: National Comprehensive Cancer Network

NCCNHR: National Citizens Coalition for Nursing Home Reform

NCDPD: National Council for Prescription Drug Programs

NCHICA: North Carolina Healthcare Information and Communications Alliance

NCHS: National Center for Health Statistics

NCHS: National Center for Healthcare Statistics

NCHSR: National Center for Health Services Research

NCI: National Cancer Institute

NCMHD: National Center for Minority Health and Health Disparities

NCNR: National Center for Nursing Research

NCPDP: National Council for Prescription Drug Programs

NCPDP: National Council for Prescription Drug Programs

NCQA: National Committee for Quality Assurance

NCSBN: National Council of State Boards of Nursing

NCTR: National Center for Toxicology Research

NCVHS: National Committee for Vital & Health Statistics

ND: doctor of naturopathy

NDA: National Dental Association

NDA: non-disclosure agreement

NDAB: National Diabetes Advisory Board

NDC: National Drug Codes

NDEERS: Native Defense Enrollment Eligibility Reporting System

NE: net earnings

NE: nurse extenders

NEI: National Eye Institute

NeoICU: Neonatal Intensive Care Unit

NF: national formulary

NF: nursing facility

NFA: no further action

NFCA: National Family Caregivers Association

NFLPN: National Federation of Licensed Practical Nurses

NFNA: National Flight Nurses Association

NFP: not-for-profit

NFSNO: National Federation for Specialty Nursing Organizations

NH: number holder (wage earner)

NH: nursing home

NHC: National Health Council

NHCAA: National Health Care Anti-Fraud Association

NHCT: National Healthcare Trust Fund

NHF: National Health Fund

NHF: National Heart Foundation

NHGRI: National Human Genome Research Foundation

NHI: National Health Insurance

NHII: national health information infrastructure

NHIP: National Health Insurance Plan

NHLBI: National Heart, Lung and Blood Institute

NHMA: National Hispanic Medical Association

NHSC: National Health Service Corp

NIA: National Institute on Aging

NIAID: National Institute of Allergy and Infectious Diseases

NIAMSD: National Institute of Arthritis and Musculoskeletal and Skin Diseases

NIBIB: National Institute of Biomedical Imaging and Bioengineering

NIC: nursing intervention classification

NICHD: National Institute of Child Health and Human Development

NICU: Neonatal Intensive Care Unit

NIDA: National Institute on Drug Abuse

NIDCD: National Institute of Deafness and other Communication Disorders

NIDDK: National Institute of Diabetes, Digestive & Kidney Diseases

NIDR: National Institute of Dental Research

NIDRR: National Institute of Disability and Rehabilitative Research

NIF: not in file

NIGMS: National Institute of General Medial Research

NIH: National Institutes of Health

NIMH: National Institute of Mental Health
NINDB: National Institute of Neurological Disease and Blindness
NINDS: National Institute of Neurological Disorders and Stroke
NINR: National Institute of Nursing Research
NIOSH: National Institute for Occupational Safety Institute and Health
NIS: Net Income Statement
NISA: National Insurance Association
NIST: National Institute for Standards and Technology
NLN: National League of Nursing
NLRA: National Labor Relations Act
NLSP: network layer security protocol
NM: doctor of naturopathic medicine
NMA: National Medical Association
NMDS: Nursing Minimum Data Set
NMHCC: National Managed Health Care Congress
NML: National Medical Library (National Library of Medicine)
NMP: non-physician medical practitioner
NMRI: Naval Medical Research Institute
NMSS: National Multiple Sclerosis Foundation
NMW: nurse midwife
NNSA: National Nurses Society on Addiction
NOA: Notice of Admissions
NOBA: Notice of Budget Authority
NOC: not otherwise classified

NOC: Notice of Change
NOC: nursing outcome classification
NOD: Notice of Determination
NOD: Notice of Discipline
NODB: National Optometric Database
NOF: National Osteoporosis Foundation
NOI: Notice of Intent
NOL: not officially lapsed
NOLF: Nursing Organization Liaison Forum
NON-PAR: non-participating provider
NON-PAR: non-practicing physician (provider)
NOS: not on staff
NOS: not otherwise specified
NOT: Notice of Termination
NP: nurse practitioner
NPA: non-par approved (approval)
NPDB: National Practitioner Data Bank
NPF: national provider file
NPI: national provider identifier
NPNA: non-par not approved
NPP: Notice of Privacy Practices
NPPIA: Non-Public Personal Information Act
NPR: Notice of Program Reimbursement
NPRM: Notice of Proposed Rule Making
NPS: National Provider System
NPSR: net patient service revenue
NQA: National Quality Award
NQF: National Quality Forum
NR: not recommended
NRA: normal retirement age
NRC: no repudiation of commitment

NRO: no repudiation of origin

NSA: National Security Agency

NSABP: National Surgical Adjuvant Breast and Bowel Project

NSC: National Supplier Clearinghouse

NSC: no significant change

NSCIA: National Spinal Cord Injury Association

NSF: National Standard Format

NSNA: National Student Nurses Association

NSR: no significant result

NTFHR: National Task Force on Healthcare Reform

NTM: notice to members

NTO: not taken out

NUBC: National Uniform Billing Committee

NUCC: National Uniform Claim Committee

NVPO: National Vaccine Program Office

NW: net worth

NWC: National Workers Compensation Reinsurance Pool

NWDA: National Wholesale Druggists Association

NYD: not yet diagnosed

O

OA: open access

OAA: old-age assistance

OACIS: Open Architecture Clinical Information System

OAM: Office of Alternative Medicine (NIH)

OAS: old age security

OASDHA: Office of the Assistant Secretary of Defense Health Affairs

OASDHI: Old Age, Survivors, Disability, and Health Insurance. See Medicare and SS.

OASDI: Old Age, Survivors, and Disability Insurance. See Social Security.

OASI: Old-Age and Survivors Insurance, or Social Security

OASIS: Outcome and Assessment Information Set

OB: obstetrics

OBQI: outbound-based quality improvement

OBRA: Omnibus Budget Reconciliation Act

OC: opportunity cost

OC: overhead cost

OCA: outstanding claims account

OCC: occupation

OCHAMPUS: Office of Civilian Health and Medical Program of the Uniformed Services

OCHIP: owner controlled health insurance plan

OCI: Office of the Commissioner of Insurance

OCIE: Office of Compliance, Inspections and Examinations

OCL: other carrier liability

OCNA: other carrier name/address

OCR: Office of Civil Rights

OCR: Optical Character Recognition

OCRO: Office of Central Operations

OCT: Office for Clinical Trials

OD: doctor of optometry

ODIO: Office of Disability and International Operations

ODM: operational data model

ODO: Office of Disability Operations

ODPHP: Office of Disease Prevention and Health Promotion

ODR: Office of Direct Reimbursement

OEI: Office of Evaluation and Inspections

OGC: Office of General Counsel

OGR: Office of Governmental Relations

OHAP: Office of HIV/AIDS Policy

OHCA: organized health care arrangement

OHMO: Office of Health Maintenance Organizations

OHRP: Office for Human Research Protections

OHTA: Office of Healthcare Technology Assessment

OIG: Office of the Inspector General

OL: operating leverage

OM: operations and maintenance

OMB: Office of Management and Budget

OMC: Office of Managed Care

OMD: oriental medical doctor

OME: other medical expense

OMG: object management group

OOA: out of area

OON: out of network

OOP: out of pocket

OP: operative report

OP: out patient

OP: over payment

OPDR: outpatient diagnostic rider

OPHC: Office of Prepaid Health Care

OPIR: Office of Program Integrity Review

OPL: other party liability

OPM: Office of Personnel Management

OPOD: Out Patient Department

OPOP: Office of Provider Operations and Procedures

OPPS: Outpatient Prospective Payment System

OR: occupancy rate

OR: operating room

ORA: Omnibus Reconciliation Act

ORAS: Office of Regional Administrative Services

ORF: outpatient rehabilitation facility

ORI: Office of Research Integrity

ORT: Operation Restore Trust

ORWH: Office for Research on Women's Health

OSCAR: Online Survey Certification and Reporting

OSEP: Office of Special Education Programs

OSERS: Office of Special Education and Rehabilitation Services

OSG: Office of the Surgeon General

OSHA: Occupational Safety and Health Administration

OT: occupational therapy (or therapist)

OTA: occupational therapy aid

OTA: Office of Technology Assessment

OTC: over-the-counter

OTR: occupational therapists

OUTH: out of office hour

OVR: Office of Vocational Rehabilitation

OWCP: Office of Worker's Compensation Programs

OWH: Office of Women's Health

P

PA: patient advocacy

PA: Patriot Act

PA: physician's assistant

PA: power of attorney
PA: prior authorization
PA: Privacy Act
PA: Protection and Advocacy for Handicapped Developmentally Disabled Persons
PAAF: Preadmissions Assessment Form
PAC: preauthorized check
PAC: Preadmission Certificate
PACE: performance and cost-efficiency
PACE: Program Advise and Consent Encounter
PACE: Program of All Inclusive Care for the Elderly
PACER: Parents Advocacy Coalition for Educational Rights
PAG: policy advisory group
PAHO: Pan American Health Organization
PAM: patient accounts manager
PAP: patient assessment profile
PAR: participating provider (supplier)
PARI: people actively reaching independence
PARP: participating physician
PAS: preadmission screening
PAS: patient appointing and scheduling
PAS: personal assistance services
PAS: publicly available specifications
PASARR: preadmission screening and annual record review
PASPR: preadmission screening patient recipient
PASS: plan for achieving self-support
PATCH: planned approach to community health

PATH: physician at teaching hospital
PBA: patient-based assessments
PBC: pro bono care
PBM: pharmacy benefits manager
PBRN: Primary Care Based Practice Research Network
PC: professional component
PCA: personal care attendant
PCCM: primary care case management
PCG: physician care groups
PCM: primary care manager
PCN: primary care network
PCO: Patient Choice Organizations
PCP: primary care physician
PCP: primary care provider
PCP: primary care provider or physician
PCPFS: President's Council on Physical Fitness and Sports
PCPM: per contract per month
PC/PM: pharmacy contract/per month
PCR: physician contingency reserve
PCRM: patient care resource management
PCRP: Prostate Cancer Research Program
PCS: personal care services
PCT: private communication technology protocol
PDC: physician-developed criteria
PDR: Physician's Desk Reference
PDT: purchased diagnostic test
PE: post eligibility
PE: post entitlement
PE: practice expense
PEBES: Personal Earnings and Benefit Statement
PEC: Pharmacoeconomic Center
PEC: preexisting condition

PEL: permanent employer leasing
PEL: physician employer leasing
PEM: Privacy-enhanced mail
PEO: permanent employer outsourcing
PEO: physician employer outsourcing
PEP: partial episode payment
PFCRA: Program Fraud Civil Remedies Act
PFE: potential future exposure
PFP: personal financial planner
PGP: prepaid group practice
PGP: pretty good protection (privacy)
PH: partial hospitalization
PH: physician hour
PharmD: doctor of pharmacy
PHC: public health clinic
PhD: doctor of philosophy
PHI: protected health information
PHO: physician hospital organization
PHP: prepaid health plan
PHP: partial hospitalization program
PHP: public health promotion
PHR: public health region
PhRMA: Pharmaceutical Research and Manufacturer's of America
PHS: Public Health Service
PHSA: Public Health Service Act
PI: physically impaired
PI: principal investigator
PI: process improvement
PIA: patient income account
PIA: personal incidental allowance
PIA: primary insurance amount
PIA: professional insurance agent
PIM: Program Integrity Manual

PIN: provider (personal) identification number
PIP: partners in policymaking
PIP: periodic interim payment
PIP: personal injury protection
PIP: physician incentive plan
PIT: pathology information transfer
PIX: patient identifier cross reference
PKAF: public key authentication framework
PKCS: public (private) key cryptography standard
PKI: public (private) key infrastructure
PL: profit and loss
PL: public law
PLR: primary loss retention
PM: preventive maintenance
PM: program memorandum
PMA: Pharmaceutical Manufacturers Association
PMCC: Performance Measurement Coordinating Council
PMG: primary medical group
PMI: Patient Master Index
PML: probable maximum loss
PMPM: per member per month
PMPY: per member per year
PMS: Practice Management System
PMV: presumed maximum value
PNA: personal needs allowance
PNO: premium notice ordinary
PNP: professional nurse practitioner
PO: by mouth
PO: physician organization
PO: Purchase Order
POC: plan of care
POC: point of contact
POCA: plan of corrective action

POCI: provider ownership compensation interest

POG: Pediatric Oncology Group

POL: Physician's Office Laboratory

POM: Physician Office Manual

PON: pocket of need

PORT: patient outcome-based research trials

POS: place (point) of service

PP: payback period

PPAC: preferred physicians and children

PPD: per patient day

PPD: Permanent Partial Disability

PPM: Physician Practice Management

PPMC: Physician Practice Management Company (Corporation)

PPO: preferred provider organization

PPR: patient–physician relationship

PPR: physician payment reform

PPRC: Physician Payment Review Commission

PPRU: Pediatric Pharmacology Research Unit

PPS: prospective payment system

PPTP: point-to-point tunneling protocol

PR: patient records

PR: peer review

PR: pro rate

PRA: Patient Reform Act

PRB: premium receipt book

PRCL: Pre Review Contingency Letter

PRD: pro rata distribution

PRG: procedure related group

PRI: Patient Review Instrument

PRIT: Physicians' regulatory issues team

PRN: when necessary

PRO: Physician Review Organization

PRO: Professional (Peer) Review Organization

ProPAC: Prospective Payment Assessment Commission

PRP: potentially responsible parties

PRRB: Provider Reimbursement Review Board

PRUCOL: permanent residence under color of law

PRW: past relevant work

PSA: patient synchronized application

PSAO: Pharmacy Services Administration Organization

PsD: doctor of physiology

PSDA: Patient Self-Determination Act

PSE: personal secure environment

PSN: provider-sponsored network

PSO: Provider Sponsored Organization

PSPA: Physician Services Practice Analysis

PSPS: Policy Statement on Payment System Risk

PSRO: Physician (Professional) Peer Review Standards Organization

PSRO: Professional Standards Review Organization

PsyD: doctor of psychology

PT: pharmacy and therapeutics

PT: proficiency testing

PT: physical therapy

PTA: physical therapy aide or assistant

PTA: prior to admission

PTMPY: per thousand members per year

PTSD: Posttraumatic stress disorder
PUF: public use files
PVH: private voluntary hospital

Q

Q: each or every
Q2H: every two hours
QA: quality assurance
QAAC: Quality Assessment and Assurance Committee
QALY: quality-adjusted life year
QAM: every morning
QAP: Quality Assurance Program
QARI: Quality Assurance Reform Initiative
QA/RM: quality assurance/risk management
QA/UR: Quality Assurance/ Utilization Review
QAS: Quality Assurance Survey
QC: quality control
QC: quarter of coverage
Qd: once a day, every day
QDWI: qualified disabled and working individual
QE: qualified eligible client
QEP: qualified eligible patient
QEP: qualified eligible person
QH: every four hours
QH: every hour
QHS: every night at bedtime
QI: qualified individual
QI: qualifying individuals
QI: quality improvement
QI: quality indicator
QID: four times a day
QIO: Quality Improvement Organization
QISMC: quality improvement system for managed care

QM: every morning
QM: quality management
QMB: qualified Medicare beneficiary
QME: qualified medical examiner
QMRP: qualified mental retardation professional
QN: every night
QNS: quantity not sufficient
QOD: every other day
QOH: every other hour
QOL: quality of life
QON: every other night
QP: as much as desired; at will
QPC: quality patient care
QPM: every afternoon
QR: quick response
QS: sufficient quantity
QUPI: quality insurance and performance improvement
QV: as much as desired

R

RA: remittance advice
RACE: Registry of Approved Continuing Education
RACER: Referral Authorization Claims Eligibility and Reports
RADT: registration, admission, discharge, and transfer
RAI: Resident Assessment Instrument
RAP: residential assessment protocol
RAPIDS: Real Time Automated Personnel Identification System
RASP: reverse application service provider
RBITU: Regional Behavioral Intensive Treatment Unit

RBNI: reported but not incurred

RBRVS: Resource-Based Relative Value Scale

RBTU: Regional Behavioral Treatment Unit

R&C: reasonable and customary

RC: reasonable charge

RC: request for comments

RCC: ratio of costs to charges

RCCA: Residential Care Center for Adults

RD: registered dietitian

RDH: registered dental hygienist

REB: Reportable Economic Benefit

Retro: retrospective rate derivation

RFA: request for application

RFC: request for consideration

RFC: residual functional capacity

RFH: request for hearing

RFI: request for information

RFP: request for proposal

RFR: request for reconsideration

RFS: request for services

RHA: regional health administrator

RHC: rural health clinic

RHHI: regional home health intermediary

RHNDPGP: Rural Health Network Development Planning Grant Program

RHP: regional health planning

RHU: registered health underwriter

RI: residual income

RIB: Retirement Insurance Benefits

RIC: rehabilitation impairment category

RICO: Racketeer Influenced Corrupt Organizations Act

RM: regression methodology

RM: risk management

RMC: rating method code

RMRP: Regional Medical Review Policy

RMUR: Retrospective Medical Utilization Review

RN: registered nurse

RNAC: registered nurse assessment coordinator

ROE: report of eligibility

ROE: return on equity

ROI: return on investment

RP: retained premium

RPCH: rural primary care hospital

RPh: registered pharmacist

RPI: residual practice income

RPIH: registered professional industrial hygienist

RPT: registered physical therapist

RPU: reduced paid up

RR: rate review

RRB: Railroad Retirement Board

RRC: Rural Referral Center

RRG: risk retention group

RRTC: Rehabilitation Research & Training Center

RT: respiratory therapist

RTC: Residential Treatment Center

RTOG: Radiation Therapy Oncology Group

RTP: return to provider

RTU: relative time unit

RUG: resource utilization group

RVSR: Rating Veteran Service Representative

RVU: relative value unit

S

SA: Society of Actuaries

SACU: Supplier Audit and Compliance Unit

SADMERC: statistical analysis durable medical equipment regional carrier

SAE: serous adverse event

SAI: Statement of Additional Information

SAMBA: Society of Ambulatory Anesthesiologists

SAMHSA: Substance Abuse and Mental Health Services

SAR: Suspicious Activity Report

SARBOX: Sarbanes-Oxley Act

SAS: Statement of Auditing Standards

SAT: security awareness training

SBC: school-based clinic

SC: survey and certification

SCCM: Society of Critical Care Medicine

SCH: sole community hospital

SCHIP: Supplemental Children's Health Insurance Program

SCIC: significant change in condition

SCM: supportive case manager

SCP: sole community provider

SCR: standard class rate

SCR: system change request

SCU: specialized care unit

SDB: Survivor's Death Benefit

SDC: secondary diagnostic category

SDI: State Disability Insurance

SDO: Standards Development Organization

SEC: Securities and Exchange Commission

SEC: specific episode of care

SEGLI: Service Employee Group Life Insurance

SEISMED: Secure Environment for Information Systems in Medicine

SEQY: summary earnings query

SERP: Supplemental Extended Reporting Policy

SFR: substantial financial risk

SFSP: Society of Financial Service Professionals

SG: Surgeon General

SGA: selling, general administrative expenses

SGA: Standard Industry

SGA: substantial gainful employment

SGNA: Society of Gastroenterology Nurses and Associates

SGO: Surgeon General's Office

SHA: secure hash algorithm

SHA: State Health Agency

SHARS: School Health and Related Services

SHCC: Statewide Health Coordinating Council

SHDPA: Office of State Health Data and Policy Analysis

SHEP: Survey of Healthcare Experiences of Patients

SHMO: Social HMO

SHP: safe harbor principles

SHTTP: secure hypertext transfer protocol

SI: Severity Index

SIB: Spouse Insurance Benefits

SIG: shared instrumentation grant

SIG: special interest group

SILS: Standards for Interoperable LAN Security

SIMS: surgical indications monitoring criteria

SIPCP: Security Incident Procedures Contingency Plan

SIR: self-insurance retention

SIR: System Incident Report

SIREN: secure in regional networks

SLA: Service Level Agreement

SLMB: specified low-income Medicare beneficiary

SMA: state Medicaid agencies

SMDA: Safe Medical Devices Act

SMI: Supplementary Medical Insurance

SMIB: Supplemental Medical Insurance Benefits

SMP: security management process

SMS: socioeconomic monitoring system

SMTP: simple mail transport protocol

SNF: skilled nursing facility

SNOMED: Systematized Nomenclature of Medicine

SNOMED-CT: Systematized Nomenclature of Medicine Clinical Terms

SO: second opinion

SO: signing official

SOAP: Subjective Objective Assessment Plan

SOB: Statement of Benefits

SOC: standard of care

SOI: severity of illness

SOM: State Operations Manual

SOP: standard operating procedure

SOP: swing out plan

SOS: site of service

SOSA: strength of support assessment

SOW: statement of work

SP: single premium

SP: single prole (died without issue)

SP: speech pathology

SP: status post

SPAP: State Pharmacy Assistance Program

SPBA: Society of Professional Benefit Administrators

SPD: summary plan description

SPIN: standard prescriber identification number

SPKM: simple public key GSS-API mechanism

SPL: structured product label

SPMI: seriously and persistently mentally ill

SPOA: single point of accountability

SPOE: single point of entry

SPP: Select Provider Program

SPR: standard provider remittance

SPWG: special work group

SRG: scientific review group

SRO: single room occupancy

SRU: small residential unit

SS: Six-sigma

SS: Social Security Act

SSA: Social Security Administration

SSDC: Social Security Disability Coverage

SSDI: Social Security Disability Insurance

SSI: Social Security Insurance

SSI: Supplemental Security Income

SSID: Social Security Insurance Disability

SSIRD: SSI Record Display

SSL: secure sockets layer

SSLP: Social Security Laws and Practice

SSN: Social Security number

SSO: Standard Setting Organization

SSOP: Second Surgical Opinion Program

SSP: Single Service Plan

SSR: Social Security ruling

SSRS: Social Security Reporting Service

ST: Speech Therapy
ST: standard treatment
STD: sexually transmitted disease
STD: short-term disability
STFCS: standard transaction format compliance system
SUBC: State Uniform Billing Committee
SVC: service
SVH: State Veterans Home
SWG: sub work group

T

TAANA: The American Association of Nurse Attorneys
TAR: Treatment Authorization Request
TAT: turn-around-time
TBA: transferred business analysis
TC: technical component
TC: total cost
TCB: trusted computing base
TCM: Total Care Management
TCP: transfer control protocol
TCS: Transactions and Code Sets
TCSEC: trusted computer systems evaluation criteria
TCU: Transitional Care Unit
TDB: Temporary Disability Benefits
TDC: total direct costs
TEFRA: Tax Equity and Fiscal Responsibility Acts of 1982–83
TID: thrice a day
TIN: tax identification number
TLS: transport layer security
TLSPL: transport layer security protocol
TM: time and materials
TO: telephone order
TPA: third party administrators

TPA: third party assessment
TPA: Trading Partner Agreements
TPHI: third party health insurance
TPO: Treatment, Payment or Health Care Operations
TPR: third party reimbursement
TQM: Total Quality Management
TR: turnover rate
TRO: Temporary Restraining Order
TS: transmissions security
TT: transfer to
TT: turnover time
TTD: teletype for the deaf
TTD: temporary total disability
TTP: trusted third party

U

UAAL: underfunded actuarial accrued liability
UAL: underfunded actuarial liability
UAP: University-affiliated program
UB: uniform bill or billing
UB-82: Uniform Billing Code, 1982
UB-92: Uniform Billing Code, 1992
U&C: usual and customary
UCAS: Uniform Cost Accounting Standard
UCD: Unemployment Compensation Disability
UCDS: Uniform Clinical Data Set
UCR: usual, customary, and reasonable
UCRS: Utilization Control Reporting System
UCTS: Uniform Claim Task Force
UDK: User-defined key
UDSMR: Uniform Data Set for Medical Rehabilitation

UEMR: Use of Electronic Medical Release

UF: unknown factor

UHCCS: unsolicited health care claim status

UHCIA: Uniform Health Care Information Act

UHDDS: Uniform Hospital Discharge Data Set

UHI: unique health identifier

UHI: unique health information

UHIN: Utah Health Information Network

UI: unearned income

UI: unemployment insurance

UIC: unit identification code

UL: unauthorized leave

UM: Utilization Management

UME: unreimbursed medical expense

UMGA: Unified Medical Group Association

UNCE/FACT: United Nations Center for Facilities of Procedures and Practices for Administration, Commerce and Transport

UN/EDIFACT: United Nations Rules for Electronic Data Interchange for Administration, Commerce and Transport

UNOS: United Network for Organ Sharing

UNSM: United Nations Standard Messages

UP: under payment

UPIN: Universal Physician Identification Number

UPL: upper payment limit

UR: utilization review

URAC: Utilization Review Accreditation Commission

URO: utilization review organization

URQA: utilization review and quality assurance

USAMRMC: United States Army Medical Research and Material Command

USAO: United States Attorney's Office

USC: United States Code (Refers to federal laws)

USFDC: United States Department of Commerce

USFMG: United States Foreign Medical Graduate

USFMSS: United States Foreign Medical School Student

USMG: United States Medical Graduate

USP: United States Pharmacopoeia

USPAP: Uniform Standards of Professional Appraisal Practice

USPHS: United States Public Health Service

USSG: United States Surgeon General

USUHS: Uniformed Services University of the Health Sciences

UWA: unsuccessful work attempt

V

VA: Veteran's Administration

VA: Veteran's Affairs

VACERT: Veterans Administration Electronic Education Certification Program

VACO: Veterans Administration Central Office

VAEB: Veterans Administration Executive Board

VAMC: Veteran's Administration Medical Center
VAN: Value Added Network
VARD: Veteran's Administration Research and Development
VBA: Veterans Benefits Administration
VC: voluntary closing
VC: variable cost
VE: vocational expert
VE: voluntary effort
VEBA: Voluntary Employee Benefit Association
VETSN: Veterans Services Network
VHA: Veterans Health Administration
VIP: Voucher Insurance Plan
VIPPS®: Verified Internet Pharmacy Practice Sites®
VNA: Visiting Nurse Association
VO: verbal order
VPN: Virtual Private Network
VR: vocational rehabilitation
VRE: vocational rehabilitation and employment
VRS: voice response system

W

W: wage earner
WARNA: Worker's Adjustment and Restraining Notification Act
WBS: work breakdown structure
WC: workers' compensation
WCB: Workers' Compensation Board

WCCO: World Conference for Cancer Organization
WCP: Workers' Compensation Program
WCVO: written confirmation of verbal orders
WEDI: Workgroup for Electronic Data Interchange
WHF-USA: World Health Foundation-United States of America
WHO: World Health Organization
WIB: Widow(ers) Insurance Benefits
WIC: Women Infant Children
WL: waiting list
WMS: Welfare Management System
WOL: Waiver of Liability
WP: waiting period
WS: workstation security
WTI: working toward independence

X

XR: x-ray

Y

YRBS: Youth Risk Behavior Survey
YTD: year to date
YTM: year to month

Z

ZBB: zero-based budgeting
ZPHMO: Zero Premium Health Maintenance Organization

BIBLIOGRAPHY

Aalseth Codebusters™. (2005). *Coding connection: A documentation guide for compliant coding* (2nd ed.). Sudbury, MA: Jones and Bartlett.

American Association of Health Plans. (1996). *Guide to accreditation.* Washington, DC: Author; 83.

American Hospital Association. (2000). *AHA guide to the health care field.* Chicago: Health Forum LLC.

Anderson, J. (1999). *Guide to state medicaid managed care laws and rules.* Sudbury, MA: Jones and Bartlett.

Anderson, J. (1999). *State-by-state laws and regulations on workers' compensation managed care.* Sudbury, MA: Jones and Bartlett.

Baker, J. J. (1998). *Activity-based costing and activity-based management for health care.* Gaithersburg, MD: Aspen.

Beaglehole, R., & Bonita, R. (1998). Public health at the crossroads: Which way forward? *Lancet, 351* (9102), 590–592.

Berne, E. (1964). Games people play: The psychology of human relationships. Penguin Books, Ltd. New York, NY.

Biblo, J. D., Christopher, M. J., Johnson, L., & Potter, R. L. (1995). *Ethical issues in managed care: Guidelines for clinicians and recommendations to accrediting organizations.* Kansas City, MO: Midwest Bioethics Center; 3–4, 8, 11–12.

Boyer, M. H. (1997). A decade's experience at Tufts with a four-year combined curriculum in medicine and public health. *Academic Medicine, 72,* (4), 269–275.

Brown, J. L. (1997). *Insurance administration.* Atlanta, GA: LOMA; 395.

Browning, C. H., & Browning, B. J. (1996). *How to partner with managed care—A do it yourself kit* New York: Wiley.

Bryce, H. J. (2001). Capacity considerations and community benefit expenditures of nonprofit hospitals. *Health Care Management Review, 26* (3), 24–39.

Canby, J. B. IV. (1995). Applying activity-based costing to healthcare settings. *Healthcare Financial Management, 49* (2), 50–52, 54–56.

Carpenter, D. O., & Conway, J. B. (1996). Optimizing professional education in public health. *Journal of Public Health Management and Practice, 2* (4), 66–72.

Chambers, L. W., Hoey, J., Underwood, J., & Bains, N. (1998). Integration of service, education, and research in local official public health agencies. *American Journal of Public Health, 88* (7), 1102–1104.

Cherry, J., & Sridhar, S. (2000). Six sigma: Using statistics to reduce variability and costs in radiology. *Radiology Management, 6,* 1–5.

Chickering, K. L., Malik, T., Halbert, R. J., & Kar, S. B. (1999). Reinventing the field training experience: Building a practical and effective graduate program at the UCLA School of Public Health. *American Journal of Public Health, 89,* (4): 596–597.

Committee on Assuring Health, Institute of Medicine. (2003). *Future of the public's health in the 21st century.* Washington, DC: National Academy Press.

Conrad, P. (1998). Worksite health promotion: The social context. *Social Science and Medicine, 26,* (5), 485–489.

Coughlin, S. S. (1996). Model curricula in public health ethics. *American Journal of Preventative Medicine, 12* (4), 247–251.

Coughlin, S. S., Katz, W. H., & Mattison, D. R. (1999). Ethics instruction at schools of public health in the United States—Association of Schools of Public Health Education Committee. *American Journal Public Health, 89* (5), 768–770.

Current Procedural Terminology. Standard Version. (2005). AMA. Chicago, Illinois.

Dacso, S. T., & Dacso, C. C. (1999). *Risk contracting and capitation answer book: Strategies for managed care.* Gaithersburg, MD, Aspen.

Daigrepont, J., & Mink, L. (2001). *Starting a medical practice.* Washington, DC: American Medical Association.

Dandoy, S. (2001). Educating the public health workforce (PMID: 11236421). *American Journal of Public Health, 91* (3), 467–468.

Deutsch, S. (1999). *The credentialing.* Sudbury, MA: Jones and Bartlett.

Diagnostic Related Groups Definitions Manual. Version 23. (2006). CMS. Baltimore, Maryland.

Dranove, D. (2003). *What's your life worth? Health care rationing … who lives? Who dies? And who decides?* Upper Saddle River: NJ: Financial Times/Prentice-Hall. New York, NY.

Eng, T. R., Maxfield, A., Patrick, K., Deering, M. J., Ratzan, S. C., & Gustafson, D. H. (1998). Access to health information and support: A public highway or a private road? *JAMA, 280* (15), 1371–1375.

Ernst & Young. (1997). *Spider graphs and charts.* New York, NY

Fine, A. (1998). *Provider sponsored organizations: Emerging opportunities for growth.* Sudbury, MA: Jones and Bartlett.

Fineberg, H. V., Green, G. M., Ware, J. H., & Anderson, B. L. (1998). Changing public health training needs: Professional education and the paradigm of public health. *Annual Review of Public Health, 15,* 237–257.

Fox, P. (1996). *Managed care and chronic illness.* Sudbury, MA: Jones and Bartlett.

Frank, C. (2000). *Physician empowerment through capitation.* Sudbury, MA: Jones and Bartlett.

Frank, L., Engelke, P. O., & Schmid, T. L. (2003). *Health and community design—The impact of the built environment on physical activity.* Washington, DC: Island Press.

Garrett, L. (2002). *Betrayal of trust—The collapse of global public health.* Hyperion Press, New York, NY.

Gerber, D. (2005). *100 questions and answers about plastic surgery.* Sudbury, MA: Jones and Bartlett.

Gervais, K. G. (1999). *Ethical challenges in managed care: A casebook.* Baltimore: Georgetown University Press.

Ginn, G. O. (1990). Strategic change in hospitals: An examination of the response of the acute care hospital to the turbulent environment of the 1980s. *Health Services Research, 25* (4), 565–591.

Goldfield, N. (1999). *Ambulatory care services and the prospective payment.* Sudbury, MA: Jones and Bartlett.

Goldfield, N. (1999). *Physician profiling and risk adjustment* (2nd ed.). Gaithersburg, MD: Aspen.

Gordon, L. J., & McFarlane, D. R. (1996). Public health practitioner incubation plight: Following the money trail. *Journal of Public Health Policy, 17* (1), 59–70.

Grazier, K. L. (1999). Managed care and hospitals. *Journal of Healthcare Management, 44,* (5), 335–337.

Grodzki, L. (2000). *Building your ideal private practice—How to love what you do and be highly profitable too.* WW Norton and Company, New York, NY.

Grumbach, K., & Bodenheimer, T. S. (2001). *Understanding health policy.* New York: McGraw-Hill. New York, NY.

Hall-Long, B. (1998). Public health staff education and training: An academic-government research initiative. *Abstract Book Association Health Services Res, 15,* 94–95.

Halvorson, G., & Isham, G. (2003). *Epidemic of care—A call for safer, better, and more accountable health care.* New York: Wiley.

Harris, T. (1967). *I'm OK, you're OK.* Harper Collins Publishers. New York, NY.

Haughton, B., Story, M., & Keir, B. (1998). Profile of public health nutrition personnel: Challenges for population/system-focused roles and state-level monitoring. *Journal of American Dietician Association, 98* (6), 664–670.

Herzlinger, R. (1994). *Financial accounting and managerial control for nonprofit organizations.* Gaithersburg, MD: Aspen.

Herzlinger, R. (1999). *Market-driven healthcare.* Reading, MA: Perseus Books.

Herzlinger, R. (2001). *Consumer driven health care.* New York: Jossey-Bass.

Himmelstein, D. U., and Woolhandler, S. (2001). Bleeding the patient—The consequences of corporate healthcare. Common Courage Press. Monroe, ME.

Hoffman-Goetz, L., & Dwiggins, S. (1998). Teaching public health practitioners about health communication: The MPH curriculum experience. *Journal of Community Health, 23* (2), 127–135.

Huggins, K., & Land, R. D. (1992). *Operations of life and health insurance companies (2nd ed.).* Atlanta, GA: LOMA; 259–260.

Hunink, M. G. M., Glasziou, A. S., Elstein, J. E., Siegel, J. W., Pliskin, J., & Glasziou, P. (2001). *Decision making in health and medicine: Integrating evidence and values.* New York: Cambridge University Press.

Institute of Medicine, Committee on Healthcare Quality in America. (2002). *Crossing the quality chasm.* Washington, DC: U.S. Government Printing Office.

Kant Patel, M. E. (2000). *Health care politics and policy in America.* Rushefsky, Sharpe. Armonk, NY.

Katz, R. (1998). *The family practitioner's survival guide to the business of medicine.* Sudbury, MA: Jones and Bartlett.

Kilpatrick, K. E., & Romani, J. H. (1995). The evolution of health administration education for public health: Responding to a changing environment. *Journal of Health Administration and Education, 13* (4), 585–595.

Kirk, R. (1997). *Managing outcomes, process, and cost in a managed care environment.* Sudbury, MA: Jones and Bartlett.

Kongstevedt, P. R., & Plocher, D. W. (1998). *Best practices in medical management.* Gaithersburg, MD: Aspen.

Kongstvedt, P. R. (2003). *Best practices in medical management: The managed health care handbook series.* Sudbury, MA: Jones and Bartlett.

Kongstvedt, P. R. (2004). *The managed health care handbook* (3rd ed.) [CD-ROM]. Sudbury, MA: Jones and Bartlett.

Krider, B. (1997). *Valuation of physician practices and clinics.* Sudbury, MA: Jones and Bartlett.

Lawrence, D. (2002). *From chaos to care—The promise of team based medicine.* Reading, MA: Perseus Books.

LeBow, R. (2002). *Health care meltdown.* JRI Press, Boise, ID.

Luke, R. D., Begun, J. W., & Walston, S. L. (2000). Strategy making in health care organizations. In S. M. Shortell & A. D. Kaluzny (Eds.), *Health care management: Organization design and behavior* (4th ed.). Albany, NY: Delmar.

Marcinko, D. E. (2000). *The business of medical practice.* New York: Springer.

Marcinko, D. E. (2001). *Financial planning for physicians and healthcare professionals.* New York: Aspen.

Marcinko, D. E. (2002). *Financial planner's library on CD-ROM.* New York: Aspen.

Marcinko, D. E. (2002). *Financial planning for physicians and healthcare professionals.* New York: Aspen.

Marcinko, D. E. (2003). *Financial planner's library on CD-ROM.* New York: Aspen.

Marcinko, D. E. (2003). *Financial planning for physicians and healthcare professionals.* New York: Aspen.

Marcinko, D. E. (2004). *The advanced business of medical practice.* New York: Springer Publishing

Marcinko, D. E. (Ed.). (2005). *Financial planning for physicians and advisors.* Sudbury, MA: Jones and Bartlett.

Marcinko, D. E. (Ed.). (2005). *Insurance planning and risk management for physicians and advisors.* Sudbury, MA: Jones and Bartlett.

Marcinko, D. E. (Ed). (2007). *Financial management for healthcare organizations.* Blaine, WA: Specialty Technical Publishers.

McCall-Perez, E. (1997). *Physician equity groups and other competitive emerging entities.* New York: McGraw Hill.

Millenson, M. L. (1997). *Demanding medical excellence: Doctors and accountability in the information age.* Chicago: University of Chicago Press.

Morrison, J. I. (1999). *Health care in the new millennium: Vision, values, and leadership.* San Francisco: Jossey-Bass.

Moseley, G. B. III. (1999). *Managed care strategies: A physician practice desk reference.* Sudbury, MA: Jones and Bartlett.

Mullah, C. (2001). *The case manager's handbook: Forms and letters on CD-ROM* (2nd ed.). Sudbury, MA: Jones and Bartlett.

Nash, D. (1994). *The physician's guide to managed care.* Sudbury, MA: Jones and Bartlett.

Nathanson, M. (2005). *Health care providers government relations handbook: Shaping policy to win* (2nd ed.). Sudbury, MA: Jones and Bartlett.

The National Coalition on Healthcare. (1997). *Why the quality of U.S. health care must be improved.* Washington, DC: Author.

Pinner, R. (1998). Public health surveillance and information technology. *Emerging Infectious Diseases, 4* (3), 462–464.

Potts, L., Scuthfield, F. D., Merrill, R., & Katz, W. (1998). *The growth of managed care: Implications for change in schools of public health.* Washington, DC: Association of Schools of Public Health.

Pryor, T. (2002). *Activity based management: A healthcare industry primer.* Chicago: American Hospital Association.

Reid, W. M., Hostetler, R. M., Webb, S. C., & Cimino, P. C. (1995). Time to put managed care into medical and public health education. *Academic Medicine, 70* (8), 662–664.

Rognehaugh, R. (1997). *The managed healthcare dictionary.* Gaithersburg, VA: Aspen; 73.

Rognehaugh, R. (1998). T*he managed health care dictionary (2nd ed.).* Sudbury, MA: Jones and Bartlett.

Satinsky, M. A. (1998). *The foundations of integrated care: Facing the challenges of change.* Chicago: American Hospital.

Saxton, J. W., & Leaman, T. L. (1998). *Managed care success: Reducing risk while increasing patient satisfaction.* Gaithersburg, MD: Aspen.

Scott, R. E. (2000). *Legal aspects of documenting patient care (2nd ed.).* Sudbury, MA: Jones and Bartlett.

Scott, R. E. (1998). *Managing healthcare demand.* Gaithersburg, MD: Aspen.

Scutchfield, F. D., Harris, J. R., Koplan, J. P., Lawrence, D. M, Gordon, R. L., & Violante, T. (1998). Managed care and public health. *Journal of Public Health Management and Practice, 4* (1), 1–11.

Singh, D. (2005). *Effective management of long-term care facilities.* Sudbury, MA: Jones and Bartlett.

Sloan, R. M. (1999). *Introduction to healthcare delivery organizations: Function and management (4th ed.).* Chicago: Health Administration Press.

Smith, O. (1906). *Modernized chiropractic.* SM Langworthy. Cedar Raids, Iowa.

Solomon, R. (1997). *The physician manager's handbook: Essential business skills for succeeding in health.* Sudbury, MA: Jones and Bartlett.

Sparrow, M. K. (2000). *License to steal: How fraud bleeds America's health care system: Vol. 2.* Westview Press. Boulder, CO.

Stahl, M. J. (1999). *The physician's essential MBA: What every physician leader needs to know.* Gaithersburg, MD: Aspen.

Steppe, A. R. (1996). Playing jeopardy with public health: An old threat for a new century. *Journal of Community Health, 21* (4), 237–239.

Tindall, A. (2005). *Guide to managed care medicine.* Sudbury, MA: Jones and Bartlett.

Tinsley, R. (2004). *Medical practice management handbook.* New York: Harcourt~Brace.

Turnock, B. J., & Handler, A. S. (1998). From measuring to improving public health practice. *Annual Review of Public Health, 18,* 261–282.

U.S. Congress, Office of Technological Assessment. (1995). *Bringing health care online: The role of information technologies* (Report no. OTA-ITC-624). Washington, DC: U.S. Government Printing Office.

Weinberg, D. A. (2001). *Code green—Money driven hospitals and the dismantling of nursing.* Ithaca, NY: Cornell University Press.

Youngberg, B. (2004). *The patient safety handbook.* Sudbury, MA: Jones and Bartlett.

Zaslove, M. O. (1998). *The successful physician: A productivity handbook for practitioners.* Gaithersburg, MD: Aspen.

Zimer, D. (1999). *Physician compensation arrangements: Management and legal trends.* Sudbury, MA: Jones and Bartlett.